D1713194

IRON*Artisans*

UNIVERSITY OF PITTSBURGH PRESS

IRON*Artisans*

*Welsh Immigrants &
the American Age of Steel*

RONALD L. LEWIS

Published by the University of Pittsburgh Press, Pittsburgh, Pa., 15260
Manufactured in the United States of America
Printed on acid-free paper
10 9 8 7 6 5 4 3 2 1

Cataloging-in-Publication data is available from the Library of Congress

ISBN 13: 978-0-8229-4762-2
ISBN 10: 0-8229-4762-5

Cover art: John Ferguson Weir, *Forging the Shaft*, 1874–77. Oil on canvas, 52 x 73 ¼ in.

Cover design: Alex Wolfe

For my good friends Bill Jones and Val Davidge

CONTENTS

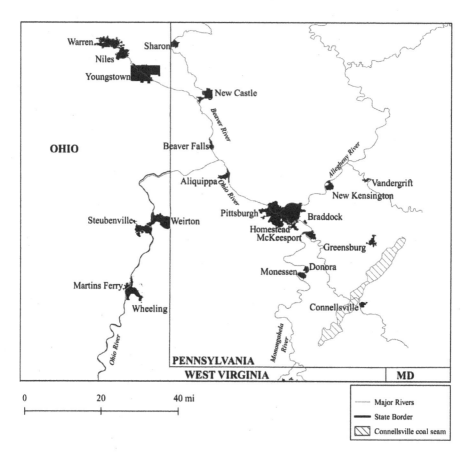

Map 1. Upper Ohio valley region. Cartography by Caroline Welter, Regional Research Institute, West Virginia University, Morgantown.

PREFACE & ACKNOWLEDGMENTS

Interdependency bound the coal and iron industries in the United States as the nineteenth century evolved, and industrialists located their steel mills near metallurgical coalfields. The most favorably located region for this kind of industrial consolidation was the upper Ohio River valley. Pittsburgh, because of its strategic location at the head of the Ohio River in the midst of the richest coal deposits in the United States, emerged early in its history as the hub of the upper Ohio valley (map 1). It was to this region, therefore, that so many Welsh coal miners and iron- and steelworkers immigrated to find employment.

I define the region as the physiographic area of Pittsburgh and its industrial hinterland within a roughly sixty-mile radius of the city. The region becomes amorphous at its periphery because it cuts across the boundary lines of three states. Nevertheless, portions of southeastern Ohio and northern West Virginia, as well as western Pennsylvania, clearly functioned within Pittsburgh's sphere of influence. Defining the region strictly within state boundaries ignores important historical linkages of the iron and steel industry connecting the hub of Pittsburgh with the numerous "spoke" industrial cities on the Allegheny and Monongahela Rivers and smaller industrial cities such as Wheeling, Martins Ferry, Steubenville, and Weirton on the Ohio River, as well as Youngstown, Ohio, and New Castle and Sharon, Pennsylvania, on the upper tributaries of the Beaver River.[1]

Before 1850, most rural and small-town areas of the upper Ohio had little contact with Pittsburgh, but the arrival of railroads, canals, steamboats, and road improvements extended Pittsburgh's economic reach throughout the tristate region. As Pittsburgh grew into a national iron and steel manufacturing center, entrepreneurs spread commercial development more widely by investing heavily in the natural extractive industries, thus spurring the construction and expansion of iron furnaces, rolling mills, nail factories, foundries, and forges. As one scholar observed, "The improved physical accessibility created by railroads and later automobiles, the centralizing forces of industrial capitalism, and the spatial extension of urban social and cultural institutions generally expanded the sphere of metropolitan influence" into every corner of the upper Ohio region.[2]

This book began to take shape more than a decade ago, when I laid out a plan to write about the industrial migration from Wales to the United States. Welsh immigration occurred in two phases and involved two different populations. First came the pre-1840s agricultural migration of farmers in search of affordable land and religious freedom. The second, between 1850 and 1910, was a much larger movement of Welsh industrial migrants who came in search of greater economic opportunities generated by the Industrial Revolution. The vast majority of the latter group were coal miners and iron- and steelworkers with a wealth of previous experience in Wales and England, where the coal, iron, and steel industries had flourished for more than a century.

Although the total number of Welsh immigrants paled in comparison with the late nineteenth-century influx from southern and eastern Europe, the Welsh provided the core of technical knowledge and skilled workers who were instrumental in the emergence of the United States as a global industrial power built on coal, iron, and steel. However, these skilled immigrants from Britain who played such a vital role in the evolution of the iron and steel industry have not received the attention they would seem to deserve. In fact, this small but critical group of immigrants has, as historian Nora Faires observed in 1989, "attracted little scholarly attention, despite suggestions that, because of their key positions in manufacturing and their traditions of labor activism before migration, they played a crucial role in the development of the region's industry."[3] Regrettably, little has changed over the ensuing decades.

Two different groups of industrial workers—coal miners and iron- and steelworkers—overwhelmingly dominated the second Welsh wave. Their stories, although intertwined, were too complex for a single book, so for analytical purposes I have treated them as two distinct groups. Consequently, in 2008 I published *Welsh Americans: A History of Assimilation in the Coalfields*, which explored the role of the Welsh in the development of the American coal industry. Several other research projects intervened after the publication of that book, but my research on the Welsh industrial migration is complete with the publication of *Iron Artisans: Welsh Immigrants and the American Age of Steel*.

Welsh metalworkers constituted one of the largest and most distinctive elements within the industrial labor migrations to the United States. Therefore, they highlight the breadth of skills, cultures, and experiences within those mass labor migrations between the Civil War and World War I. For that reason, the fulcrum of this study is located at the intersection where the various "transnational" strands of immigration history, ethnic history, and labor and social history converge. It demonstrates the continuity and change within both an internal and comparative framework and analyzes how Americanization worked within a small, relatively privileged, working-class group.

An abundance of evidence demonstrates that the Welsh, like immigrant miners from other ethnic groups, did not discard their identity upon arrival. Nor was communication with the homeland severed. A large volume of both personal and professional information was constantly shared between Welsh iron- and steelworkers in America and their relatives, friends, and colleagues back home. Exploring this transfer of knowledge and skills between the United States and Wales reveals the transnational relationships binding not only Welsh Americans with their compatriots in Wales but also the American and Welsh iron and steel industry.

Generally, the English and Scots were simply absorbed into American society because Americans were either ignorant of or unconcerned with the cultural differences among them. The Welsh, who often spoke a different language, were more difficult to ignore. Yet Americans absorbed the Welsh just as readily and for the same reasons. Most white Americans were of British birth or heritage during this nativist period when white Anglo-Saxon Protestants felt threatened by the "Other"—the despised Asians and Africans, as well as the millions from southern and eastern Europe. All British immigrants were received as welcome reinforcements to the nation's original white stock. Even though Welsh American leaders sought to retain their national identity by preserving the Welsh language and transplanting chapel styles and cultural festivals from Wales, they lasted for a generation or two before being swallowed into the American mainstream. Moreover, natives regarded the Welsh as ultra Protestant, a good counter to the tide of Catholicism being brought in by the southern and eastern Europeans beginning in the 1880s. Because the Welsh were skilled and old stock, Americans assigned to them a higher social status than the Europeans whom they regarded as poor, low-skilled, and cheap labor and therefore less worthy in the American social calculus.

And then there were the native-born African Americans. Their numbers were comparatively low prior to the Great Migration from the South that became a large-scale movement during World War I. Still, several hundred Black steelworkers were employed in western Pennsylvania mills, primarily in Pittsburgh and Allegheny County. The vast majority of them were laborers, but a few of them were skilled puddlers, heaters, and rollers. Skilled or unskilled, however, and in keeping with the endemic racism in Jim Crow America, employers and white steelworkers actively discriminated against them. The Welsh were implicated in this behavior as members in, and leaders of, two steelworker unions, the Sons of Vulcan and the Amalgamated Association of Iron and Steel Workers, that barred Black Americans from membership in the belief that doing so would protect the jobs of white workers.

In what is now a familiar story, the Welsh belonged to the "old stock" immigrants who were therefore considered white immediately upon arrival. They confronted none of the discriminatory obstacles thrown up before the "new immigrants" who, although Caucasian, were accorded few of the privileges reserved for white arrivals because of their low social status. At the bottom of the social hierarchy, racism dictated that Black Americans were never to enjoy the privileges of native-born white Americans.

Finally, although Welsh industrial workers generally were literate in Welsh and/or English, the written record they left for historians is too sparse and scattered to allow for systematic analysis. There are a few digitized collections, such as the Wales-Ohio Project and the Wales-Pennsylvania Project, available at the National Library of Wales. Interesting as they are individually, however, the collections themselves are composed of disaggregated historical documents and artifacts, most of which refer to Welsh immigrants generally, rather than to iron- and steelworkers specifically.

Fortunately, the Welsh Newspaper Project at the National Library of Wales has been digitized. It provides a wealth of information relating to the personal and professional lives of Welsh iron- and steelworkers in a searchable archive of 120 Welsh newspapers published between 1804 and 1919, with a total of 1.1 million pages containing more than 15 million individual articles. Many of the newspapers in the iron, steel, and tinplate towns of South Wales carried daily and weekly columns on the industry in Wales and the United States. They also published an array of correspondence from workers who had made the Atlantic passage to America and reported on

Welsh immigrant families, communities, and working conditions. Travelers, sojourners, permanent transplants, and family members often wrote letters to their hometown newspapers, confident that family, friends, and former coworkers hungry for news from America would read their open letters. Industrialists and professional reporters covering the metal industries also took extended investigative tours of American plants and their associated Welsh communities, and their reports add further detail to this epistolary archive. The massive volume and variety of material in these digitized newspapers can be difficult to navigate, not to mention excessively time-consuming to use, so I have provided very complete citations for researchers who wish to consult these sources. Difficulties aside, this extensive inventory of personal and professional correspondence yielded a substantial tranche of otherwise unavailable primary sources, as will become apparent in the pages that follow.[4]

All scholarly researchers are dependent on libraries, and I am no exception. The research for this book was conducted off and on over many years in libraries great and small, general and specialized, near and far. In Wales, Cardiff Central Library, Cardiff University Humanities Library, and the National Library of Wales in Aberystwyth were of first importance. In the United States, a number of large research libraries were most helpful, both in person and through their interlibrary loan services, including the Library of Congress, University of Pittsburgh Libraries, Penn State University Libraries, and West Virginia University Library. Community-level libraries provided valuable localized information on Welsh steel communities. They included the Mahoning Valley Historical Society and the Youngstown Historical Center of Industry and Labor, both in Youngstown, Ohio; Rodman Library, Alliance, Ohio; Warren-Trumbull County Library, Warren, Ohio; New Castle Public Library, New Castle, Pennsylvania; and the Ohio County Public Library, Wheeling, West Virginia, to name a few. To these institutions I extend my sincere, if belated and inadequate, appreciation.

I am pleased to acknowledge my gratitude to the Regional Research Institute at West Virginia University and its director, Randall Jackson, who arranged for a geographic information systems expert to prepare several maps that appear in this book. Caroline Welter created excellent maps of the upper Ohio valley region, ironworks in South Wales, 1860, and tinplate works in South Wales, 1700–1956, and I am most appreciative of their generous assistance.

Finally, I wish to pay tribute to the readers of the manuscript for their very helpful reports. And, as always, I want to express my heartfelt thanks to Susan E. Lewis, whose skillful readings significantly improved the final manuscript.

IRON *Artisans*

1

The Transplanted

During the first century and a quarter of its existence, the United States received between thirty-five million and forty million mostly European and British immigrants seeking land, economic opportunity, and political and religious freedom. The nineteenth century was by far the high-water mark of this incoming tide of humanity. During the second half of the nineteenth century and first decade of the twentieth century, Wales came closest to experiencing a mass migration to the United States. Nevertheless, to use historian Alan Conway's memorable phrase, compared with the "big battalions from the continent of Europe and from England itself, the Welsh formed little more than a corporal's guard."[1] During this period a vast majority of the Welsh immigrants were coal miners and iron- and steelworkers whose historical significance rests on their strategic contributions to America's industrial development rather than their numbers.

Welsh Immigration

A clear understanding of the Welsh experience in America requires an interpretive framework that accounts for the fragmented identities others attached to incoming migrant groups and the identity embraced by the immigrants themselves. The term "immigrant" is packed with meanings constructed by natives and marks newcomers as not one of "us." Unfortunately, there is no convenient term to replace it. Scholarship on immigration reflects the era during which it was written. During the early twentieth century, US scholarship was stamped by concerns over the potential for assimilating the great diversity of humanity entering the country during that period. Historians such as Carl Wittke were optimistic that the European nationals arriving from southern and eastern Europe would eventually be assimilated because of America's ability to absorb different peoples and meld them into one. America was a "melting pot," and immigration and assimilation were thought to have played a critical role in forging the American character.[2]

Beginning in the 1960s, revisionists abandoned this homogenizing paradigm and focused instead on race, ethnicity, and cultural pluralism. Even by the late 1930s, Marcus Lee Hansen was reminding scholars that, although British culture was dominant in the United States, it was only one of many cultures that had shaped the nation. Realizing that immigration and assimilation constituted a two-way street, scholars devised new conceptual approaches to explain the intercontinental mass movement of people. Richard A. Easterlin's "push-pull" model explained immigration within the processes of economic modernization. Rapid industrialization in the United States created a great demand for labor while at the same time undermining the ability of other nations to sustain their own people. American scholars of this generation concentrated on particular ethnic cultures and communities, portraying immigrants as either "retainers" of their culture within ethnic enclaves or as "modernizers" who abandoned the old culture for the new for rational economic reasons.[3] In both cases, historians were preoccupied with conflict between immigrants and native-born Americans and how immigrants actively protected their own cultural identities rather than conform to mainstream American values.

John Bodnar's *The Transplanted* (1985) synthesizes immigration and assimilation within the framework of capitalism and explores how Old World values were adapted, rather than abandoned, in the New World. He locates this dynamic within the family, community, and workplace, a personal world further influenced by class, kinship, and ethnicity. Bodnar might be described as a "soft pluralist" who regarded cultural differences as intrinsic assets, as opposed to the "hard pluralist" who is concerned with class rather than culture, as well as the issues of struggle and exploitation.[4] Bodnar's thesis is that immigrants were pragmatic about the culture they brought with them, retaining what was useful from the old culture and adopting what they found useful in the new.[5]

Since the 1990s the drumbeat in immigration history has been for scholars to expand their approach beyond the United States and the nation-state in order to articulate the field within its global context; this is a "transnational" approach that studies movements and forces that cut across national boundaries. Historian Kevin Kenny asserts that two approaches to immigration history emerged from the effort to avoid the dead ends inherent in a singular focus on either the nation-state or cultural enclaves. The "transnational" approach looks for "reciprocal interactions . . . among globally scattered communities." The "cross-national" approach, on the other hand, "examines specific similarities and differences in the experiences of similar migrants who have settled in different nations." Kenny argues that neither perspective by itself will yield satisfactory results. Comparisons based on nationality do not "capture the fluid and interactive processes at the heart of migration history." The transnational approach alone, however, does not account for the persistent power of nation-states to attract loyalty or for the sharp regional, cultural, and political differences that may fragment a single nationality, such as the Scots, Welsh, and English, not to mention the Irish, within Great Britain.[6]

This study examines continuity and change among Welsh immigrants within the framework of the Welsh homeland and the American hostland. The transatlantic transfer of Welsh culture and skills and how the migrants adapted them to American circumstances in order to succeed is the major theme in this study. It is therefore built upon the conceptual foundation of both the transnational and the cross-national perspectives, both being vital to understanding immigration and assimilation into American society. Unlike what occurred during the southern and eastern European mass migrations, Americans either welcomed migrants from Britain or did not feel a need to comment on their presence. In his popular book *The American Commonwealth* (1888), James Bryce claimed that the English, Welsh, and Scottish migrants were "absorbed into the general mass of native citizens" and tended to "lose their identity almost immediately" in the United States. Although they numbered in the millions, their political footprint was invisible because they had "either been indifferent to political struggles or have voted from the same motives as an average American."[7]

Andrew Carnegie came a step closer to the truth in *Triumphant De-mocracy* (1886), asserting that the British held a privileged position in the United States because they played a leading role in building the country. Migrants from Britain, like the Welsh immigrant David Thomas, credited as the "father of the anthracite iron industry in America," not only created the industries but, as industrial workers, they had performed much of the labor as well. Carnegie claimed that British immigrants held a monopoly on industrial invention and the skills needed to run those industries. In the nineteenth century almost half of the manufacturing workforce was from Britain, while Americans were primarily engaged in agriculture. Moreover, this near monopoly in manufacturing and the skilled trades was passed on to their children.[8]

In this era of aggressive racism, nativism, and Anglo-Saxonism, many (and probably most) Americans regarded southern and eastern Europeans, not to mention Asians, Africans, and even Black Americans, as too alien to be assimilable. On the other hand, British immigrants were seen as, and thought of themselves as, "valuable reinforcements" to the British stock that had established the United States. They occupied an ambiguous status between native and immigrant but were comfortable living among "cousins" though not necessarily feeling at home. Within Great Britain the "British" identity was constructed to meet the needs of empire by incorporating the distinct nationalities of the English, Welsh, and Scots, and it represented expansion, global power, imperialism, and, for some, the civilizing of "hea-thens" in remote places. However, British emigrants did not always share this identity in equal portions. The Scots and Welsh each maintained their own distinctive cultural and national identities in the United States in a way the English did not, even though Americans drew little distinction between them. The paucity of scholarship on the subject indicates that, at least in the literature, the British would seem to have been, in Charlotte Erickson's apt phrase, nearly "invisible immigrants" and, to use another historian's poignant phrase, "white on arrival."[9]

While the immigrants who arrived in America during the seventeenth and eighteenth centuries were predominantly from the British Isles, it was the transportation revolution of the mid-nineteenth century that trans-formed emigration in British history. Steamships greatly reduced the perils of sea travel and made migration a much less irreversible decision, while in America railroads opened the interior to settlement and development. The cost of transportation also fell, opening emigration to ordinary workers who sought to improve their lives by moving abroad. Industrialization in the United States attracted skilled British workers, who quickly took advantage of the new opportunities. Their privileged status was reflected in the immigrant experience of Welsh ironworkers, whose identity was anchored in their unique work culture, nineteenth-century Welsh nationalism, religion, politics, cultural practices, and labor-industrial relations. Their reception and social position, however, stood in stark contrast to the experience of the millions of southern and eastern Europeans who entered the US labor market at the lowest rung. The result was a stratified and segmented labor market rather than actual job competition.[10]

Welsh immigration to the United States was chronologically, geographically, and occupationally concentrated. Eighteenth- and early nineteenth-century Welsh immigrants to the United States were primarily farmers seeking better land. By far the greatest influx, however, came in oscillating waves between the 1840s and 1900 with the migration of industrial workers.[11] The 1900 census recorded the presence of Welsh in every state of the Union, but they were concentrated in particular states. Out of a total 267,000 Welsh-born immigrants and their children in the United States (93,744 immigrants and 173,416 children of immigrants), 100,143 of them lived in Pennsylvania alone. Ohio was a distant second with 35,971. These two states also contained the two largest concentrations of Welsh in the coal and iron districts. More than 40,000 lived in adjacent Lackawanna and Luzerne Counties, where Scranton and Wilkes-Barre, respectively, are the major towns. Of the 35,971 Welsh in Ohio, 24,312 lived in the coal and iron districts of northeastern Ohio and along the Ohio River.[12]

The British statistics on those immigrating to the United States between 1871 and 1920 showed 3.0 million English and Welsh together, 650,000 Scots, and 2.2 million Irish, a much larger number than the official count of the US census. The data discrepancy is a casualty of the differences in the American and British definitions of an "emigrant" and an "immigrant." Until 1909 the United States counted only steerage passengers as immigrants, and a significant number of British had booked second- or even first-class passage to America. Until 1914, on the other hand, the British government classified all passengers as emigrants whether or not they intended to remain in America. Therefore, the American figures are too low while those of the British are too high. Also, the British did not differentiate between the

Welsh and the English, while in 1860 the US government became the first to recognize the Welsh as a distinct nationality. Further confounding the calculations, the British did not enumerate returnees until 1895, and the United States did not record those who returned to their native land until 1908. Because the migrants' motives were undocumented, there is no way to distinguish between immigrants and sojourners. Due to undercounting, the actual figures were undoubtedly higher. Nevertheless, it is clear that far more English, Scots, and Irish came to America than did Welsh, both numerically and as a percentage of their respective national populations. Between 1881 and 1931, Wales lost to the United States an average of fewer than 7 per 10,000 of population, whereas England lost 14, Scotland 25, and Ireland 89 per 10,000. As may be seen in table 1.1, the vast majority migrated between the Civil War and World War I. The number of Welsh-born immigrants in the United States was 29,868 in 1850 and peaked in 1890 at 100,079. On the other hand, that same year the English-born outnumbered the Welsh nine times over, the Scottish-born two and a half times, and the Irish-born by more than eighteen times.[13]

The historically interesting question is why the Welsh migration represented but a trickle relative to the emigration from other countries of the British Isles, both in absolute numbers and as a percentage. Why were the Welsh less likely to emigrate even though the conditions that stimulated emigration elsewhere in the British Isles also were present in Wales? The answer is found in the growth of the Welsh industrial economy and its articulation with the British and American economies. During the second half of the nineteenth century and beginning of the twentieth century, emigration from Britain and investment in the United States were positively correlated. When British capitalists invested in the US industrial expansion, economic activity at home stagnated and excess labor migrated to the United States. When British capitalists invested at home, the reverse occurred—emigration declined and internal migration to British urban-industrial centers accelerated. During the entire period between 1851 and 1911, Great Britain lost population through immigration, mostly to the United States, but departures fluctuated with each economic cycle and were reflected in the peak periods of 1851–1861, the 1880s, and 1901–1911.[14]

The South Wales coal and iron district had migration patterns that were the opposite of the English, Scottish, and American patterns. Emigration from Wales spiked in the 1860s and increased again in the 1880s, but the

Table 1. British-born population of the United States, 1850–1920

Year	Total population	Total foreign-born	English	Welsh	Scottish	Irish
1850	23,191,876	2,244,602	278,675	29,868	70,550	961,719
1860	31,443,321	4,136,175	431,692	45,763	108,518	1,611,304
1870	38,558,371	5,567,229	555,046	74,533	140,835	1,855,827
1880	50,155,783	6,679,943	664,160	83,302	170,136	1,854,571
1890	62,947,714	9,249,560	909,092	100,079	242,231	1,871,509
1900	75,994,575	10,341,276	840,513	93,586	233,524	1,615,459
1910	91,972,266	13,515,886	877,719	82,488	261,076	1,352,251
1920	105,710,620	13,920,692	813,853	67,066	254,570	1,037,234

Source: Berthoff, *British Immigrants in Industrial America*, 7, citing US Bureau of the Census, *Sixteenth Census of the United States*, 1940, 2:43.

losses were more than offset by the population gains from in-migration as Wales absorbed population at a rate second only to the United States. Nearly the opposite occurred in England and Scotland. Wales's distinctive migration pattern is directly related to the growth of the South Wales coal, iron, and tinplate industries during the second half of the nineteenth century. Because of this rapid industrialization, the surplus rural population, as well as tens of thousands of British in-migrants, entered the local workforce. In effect, the South Wales coal, iron, and tinplate industries held back what might have been a flood of immigration to the growing economies of England and the United States. Industrial expansion in the coal and iron district of South Wales helped to stem the flow of migration by absorbing surplus rural laborers who could simply move to the nearest urban-industrial center rather than cross the Atlantic.[15] This migration pattern did not exist within other "Celtic Fringe" nations, particularly Ireland, where no similar expansion of industry provided the rural poor with industrial employment opportunities.

The option of migrating to the South Wales coal and iron district explains why tens of thousands, rather than hundreds of thousands, of Welsh emigrated; it was a significant movement but not a diaspora. The influence of the Welsh migration in the United States, however, far surpasses the weight of its numerical measure. These largely skilled workers followed ethnic, family, and occupational networks in the coal and metal industries within their trades of expertise. According to the US Immigration

Table 1.2. Immigrants to the United States from the British Isles, 1875–1920

Country origin and time period	Immigrants to US with occupations	Percent skilled	Percent laborers	Total immigrants to the US	Annual rate of immigration per 10,000 mean population
WALES					
1875–1880	1,374	54.4	26.0	-	-
1881–1890	5,682	48.4	34.7	12,640	8
1891–1900	5,005	54.3	20.9	11,219	6
1901–1910	11,708	61.6	11.5	18,631	8
1911–1920	9,988	57.0	6.6	15,379	6
(Avg.)		(55.1)	(20.0)		
SCOTLAND					
1875–1880	19,471	51.8	13.6	-	-
1891–1900	28,006	53.6	12.2	60,046	14
1901–1910	86,976	62.2	22.1	133,338	29
1911–1920	100,824	52.2	5.2	164,131	34
(Avg.)		(52.6)	(15.3)		
ENGLAND					
1875–1880	92,602	39.8	31.9	-	-
1881–1890	319,118	34.7	42.5	644,680	25
1891–1900	128,107	52.4	16.0	224,350	8
1901–1910	237,227	62.3	12.4	387,005	12
1911–1920	271,181	52.5	13.0	419,526	12
(Avg.)		(48.3)	(23.2)		
IRELAND					
1875–1880	97,639	14.0	49.6	-	-
1881–1890	382,368	9.2	58.0	655,482	123
1891–1900	280,054	9.2	35.8	404,045	88
1901–1910	316,340	15.0	45.3	371,772	84
1911–1920	187,902	29.3	18.0	240,041	55
(Avg.)		(15.3)	(41.3)		

Sources: Compiled from B. Thomas, *Migration and Economic Growth*, table 81, 269–72; B. Thomas, *Welsh Economy*, table 3, 11. *Notes:* Percentages are rounded to the nearest tenth of a percent. Semiskilled workers were not represented in the breakout data; they were often learning one of the skilled trades associated with the iron-steel-tinplate industries. For Ireland, the percentage of immigrant "servants" (generally women) was higher than that of "common laborers" (generally men).

Commission of 1907–1910, only 15 percent of all immigrants working in industry had been industrial workers in their native countries, but a much larger proportion of the British resumed their previous trades when they arrived in America: 58 percent of the Welsh, 50 percent of the English, and 36 percent of the Scots. The percentage was even greater among the British iron-, steel-, and tinplate workers. Fully 72 percent of the Welsh resumed their previous occupations in the United States, while 48 percent of the English and 43 percent of Scots did so—a very high percentage compared with 21 percent of the Swedes and 17 percent of the Germans, two other nationalities with a significant presence in the US steel industry.[16]

Of the immigrant Welsh workers with identifiable occupations, 75 percent were concentrated in the coal mining and iron and steel industries. Census data do not identify actual occupation by ethnic group, thus precluding a precise number for Welsh in the metal industries. However, the census data demonstrate that two-thirds of the Welsh workers who entered the United States between 1881 and 1920 were "professional" and or "skilled" (table 1.2). The "semiskilled," often in training for skilled occupations in the metal industries, were not included in the breakout tables.

David Davies, editor of major daily newspapers in Cardiff and Swansea and a very knowledgeable observer of the South Wales metal industries, toured the Welsh mill communities in the United States in 1897–1898. He estimated that there were "7,000 Welshmen employed at American works."[17] Davies certainly undercounted the total, however, for the semiskilled and laborers would have been nearly invisible to him. A closer estimate for the total number of Welsh-born workers in the US steel industry at the turn of the twentieth century would have easily reached more than 10,000 of the total 125,000 steelworkers in the country. Male Welsh immigrants were overwhelmingly married with children, so a conservative estimate of the Welsh-born steelworkers and their dependents would not have registered below 40,000. Nevertheless, even if the official count were doubled or tripled, the fact remains that the number of Welsh in the United States was small in comparison with other nationalities.

According to a leading expert on Welsh emigration, "The popular impression that Welsh workers flocked to the United States in the latter half of the nineteenth century is a myth. In the decade 1881–1890, when the absorptive power of the United States was at a peak, the effect on Wales was hardly noticeable." The annual rate per ten thousand British Isles immigrants with identifiable occupations was only three for Wales, twelve for England, twenty for Scotland, and seventy-seven for Ireland.[18] Historian Rowland Tappan Berthoff's observation that the nineteenth-century British migration to the United States "ran not in a broad, undifferentiated stream but rather in many parallel channels" has particular poignancy for the Welsh. According to Berthoff, few of them were likely to cross the Atlantic unless they expected to find work in their chosen trade. The historical significance of the Welsh migration, therefore, lies not so much in its numbers as in the fact that they were skilled in crafts and management and "directly transfused the skills and experience of the premier industrial nation of the early nineteenth century into the veins of the rising giant of the twentieth."[19]

On arrival in the United States, the Welsh flocked to colonies of compatriots where they would be welcomed by relatives and friends, as at the Lonaconing ironworks in Maryland, where it was reported that the workers were "all uncles and cousins."[20] The 100,079 Welsh-born residents of the United States in 1890 were widely dispersed, as shown in map 2. The Reverend R. D. Thomas counted two hundred Welsh settlements in 1870, all of them small except for those contained within in urban-industrial centers, such as Scranton, Wilkes-Barre, Pittsburgh, and Youngstown. The industrial migrants were concentrated in the coal and iron centers of Pennsylvania and Ohio, where nearly one-half of all the Welsh lived, while the Welsh agricultural migrants were concentrated in Ohio and Wisconsin. Welsh migrants nearly always settled north of the Mason-Dixon line because the demand for industrial labor was strongest in the North. Four of every five Welsh immigrants lived in Pennsylvania, New York, Ohio, or Wisconsin in 1880. As late as 1900, after decades of American westward migration, two of every three Welsh still lived in these states, plus Minnesota.[21]

Welshmen and their families set out for the coal, iron, and steel districts of western Pennsylvania and Ohio. Johnstown, in Cambria County, Pennsylvania, grew under the stimulus of a major steel mill, and satellite coal mining communities provided the great quantities of coal consumed by the furnaces. The large Welsh colony of a thousand or more that had congregated around the mills and mines prompted one Welsh immigrant to call the Cambria Iron Company works the "Dowlais of America," referring to the largest ironworks in Wales.[22] By midcentury the iron and coal industries had also established an embryonic presence in Ohio, and

Map 2. Locations of Welsh-born persons living in the United States, 1890. Each dot represents one hundred persons. After R. Lewis, *Welsh Americans*, 49.

the number of industry enterprises expanded rapidly in that state during the Civil War and postwar years. In the northeastern Ohio triangle of the industrial cities of Youngstown, Cleveland, and Canton, thousands of Welsh iron- and steelworkers arrived between the 1850s and the 1890s. In many of these towns the Welsh occupied a prominent presence; a native of the Welsh "tinplate capital" of Llanelli reported that Youngstown was the "Welsh metropolis of America."[23]

In many respects the story of William H. "Bill" Davey was typical of the Welsh steelworker who immigrated to America during the period when the tinplate industry was first established in the United States. Davey's family had been engaged in steel and tinplate manufacture for generations, his father as a heater and his grandfather as an engineer in the same works. Davey was born in 1873 in Briton Ferry, Glamorganshire, South Wales. His father moved his large family to Pontypool to find work when the Briton Ferry works closed for lack of orders. Then, when Bill was fifteen, a shutdown in the mill finally prompted his father to move to the United States, where he had wanted to go for some time.[24]

His father's siblings had preceded him in making that move, so his was not a reckless act of desperation. At Demmler, Pennsylvania, near Pittsburgh, the elder Davey took a position in 1888 as a roller in the U.S. Iron and Tinplate Manufacturing Company's blackplate mill, and his entire family soon joined him. Bill Davey became an opener on the hot mills and later a screwboy (one who assisted several skilled men at a time). At seventeen he became a heater for his father and at twenty went to work as a roller at the Falcon Tin Plate & Sheet Company in Niles, Ohio. From then on he followed the "tramping artisan" tradition so common among the skilled ironworkers and tinplaters of this period, moving on to Crescent Works in Cleveland, to Canal Dover, Cambridge, Youngstown, and then Martins Ferry, Ohio. His first position as manager was at McKeesport Tinplate Company, but from there he moved to become manager at McClure Tinplate, then Carnahan Tinplate in Canton, Ohio. Bill and two of his brothers constructed the Massillon Rolling Mill and then bought Carnahan, which they sold to Republic Steel in 1935. While becoming a manager and then owner was not typical for Welsh immigrants in the American industry, neither was it an unusual career trajectory.[25]

Bill Davey's reminiscences were published in Roy Rutherford's *Romancing in Tin Plate*, an excellent technical history of the industry.[26] Davey's reminiscence reveals the wide network of acquaintances that prevailed among the early Welsh tinplate communities in the United States. For example, one of the most important improvements in the tinning process was developed by Edmund Morewood in 1866, when he invented the patent rolling of tin plates as they left the tinning pot. Hand-dipping was replaced by the Morewood pot, which consisted of a pair of submerged revolving rollers in a pot of hot grease. The plates passed between the rollers, thus regulating the amount and evenness of the tin coating. Submerged rolls would eventually be utilized throughout the operation, thus eliminating hand labor except for the initial feeding.[27] "By a peculiar coincidence," Davey reminisced, "this family of Morewoods and my father and mother were playmates together as children in Briton Ferry, Wales. They were later employed by the same company and at the same works which was known as the Vernon Tin Plate Company."[28]

Davey knew and kept track of the Welsh workers who succeeded in the American tinplate industry. He noted, for example, that the Baltimore Tin Plate Company, located at Locust Point, in Baltimore, Maryland, was purchased by the American Tin-Plate Company trust, which almost immediately closed its doors. Bosses at the works were Jimmie Michaels, William Thomas, John Jones, and John Taylor, all from Briton Ferry, Wales. Davey also recalled that the Stickney Iron Works, another tinplate plant erected in Baltimore, was superintended by John Embright, "whom I worked for as a boy." Davey went on to mention other Welsh managers at numerous other mills. Substantial Welsh communities developed in the Indiana gas belt, in towns such as Elwood and Gas City, and Davey came to know the operators of these mills when he served as financial secretary of the Amalgamated Association of Iron, Steel and Tinplate Workers. The mills in Indiana produced a number of prominent men in the industry, many of them Welsh, Davey recalled. One was Charlie Hook, who chaired the board of the American Rolling Mill Company. Another was W. P. Lewis, a mill superintendent who later returned to Wales to manage the tinplate works at Cwmavon. Davey's brother-in-law, John M. Jones, was superintendent of the works at Montpelier, Indiana, and later built the tinplate plant of the Bethlehem Steel Company at Sparrows Point, in Maryland. Davey also affirmed that Welsh immigrants generally followed the chain migration pattern, with friends and relatives providing new immigrants with a base of support, including occupational news and contacts. The home of Davey's parents served as one of these way stations, Davey recollected, noting that "our home at McKeesport, Pa. seemed to be the rendezvous for all those who came from Wales looking for a job."[29]

During this early period the separation between the skilled workforce and management was narrow, for skilled tinplate workers were responsible for the production and quality of the product. Among the Welsh immigrants, however, there was a distinction between those who were skilled and those who were not, and especially those who never would be. Their behaviors were apparent in how they related to management and personnel issues. As one of the elites, Davey reflected this attitude: "A lot of our friends from the other side came over here and got into disrepute, especially antagonistic toward the operator insofar as the union was concerned. Many of these meetings ended in brawls, and a lot of our Welsh tin workers got into bad grace because of some of these habits. In fact, one crowd went out to Gas City and in saloon parlors were known as the 'Dirty Dozen.'" Davey observed that William C. Cronemeyer "became very much disgusted by these tactics and Welshmen seemed to be imbued with the idea that anybody who ventured into the tin plate business was an invader and resented it." Cronemeyer decided he could find more amicable workers in Germany than in Wales or England and, "in direct violation of the immigration laws at that time, brought back a large number of German workers." Davey observed that they became very good workers and citizens, but "for a long while only those from Wales and England were efficient workers; others had been tried unsuccessfully." The Welsh, of course, were outraged, and "while the Germans were not up to the standard of the Welsh worker, it did not take long for them to become efficient."[30]

By the time of this reminiscence, the exact date of which is not clear, Bill Davey sounded very much like an American, declaring that "the tin plate market was already here and all we had to do was take it away from the Welshman."[31]

The notion that the Welsh were much less likely to emigrate than the English or Scots does not fit comfortably into the popular perception of the Welsh, as historian Gwyn Williams has observed. Welsh American émigrés occupied a special place in Welsh life because they were literally and figuratively family. The farmers, colliers, and steelworkers who missed their family and friends subscribed to local and trade newspapers and wrote letters, and, after transatlantic transportation improved, many returned home to visit. Industrial modernization had fractured their families, but locations where they settled, such as Scranton, Pittsburgh, Youngstown, and other, smaller mill towns, became virtually household names in Wales. The idea that relatively few Welsh emigrants went to the United States contradicts received wisdom in Wales because there are few families, and hardly any extended families, that do not include an American branch.[32]

In addition to the small size of the Welsh migration and the inadequate statistical data constraining historians of the Welsh American experience, the written record left by Welsh Americans themselves is scant and sometimes misleading. These writings often exaggerated the number of Welsh in the United States, as well as the extent of their contribution to the country. Among the more colorful of the claims repeated again and again in print was that a Welsh royal named Prince Madoc had sailed west from Wales and "discovered America" in the twelfth century. Some were convinced that the Mandan Indians, Native Americans of the northern Great Plains who supposedly spoke Welsh, were descendants of Madoc. Unfounded myths, along with the boasting of the "most eminent" Welsh Americans, did little to bolster meager historical documentation and obscured the real experience.[33] Such filiopietistic writing appeared at the height of the Welsh migration in the late nineteenth and early twentieth centuries in popular Welsh American periodicals like *Y Drych*, *The Druid*, and *The Cambrian*. "The ever constant overwhelming praise of the Welsh" was "nauseating," the Welsh American William Howells declared to *The Druid* in 1909. The editor dismissed Howells's objection, suggesting that he medicate his indigestion.[34] These periodicals presented the Welsh as positive reinforcements to the American Anglo-Saxon nation, unlike the southern and central European immigrants, and they extolled the Welsh as the most religious, dependable, thrifty, and abstemious of people.

Moreover, the Welsh migration to the United States was overwhelmingly composed of working people who left no caches of manuscript records or personal papers. Therefore, despite their inherent biases, periodicals are one of the most important sources for studying Welsh America. Even though they must be used with caution, the ethnic newspapers and magazines served an important function in the transition from the Old World to the New. The editors might have been motivated by ethnic pride, but the published biographical profiles of prominent individuals in many cases provide the only historical record of their lives. Most significant for the social historian are the letters and articles submitted by otherwise ordinary Welsh immigrants living in scattered and otherwise disconnected communities. From these sources can be gleaned local community news, as well as the state of local industry, conditions, and employment. The letters and articles helped to maintain the ethnic networks that facilitated and, to a degree, determined the direction of Welsh migration and settlement in America. Moreover, the periodicals gave Welsh Americans a more powerful collective voice than their actual numbers would have suggested.

Forces Energizing Preindustrial Migration

Americans and the Welsh may think of the industrial migration of the mid- to late nineteenth century as the historical tissue connecting the two places, but the links actually stretch back to the origins of the United States. Although an indeterminate number of Welsh traveled to the American colonies, they were few in number and they went as individuals.[35] The earliest immigrants were people with some means and a broader political and religious consciousness than is generally ascribed to poor rural migrants. Several prominent nonconformist members of the clergy with a wide following in Wales, as well as a deep understanding of American affairs, embraced the American Revolutionary War and took the lead in defending it from opponents in Britain. In his *Observations on the Nature of Civil Liberty* (1776), the dissenter Richard Price anticipated Thomas Paine's application of the "rights of man" to the American Revolution, and David Williams, another Welsh dissenter who knew Benjamin Franklin, also advanced an intellectual defense of the Americans in *Letters on Political Liberty* (1782). Both argued for the God-given right to national self-determination, and Williams went a step further by advocating universal manhood suffrage, the ballot, payment of MPs, annual parliaments, and smaller constituencies—all reforms that presaged the Chartist manifesto. The identification of America with radical democratic ideals had a strong appeal in Wales, particularly when expressed by these highly respected religious leaders. While these revolutionary ideas did not stimulate emigration, they did place the United States in the mix of legitimate alternatives for Welsh settlement.[36]

Welsh emigration in the long nineteenth century was divided into two phases, the first an agricultural migration from 1815 to the 1840s and then an industrial migration between 1850 and 1920. The Welsh agricultural migration was generated by major social and economic changes on the land similar to those stimulating the mass migrations in Europe following the Napoleonic wars. For most of the nineteenth century, according to historian Alan Conway, Wales was two nations. The rural areas were occupied by a "Welsh-speaking, non-conformist, politically Liberal Welsh peasantry and an English-speaking, Anglican, politically Tory land-owner class." In the industrial districts "the same linguistic, ethnic, religious, and political differences divided the foundry men from the ironmasters." This division was more or less true for the colliers who were employed in the mines belonging to the iron companies. In the heavily capitalized segments of the iron and coal district of South Wales, the Royal Commission on the State of Education in Wales emphasized this division in 1847: "In the works the Welsh workman never finds his way into the office. He never becomes either clerk or agent. . . . Equally in his new, as in his old, home, his language keeps him under the hatches, being one in which he can neither acquire nor communicate the necessary information. It is a language of old-fashioned agriculture, of theology and of simple rustic life, while the entire world about him is English."[37]

Wales was therefore unprepared for the great population explosion that began in the early nineteenth century and had doubled the number of inhabitants of Wales by midcentury. The dramatic increase in the price for corn during the wars with France between 1793 and 1815 precipitated the enclosure movement and led to the enclosure of the uplands formerly regarded as suitable only for the poor. Welsh farmers removed from the moorland grew into an "army of landless farm laborers" forced to migrate to the burgeoning South Wales coal and iron district or to immigrate to the United States, where cheap land was available.[38]

Corn prices collapsed with the end of war, and economic depression ensued. By 1817 Wales had entered a period of famine. The normally conservative Welsh peasants became radicalized, and their grievances exploded in the Rebecca Riots following passage of the Highways Act of 1835, which initiated a turnpike system in Wales, maintained by tolls collected at gates erected every few miles. The tolls laid an excessive financial burden on the already strapped farmers, and they were quick to demonstrate their distress. The first riot erupted in 1839 in western Wales and spread to South Wales during the early 1840s. Like the better-known rural violence of the Whiteboys, Ribbonmen, and Molly Maguires in Ireland, Welshmen disguised in women's clothes and with their faces blackened set about destroying the tollgates and driving off the keepers and constables who attempted to protect them.[39]

The agrarian unrest had major implications, as the Welsh became much more politically conscious. The nonconformist ministers emerged from the smoke of cultural warfare as the uncontested leaders of the people in the struggle against the Anglican, English-speaking, Tory landowners who still controlled society. The rising tide of Welsh nationalism broke in full force over the Treachery of the Blue Books, an inquiry conducted for Parliament by the Royal Commission on the State of Education in Wales and resulting in a report released in 1847. The three commissioners were English Anglicans ignorant of the Welsh language and culture, and they managed to insult patriotic Welsh with their arrogant conclusions that the language, culture, and institutions of Wales were inferior. The report was received in Wales with bitter indignation, and it galvanized the Welsh behind the nonconformist ministers who launched a counterattack against English imperialism.[40]

The Treachery of the Blue Books shifted the balance of power in the political struggle for the hearts and minds of the Welsh-speaking population in favor of the nonconformist ministers, who rose up in unison to denounce the Blue Books, and they brought the issue of disestablishment of the Anglican Church as the official state church to the forefront of Welsh politics.[41]

In this context, one can readily understand why the idea of establishing a new Welsh nation abroad, one that would preserve the language and culture of Wales, gained urgency during the nineteenth century. Nonconformist ministers, such as Morgan John Rhys, Benjamin Chidlaw, Samuel Roberts, and Michael D. Jones, played a prominent role in this movement that led thousands of Welsh to establish new colonies in the United States and, in Jones's case, in Argentina's Patagonia region.[42]

Undoubtedly these promotional activities stimulated interest in and general awareness of emigration among the rural Welsh population. The vast majority of those who left for America went for pragmatic rather than idealistic reasons. Even though the vast majority did not seek an exclusive Welsh existence, the pre-1840s agrarian migrants tended to join family and friends in the Welsh agricultural communities of Pennsylvania, New York, and eastern Ohio, where they continued their familiar practices with little interference. Welsh settlers followed the American western agricultural migration into the fertile flatlands of the Midwest. Large concentrations of Welsh settled in Wisconsin, and others moved on to Iowa, Missouri, and Kansas. Compared with other immigrant groups, however, their numbers were small, and the farther west the Welsh migrated, the more dispersed they became. It is also clear that they emigrated individually or in family groups, relying on family to assist them in settling the new land. However, one section of the United States that Welsh farmers avoided was the South, because they found slavery repugnant, cheap land was scarce, and there was little demand for their labor in a region dependent on oppressed Black workers. The 1860 census reported that fewer than 500 of the 45,500 foreign-born Welsh lived below the Mason-Dixon line.[43] Occupying a unique place in the history of Welsh emigration in the mid-nineteenth century was the large number of Mormon converts who settled in Utah. The Mormon scholar Douglas Davies claims that in 1887 the Welsh population reached nearly 17,000, or about 15 percent of the population in Utah, while another authority finds this figure too low, estimating that the Welsh population was closer to 25,000.[44]

Industrial Migration within Wales

As the rural economy rebounded in the 1850s and 1860s, emigration from rural Wales to the United States faded. Prosperity did not last long, however, for in the late 1870s the Welsh countryside was plunged into a severe

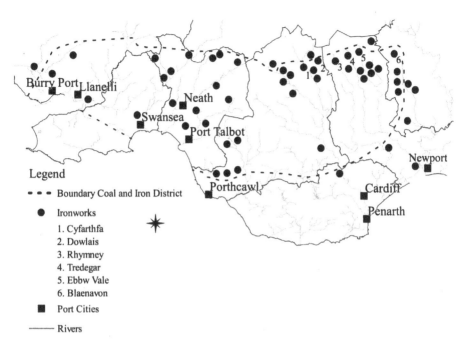

Map 3. Ironworks in South Wales, 1860. Cartography by Caroline Welter, Regional Research Institute, West Virginia University, Morgantown.

depression that lasted for the next two decades. Once again poverty forced people to migrate, but this time many went to the rapidly expanding South Wales coal and iron district.[45]

In the nineteenth century Welsh industry was defined regionally. Slate mines and quarries dominated the northwestern county of Gwynedd; Cardiganshire was noted for its woolens manufactured in small shops and homes throughout the western counties. Copper was smelted in the lower Swansea Valley, and to the west in Llanelli and adjacent towns the Welsh tinplate industry dominated British production to the point of monopoly. But it was the ironworks, born out of the demands of the almost continuous wars with France from 1757 to 1815, that emerged as the dominant industry in Wales during the first half of the nineteenth century. Eight great ironworks, as well as numerous smaller ones, sprang up to cast guns and munitions. At the center of the iron industry stood Merthyr Tydfil, the "Iron Capital of the World," encircled by the giant Cyfarthfa, Dowlais, Penydarren, and Plymouth works.[46]

By midcentury, the advantages of location at the upper rim of the South Wales coalfield dimmed as the ores played out and technological changes forced the iron industry to move down the valleys to the coast. The South Wales coal industry became the engine of the Welsh economy during the last half of the nineteenth century.[47] The industrial transformation of Wales in the nineteenth century is documented statistically by the growth in population, from about half a million in 1800, 80 percent of whom depended on agriculture, to more than 2.5 million in 1914, 80 percent of whom lived in urban areas and were employed in nonagricultural pursuits. By 1850 the number of industrial workers had already passed that of farmers, and, by 1910, 388,000 people had abandoned the Welsh countryside, primarily for the South Wales iron and coal industries. Most of the workforce was Welsh at midcentury, but during the last half of the nineteenth century Wales became an importer of labor. By the first decade of the twentieth century, the population of Glamorgan County had surpassed one million, and fully one-third had been born outside the country.[48]

Prior to industrial expansion in the nineteenth century, Wales was overwhelmingly pastoral, and the workforce that gathered in the new coal and iron towns lacked a tradition of class cohesion.[49] During the crisis years of depression and the First Reform Bill, 1829–1831, the working class in Wales began to take shape as a national force. The rising class consciousness peaked with the Merthyr Tydfil Rising of May 1831, when the workers took over the city for four days; authorities regained control only after three pitched battles with military troops. Eight years after the Merthyr Rising, Chartism, the first attempt to build an independent political party representing the interests of the working classes, took root in the Welsh valleys.[50] The Chartists took their name from their charter, first published in 1838, demanding universal manhood suffrage, annual parliaments, the secret ballot, abolition of property qualifications for members of Parliament, payment to MPs, and equal electoral districts. When soldiers fired on the Chartists' ill-fated march on Newport in 1839, the result was twenty-two deaths and three leaders transported to the Australian penal colony. Yet, in spite of these losses, the workers of the coal and iron district had established another milepost on the road to solidarity.[51]

Despite the labor unrest, militant trade unionism (with which Welsh coal miners and iron- and steelworkers became synonymous in the twentieth century) was slow to find organization. For most of the nineteenth century,

Welsh miners and foundry workers were not ideological radicals; in fact, they were preoccupied with wages even to the exclusion of hours of labor, safety, and working conditions.[52] It was this preoccupation with wages that shaped their attitudes toward unionism. When unions promised to have wages raised, workers joined; when they failed to keep that promise, workers lost interest. Consequently, no permanent industry-wide labor organizations were established in Wales until the 1890s. Many reasons have been offered for the difficulties confronting the early unions, but the idea that workers and employers shared a common interest in keeping the works operating weakened the development of unions. In the 1870s the automatic wage regulator, the sliding scale, and the regulatory committee were mechanisms established to deal with grievances, and these undoubtedly weakened the perceived need for strong labor unions. Also, the nonconformist religious denominations, which had particularly strong representation among the mine and mill workers, opposed the unions. The strike weapon was therefore the only instrument left to the miners, and for most of the century it was used in generally unsuccessful attempts to prevent a cut in wages, rather than to seek wage advances.[53] The ironworkers embraced the sliding scale because it brought an end to the turmoil in the South Wales coalfield and removed the wage rate from the arbitrary actions of the employers. It also undermined the need for a strong labor union.[54] The commitment of Welsh ironworkers to the sliding scale and the arbitration of grievances was therefore deeply rooted in their experience in Wales.

The great influx of people seeking employment in the burgeoning South Wales coal and iron district came primarily from rural Wales; most were displaced agricultural laborers who brought with them their own traditions and religious practices. In the years prior to the 1850s, Protestant Nonconformism, as represented by the Unitarians, Congregationalists, Presbyterians, Baptists, Calvinistic Methodists, and Independents, characterized the religion of the Welsh. Many Welsh rejected the Church of England as an imposition and symbol of their subordinate position to England. Also, they found comfort in the simplicity of the denominational structure of Nonconformism, in which control rested with the local congregations. Therefore, 87 percent of them attended nonconformist chapels while only 9 percent of Welsh churchgoers attended the Church of England.[55]

Nonconformism attracted many talented Welsh ministers. Its antiestablishment stance carried within it the roots of Welsh nationalism, but what made Nonconformism the religion of Wales were the nonreligious institutions created and then transported to America. Dissenting chapels became educational centers for working-class children and adults (whom British institutions ignored) by operating tuition-free day schools and Sunday schools. Moreover, unlike the Anglican churches, which were strictly devotional spaces, the nonconformist chapels also served as community centers, providing educational activities such as lectures, eisteddfodau, concerts, and readings, as well as serving as meeting places.[56] The dissenting denominations emphasized the "centrality of individual responsibility and worth, and claimed that individual evils were responsible for the social iniquities of the period," not the capitalists, not the economic system, not the complicity of government. The emphasis was on personal respectability rather than social change. Therefore, with the exception of the free-thinking Unitarians, the nonconformist denominations were either lukewarm or hostile to the social revolts of the day, such as the Rebecca Riots, the Merthyr Tydfil Rising of 1831, and the Chartist movement.[57]

The growing importance of Disestablishment, or the movement for religious freedom and independence for the nonconformist denominations from the official state church, offered another point of convergence for labor and dissenter radicalism. With greater representation in Parliament, reformers could support the repeal of laws that prevented freedom of religious expression.[58] Notwithstanding the stirrings of conscience among some individual clerics, official Nonconformism in Wales took no stand on social or political issues unless they directly affected the denominations, so nonconformist ministers seemed indifferent to the social problems that affected the tens of thousands of their adherents. The struggle between labor and capital intensified as the nineteenth century waned, but most nonconformist leaders seemed blind to social injustice. One worker complained that, "instead of giving men justice," the ministers attempted to make workers "more sober, humble, and contrite in heart." The chapels were good for "Psalm singing, tea meetings, and pious sentiments," he continued, but "their influence is always on the side of the oppressors, the capitalists." The split in Wales between the radical dissenters and traditional nonconformist ministers resurfaced in the United States.[59]

Bound for America

It is against the backdrop of poor living and working conditions, the unpredictability of employment and wages, and the growing power of

Nonconformism that the emigration from the Welsh coal and iron district must be understood. Ethnically, these families were very cohesively Welsh, culturally not far distant from rural Wales, and bound together by a common language. Many industrial workers were still capable of returning to the land, but increasingly most mine and mill workers were the children of migrants who had known only industrial life. Therefore, when economic difficulties mounted, the lure of a rapidly industrializing America, where skilled labor was in demand and an abundance of cheap land was still available, proved irresistible for many. After decades of nonconformist ministers' letter writing, newspaper exchanges, and lectures on the advantages offered by the United States, the Welsh were fully apprised of political and economic developments there.

The Civil War caused great apprehension in Wales and dampened the emigration spirit until it became clear that the Union would prevail. The Welsh clergy and the press spoke in a unified voice against slavery, and public opinion in Wales was strongly supportive of the Union during the Civil War, which they viewed as a struggle to end the evil of slavery. Prior to the war, nearly all Welsh immigrants had settled in the northern states, at least in part because of their abhorrence of slavery. Almost without exception, therefore, those who fought in the war enlisted in the Union ranks. Prior to 1863, President Lincoln occasionally was chastised in the Welsh press for not emancipating the slaves.[60] Even with the disruptions in transportation, however, a number of Welsh workers, most of them skilled ironworkers and colliers, embarked for the United States during the war years. American workers were being drafted into the military, so newly arrived British replacements readily found work at high wages. The *Merthyr Telegraph* editorialized on the reasons for the emigration of industrial workers, noting first low wages, followed by a glut of labor in the mines and mills, and the almost constant strife between workers and operators over low wages and poor living and working conditions. Consequently, even with the attendant risks, the potential for prosperity in the United States was preferable to the certain misery of remaining at home.[61] The outflow strengthened as the war proceeded, and its conclusion in 1865 triggered a surge of Welsh migrants heading for the United States.

By the end of the 1860s, however, there was a growing concern in the South Wales coal and iron district over a perceived mass migration. It was not in Merthyr's interest to export its best workers, city newspapers pointed out, for local industry would be deprived of their services, while, at the same time, they would be in the United States helping to advance the industrial interests of Merthyr's competitors. The *Merthyr Telegraph* editorialized in 1869 that, with the "excessive course of depletion" from the coal and iron district, "we lose our best workmen and our competitors gain their services; and while we suffer they are advantaged."[62] The *Merthyr Express* complained in 1868 under the headline "Emigration: Its Advantages and Disadvantages" that people were still keen to go abroad, and "our best men have been scattered to the four corners of the earth."[63] By the end of the decade, the emigration "contagion" had been resurrected as a criticism of the owners of industry for neglecting their civic responsibilities by not paying their skilled workers a proper wage or giving them the respect they deserved.[64] Historian William D. Jones suggests that Merthyr Tydfil is best understood as a "transnational" city. The press played an influential role in constructing an international Merthyr and nurturing an awareness of a wider world with the town at its nerve center. The city's newspapers carried news of former residents, printed letters from them, and reprinted extracts from overseas newspapers sent to them by emigrants.[65]

By 1868 South Wales had many emigration societies, particularly in the coal and iron towns at the heads of the Taff, Cynon, Rhondda, and Rhymney Valleys, where there was serious economic distress and a significant number of people were leaving, mostly for the United States.[66] Two societies were launched in Merthyr in 1868: the Merthyr Tydfil Emigration Society and the Cambrian Emigration Society, both organized by workers themselves and both hoping to relieve the labor surplus.[67] The historical significance of both organizations, as well as others like them, is in the evidence that many industrial workers in South Wales, as in Britain generally, considered emigration to be a legitimate alternative during times of economic stress. The emigration societies provided assistance to members who emigrated, but the greatest majority of those who migrated to the States did so with their own funds and relied on their own networks of family and friends to make the passage.[68] In 1869, *The Times* of London observed that it was disheartening to witness the "large number" of skilled working men "constantly leaving the coal and iron district of South Wales from Merthyr, Aberdare, Pontypool, and other centres of population." Each week 100 to 120 were departing, and "the passage money of a large number of them has been paid by relatives and friends who left their native home years ago, and who have since so far prospered as to be able to render this assistance to their connexions. As usual a large majority of the emigrants are leaving for the United States."[69]

The emergence of emigrant steamship lines as a mature business transformed traveling conditions and significantly lowered the barriers to crossing the Atlantic. Steamships first plied the Atlantic in the 1840s, but they carried only a few cabin passengers who could afford the trip. In 1856, 96 percent of all British passengers entering the United States through New York City arrived by sailing vessels, mostly American packets. The rapid shift to steam had important repercussions on the emigration business. By 1865 nearly three-quarters, and in 1867 more than 90 percent, of British passengers bound for North America arrived by steamship. By the end of the decade travel by sail was a thing of the past.[70]

Large-scale migration to the United States would not have been possible without the shift to steam because crossing the Atlantic Ocean in a sailing ship was a monumental psychological barrier for most people. Passage from Liverpool to New York took about five weeks by sail, and foul weather could easily lengthen the voyage to fourteen weeks. Steamships reduced the length of the voyage to two weeks or less, were more reliable, and provided a far less traumatic experience than sailing vessels. They made the world smaller so that crossing the Atlantic seemed less irreversible; if one were disappointed with America or wanted to visit family, returning was not unreasonable or impractical. Travel by steamship also made seasonal migration possible for workers who could sojourn to the States when work was scarce in Britain and return home when the economy recovered.[71]

Reporting on the departure of emigrants from Beaufort, at the head of the Ebbw Fawr valley in Monmouthshire, a Merthyr newspaper account observed that "the difficulty of getting to America is of little moment or consideration," for the journey to America "is now looked upon as a mere excursion."[72] Typically, married men would precede their wives to the States and, once they had earned sufficient money, would send steamship passes so their families could join them. In October 1869, the *Baner ac Amserau Cymru* correspondent in Aberdare reported that scores of wives were leaving the train station to join their husbands in America.[73] Even under the best of circumstances, departures were dramatic, disruptive events for families and communities. Farewell and departure rituals, sometimes with concerts, poetry reading, and speeches, provided the emigrants a proper send-off, but they also testify to the impact of emigration on the family and community. Large crowds often escorted emigrants to the train station amid exhibitions of great joy and sorrow. A newspaper reported in 1869 that hundreds of Aberdare residents paraded in the streets, cheering and waving handkerchiefs in a farewell to a party of emigrants.[74]

Emigration triggered social repercussions in Wales and America on a very personal level. Families were the principal links in the networks that supported the chain migration and forged transnational identities among families in both Wales and the United States. It created distinctive ethnic occupational communities in the United States that, as long as memory and communication lasted, made America an extension of "home."

2

Transnational Institutions

The Welsh had been coming to America since the eighteenth century, and by the mid-nineteenth century the economies of Wales and the United States had been bound together by commerce, capital investment, and labor exchange. Beyond the belief that immigrants could elevate their economic positions in America, Welsh immigrants also were attracted by the social and political ideals that elevated democracy over aristocracy and, most importantly for the dissenting non-Anglican Welsh, the absence of an official state church. These themes were emphasized repeatedly in Welsh American publications promoting the idea that the Welsh were contributors to the American ideal of success. Welsh writers and intellectual leaders proclaimed that success was achieving middle-class security, and they promoted the employer-friendly notion that Welsh workers were economic partners in the capitalist enterprise rather than ideological antagonists. For these bourgeois writers, upward mobility and financial success were the primary measures determining whether immigrants had achieved the American dream.

Welsh immigrants who had been attracted by the American iron and steel industry ultimately created transnational cultural spaces in mill communities where they settled, and they carried with them cultural markers that generally worked against other immigrants. In addition to speaking another language, the Welsh maintained their own national church denominations, which conducted the liturgy in the Welsh language. Welsh communities tended to cluster around these churches, and their tendency to marry and to employ workers from their own group exposed them to charges of "clannishness." The migrants from Wales also had their own fraternal orders and literary societies, and they brought with them the eisteddfod, a unique cultural festival usually conducted in the Welsh language. Although Americans took note of various Welsh cultural distinctions, such things did not prompt the serious negative reactions to cultural expressions that southern and eastern European immigrants experienced.

Unlike so many of their agricultural counterparts, few industrial workers who emigrated from Wales had the conscious intention of preserving Welsh culture in a new land. They settled together because mill workers congregated around the iron and steel mills that employed them, and being close to family and friends who helped ease the transition to life in America was particularly important for monoglot Welsh immigrants. Nevertheless, to the degree circumstances allowed, lifeways in the Welsh American settlements had been transplanted from Wales. How conscious the immigrants were of this process very much depended on the degree of importance they placed on Welsh national identity before they left their homeland. Large sections of South Wales had become heavily anglicized by the nineteenth century as industrialization drew Wales into the greater commercial and political dynamics of the British Empire.

The Welsh Language

The migration of rural monoglot Welsh into the industrial centers of South Wales reinforced traditional culture within the new coal and iron communities. As with other immigrants who often found their national identity when they became a minority in the American polyglot of peoples, so too did many of the Welsh. The kind of community in which the immigrants settled, however, was crucial. In the large cities, like New York or Philadelphia, they would simply disappear into the large, diverse population. Even in a city like Pittsburgh, where the Welsh played an important role in the steel industry, their presence was overshadowed by other, larger ethnic populations. In small- and medium-sized towns and cities, however, the Welsh language and churches persisted into the twentieth century.[1]

The cultural background of the Welsh and other British immigrants pre-sented far less formidable barriers than those encountered by other foreign immigrants. The majority of the Welsh were at least able to speak English, shared common legal and political traditions, were devout Protestants and skilled industrial workers, and generally mirrored American middle-class values and aspirations. As one historian observed, most British immigrants passed almost unnoticed into American life; the "immigrant problem" had nothing to do with the English, Scots, or even the more "clannish and foreign-speaking Welsh." The British generally escaped ridicule from Americans. Derogatory names like "micks," "dagoes," and "hunkies" were never attached to British immigrants. The Welsh might object to being called "Taffy" or "goat," but few Americans used these terms at all, and fewer still either understood or intentionally used them as epithets. Welsh immi-grants generally were inclined to band together in their own communities, but they seldom lived apart from Americans and were never segregated by law or custom.[2] As one knowledgeable Welsh observer commented, "The Welshman somehow does not regard himself as a foreigner in the States, and reserves the appellation for races which are not of Anglo-British origin."[3]

Although one might expect that their language would have served as a hurdle to acquiring American citizenship, a higher proportion of Welsh became fully naturalized citizens than the English or Scots. In fact, only 7 percent of Welsh immigrants had not applied for citizenship in 1900, whereas 13 percent of the English and the Scots had not. The Welsh ex-hibited a higher proportion of fully naturalized citizenship than migrants from any other nation. In 1920, 72.9 percent of the foreign-born Welsh were naturalized American citizens, whereas the percentage for all foreign countries combined was 47.2 percent. They were no less attached to their homeland, but they were not equally loyal to the British Crown and were not reluctant to renounce their allegiance to the Crown when taking on American citizenship. Measuring return migration with anything like pre-cision is impossible because of the way statistics were, or were not, collected in the nineteenth century, but scholars estimate that only 13 percent of the Welsh and Scottish, and 21 percent of the English, in the United States returned to their homelands between 1908 and 1923. This is an extremely small percentage compared with eastern and southern Europeans.[4]

Mill towns were fertile incubators of a distinctive Welsh and work-based culture. Iron and steel mill life was reproduced in the nineteenth century by fathers who transferred their knowledge of the craft to their sons by taking them into the mills as boys. Mill culture was distinguished, therefore, by not only the unique bonds formed as a result of shared difficulties and the dangers of the job itself but also because it was welded together by intergenerational, interfamilial, and intraethnic dependencies. Moreover, it was very difficult to shift from one trade to another without a sponsor. Those who belonged in the community were born into either this culture or a very similar one.

The Welsh language was a distinctive cultural carryover that the Welsh brought with them to the United States. It unified people from different places and experiences in Wales and bound them as a group to withstand the disintegrative forces that threatened the identity of all immigrants. The Welsh language carried less significance in industrializing South Wales because of the great influx of English speakers during industrialization. Once in America, a person who had the ability to speak, read, and write Welsh possessed a key measure of "Welshness" among those who took tradition seriously. The most distinctively Welsh immigrant settlements and institutions in nineteenth-century America were those in which the Welsh language was the primary medium of communication. In the 1860s and 1870s, when the first generation to arrive in America had reached significant proportions, most still spoke their native language at home and with friends.

The Welsh language survived longest in the large rural settlements of Ohio and Wisconsin, as well as in the coal and iron district settlements where a critical mass could maintain traditional Welsh-language institutions. Such settlements were common in Carbon, Luzerne, and Lackawanna Counties in Pennsylvania, where in 1890 there were thirty-seven thousand natives of Wales residing in Scranton, Wilkes-Barre, Carbondale, and numerous other industrial communities.[5] Similarly, thousands more resided in Pittsburgh and satellite towns of the upper Ohio valley coal and iron region, and undoubtedly most of them were conversant with the language of their homeland. In the Welsh coal and iron communities of northeastern Ohio near Youngstown, as well as the southern Ohio rural-industrial communities in Gallia, Jackson, and Perry Counties, the native tongue was also ubiquitous among the first generation. The numerous churches with Welsh-language worship in these districts support this conclusion.[6]

Religious Denominations

The Welsh language exerted its greatest influence through the cultural institutions and societies the Welsh immigrants established in the United States, none more important than the church. As the newcomers settled into communities, the Welsh chapel was not long in arriving to serve their spiritual needs, and in the good old "mother tongue."

The evangelical camp meetings that swept colonial and antebellum America in the First and Second Great Awakenings of the early nineteenth century were initially a British form of Methodism brought to the colonies by the revivalist preacher George Whitfield. The camp meetings were Americanized on the frontier and then reexported to Britain in the early nineteenth century by American revivalists. In Britain, the Calvinists, who preached predestination (that God had preordained human affairs), were far more successful in converting the Welsh during the great revival meetings than were John Wesley's Methodists, who did not accept predestination. By the 1850s, half of the Welsh population had adopted a Calvinistic form of Methodism and rejected the established Church of England, a noteworthy circumstance because nonconformists were much more likely to emigrate. The religious preferences of British immigrants to the United States between 1845 and 1855 reveal the following denominational distribution: Church of England/Episcopal, 12.6 percent; Presbyterian, 19.7 percent; and nonconformist, 67.7 percent. Of the last group, 44.7 percent were Methodist; 10.2 percent Congregational; 4.6 Baptist; and 8.2 percent followed other faith traditions, being Catholics, Mormons, Independents, Unitarians, Quakers, Universalists, and so on.[7]

Some features of Methodist nonconformity prepared its adherents for emigration. It was less encumbered by central organizational structure than the continental denominations and could therefore function independently, thus allowing Methodists in America a wide latitude in which to practice their religion. Among the nonconformists, Methodism had a particularly dramatic behavioral impact on believers, who were exhorted to greater diligence at work, frugality, and ambition for upward social mobility in order to fulfill God's grand plan. The poor and the working classes were receptive to Methodism and found in its teachings a way out of poverty. That road often led to America.[8]

The number, denomination, and location of Welsh churches mirror the dispersal of the Welsh American population in the nineteenth century. As many as 85 percent of those who attended church in nineteenth-century Wales were Protestant nonconformists, as were the vast majority of nine-teenth-century Welsh immigrants. Nearly all of the immigrants to America were associated with the Calvinistic Methodists (or Welsh Presbyterians), the Congregationalists, or the Baptists. The Reverend R. D. Thomas's gen-erally reliable survey of Welsh church distribution and attendance in the United States counted 384 Welsh churches in 1871, with a total attendance of 50,053 distributed as follows: 20,200 (40.2 percent) attended 152 Calvinistic Methodist churches; 20,828 (41.6 percent) attended 154 Congregationalist churches; 8,595 (17.2 percent) attended 71 Baptist churches; and 430 (.08 percent) attended 7 Wesleyan Methodist churches (which rejected predes-tination). All of these churches were led by Welsh clergy members who were conscious of their national identity, preached in Welsh, and maintained communication with their native land.[9]

The Calvinistic Methodists tended to be more prevalent in the agricul-tural communities and the Midwest, reflecting church preference in western Wales, where many of these immigrants originated. The Congregational-ists, on the other hand, were most numerous in South Wales and therefore had a stronger presence in the industrial states, particularly Pennsylvania and Ohio. The Baptists were a smaller denomination, but they also were disproportionately concentrated in Pennsylvania and Ohio.[10]

The chapel was the defining element of the "Welsh way of life," both in the rural-agricultural as well as in industrial settlements. The Welsh way was decidedly puritanical. It demanded a rigid observance of the Sabbath, temperance and preferably abstinence, and austerity in church and daily life. Ideally, most of one's leisure time was taken up by the church. Sunday from 9:00 a.m. to 8:00 p.m. was strictly set aside for church activities.[11] Preaching in the Welsh language, however, undermined the church's lon-gevity. Owen Morgan, an immigrant from Pontypridd, reported in a Cardiff newspaper under the pseudonym "Morien" that religion was "flourishing" among the Americans but not among the Welsh, who were leaving the Welsh-language chapels for those with services conducted in English. "It appears to me," he observed, "that the Welsh cause in this country is dying rapidly. Nothing, in my opinion, will sustain the Welsh language—neither worshiping in that tongue, Welsh newspapers, magazines, nor national rites nor customs will do it." The reasoning behind Morgan's dire prediction was that the children would grow up to be Americans, speak their language, assimilate, and adopt American social customs of what was after all their native land.[12]

Sunday school was a Welsh invention and foundational to their religion. It also played a vital role in bringing literacy to the Welsh by providing an elementary education at a time when it was not generally available in Wales. Classes were organized by age, with topics of study appropriate for each level. Students learned to read from the Welsh Bible, grew up learning it backward and forward, and used it to understand the world. The Sunday school, therefore, not only taught church members to read but prepared them to be biblical scholars capable of reciting long passages by heart. It also produced the next generation of Welsh spiritual leaders, in a distinctively Welsh mold. Welsh ministers could count on preaching to a congregation well versed in sacred scripture and one that measured the minister's oratorical skill and biblical knowledge by a lofty standard.[13]

"Gomerian," the Pittsburgh correspondent for *The Druid*, reported that even in non-Welsh churches in neighborhoods where the Welsh were numerous, there was a strong Welsh stamp on their affairs. He reported that the Reverend R. C. Morgan occupied the pulpit of the Loring Avenue Baptist Church in the West End. "The Welsh element is quite strong in the congregation," he reported, and it was the home church of several Welsh union leaders. The presenter was John Williams, the secretary of the Amalgamated Association of Iron, Steel, and Tinplate Workers and a brother of Reverend R. T. Williams, former pastor of the Carnegie Baptist Church. John Williams's father and his brother, Reuben, "another eminent official" of the Amalgamated Association, also worshiped at the Loring Avenue church. Another active member of Loring Baptist was the Amalgamated Association leader Ben Davis, editor of the *Amalgamated Journal*, who had "a host of Cymric friends in many states." "Gomerian" observed that it was "no wonder Reverend Morgan felt quite at home, and that he was imbued during his discourse with genuine Welsh 'hwyl.'"[14]

One observer illustrated the difference, perhaps more aspirational than realized, between the English and Welsh pulpit. The English, he wrote, were "high platform men wearing high vests and standing much upon their dignity," whereas Welsh ministers were "low platform men," self-respecting and yet "always in sympathy with the people."[15] Nothing less would do in a Welsh American working-class community. The ministers also generally sided with the workers in times of trouble, and especially during strikes they identified themselves with the class-consciousness of workers. Writing of the 1909 Amalgamated Association strike, the Reverend W. J. John from the mill town of New Castle, Pennsylvania, declared that "the sufferings of the mill men who are thrown out of employment by the arbitrary and unjust actions of an arrogant trust [United States Steel Corporation], affects every individual in the community in purse or in person." Reverend John asked rhetorically why the United States Steel Corporation would want to crush the union and answered that the reason was "pure selfishness. The men who are now on strike were employed in this industry in New Castle before ever the trust was formed, and they were union men, in union mills, before the trust was chartered, and they are the men who taught the trust to make tin[plate]." The strikers would therefore fight for freedom, as did their forefathers, against the "iron hand of a heartless and tyrannous trust."[16]

Welsh churches also provided the venue for the congregational singing that Americans associated so closely with the Welsh that it was thought to be innate to them. Sung in four-part harmony from hymnals using the "tonic sol-fa" musical notation, the hymns were drawn from a large storehouse of material written and composed by Welsh musicians. One of the greatest of them, William Williams Pantycelyn (1717–1791), a leader in the eighteenth-century Welsh Methodist revival, wrote more than one thousand hymns. From generations brought up in this culture emerged the famous Welsh choirs, male choruses, and musical competitions that so many regarded as distinctively Welsh.[17] Declaring the centrality of the church in Welsh culture and institutional life is not to claim that its teachings were universally followed. The religious census taken in England and Wales in 1851 documented that nearly half (47.67 percent) of the population of Wales claimed no denomination at all.[18] Industrial emigrants bound for the United States were therefore as likely to be unchurched as they were to be devout. The constant refrain against "demon rum" in the Welsh American press suggests that the underside of Welsh culture was not as respectable as the churches would have liked. According to Reverend R. D. Thomas's figures, less than half (43.25 percent) of Welsh Americans attended the Welsh churches. While some undoubtedly attended American churches, it is clear that a large segment of the Welsh American population was not attending church.[19]

For Methodists and other nonconformists, religion was the basis for living moral lives, and temperance was essential to that end. Britain and the United States shared a transatlantic temperance movement that originated among American evangelicals and then spread to Britain—another linkage that helped to ease the Welsh nonconformists into American life. Immigrants did not support temperance wholeheartedly, however, and both coal and iron communities were notoriously committed to their beer.[20] The perceived "lack of morality" among the Welsh was one of the great concerns expressed publicly by "respectable" Welsh in Wales as well as in America. A newspaper article published in 1870 declared that morality in Hyde Park (the Welsh section of Scranton) was second only to Sodom and was "the equal of Gomorrah." Saloons were "as numerous as the frogs of Egypt." Responsibility for this state of affairs, according to the author, fell upon the shoulders of Welsh men and women from the ironworks towns of Tredegar, Rhymney, Dowlais, Merthyr, and Aberedare "who have recently arrived from there or within the last two years. The scum of the works of Wales has been shipped to Hyde Park." The remedy offered for this deplorable state of affairs was that ministers from Wales should serve as temperance missionaries among the nonabstemious of Hyde Park, to show them the light.[21] Interestingly, during this period a section of Pontlottyn was locally known as "Sodom," and a conjoining section of Rhymney was called "Gomorrah."

Undoubtedly there was some exaggeration in these articles in order to make the point, but there is also an abundance of evidence that popular culture among Welsh ironworkers was something quite different from what the ministerial profession had in mind. Although the pietistic platitudes and preachments bordered on self-aggrandizement, there is no doubt that drunkenness, disorder, and other social problems created a sense of urgency among the advocates of temperance. Nineteenth-century America was a rough-and-tumble society, and drunkenness was just as prevalent among the Welsh as it was among Americans and other ethnic groups in industrial communities. The saloon and the church vied for the workers' loyalty both in Wales and in America, and temperance crusaders faced an uphill struggle as unrelenting as that challenging Sisyphus. Still, Welsh prohibitionists continued their fight for decades, right up to passage of the Eighteenth Amendment in 1919, which ushered in Prohibition.[22]

Welsh ministers were joined in the temperance crusade by the "respectable" citizens of the community. J. L. Phillips of Girard, Ohio, a mill town near Youngstown, reported to *The Druid* in 1909 that a "bitterly contested" local option election had been waged in Mahoning County, and it had been decided in favor of the "wets," meaning Youngstown would be wet for three more years. "It is a source of regret that the low, unintelligent naturalized citizens should hold the balance of power in these elections," he wrote, for they did not "contribute to the wealth or help bear the burden of taxation, nor have any tendency whatever to the moral uplifting of a community." Phillips, like so many other Welsh Americans, obviously did not think of himself as an immigrant. From their perspective, European immigrants were irresponsible and unworthy of citizenship. The Welsh, on the other hand, were respectable citizens and undeniably worthy of being Americans.[23]

While the Welsh church served as the principal transitional institution for the first generation of immigrants, as well as the single most unifying cultural institution in Welsh American communities, it did not initiate communities so much as follow them. This state of affairs represented a major difficulty for all denominations, because just as soon as the churches were established the Welsh managers and mill workers moved on to another location, leaving the ministers to follow or face deserted pews.[24]

Eisteddfod and *Gymanfa Ganu*

The Welsh immigrants also transplanted the eisteddfod, a cultural institution second only to the chapel in importance. The origin of the eisteddfod (phonetically, "ice-steth-vod"; literally, "session"), a uniquely Welsh gathering, celebrated the talents of poets, writers, and musicians as they competed for prizes. The first such competitions to be called by that name began in the fifteenth century but declined in popularity as the gentry who sponsored them became anglicized and lost interest during the sixteenth and seventeenth centuries. Interest was resurrected again in the eighteenth century, particularly by the poet Iolo Morganwg, whose efforts led directly to the blossoming of Welsh cultural nationalism in the nineteenth century. By the end of the nineteenth century, the Royal National Eisteddfod had become institutionalized in Wales, and the tradition continues to the present.[25] The Gorsedd of Bards of Great Britain, a society also founded by Morganwg and closely associated with the eisteddfod, is still composed of leading poets, musicians, and other prominent Welsh figures. Membership is given only after passing demanding examinations or for making outstanding contributions to Welsh culture. As an organization, the Gorsedd set very high standards of performance, but even though it has representation on the International Eisteddfod governing board, the Gorsedd has no administrative function.[26]

The first recorded eisteddfod in the United States took place in the iron and rolling mill town of Carbondale, Pennsylvania, on Christmas Day in 1850. Others soon followed during the 1850s in Pittston and Scranton, Pennsylvania, and elsewhere. Beginning in the 1860s, eisteddfodau (the plural of eisteddfod) were held in many Welsh American communities, usually on Christmas Day and New Year's Day. As the nineteenth century waned, these events gradually shifted away from primarily poetry and literary competitions in the Welsh language and began to emphasize choral music, particularly the great choir competitions. The coal and iron districts of Carbondale, Scranton, and Wilkes-Barre, Pennsylvania, the Pittsburgh and upper Ohio valley, and the Mahoning Valley cities of Warren and Youngstown, Ohio, to New Castle, Pennsylvania, were the great centers of eisteddfodic enthusiasm.[27]

The eisteddfod served several important social functions in the Welsh community. It nurtured local literary and musical talent by providing a competitive venue and a purposeful goal for Welsh writers and choirs whose ambition was to win the eisteddfod. It also provided intellectually rewarding activities for the community—performers and audience alike—and was often referred to as the "university of the poor." Since the event was not segregated by sex or class, the entire community was served, as well as unified by, the eisteddfod. The popularity of these events is evident in the attendance and the number of them, especially in the larger Welsh centers. In 1877, Luzerne County, Pennsylvania, hosted three large eisteddfodau within eight days of each other, all of them well attended. One observer compared Luzerne County with Glamorgan County in Wales, and the eisteddfodau at Hyde Park, Plymouth, and Pittston with their counterparts at Aberdare, Pontypridd, and Mountain Ash, Wales. Commenting on the local eisteddfod in 1871, the *Scranton Republican* reported that Welsh locals of every stripe were present but "mostly those with brains, religious and non-religious, rich and poor, sober and a sprinkling of jesters."[28]

It would be difficult to overestimate the significance of the eisteddfod, and the culture that supported it, for aspiring Welsh writers, poets, and musicians in nineteenth-century Wales. The same may be said for Welsh America between the Civil War and the Great Depression. Countless performers got their start by entering the eisteddfod competitions, which ranged from small local affairs to major national events. Participants were not confined to a particular class. Indeed, the working class probably derived the greatest benefit from these events because they provided an avenue for artists to develop their talents. Few achieved the kind of fame and success afforded by the eisteddfod that Joseph Parry did, but his life serves as an example of what was possible.

Joseph Parry (1841–1903), a musician and prolific composer, is best known for writing "Myfanwy" and "Aberystwyth" and as the first Welshman to compose an opera, *Blodwen*, in the Welsh language. Parry was born in Merthyr Tydfil, and by age twelve he was working at the puddling furnaces at the Cyfarthfa Iron Works. In 1854 the family immigrated to Danville, Pennsylvania, where his father, Daniel, had immigrated the year before and found employment as a roller in the Danville rolling mill locals called "Old Rough and Ready" after President Zachary Taylor. Young Joseph Parry immediately entered the same rolling mill as a "puddler's boy" for a Welsh heater, John M. Price, who became Parry's music teacher. A rolling mill was a dangerous place, and Parry was fortunate to avoid injury or death on at least two occasions—once when a boiler exploded, killing a companion working at Parry's side, and once from a broken flywheel. Parry survived to become a puddler himself.[29]

Parry's greatest love was music, but, like most working-class immigrant boys, he had little time or money to study music. A born musician, Parry learned the basics from a coworker, and before long he could play several instruments and was serving as the organist at the Mahoning Presbyterian Church in Danville. In 1861 he took first prize at the Utica eisteddfod for an anthem he wrote. A few years later he submitted another anthem to the National Eisteddfod in Wales, and the adjudicators awarded him first prize. At the national contest in 1865, Parry was offered a seat in the Gorsedd of Bards and given the title "Pencerdd America" (Chief Musician of America).

The spectacular career of the puddler from Danville had been launched. Recognizing his unique talent, supporters established a fund for Parry so he could study music, and in 1868 he and his wife and children arrived in England, where he began his studies at the Royal Academy of Music. He continued his formal studies in 1871, when he entered Cambridge University, and later became the first Welshman to be awarded both the MusB and MusD at that institution. Parry taught at Aberystwyth University for several years before accepting a chair at Cardiff University in 1888. He composed a prodigious volume of music over the years, and, although he had become an American citizen in 1859, he spent the rest of his life in Penarth, Wales. When he died, more than seven thousand people lined the route as the cortege made its way to the burial ground.[30]

The large size of some of the eisteddfodau, as well as their cultural distinctiveness, caught the attention of the non-Welsh population. Commenting on a forthcoming eisteddfod in 1875, the *Scranton Republican* poked gentle fun at the Welsh by announcing that a "polysyllabic tournament" was scheduled in which attendees would be overcome by an "orthographic epidemic." If the local newspaper had a bit of fun with the Welsh, it was not lacking in respect. Several weeks later the same newspaper determined that the national eisteddfod to be held in Hyde Park that year "will be a great credit not only to the Welsh people; it will reflect honor on this city. There is no class of people who place a higher estimate upon the advantages of intellectual culture than the Welsh and however limited the opportunities of a community composed of this nationality, it will abound in organizations and societies for music, literature, oratory and the lesser sciences."[31]

As the center of the Welsh population moved westward and domination of heavy industry shifted from iron to steel, Pittsburgh and the upper Ohio valley region became the center of eisteddfodic activities. As early as 1888, the Pittsburgh eisteddfod attracted between five thousand and six thousand visitors and was supported by the city's prominent Welsh, such as event president John Jarrett, former head of the Amalgamated Association of Iron and Steel Workers and US consul at Birmingham, England. Previous presidents had included the wealthy businessman Thomas C. Jenkins and the general superintendent of Andrew Carnegie's Edgar Thomson Steel Works, Captain William R. Jones.[32] The Pittsburgh eisteddfod of 1903 was expected to attract twenty-five thousand people, from all parts of the United States, Canada, and Wales. Charles Schwab, president of US Steel, was expected to attend, as was Samuel "Golden Rule" Jones, the mayor of Toledo, referred to as "the greatest Welshman in the country."[33]

In 1912 Welsh American leaders in Pittsburgh believed that their time in the spotlight had arrived. The 1913 International Eisteddfod was to be held in Pittsburgh, and Robert H. Davies (who wrote under the name "Gomerian") traveled to Wales, where he obtained permission from the Gorsedd of Bards of Great Britain to establish the American Gorsedd. The prominent Welsh Pittsburghers behind this effort intended for the American Gorsedd to be the "single most important Welsh organization in America." Instead, it gave voice to what the Gorsedd regarded as "the value and nature of being Welsh in America."[34] The founders of the American Gorsedd hailed from the comfortable Pittsburgh neighborhood of North Oakland, rather than the smoky neighborhoods near the mills. These men purchased the influential Welsh American newspaper *The Druid* and moved it from Scranton to Pittsburgh in 1912. Along with the 1913 International Eisteddfod and formation of the American Gorsedd, they planned to concentrate all "Cymric interests under the same roof and make the Gorsedd home a mecca for all Welsh pilgrims." This vision was realized on St. David's Day in March 1919, when a banquet and concert were held to dedicate the new Pittsburgh headquarters of the American Gorsedd. It occupied an entire floor of a large downtown building and included an assembly room, library, and offices for *The Druid*.[35]

The *gymanfa ganu* (phonetically, "ga-man-va-gan-nee"; translated loosely as "singing festival") was another uniquely Welsh institution that made the passage from Wales to America. The first known gymanfa ganu as an independent singing festival took place in Aberdare, Wales, in 1859 and quickly grew in popularity in Wales and then the United States. As Americanization progressed, English replaced Welsh as the language of the eisteddfod, and thus some of the original cultural significance of the eisteddfod was lost. This opened the way for the musical portion of the festival to become the dominant feature and for the gymanfa ganu to replace the eisteddfod in the early twentieth century as the most popular cultural festival in Welsh American communities. Members of Welsh churches traditionally gathered to sing at rotating host churches. The tonic sol-fa method of music reading, taught to children in Welsh Sunday schools, greatly facilitated the gymanfa ganu. In 1929 the National Gymanfa Ganu Association was founded in Niagara Falls, New York, and it was led by officers of the St. David's Society of Youngstown.[36]

▶ Fig. 2.1. Program cover, Pittsburgh International Eisteddfod, 1913. University of Pittsburgh, Historic Pittsburgh Digital Collection.

PROGRAM of the

PITTSBURGH INTERNATIONAL EISTEDDFOD

CAPTAIN WILLIAM R. JONES.

PITTSBURGH. PA.
JULY 2-3-4 and 5-1913.

PRICE 25 CENTS

The festival was especially popular in smaller coal and steel mill communities. Like the eisteddfod, it not only reinforced cultural identity but also provided important leisure-time activities for mill workers and their families in places where cultural opportunities often were limited. Also like the eisteddfod, it was open to men, women, and children alike, and, in bringing people of similar interests together from outside the community, the festival also expanded the social world of working families. Unlike the eisteddfod, however, the gymanfa ganu was not competitive at all. Its sole purpose was for participants to congregate and sing hymns, and eventually a mix of secular music written for chorus was added to the event.

Reinforced by the church, eisteddfod, and gymanfa ganu, choral singing was a significant part of the daily life of Welsh Americans. The awe-inspiring exhibitions of four-part harmony delivered by Welsh choirs attracted attention wherever they occurred. In the 1830s, for example, it was reported that residents near Carbondale, Pennsylvania, who heard "the strong minor chords of Welsh hymns on the frosty night air for the first time, got out of bed to listen."[37]

Welsh American Societies

Welsh Americans also established benevolent and cultural societies to address secular needs not served by their religious institutions. Like nineteenth-century Americans generally, the Welsh joined fraternal orders and benevolent societies for a sense of belonging, as well as for the insurance policies these societies offered, which provided members some measure of security against the financial calamities associated with serious accident, protracted illness, or death. The Welsh Society of Philadelphia, the oldest of the benevolent societies, founded in 1727 and still in existence, aided Welsh immigrants who found themselves desperate in a strange city. The society aided them by providing food, clothing, and lodging, as well as by helping them find work or reach their destination. Others with similar benevolent missions included the Welsh Benevolent Society of Utica and Vicinity, founded in 1849, and the Cambrian Benevolent Society of Chicago, founded in 1854. The Independent Order of True Ivorites was founded in Wrexham, Wales, in 1836, and named for Ifor Hael (Ivor the Liberal), a fourteenth-century Welshman whose generosity and deeds of kindness elevated him to legend. The American Order of True Ivorites was founded in Pittsburgh in 1848 by immigrants who had been members in Wales, and chapters soon sprang up in Welsh American settlements. The Ivorites provided health and death benefits for members and assistance to other Welsh families in times of need. Cultural and social activities were also sponsored by the lodge.[38]

Every Welsh American community had its St. David's Society and/or Cambrian Club to take the lead in celebrations of Welsh heritage. Perhaps one hundred or more of these societies existed in the United States at one time or another. The most numerous of the Welsh societies were those that sponsored concerts, banquets, speakers, readings, and other social and cultural events. Most important, they led celebrations on March 1 for St. David, the patron saint of Wales, and during the summer sponsored Welsh Days at community parks. These were major events on the Welsh American calendar, as well as holidays from work. An editorial written by "Cymro" (meaning "Welshman") appeared in *The Druid* in 1908 urging Welsh Americans to work on St. David's Day. But, the editor retorted, the newspaper claimed that "none of the big companies will expect a Welshman to work that day," pointing out that "Cymro" was a foreman, which apparently was sufficient explanation.[39]

The St. David's Society of Pittsburgh had 1,000 members in the city and surrounding Allegheny County before it was forced to disband during the depression of the mid-1890s. It was reorganized in 1898 with 250 charter members as "a social and political society" that focused its attention on the advancement of "Welshmen as Americans."[40] Certainly, there was a critical mass of Welsh from which to recruit because Pittsburgh and Allegheny County were home to an estimated 20,000 Welsh people and their offspring.[41] Like most branches of the St. David's Society, the Pittsburgh branch was led by some of the most prominent Welsh members of the community. The society met on March 1, 1887, to celebrate St. David's birth, and the program was led by Miles S. Humphreys, a former grand master of the Sons of Vulcan and a Labor Party member of the Pennsylvania legislature. John Jarrett and Captain William R. Jones were among a number of other prominent community figures who had held leadership positions in the society.[42]

Youngstown and other mill towns in the district also supported active St. David's Societies that invited respected Welsh and Welsh American figures to speak or perform at their events. In the summer of 1894, for example, Anthony Howells, the prominent Canton, Ohio, business-man-politician and US consul at Cardiff, was the society's guest. He spoke to members and friends about life in that nation's capital. Like many of these meetings, Howells's comments were shared with outlets in South Wales.[43] And in 1909, the Youngstown St. David's Society invited Thomas L. Lewis, president of the United Mine Workers of America, to address the membership.[44]

The Welsh immigrant households of mine and mill towns in the Youngstown district supported more than one Welsh heritage society. The Welsh Pioneers Society of the Counties of Trumbull and Mahoning, for example, sponsored the annual Welsh reunion picnic held during the summer at local parks. These gatherings were very popular and drew Welsh people from near and far. Fully ten thousand people were present at the reunion in 1898. Participants old and young could choose from such activities as baseball, races, contests, recitations, and, of course, musical entertainment. As was the case at St. David's Society meetings, the Welsh language was on full display whenever possible. Thus, the typical Pioneers Society meeting always had recitations and hymn-singing in Welsh.[45]

At a time when all music was still performed in front of a live audience, numerous community choral societies were organized, often by the local Welsh cultural society. Some of them were well known, even famous in their day, among them the Cymrodorion Choral Society of Scranton, led by the famous composer Daniel Protheroe. Perhaps the most renowned among them all was the Orpheus Glee Club of Wilkes-Barre, which won national acclaim.[46] Nearly all societies either organized their own Welsh choir or sponsored one, because it served as a popular venue for celebrating Welsh heritage and because most societies incorporated music into their regular meetings. The Follansbee, West Virginia, St. David's Society sponsored a glee club in 1909 that had been "organized here some time ago."[47] Similarly, the New Castle Male Chorus arranged for a concert upon the return of Agnes Parry (unrelated to Joseph) from her studies at the Royal Academy of Music in London.[48]

Touring Welsh choirs from the homeland had become commonplace in Welsh American communities by 1890. After winning first place at the International Eisteddfod at the World's Fair in Chicago in 1893, a "celebrated Welsh choir of lady singers" presented a concert in Pittsburgh as part of its triumphal tour. According to a local newspaper, "The Welsh people made the mistake of their lives in not securing the biggest hall in the city," because they were unable to accommodate the overflow audience that turned out at the Fifth Avenue Congregational Church. "The main auditorium was packed to suffocation, gallery and aisles a solid mass of humanity, stairways and corridors choked with people, and still they came until all ante-rooms below were filled, the vestibules thronged, the churchyard as full as could be without breaking down the fences, the street blocked, and every passing car stopping to add to the aggregation." The reporter doubted that any musical troupe was "ever received here with such enthusiasm as greeted these winsome Welsh maidens."[49]

In 1909 the Llanelli Royal Choir met with "a most gratifying run of success in its tour of the American states," a Llanelli newspaper reported. The tour had already taken the singers to large cities such as Chicago, Milwaukee, and Pittsburgh, and after performing in Ohio the choir was headed for Scranton, where it was booked every day in November and right up through Christmas.[50] In 1914 the Gwent Glee Singers, "the best aggregation of singers which Wales has sent over in the past twenty years," came to the United States on their second tour. Local Welsh societies sponsored each stop on the tour.[51] The local Welsh society of Morgantown, West Virginia, a tinplate town, sponsored a "grand concert" of the Cambria Glee Singers in 1911. In the steel manufacturing town of Alliance, Ohio, the first of a winter series of entertainments was presented at the Welsh Calvinistic Methodist Church in December 1914, *The Druid* announced, and these programs were "anxiously looked forward to and well attended."[52]

Touring singers were amazed by the enthusiasm that greeted them in the United States. On returning to Wales, one singer recounted for the *Merthyr Express* how the émigrés were "ten times more Welsh than they were at home. They are Welsh to the core and will travel hundreds of miles to hear anything Welsh."[53] Some tours ended on a note far beyond enthusiasm. Such was the case of Rachel Thomas, formerly of Mountain Ash, Wales, following a November 1909 concert of the Cambria Glee Society in Morgantown, West Virginia. "Miss Thomas's sweet contralto voice captivated among others, John Protheroe, a native of Llanelli, who holds a responsible position in the tinplate works. In three weeks the couple were married, and the honeymoon was spent at Pittsburgh. It is hoped that Mrs. Protheroe will become a familiar figure on the local concert platform," a Cardiff newspaper commented.[54] The Royal Welsh Ladies' Choir's 1908 tour was led by "Madame Hughes-Thomas" and was accompanied by her husband,

Edward Thomas, also known as "Cochfarf" (Redbeard), who was a member of the Gorsedd of Bards of Great Britain and a senior Cardiff city council member. The Thomases "formed an enthusiastic opinion of the American people, cosmopolitan as they are by extraction," and were overwhelmed by the graciousness of their reception. At a Thanksgiving Day concert in Pittsburgh the audience was "insatiable in their demands," and the choir "encored seven items on the programme."[55]

Newspapers and Periodicals

Welsh American newspapers and magazines were established to maintain some continuity of personal and group identity by providing subscribers with news from the old country, and they served a unifying purpose for the highly mobile ironworkers. The tramping artisan could easily lose contact with former family and friends, and the Welsh American periodicals are replete with the comings and goings of ironworkers.[56] Correspondents submitted news items to the periodicals, sometimes on a regular basis over an extended period of time, concerning their respective Welsh communities. This method of communication made it possible for widely scattered families to gain information about relatives and friends living elsewhere. Access to the periodicals also helped the relatively isolated Welsh communities to keep the immense geographic scale of their dislocation from overwhelming them. Sharing the names of community residents, their Welsh hometowns, their relatives, and their known employment history brought the enormity of their migrations down to a manageable "it's a small Welsh world" scale. Published by *The Druid* in 1911, the following narrative, submitted by a South Wales immigrant then living in Youngstown, suggests the importance of personal connections:

> I [recently] talked to Mrs. William Davies [and] after a short time I asked her where she hailed from. "South Wales," she said. "What part," I inquired, "Swansea, or Abertawe, as we Welsh call it." "Oh, whereabouts in Abertawe?" I inquired. "Landore or a little place called Plasmarl, near Landore." "Oh, indeed, which of the houses did you live in?" I asked. "Between Rees and Edwards' grocery stores." By this time she found that I was familiar with the locality. We lived within a few yards of each other, and left there within twelve months of each other for the States. . . . The writer ["F. T."] has a

father, brother and sisters, and a host of acquaintances scattered all over the United States who will read this little story with a great deal of interest, and will be glad to learn that Mr. and Mrs. William Davies of Plasmarl is still on earth and well and hearty. They desire to be remembered to their old acquaintances.[57]

One newspaper in particular, *Y Drych* (The mirror), actively sought to construct an ideology of Welshness for Welsh Americans that was grounded in the language. *Y Drych* was one of twenty-one newspapers serving Welsh America between the 1830s and the 1920s. It closely resembled the other Welsh-language newspapers in America and, to a degree, the other 1,163 immigrant newspapers published in America in 1900. Its peak circulation of 12,000 at the turn of the twentieth century represented approximately 10 percent of the recorded Welsh-born population. *Y Drych* enjoyed an exceptional longevity. The life span of most Welsh American newspapers and periodicals was a few years or even less, but *Y Drych* survived for a century and a half, from 1851 to 2001, making it one of the longest-running ethnic newspapers in American history. Most of the Welsh newspapers accommodated their content to a mixed readership and offered a blend of English and Welsh text, but *Y Drych*'s most distinctive feature was that it published only in Welsh for its first seventy or eighty years.[58]

During its years of publication between 1907 and 1939, *The Druid* was *Y Drych*'s chief competitor. Given that Welsh immigrants were increasingly from the coal and iron district of South Wales, where the language was in decline, rather than the western part of the country, where it was still strong, the decision to publish in English made sense. The all-English policy undoubtedly explains *The Druid*'s popularity and wide distribution. In 1912 a Welsh cohort led by James J. Davis, a Welsh iron puddler who subsequently became US secretary of labor and then senator from Pennsylvania, bought the newspaper and, as mentioned previously, moved it from Scranton to Pittsburgh.[59] *Y Drych* and *The Druid* both had strong circulation throughout the Welsh settlements in America, including the coal and iron districts.

So too did the most important and successful of the Welsh American magazines, *The Cambrian*. It was one of sixty-five journals Welsh American journals published between the 1830s and the 1920s. A monthly and later bimonthly published between 1880 and 1919, the all-English periodical was widely circulated in the Welsh communities throughout the United States. The numerous letters from readers located in mill towns is a strong indication of *The Cambrian*'s popularity among Welsh ironworkers. Similarly, each issue carried a page listing their agents by community, and a large number of these agents resided in the iron and steel producing centers. Reverend E. C. Evans, editor of *The Cambrian*, confronted the language issue head on in an 1893 article outlining the difficulties of confining Welsh nationality to the "narrow limits of the Welsh language." Birth, descent, and speech all bound people, including the Welsh, but "must a person be able to speak the Welsh language" to be considered Welsh? In Evans's opinion, it was not a prerequisite. "The Cornish, Scotch, and Irish people have adopted English, and the children of English, Irish, French, Italian and Jewish parents residing in Wales speak Welsh fluently and identify themselves with national movements without becoming Welsh people." On the other hand, Evans observed, there were many in Wales and America who were "thoroughly Welsh by birth and lineage" but did not understand the Welsh language.[60]

National identity, Evans recognized, was a complex matter. Between the extremes of the Welsh language as the only marker of Welsh identity and the complete loss of Welsh lineage and identity were gradations of identity that should be acknowledged. Evans designated several classes: those born in Britain or Wales, American-born Welsh who speak Welsh, American-born Welsh and their descendants who identify themselves as Welsh but do not speak the language, and Welsh descendants in America who have lost their Welsh identity and knowledge of their lineage. The census data were therefore totally inadequate for establishing the number of Welsh in the United States, Evans claimed, and of no value at all in determining how many either spoke the language or had shifted to English during this period. By breaking down Welsh Americans into these categories of identity, however, Evans calculated that, of the estimated total of 400,079 Welsh and Welsh descendants in the United States, only about one-quarter of them spoke Welsh in 1890, and that number was falling.[61]

The division over the role of language in Welsh identity revealed the broader underlying cultural dissonance among the industrialized, anglicized Welsh of South Wales and the more traditional populations of North Wales and western Wales. These regional differences were carried across the Atlantic and magnified by the forces of assimilation in America. *The Druid* and *The Cambrian* published only in English, reasoning that the Welsh were now in the United States, where English was the lingua franca, and, in order to facilitate their chances for success, the Welsh should accept the inevitable and learn to speak English.[62] On this point *Y Drych* vigorously objected. The newspaper promoted the idea that the Welsh should become Americanized in order to take full advantage of the opportunities that came with citizenship, but doing so did not require them to abandon their own language and customs.[63]

The language embodied the very essence of being Welsh, according to *Y Drych*, which editorialized that "in accordance with an unwritten but inflexible law, a man cannot be a Welshman without knowledge of Welsh. . . . The Welsh will surely lose themselves in and melt into the American nation when the language is lost."[64] Attempts to define ethnicity in essential traits, in a manner that defines culture as static, fixed, and immutable, rather than dynamic, interactive, and changing, is a kind of ethnic absolutism modern scholars no longer accept. The predominant voices speaking from the Welsh ethnic newspapers reflected this absolutist understanding of culture, but *Y Drych* went a step further, enshrining the Welsh language as the dominant marker of Welshness in both Wales and the United States.[65]

The particular kind of American that these ethnic newspapers promoted to the Welsh was not to be available to all immigrants. All three drew a line when it came to the "new" immigrants from eastern and southern Europe flooding into the iron and steel centers, but *Y Drych* was particularly emphatic. In an 1888 article headlined "Peryglon Ymfudiaeth" (The perils of immigration), the newspaper stressed that America must be kept for Americans and that such a goal could be achieved only by excluding people of Asian, African, or southern and eastern European origin. Similarly, an 1893 issue carried an article declaring that the Welsh were entitled to be part of the great American nation, but it also warned that "it would be futile and foolish to argue that all the tribes and nations of our Republic should melt into each other. Would it be appropriate for Gomer's race to mix with the black Negro and the red Indian, or the bloody Dago?"[66]

The immigrant conundrum that faced the Welsh also confronted the press that served them. On the one hand, pluralism allowed ethnic groups to retain their identities and gave the ethnic press a reason to exist, but assimilation offered the greatest opportunities for the social and economic advancement that the groups presumably came to America to find. On the other hand, assimilation undermined the purpose served by the press. Published in English, *The Cambrian* and *The Druid* avoided the pitfalls by unambiguously embracing the English language without diminishing the value of Welsh. *Y Drych*, on the other hand, advocated that the key reason for assimilation into and loyalty to the United States was that this country offered Welsh immigrants the benefits of citizenship even as they remained Welsh in language, religion, and culture. As historian William D. Jones has observed, those readers, writers, and editors of the Welsh press were searching for ways to become Americans without surrendering their own culture.[67]

Welsh American periodicals certainly filtered reality. Reliance upon the Welsh language screened out those who could not read it, and the Welsh press took no notice of social and labor problems in the iron and steel industry, filling their pages instead with biographical treatments of successful skilled workers, managers, and men working in business. Little or no news beyond the Welsh community networks of church-goers, merchants, and professionals found space in their pages. William D. "Bill" Jones has characterized *Y Drych* as the newspaper of the "Welsh language elite." He astutely observes that they represented a "thin layer of immigrant intellectuals" managing a "White-Anglo-Saxon-Protestant newspaper in Welsh," whose project was constructing the "whiteness," and therefore the "Americanness," of the Welsh.[68]

It is in the nature of memory to be nostalgic about the past, and nostalgia was common among immigrants whose enthusiasm for their new world was tempered by their loss of the familiar old one. Cultural institutions such as the church, musical festivals, ethnic societies, and the press helped the immigrants to resolve what it meant to be Welsh American. They constructed a Welsh American identity built on nonconformist Protestantism, republicanism, the Welsh language, sobriety, respectability, self-improvement, and social mobility. These values not only preserved the immigrants' version of "Welshness" but also prepared the way for assimilation on their own terms.

Immigrants from the British Isles did not share the same experiences on the road to becoming Americans. From the beginning, Americans treated the Irish as an "ethnic" group distinguished from the English, Welsh, or

Scots. The sheer number of Irish immigrants was remarkable, even alarming, at its peak during the Irish Famine, when between 1845 and 1855 nearly 1.5 million Irish entered American ports. Together with German Roman Catholics displaced by the "Hungry Forties," they became America's first significant ethnic group. Historian Kerby Miller argues that the prefamine Irish came to America seeking political independence and economic advancement, but after the famine Irish America evolved into a culture of exiles who had been forced to abandon their homeland by an oppressive British government. At that point it was only a short step from economic rationalism to a political culture of Irish nationalism. The Protestant Irish, on the other hand, took an easier path to American acceptance by redefining themselves as "Scotch Irish," emphasizing their Britishness as a way to distinguish themselves from their Catholic compatriots.[69]

Unlike Irish American identity forged by poverty and British oppression, identities of the English, Welsh, and Scots were rooted in the insecurity of an industrializing economy at home and fears for their children's future. Their Britishness posed few barriers to Americanization, and, according to historian Alexander Murdoch, they viewed themselves "not so much as 'invisible' but as 'exceptional'; neither native 'Yankees' nor really immigrants, they saw themselves as valuable reinforcements to the British 'stock' that built America."[70] Murdoch argues that, despite their best efforts, the first-generation immigrants were never "really wholly American." In the United Kingdom (after 1903) national identities were based on England, Scotland, or Wales, and loyalty to the Crown (however tenuous). Among themselves, what distinguished British immigrants in the United States during the late nineteenth century was less their national identity within the United Kingdom than their having been from Glasgow, Cardiff, or Manchester. "This reflected," Murdoch argues, "the growing urban element in British emigration after 1860." He concludes that "Welsh-American and Scottish-American immigrants and their children participated in hyphenated Americanism in a way that was rare in the English-American community" because of the nationalist movements in Scotland and Wales.[71] However, Americans generally were either unaware, or placed little importance on, the otherwise significant distinctions between the English, Welsh, and Scots; unlike the Catholic Irish, they were simply British cousins.

As Welsh immigrants became Americanized, their transplanted institutions and customs went into decline and then all but disappeared. Over time the Wales homeland they remembered existed only in memory. Their children had no memory of Wales to perpetuate and no history of discrimination or struggle for survival to generate the kind of distinctive experience that would continue to unite them. Consequently, within a generation hardly a ray of light could pass between what it meant to be "Welsh American" and "American."

3

Early American Iron and the Welsh Plan

Geographer Anne Kelly Knowles, in her research on the American iron industry during the antebellum era, has found that "Welsh puddlers and rollers cropped up at almost every rolling mill," and even though "the Welsh did not outnumber English iron artisans in the United States, they brought a distinctive ethnic-occupational identity" to the industry. "Time and time again in manuscript correspondence and printed reports," Knowles found references to Dowlais and Cyfarthfa. These were two of the largest iron companies in South Wales, and they "epitomized modern ironmaking to contemporaries because they were among Britain's first fully integrated ore-to-rail operations."[1]

Even a general calculation of the number of Welsh, or any other immigrant group, employed in the American iron industry prior to the Civil War would be impossible because the sources simply are not available to make that determination. Moreover, the iron industry changed with the growth of the nation. At the beginning of the nineteenth century the iron industry, like the American population, was concentrated east of the Appalachian Mountains within a few days' wagon haulage from the major urban centers, such as Philadelphia and Baltimore. On the eve of the Civil War, ironworks had been erected near most of the large ore deposits all the way to the

Mississippi River. Unlike Great Britain, however, America's high-grade ore deposits did not correlate with seams of metallurgical coal. The exceptions were in portions of eastern Ohio, western Pennsylvania, and western Virginia in the upper Ohio River watershed. It was no accident, therefore, that the iron industry quickly spread its roots into this region.[2]

Most antebellum ironworks produced pig or bar iron to be forged into a variety of household iron wares, as well as horseshoes, wheel rims, nails, and farm implements. Demand for these products was in local markets clustered into geographical regions, and blast furnaces were typically located in rural hamlets or villages close to the natural resources. On the other hand, rolling mills generally were located on waterways closer to urban areas, to facilitate the distribution of finished products.[3]

In some larger towns and urban communities, such as Wheeling (in what is now West Virginia) and Pittsburgh, Catasauqua, and Danville, Pennsylvania, for example, iron represented the dominant industry and the major employer. Pittsburgh was home to the largest concentration of rolling mills, and Wheeling was known as "Nail City." Catasauqua, established in 1839, was dominated by the Lehigh Crane Iron Company, which in 1856 employed 650 men in the production of anthracite pig iron. Welsh immigrants dominated ownership as well as the skilled and managerial positions at the Lehigh Crane ironworks. Danville's Montour Iron Company was one of the few antebellum iron communities with both anthracite-fired blast furnaces and rolling mills. In 1850, Danville's 3,302 residents included hundreds of Welsh, English, and Americans in the skilled jobs, while Irish were the most numerous among other immigrants employed in unskilled labor. Of the six ironmasters in Danville, three were American, while the other three were from England or Wales.[4]

Urban iron communities had a larger and more ethnically mixed workforce than the small frontier villages that grew up around forges (for hammered iron) and bloomeries (for raw iron). Pittsburgh attracted immigrant Welsh, English, and Irish ironworkers during this period, and the dominance of the Welsh and English in the skilled positions at the city's rolling mills initiated a chain migration of friends and relatives. Iron-making centers like Pittsburgh and Danville became destinations for immigrating Welsh ironworkers who, like Welsh coal miners, were more apt to see greater opportunity in coming to a place where they found significant numbers of their own compatriots. In the larger iron towns, Welsh immigrants found

Welsh-language chapels and Welsh storeowners, employers, and bosses, which greatly facilitated their transition to life in a new country. Mixing with other ethnic groups only heightened their own Welsh identity and the work culture they transplanted to America.[5]

Although antebellum iron-making communities differed considerably, they all experienced chronic shortages of the skilled labor required to operate an ironworks. Dependency on workers with particular skills naturally set owners and managers at cross-purposes with craft workers over control of their labor. American managers often complained that skilled Welsh ironworkers were too independent, clannish, and inclined to drunkenness. During periods of expansion, however, ironmasters found it nearly impossible to replace skilled men whose work or behavior they found objectionable. Many Welsh ironworkers and coal miners who emigrated in the 1830s had been politicized by the democratic reforms advocated by the Chartist movement, particularly universal manhood suffrage, the secret ballot, and annual elections to Parliament, which culminated in the uprising of Welsh miners and ironworkers in 1839. Welsh ironmasters responded by locking out union workers and suppressing armed protests. This and similar political upheavals across Britain heightened the class-consciousness of coal and iron workers.[6]

Early Development of American Iron

The American economy of the eighteenth century was predominantly agricultural, but the seeds of industrialization began to germinate during the last half of the century, prior to the American Revolution. By 1775, the American colonies had become the world's third-largest producer of unfinished iron, accounting for about 15 percent of the total world output, or an estimated thirty thousand tons annually. Britain's mercantile trade policy and colonial law forbade the exportation of American iron, so most of this iron probably found its way into domestic consumption through the local manufacture of iron wares.[7]

Before the outbreak of the Revolutionary War, the number of iron furnaces and forges in the American colonies was estimated at 257. Maryland and Virginia possessed about one-quarter of those ironworks and Pennsylvania, another quarter of the total. In production, however, no ironworks in Pennsylvania compared in production capacity to Maryland's Principio Iron Company or the Baltimore Iron Company, two of the largest industrial enterprises in colonial America.[8] It was not until the Revolutionary War that Pennsylvania ironworks began to produce iron at a rate comparable with that of the Principio and Baltimore companies. Expansion of the Pennsylvania iron industry during and after the revolution, however, was nothing short of phenomenal. During the six decades between 1716 and 1775, 73 ironworks were erected in Pennsylvania; in the quarter century between 1775 and 1800, 94 furnaces and forges had been erected.[9]

Toward the end of the eighteenth century, the British iron industry underwent a technological revolution that changed the nature not only of iron manufacture but eventually of all industry and society itself. It began with the introduction of coke as a blast furnace fuel in place of charcoal. Once adopted, coke swiftly transformed the British iron industry from being a high-cost to a low-cost producer of unfinished iron. In contrast, the United States remained a high-cost producer of iron because its manufacturers continued to use the old technology. Nevertheless, the American industry continued to grow in absolute terms. By the 1830s, US production of pig iron had increased to about two hundred thousand tons, nearly a 700 percent increase over production at the beginning of the Revolutionary War era.[10]

During the eighteenth century, the so-called indirect process of smelting and forging prevailed in Britain and America. The process involved a blast furnace, which was a large stone structure the inside of which was a bottle-shaped container for smelting iron ore and fuel. Under intense heat the oxygen was banished from the ore, and carbon released from the charcoal took its place. The resultant alloy, known as pig iron, could be reheated and worked into various shapes.

At the forge, pig iron was refined by alternately heating it in a hearth until malleable and then beating it with a large, water-powered hammer that pounded out the impurities in the form of slag. The process required a great deal of labor, and only a small quantity of iron could be produced at one time.[11]

By the end of the eighteenth century, British inventors had replaced charcoal with coke as a fuel, and refining pig iron by hammering had given way to puddling and rolling. Puddling involved the use of a new kind of furnace called the reverberatory furnace, in which iron was separated from the fuel by a low wall. Because the fuel and iron did not come into contact, a fuel less pure than charcoal, such as anthracite coal, could be used without contaminating the metal. Although too impure to use for traditional methods of refining, coke (coal from which gas has been expelled under heat) was ideal for puddling. Instead of removing the iron from the fire for hammering, now the furnace worker, or puddler, manipulated the iron through ports in the furnace wall, performing a sort of stirring motion, or "puddling." Moreover, the great increase in the amount of heat permitted by the reverberatory furnace made it possible to replace hammering with the rolling mill, a new system that forced the malleable iron through grooved rollers that could be adjusted to press the desired shape. Puddling and the rolling mill were usually adopted together in the United States, since puddling produced an iron with a high slag content, which had to be literally "squeezed" out as the iron passed through the rollers.[12]

Puddling and rolling were developed in Britain, and, because the process cut labor and fuel costs, British iron manufacturers had adopted the new technology by the late eighteenth century. Ironmasters in the United States, however, continued to rely on the traditional charcoal blast furnaces. Until technical refinements in furnace construction were developed during the second decade of the nineteenth century, puddling furnaces wasted too much of the blast. Also, charcoal was nearly free of sulfur, and, once burned, its ash consisted mostly of the lime needed to smelt iron. Moreover, good anthracite coal and coke were difficult to find in early nineteenth-century America, and neither coal nor coke produced iron as hard as that made with charcoal. The lack of adequate overland transportation facilities for shipping large quantities of iron, as well as the inertia wrought by tradition, were further deterrents to the adoption of the new technology by American ironmasters. Perhaps the most important reason mineral fuels did not find immediate acceptance in America was the abundance of timber for charcoal. Even the seemingly endless forests of the early republic period, however, could not continue to supply the insatiable demand of the charcoal iron industry. Only the growing scarcity of wood in traditional iron-producing centers precipitated the conversion to mineral fuels in the United States.[13]

Although few technological changes took place in the American iron industry prior to the 1830s, by the late antebellum era earnest experimentation with anthracite and coke fuels, steam power for blowing engines, and hot-blast furnaces had begun. The term "hot blast" referred to air passed through a chamber where it was heated and then forced into the furnace by a "blowing engine" composed of one or several pistons driven by water or steam power. The hot air rose faster than cold air from the bottom to the top of the furnace, making it more efficient by increasing the draft and therefore the heat as well.[14]

During the two decades preceding the Civil War, the increasing demand for iron due to railroad construction, building construction, and the general quickening of the industrial pulse stimulated the adoption of the new technology in other areas as well. The machinery and supplementary works that constituted rolling mills tended to appear in cities where profitable markets existed and trade with the countryside could be conducted with facility and profit. Rolling mill centers arose in the eastern coastal cities from Richmond to Boston, where railroad and port facilities were readily available. Other ironmasters chose to erect rolling mills near the iron ore deposits, in proximity to furnaces and forges, as they did in Britain.[15] Adoption of the new technology reflected the trend toward large-scale units of production and the centralization of the new ironworks at strategic points within the transportation network.[16]

The South

Prevailing geographic and economic circumstances created regional iron industries in antebellum America. On the eve of the Civil War, the South had only about one-quarter of the capacity for iron production as the North, and its efforts to increase that capacity were handicapped by the scarcity of skilled labor. Southern ironworks were generally smaller, with less mechanized furnaces, forges, and bloomeries widely dispersed across the landscape. Few were the puddlers, rollers, heaters, or furnace workers, and fewer still were those who understood the use of mineral fuel for iron smelting. While northern ironmasters actively sought skilled British labor, very few of their counterparts in the South did so. An exception was the Etowah Iron Works in northwest Georgia. In 1848–1849 Etowah attempted to integrate operations by added a rolling mill to the forge and blast furnace, and the managers hired a number of skilled men from England, Wales, Scotland, Germany, and the northern states. Nevertheless, the vast majority of the workers at southern ironworks were enslaved persons, and this preference for enslaved labor repelled the influx of new technology, as well as workers and managers with the requisite knowledge and skills. Consequently, the southern iron industry was slow to develop, and the labor force remained regional and isolated.[17]

The southern ironmasters' reliance on industrial slavery was in direct conflict with their need of skilled labor, and the struggle for a compatible labor policy played out in full force at the Tredegar Iron Works in Richmond, Virginia, the largest ironworks in the region. Welshman Rhys Davis, who previously was employed at Cyfarthfa in Merthyr Tydfil, was recruited to supervise construction of Tredegar's rolling mill in 1838. It was constructed to the standard of Tredegar Iron Works in Tredegar, Wales, another heads of the valleys iron town near Merthyr Tydfil. The managing owner of the Richmond firm, Joseph R. Anderson, a firm believer in the use of an enslaved workforce, was determined to reduce his dependency on white labor generally, and independent skilled immigrants specifically, to ensure management's control at the point of production. To that end, in the 1840s Anderson made a failed attempt to replace white puddlers and rollers with their enslaved apprentices. Anderson's belief that industrial slavery was the solution to finding a tractable labor force immediately encountered the realities of running a large, complex manufacturing operation, and necessity forced him to employ even more white northern and British immigrant workers. In fact, during the Civil War, Tredegar employed more European workers than some of the ironworks in the North. In 1864, 47 percent of rollers, 43 percent of machinists, 33 percent of engineers and designers, and 29 percent of its skilled foundry and forge workers were foreign born.[18]

Welsh immigrants refused to compete with slave labor, believing that it would diminish the value of their own labor, and they believed slavery was immoral, so they generally avoided the South. Some skilled Welsh ironworkers and managers nevertheless did venture into the region. A colony of skilled Welsh workers grew up around the rolling mill in Knoxville, Tennessee, owned by Welshmen Joseph Richards and David Richards. The Knoxville Iron Company was not incorporated until 1868, but it had its origins during the Civil War, when Confederates attempted to operate a furnace and rolling mill in the town. The company failed because of the lack of skilled workers. After Union troops occupied Knoxville, Captain Hiram S. Chamberlain put the works into operation to supply iron implements for the army. After the war, Chamberlain brought the mill back into operation, and in April 1866, brothers David, Joseph, and William Richards, along with Daniel Thomas and Thomas D. Lewis, all of whom were experienced Welsh-born ironworkers, became partners with Chamberlain in the Knoxville Iron Company. Lewis opened the company's coal mines at Coal Creek, about thirty miles from Knoxville.[19]

Only an incomplete picture can be formed of how many Welsh families were lured to the Knoxville Iron Company by the Welsh owners. A letter written in 1873 to David Richards, a state senator at the time, by an acquaintance back in Wales praised the Richards brothers for being "pioneers of the Welsh nation to the State of Tennessee" and for their success in "drawing a great many industrious and religious Welshmen after you hither."[20] In 1870 the company reportedly employed 150 men in the plant, which included the rolling mill, foundry, machine shop, and a nail factory, and another 50 men at the Coal Creek mines.[21] Another newspaper report stated in 1871 that the company employed 160 "mostly Welshmen trained to the business from boyhood."[22]

David Thomas's influence was felt in the iron industry for much of the nineteenth century, not simply because he was the "father of American anthracite iron" but also because of his technical knowledge. Due to confidence in his ability and in an entire generation of Welsh American ironmasters that he trained at Catasauqua—men who went on to shape the future of the industry—Thomas's historical significance stretched far beyond the anthracite region and the antebellum period. The men Thomas trained carried their technical knowledge and practical skills to the newly opening fields farther south and west, where they obtained prominent positions through their connections with the informal ethnic network rooted at Catasauqua.

No more illustrative case exists than that of Giles Edwards of the rising Birmingham, Alabama, coal and iron district. A prominent Welsh ironmaster with career-long membership in the Wales–David Thomas–Pennsylvania network, Edwards had been born in Merthyr Tydfil in 1824, in the shadow of the world-renowned ironworks of Dowlais, Cyfarthfa, Plymouth, and Penydarren. Having received his training in the shops of Dowlais, he had become an expert at drafting by 1842, when he immigrated to Carbondale, Pennsylvania, where he made the drawings and supervised patternmaking for the first mill constructed in the city. There he met his future wife, Salinah Evans, the daughter of Welsh immigrants from Tredegar. The quality of his work drew the attention of David Thomas, who enticed Edwards to move to Catasauqua and serve as patternmaker for the Lehigh Crane Iron Works. While there, David Thomas's famous technical library on iron-making was available to Edwards, and he took full advantage of the opportunity to further his education. A few years later, in 1855, he assisted in the construction of the Thomas Iron Works at Hokendauqua. That year Edwards was chosen to be a blast furnace supervisor at the Cambria Iron Works in Johnstown,

Pennsylvania. Here he was befriended by Cambria's prominent ironmaster, John Fritz, and in 1858 Fritz recommended him to supervise construction of the Bethlehem Iron Company's rolling mill at Bethlehem, Pennsylvania. The following year, Fritz again provided Edwards with a recommendation that landed him the job as superintendent in charge of reconstructing Bluff Furnace in Chattanooga, Tennessee, the first furnace in the southern Appalachians to successfully use coke to smelt iron.[23]

Even though the vast majority of the Welsh whom Giles Edwards encountered were decidedly pro-Union, he cast his fate with the South during the Civil War and afterward. His motives for doing so, whether out of political sympathy, for health reasons, career opportunities, or some portion of all of these, are a matter of conjecture. Of the early Welsh ironmasters who remained in the South after the war, Edwards was the most successful. Having moved from Chattanooga to Alabama during the war to supervise the newly rebuilt Shelby Iron Company's works, which was the only integrated ironworks in the Deep South until after the Civil War, Edwards remained in Alabama for the rest of his life. By 1883 Edwards had moved to Oxmoor, then about six miles south of Birmingham, where he served as superintendent of the Eureka Iron Works, which was supplied with coke from compatriot Llewellyn Johns's Pratt Mines.[24] Members of the Thomas family were frequent guests at the Edwards home. In fact, it was at the invitation of Giles Edwards that David, Samuel, and Edwin Thomas came south for the first time to purchase mineral lands. The Thomases' southern interests would evolve into the Republic Iron and Coal Company and, eventually, Republic Steel.[25]

Edwards and his wife, Salinah, retained their Welsh identity. According to Ethel Armes, writing in 1910, they spoke Welsh at home. Edwards subscribed to a Welsh-language newspaper, probably *Y Drych*, throughout his life, and Armes claimed that one of his unnamed "intimate friends" was a "Welsh bard." Never in good health as a result of breathing in noxious furnace fumes, Edwards died prematurely in 1893.[26]

Edwards's views on race and labor issues demonstrate just how southern he became. He testified before the Senate Committee on Labor and Capital in 1883 that the "unreliability" of labor was the principal problem confronting southern industrialists, and he foresaw very little possibility of remedying the problem. Edwards explained, "You see the bulk of the entire labor force here is colored." In other words, he believed that Black workers

were "shiftless," one of the important building blocks in the ideology of race
control upon which the system of segregation was built. Still, he thought it
best to train them rather than to import white labor. The reason is not difficult to understand if one bears in mind that, in Alabama, African American
laborers were paid one-third less than their white counterparts by legislative
edict, and, not coincidentally, Black workers were politically powerless to
resist. Twenty years in the South had only reinforced Edwards's beliefs about
the role of African Americans in society: "I do not see any hope in the world
for them while they are together in large numbers" until they are "brought
in contact generally with the superior race," he testified. Welsh Americans
like Edwards deviated dramatically from the overwhelming majority of his
ethnic counterparts who abhorred slavery as well as the system of racial
segregation that replaced it and therefore refused to venture below the Ohio
River. They were not alone among immigrants. Even destitute European
immigrants found the South inhospitable to free labor, and most were not
attracted by the prospect of competing against a disenfranchised, semifree
industrial reserve of Black laborers.[27] On the other hand, Welsh managers
were afforded the opportunity for personal advancement in the region's iron
and steel industry if they were willing to accommodate to the protocols of
southern race relations.[28]

Hanging Rock District

The experience of Welsh ironworkers and the industry they fostered varied widely by region, a point vividly illustrated by the colony of Welsh
immigrants from Cardiganshire, in western Wales, who settled in Gallia
and Jackson Counties, Ohio. The first settlers were on their way to a new
agricultural settlement of Welsh immigrants that had been established at
Paddy's Run, near Cincinnati, Ohio, in 1818. While en route, these first
families, who became known as the "1818 Welsh," found themselves stranded
at Gallipolis, a river town about halfway between Wheeling and Cincinnati. The locals welcomed them, so they decided to stay. In 1835 additional
families joined the settlement.[29]

The Cardiganshire migrants had been farmers in Wales, and they went
to Gallia and Jackson Counties specifically to acquire better land. By 1850
the three townships with the largest number of Welsh settlers contained
a total of 316 Welsh households, 328 American-headed households, and

23 households headed by English, Irish, or German immigrants. Demonstrating the reason they emigrated from Wales, a greater proportion of the Welsh households owned land than the other groups, and few were tenant farmers.[30] Jackson and Gallia Counties were on the northern edge of the Hanging Rock iron district, which in the late 1830s was "on its way to becoming the leading charcoal iron-producing region west of the Alleghenies," according to the historian of this community, Anne Knowles. The furnaces were rural enterprises requiring labor, provisions, and raw materials, which the local landowners and farmers readily supplied. The vast majority of Welsh families engaged in farming, but the growing iron industry provided work and ready cash to young men who were not inclined to be farmers.[31] A charcoal furnace consumed an estimated 300 to 350 acres of forest for charcoal-making each year, which, from the farmers' point of view, opened up land for agriculture. Small-scale iron production was also instrumental in the early stages of industrialization in the Ohio valley, where it served specialty markets such as machine shops and manufacturers of iron wares.[32]

Engagement of the Welsh farmers in the Hanging Rock charcoal iron industry fostered a community that differed from other Welsh agricultural settlements. In Knowles's phrase, it was "a novel form of community-based venture capitalism" that emerged in 1854, when "a large number of Welsh families" joined forces to erect and operate three charcoal iron furnaces: the Jefferson, Cambria, and Madison.[33] In this arrangement, Welsh farmers deeded their land to the furnace companies in exchange for shares of company stock, a method that guaranteed the furnace companies' rights to timber and minerals. Each of the Welsh furnace companies was launched with between thirty and sixty shareholders, nearly all of them Welsh. Knowles estimates that in 1854–1855 about one-third of the Welsh in the settlement were invested in one of the iron companies.[34]

Unlike the pattern of ownership of American furnaces, in which a few individuals owned a controlling percentage of the shares, ownership of the Welsh furnaces in the Hanging Rock district was widely dispersed among shareholders, each of whom owned shares in only one of the furnaces. Initially, the construction and operation of the Welsh furnaces was performed overwhelmingly by Welsh workers, with their in-kind hours recorded and subsequently transferred into stock. The workers accepted this arrangement, Knowles asserts, because management and workers shared a common ethnic-cultural identity based on trust and mutual cooperation. The Jefferson furnace proved to be the most successful and long-lasting. It was the last charcoal iron furnace to produce pig iron in Ohio and did not close down until 1916.[35]

By the Civil War, the Welsh workforce had already begun to decline at the Welsh furnaces. They had performed a majority of the work in the mid-1850s, but by 1860 nearly 60 percent of the "rough work" was being performed by non-Welsh workers and 27 percent by Welsh labor. In 1870 the division of labor was even more pronounced, with the remaining Welsh predominating only in the skilled and managerial ranks. Conversely, after 1850 and 1870 growing proportions of the merchants, teachers, and other professionals in the iron communities were Welsh. Knowles concludes that the Welsh withdrew from the iron industry because they did not need to expose themselves to the hard, dangerous work and, more important, because their standard of living allowed them to leave the industry for other employment.[36]

The American iron industry was still in the developmental stage during the period before the Civil War, and therefore the level of technological sophistication varied by region as it expanded unevenly westward. Iron manufacture advanced quickly across the Alleghenies after David Thomas first burned anthracite coal in his furnace at Catasauqua. This rapid spread was stimulated by the discovery of coking coal in the greater Pittsburgh region of western Pennsylvania, eastern Ohio, and northern (West) Virginia. Technological advancement and the inability to attract a skilled labor supply because of the South's reliance on unfree labor arrested the industry's development in that region until well after the Civil War. The Hanging Rock iron district in southern Ohio was in its infancy during this period, while technological developments advanced in the areas farther to the east. Therefore, Welsh ironworkers trained in the more advanced methods used in Britain were overwhelmingly attracted to the coal and iron districts of northeastern and western Pennsylvania, where ironmasters experimented with the fully integrated units of production utilizing the latest technology. Importing Welsh designs and methods to America was in its introductory stage during the first half of the nineteenth century, and use of those technologies would not reach maturity until after the Civil War.

Pennsylvania and the Welsh Plan

Achieving economic self-sufficiency by developing its own domestic manufactures was a goal of the United States from the founding of the republic.

Fig. 3.1. Dowlais Ironworks. Illustration by George Childs, 1840. People's Collection, National Museum of Wales.

During the antebellum period the stimulus for doing so was the construction of railroads to create a national market system. To this end, mass-produced iron would lead the way, even more so than in Britain, by providing a supply of rails and locomotives needed to connect a vast underdeveloped nation. This goal could only be achieved, however, with coal-fired blast furnaces. American entrepreneurs generally looked to the ironworks of Cyfarthfa and Dowlais as models to emulate because of their size, integrated production, and the low per-ton operating costs achieved through new technologies. Cyfarthfa applied the very latest puddling and rolling processes, and by the 1790s it was being regarded as the most productive ironworks in the world.[37]

To erect their new ironworks, American entrepreneurs (called "adventurers" at the time) who attempted to transfer Welsh technologies and construction hired skilled Welsh and English workers because of the knowledge they brought "under their hats." Knowles highlights several problems posed by this approach to transferring coal-fired technologies to America. The most important were the qualitative differences in the chemical composition of

Fig. 3.2. Cyfarthfa Iron Works, 1870s. People's Collection, National Museum of Wales.

mineral resources; these differences affected the quality of iron produced. Second, the locations of ore, limestone, and coal deposits were more widely dispersed in the United States than in Wales, making it harder to replicate integrated works such as Penydarren and Cyfarthfa in Merthyr Tydfil. In Wales those deposits were all readily at hand at the heads of the valleys running north-south to the port cities of Newport, Cardiff, and Swansea. These massive ironworks were constructed to integrate each stage of production. As a historian of Merthyr iron points out, they were designed so that "each successive operation followed its predecessor in a continuous flow downhill, following the contours of the valley location." Nearby Dowlais also was planned in a similar operational sequence from the furnace backward up the valley to the mines and forward, down the Taff Valley, to the Cardiff docks.[38]

Another obstacle confronting American ironmasters was their failure to take into account the greater independence of skilled British ironworkers, who were free to make production decisions as they deemed appropriate. As Knowles points out, "strong regional identities reinforced loyalties rooted in class, occupational, and ethnoreligious identities," particularly among Welsh-speaking migrants from the countryside living in iron and coal towns such as Merthyr and Tredegar, who "created a distinctly Welsh industrial culture." At the ironworks, as well as iron ore and coal mines, men worked in crews composed of friends and relatives. This practice was encouraged in Wales to foster an efficient workforce, but in the United States it was often viewed as "clannish" and placing too much control over production in the hands of workers. Another difficulty in transferring the Welsh plan to America was that ironworks in Wales were located in urban centers. When those workers immigrated to the United States, they often were disgruntled to find themselves isolated in remote rural settings. American entrepreneurs also confronted a transportation system that was uneven at best. In Wales the distances between manufacturing sites and the markets were not great, whereas in the United States the geographic scale could be vast relative to the rudimentary modes of transportation available. In addition, the Industrial Revolution had brought canals and railroads to Britain a half century earlier than in America. Canals could operate year round in Britain, but in the United States they iced over during the winter months, requiring their closure.[39]

In the 1830s came the first attempts in the United States to break away from the small-scale charcoal furnaces of the colonial and frontier eras and to build ironworks along the lines of the fully integrated Welsh plan. Knowles has documented the first attempts to transfer Welsh iron-making technology during this period. One of the first occurred at Farrandsville in central Pennsylvania along Lycoming Creek, a tributary to the Susquehanna River. In 1832 several Boston investors purchased the Lycoming Coal Company, which immediately ran into trouble from the high cost of transporting its coal by "arks" down the Susquehanna River. In the vain hope of remaining solvent, the company decided to use coke to fire its furnaces.[40]

Also, Welsh workers were recruited to operate the new ironworks. A son of one of the Lycoming investors was an iron commission merchant in London and a major exporter of British iron. Gerard Ralston's personal relationships with Welsh ironmasters had led him to marry the daughter of William Crawshay, the owner of Cyfarthfa Iron Works. Ralston contacted several prominent Welsh ironmasters in an effort to find a suitable supervisor for the Lycoming ironworks. He finally secured a commitment from Edward Thomas, a skilled employee of the Plymouth Iron Works in Merthyr.[41]

Arriving at Farrandsville in November 1835, Thomas found puddlers and rollers imported from Wales and England, and several more arrived shortly thereafter. Because Thomas failed to put the furnace into blast, the owners replaced him with a Scotsman in 1836. The new man failed as well, but, under the supervision of another Welsh immigrant, Benjamin Perry, formerly a manager at the Pentwyn Iron Works in Abersychan, the company's furnace was finally put into blast. In the end, the Lycoming Coal Company failed, not so much because of the skilled men they recruited to supervise and operate the ironworks but from poor management. Other contributing factors were the remoteness of the settlement and the dissatisfaction of the British workers with the lack of simple amenities to which they were accustomed. As a result, the company's assets were auctioned off between 1838 and 1840.[42]

About the same time, the George's Creek Coal and Iron Company was also attempting to develop an ironworks along the Welsh plan. The company built the Lonaconing furnace on George's Creek, about six miles south of Frostburg in the western Maryland panhandle, to produce merchant bar for secondary manufacturers of iron products, railroad iron, and heavy castings. With high hopes, one of the partners predicted that the time would come when western Maryland would be "looked upon as the Wales of North America."[43]

The George's Creek coal mines and ironworks would never have been confused with the ironworks in Wales that they were intended to emulate, but neither was the combined enterprise a complete failure like the works at Farrandsville. The company's furnace produced a high grade of coke iron, and demand for its coal continued for well over a century. One of the key distinctions between the Lonaconing and Lycoming works was the ability of its Welsh supervisors. John Steele was recruited from Wales in 1837 to oversee the Welsh coal miners at Lonaconing on the recommendation of a manager at the Penydarren Iron Works in Merthyr Tydfil. David Hopkins, a Welsh foundryman, took charge of erecting the first of four planned blast furnaces. Two more Welshmen, John Thomas and John Phillips, arrived a month later to serve as keepers of the furnace and supervise filling and tapping the furnace stack. The ethnic divisions at Lonaconing are not clear, but apparently Germans were employed in the ore mines and limestone quarries, Welsh held the coal mining and skilled ironworker positions, and native-born Americans worked at the other crafts, including carpentry and masonry, and as general laborers. Labor relations were fractious at the works for similar reasons as at Lycoming and Lonoconing, that is, workers had too little in the way of healthy entertainment and far too much cheap liquor was available to a relatively young male population.[44]

Although the George's Creek Coal and Iron Company never realized its goal of creating an integrated operation patterned after the famous Welsh furnaces, Knowles demonstrates that the ethnic solidarity of the Welsh in key management and skilled occupations laid the foundation for a cohesive workforce based on mutual trust and cooperation. This advantage apparently was not sufficient, however, to save the company; it ceased operation after building only one furnace stack. The main causes of its demise were the panic of 1837, which lasted several years, and the high cost of skilled labor, which had to be recruited abroad and transported to the United States.[45]

Other attempts were made to construct integrated ironworks in antebellum America, some more successful than others, but information on the composition of their workforces is insufficient to allow accurate assessment of the role of any particular ethnic group in their operation. The Mount Savage Iron Works, for example, was funded by British and American investors and constructed in Maryland on George's Creek, upstream from the Lonaconing facility. It represented the nation's first ironworks integrated from raw materials through finished product. Chartered in 1837, Mount Savage had two coal-fired furnace stacks and a rolling mill by 1845 and was one of the first to produce T-rail for railroads. Like other American ironworks unable to compete with Welsh rail, Mount Savage was also forced to shut down.[46]

Anthracite Iron

The slowness of American ironmasters to embrace coke as a blast furnace fuel raises the question of why Americans resisted its adoption and continued to use charcoal fuel. America's anthracite deposits are limited and highly concentrated in northeastern Pennsylvania, on the eastern side of the Allegheny Mountains. Anthracite's chemical makeup closely resembles coke, so when mineral fuel was substituted for charcoal east of the Alleghenies, it was anthracite coal. By 1854, the amount of anthracite pig iron had jumped from zero to 45 percent of US production.[47]

The explosive growth of the anthracite coal industry would not have been possible without the discovery of how anthracite could be used as fuel for smelting iron. The anthracite sold in the 1830s was for household heating, but leaders in the coal and iron industries were busy exploring smelting techniques that used raw anthracite as fuel. The traditional "cold-blast" method, which forced outside air into the furnace, chilled the interior to below the ignition point of anthracite. The "hot-blast" design forced hot air into the furnace, elevating the temperature enough to smelt iron, a process that was much more efficient than the traditional cold-blast method. George Crane, an English furnace owner, had been trying unsuccessfully since 1826 to smelt iron with anthracite in the cold-blast furnace at his Ynyscedwyn Ironworks, located in the village of Ystradgynlais, thirteen miles up the river Tawe from Swansea, South Wales. In the early 1830s, he sent his ironmaster, David Thomas, to Scotland to observe James Neilson's recently patented method for heating the blast. On returning to Wales, Thomas built a hot-blast furnace and successfully smelted iron with anthracite at the Ynyscedwyn works in 1837.[48]

Two competing companies in Pennsylvania followed these developments closely and eagerly anticipated the adoption of the new techniques in the United States. Josiah White of the Lehigh Coal and Navigation Company, located at Mauch Chunk, had been experimenting with making anthracite iron for more than a decade. In 1838 Lehigh Coal enticed ironmaster David Thomas to Pennsylvania to build a furnace based on the new technology. Thomas began work on the new furnace in July 1839 at Catasauqua, near Bethlehem, and successfully put it into blast in July 1840.[49] Meanwhile, a competing Pottsville group also learned of the successful trial at Crane's South Wales works, and during the winter of 1837–1838 they began planning the construction of a furnace. Where they obtained the technical knowledge to construct the works is unclear, but Welsh coal miner Richard Jones was reported to have returned to Pottsville from a visit to the Ynyscedwyn works in April 1838 bearing samples of coal, iron ore, and pig iron. The following year David Thomas provided the Pottsville "adventurers" with the technical knowledge to build the Pioneer furnace on the same plan used at Catasauqua. Benjamin Perry, a Welsh furnace manager familiar with the Ynyscedwyn works back in Wales, was employed as overseer. The Pioneer furnace was operational in October 1839, and the Lehigh Crane furnace at Catasauqua went into blast in July 1840. The new technology not only transformed the iron industry but also led to a huge boost in anthracite coal production, initiating America's rise as an industrial power and David Thomas's anointing as "father of the anthracite iron industry."[50]

Fig. 3.3. David Thomas, "Father of American Anthracite Iron." Reproduced by permission from Hagley Museum and Library.

L. Crepox. lith.   Anh of P.H.Oihson, Brlishast.   P.S.Davol & Son's lt'h Phil.

LEHIGH CRANE IRON WORKS, Catasauqua, Lehigh Co.
John Thomas, Superintendent

Fig. 3.4. Lehigh Crane Iron Works, Catasauqua, Pennsylvania, ca. 1850s. Library of Congress.

Following Thomas's lead, the new technology spread quickly throughout the anthracite fields in eastern Pennsylvania, making that region the nation's leading producer of iron. Montour erected its first anthracite furnace in 1839, and a decade later it had two anthracite furnaces and two extensive rolling mills. Within a twelve-mile radius were five additional anthracite furnaces and a hot-blast charcoal furnace. In 1845 the Montour Iron Works became one of the first to manufacture T-rail in the United States, and during the antebellum period it was the major producer of T-rail in the United States. Danville claimed 3,302 residents in 1850, including hundreds of English, Welsh, and American puddlers, rollers, heaters, molders, machinists, and miners, joined by smaller proportions of Irish, Scottish, German, French, and Nova Scotian ironworkers. Three of the six ironmasters were Americans, while the other three were English and Welsh. In an interesting aside, Danville was also home to an immigrant puddler from Merthyr

Fig. 3.5. Montour Iron Works, Danville, Pennsylvania, ca. 1855. F. V. Lahr after James Queen. Reproduced by permission from Palmer Museum of Art, Pennsylvania State University.

Tydfil—Joseph Parry, the famous composer of Welsh choral music.[51] Reverend R. D. Thomas visited Danville in 1872 and noted that there were "many iron works where a large number of Welsh have worked for years." At the time of his visit Reverend Thomas observed that at one time Danville was home to a Welsh population of about 500, but many of the Welsh had since departed.[52]

Not until 1853 would an American ironworks approach the scale of Cyfarthfa's six furnace stacks, and Dowlais's sixteen were beyond imagination. That year four anthracite blast furnace stacks were erected by the Lackawanna Iron and Coal Company at Roaring Creek in Scranton.[53] In the 1840s, Slocum Hollow, the rural area where the city of Scranton emerged as an industrial center the following decade, was on the frontier of the new industrializing America, a place where the battle for "American independence from English iron would be fought and won."[54] The location was strategically significant for the growth of iron production, with all of the necessary raw materials abundant and available for iron-making: iron ore, sulfur, limestone, and anthracite coal. The opportunities attracted the inspection of Seldon Scranton and his brother George, who purchased the property in 1840 and built a blast furnace and a nail works. George had been the ironmaster of Oxford Iron Furnace in New Jersey, so he complemented Seldon's business acumen with a level of technical knowledge that created an amazingly successful partnership.[55]

The Scrantons blew in their new blast furnace in 1841 and 1842, prompting Seldon to go to Danville, where he could hire someone with experience making anthracite iron. He found his man in John F. Davis, a native of Tredegar, South Wales, who soon put the furnaces into blast. As historian William D. Jones observes, Davis's "ironmaking magic succeeded where Yankee exuberance had failed," illustrating why Welsh technical skill was such a sought-after commodity.[56]

In the mid-1840s, the Scrantons shifted to the mass production of iron rails. At this time, British iron companies were under heavy demand for rails as railroad expansion continued in Britain, and a dramatic increase in the price of rail made it profitable enough to lure American manufacturers into the market. These conditions were particularly fortuitous for producers in eastern Pennsylvania. In fulfilling their contract with the New York and Erie Railroad in 1848, the Scranton brothers were the first to mass-produce T-rails in America, and the city named for them emerged as a major iron-producing center. In the mid-1850s, the Lackawanna Iron and Coal Company was one of the largest rail manufacturers in the nation.[57]

Scranton was surrounded by coal mines and ironworks in the northern anthracite field of Luzerne and Lackawanna Counties, which in 1900 contained 16,284 people born in Wales. Coal mines and ironworks employed an overwhelming majority of them, but the number of Welsh employed by the iron companies remains to be calculated.[58] Scranton hosted the largest concentration of Welsh in the United States. Reverend Thomas estimated that five thousand Welsh were clustered primarily in the Hyde Park neighborhood, but he only mentions their work in the local coal mines even though large numbers of them must have worked in the local machine shops and ironworks.[59] In addition to the lack of data, one of the greatest difficulties in establishing an accurate count of the Welsh in a particular location or worksite is the frequency of their moves from job to job in the "tramping artisan" tradition.

Nevertheless, there is no question that large numbers of Welsh were attracted to the growing coal and iron industries of Scranton beginning in the mid-1840s. Evan Williams was employed to supervise the Lackawanna Company's mines in 1844, and John R. Williams, a Welsh immigrant working in Wilkes-Barre, was recruited to supervise the rolling mill founded by the Scrantons in 1846; it was this mill that rolled the first T-rail. With their own nationality in charge, the number of Welsh increased dramatically through chain migration and the recruitment of Welsh workers by Lackawanna's long-serving Welsh superintendent of mines, Benjamin F. Hughes. By 1870, the city had 4,177 Welsh-born residents, who made up almost 12 percent of its population of 35,092.[60] Newer iron-producing centers like Johnstown, Pennsylvania, also were operated disproportionately by Welsh workers.[61]

In 1857 a foreman at a South Wales ironworks told an American traveler that "within the decade a score of men out of the mill's two hundred—'the pick of their workmen'—had left for the States; he himself 'had many kindred in America and expected to join them in the spring.' Welsh furnacemen could speak as familiarly about 'Pottsville, and Catasauqua, Hanging Rock [Ohio], or Johnstown as if those places were . . . Ebbw Vale, Ynyscedwyn, Pontypool, and Rhymney.'"[62]

Pittsburgh District

Eastern Pennsylvania was the center of iron-making in antebellum America, but by midcentury the industry's center was already shifting west of the Allegheny Mountains to the Pittsburgh district. Pittsburgh was a wilderness in 1750 and still a crude log settlement at the time of the American Revolution. The first census in 1790 recorded only 376 residents, but more quickly followed. With a population exceeding 5,000 by the end of the War of 1812, Pittsburgh became the largest town in what was then the American West. By 1820 the population had grown to 7,500, and industrial concerns, particularly the manufacture of iron, began to overtake commercial enterprises.[63]

Pittsburgh's location at the confluence of the Allegheny and Monongahela Rivers made it the "gateway to the West" for settlers traveling down the Ohio River. The city's iron manufacturers who provisioned those settlers with the implements they required on the frontier were supplied with raw iron by the numerous operators of small, local ironworks. By the Civil

War, an intricate railroad and river network would integrate the triangular area around the upper Ohio River, defined at its points by Pittsburgh, Youngstown, Ohio, and Wheeling, West Virginia, into what has been appropriately called the "Iron Valley."[64]

Iron was an important commodity on the frontier, and iron foundries, along with gristmills and sawmills, were among the first craft industries to be established. In 1804 the first iron foundry located in Pittsburgh began production of hollow ironware for the local market. By 1814, four other foundries, three nail factories, and the first local rolling mill had been established. Four years later came the Union Mill, the first rolling mill with its own puddling furnaces. By 1826 Pittsburgh's eight foundries and six rolling mills were employing several hundred people and supplying finished iron products to the growing settlements along the Ohio River.[65]

These early works were not integrated operations because they neither made their own pig iron nor puddled their own blooms. Instead, pig iron was hauled into the city from charcoal furnaces in the hinterland. This situation would change, however, during the two decades preceding 1850. At the midcentury mark, Pittsburgh's population reached 46,601, and an additional 21,262 residents lived across the Allegheny River in what was then Allegheny City. Nine rolling mills and eighteen foundries were in operation in both cities in 1836, and, despite the panic of 1837 and a major fire in 1845, the number of rolling mills reached twenty-five in 1856. Still, no pig iron was produced in Pittsburgh.[66]

The United States was blessed with a seemingly unlimited supply of bituminous coal, but not all bituminous coal produces the quality of coke required for iron production. Bituminous coal is found primarily on the western side of the Allegheny Mountains, so, before the Pennsylvania Railroad reached Pittsburgh from Philadelphia in 1852, it was not feasible to ship large quantities of anthracite across the mountains. When western ironmasters adopted the new fuel technology, therefore, it was coke they embraced. Until after the Civil War, the "Iron City" of Pittsburgh was dominated by rolling mills, foundries, and forges rather than furnaces producing pig iron.[67]

The development of the Connellsville coalfields southeast of Pittsburgh changed the equation dramatically. The Connellsville seam contained bituminous coal uniquely suitable for coking, thus enabling the western ironmasters to adopt the new mass-production technologies.[68] As early as 1759, colonists were aware of the bituminous coal deposits in western

Pennsylvania; they could not have known then that the rich seams underlying the recently platted town of Pittsburgh fanned out in a sixty-mile
radius. By the early nineteenth century, Pittsburgh coal was being exported
to the new towns springing up along the Ohio River and being used for
blacksmithing and domestic heating. Both charcoal and coke were made by
covering a pile of timber or coal with earth, leaving holes to vent the gases
while it smoldered. This process was later greatly improved by development
of the coke, or beehive, oven. By 1817 Colonel Isaac Meason was using coke
at his forge, where, according to tradition, the Welshman Samuel Lewis
supervised the construction of the puddling furnaces and perhaps shared
his knowledge of coke production.[69]

Thomas C. Lewis immigrated to America in 1815 from Merthyr Tydfil, where he worked as a puddler and a roller of iron bars. Iron that was
puddled and then rolled instead of hammered into bar produced a higher
grade of ductile wrought iron than the method then employed by American ironmasters. By the 1790s the process had been successfully installed
at Cyfarthfa Iron Works, where Lewis probably gained his knowledge of
the process. Eastern Pennsylvania ironmasters regarded these innovations
with skepticism, but the western Pennsylvania ironmaster Isaac Meason
embraced them. Meason entered an agreement with Lewis to construct
and supervise a new ironworks using these methods at Upper Middletown,
Fayette County, near Uniontown, some fifty miles southeast of Pittsburgh.
Thomas Lewis then enlisted his four brothers in the enterprise, and George
(rolling mill), Samuel (heater), James (catcher), and Henry (clerk) arrived in
1816. Samuel C. Lewis, the supervisor's fourteen-year-old son, also labored
at the works. David Adams, puddler, and James Pratt, finisher, were friends
of the Lewises and came with the brothers from Wales. The ironworks went
into operation in September 1817, but it was partially destroyed by flooding
in 1831, and a new works was erected in Brownsville, Pennsylvania.[70]

One of the first important antebellum ironworks constructed in Pittsburgh was Vesuvius Iron, built in 1846. The owners had no knowledge of iron
manufacture, so they hired James and George Lewis Jr., the sons of George
Lewis, known as the "Welshman who rolled the first bar of iron in America."
George Sr. had trained his sons well in the art of iron manufacture. After
immigrating to America in 1816, he became superintendent of Pittsburgh's
Union Rolling Mill in 1823 and later served as superintendent of two other
prominent antebellum ironworks—the Sligo Works and the Juniata Mill.[71]

Thomas Lewis and his family played a pivotal role in the development of the early iron industry by introducing the new technology that would initiate the American Industrial Revolution. Thomas became known as the man who built the first puddling furnace and rolling mill in the United States, and brother George, who rolled the first bar of iron in America, by 1825 was operating the Dowlais Mill at Pipetown, Pittsburgh. His sons George and James C. Lewis built the Lewis, O'Hara & Lewis Rolling Mills at Sharpsburg, near Pittsburgh, in 1846.[72]

In the early 1830s, Norton's Iron Works in Connellsville used coke that was made in a stone coke oven, possibly the first in the region. During the 1840s, the Great Western Iron Company at Brady's Bend, about sixty miles up the Allegheny River from Pittsburgh, began to produce coke iron, and other companies in the region soon followed. The Civil War saw a major spike in demand for iron, and the higher prices encouraged iron makers to invest in another technology that increased production. The hot-blast furnace overcame the disadvantages of using regular air to fan the flames by substituting heated air, which helped to maintain the high temperatures necessary to smelt iron. Development of the Bessemer process for converting pig iron into steel made it possible beginning in the 1870s to mass produce steel, further stimulating the demand for pig iron and thus for western Pennsylvania coal as well. Transportation improvements were the final component in the construction of the Pittsburgh coal and iron region as a leading industrial center. Pittsburgh's location at the headwaters of the Ohio River facilitated barging bulky raw materials to the city's industries, and the railroads required to haul iron and steel to metal manufacturers all over America became a reality during the decades after the Civil War. A measure of the resulting expansion is the number of coke ovens, which by 1882 had reached 8,400, and coal production in the coke region grew 300 percent between 1870 and 1884.[73]

At least a half dozen new mills were erected in Pittsburgh during the late 1840s and 1850s. One of them was the Birmingham Rolling Mill, owned by William J. Lewis and John Phillips in the late 1850s. Lewis was born in Pittsburgh in 1832, the son of Welsh immigrant parents who arrived in Pittsburgh in 1828. William was a young boy when his father died. At fifteen he was apprenticed as a roll-turner at the Birmingham plant, where he worked for eight years before becoming the superintendent at another mill. At the age of twenty-eight, he joined in partnership with his brother-in-law, John Phillips, as owners of a small nut and bolt factory and then the Birmingham Rolling Mill. Phillips was a Pittsburgh native whose father was a blacksmith. Lewis was inventive and patented several improvements in iron-working machinery, including a machine that made nuts and bolts.[74]

The most important of these new Pittsburgh firms, however, was the American Iron Works, which began operations in 1850 along the left bank of the Monongahela River. The company was in financial difficulty when Benjamin F. Jones and Samuel Kier took over the plant, but Jones had a genius for iron manufacture and turned the company around overnight. Although Kier was a source of financial support, Jones sought additional capital through an alliance with James Laughlin, an Irish immigrant who made his fortune in Pittsburgh and married into the city's elite. With Laughlin's deep financial resources, Jones transformed the American Iron Works into one of the major ironworks in antebellum America. At first the pig iron was purchased from works owned by the Laughlin family near Youngstown, but in 1861 Jones constructed the Eliza Furnace on the opposite bank of the river from the American Iron Works. Eliza Furnace was only the second blast furnace in the city. With a blast furnace, rolling mills, warehousing, and a sales office in Chicago, American Iron was an integrated, high-volume operation. Moreover, it employed professional managers, established bureaucratic systems, separated ownership from management, and adopted strict procedures for accountability. In short, the company was a leader in the development of the modern corporate form of organization.[75]

Welsh ironworkers accepted the uncertainties of leaving the relative security of their homeland when they crossed three thousand miles of ocean in exchange for the chance of a more promising future. Their lives depended on the ironworks, and the ironworks required their skills. Consequently, skilled men formed a relationship of reciprocal dependency with owners and managers, and they took a proprietary interest in upholding the high standards of their craft, the profitable operation of the mill, and the quality of its product. The emergence of a modern iron industry in an urban industrial center, however, fundamentally altered capital-labor relations that had prevailed under the "craftsmen's empire" by shifting control over production from skilled labor to management. Workers were not slow in understanding the threat to their ability to control their own labor.

As might be expected, the puddlers were the first to resist this threat. Puddlers worked in mills making iron rails, and their counterparts, the boilers, performed the same task in mills manufacturing merchant iron. Consequently, where specificity is not important, the two groups are often simply called puddlers. They occupied a position between management and labor, performing some roles that could be seen as managerial, such as hiring and paying their own helpers. They alone determined when the iron was ready, and managers assented to their judgment. At midcentury, before there were unions, puddlers were the natural leaders of the ironworkers, and when capital attempted to impose its will on ironworkers, puddlers led the resistance. They did not always win, but they played a crucial role in resolving capital-labor conflicts. The Pittsburgh rolling mill strike of 1850 illustrates the point.

In December 1849 the management of Lorenz, Sterling and Company informed the ironworkers of a 25 percent reduction in wages stemming from depressed economic conditions and from a reduction in the protective tariff of 1846 that resulted in British competitors gaining a decided market advantage. Other manufacturers followed suit and lowered their wage scales.[76] Solidarity was demonstrated when some two hundred puddlers held a mass meeting, collectively resolved to reject the wage reductions, and then went out on strike. It is worth noting that the striking puddlers' first response was not to organize a union but rather to organize an association to purchase company stock. This kind of association would have given them a voice in the management of mills and a share of the profits, indicating that the puddlers assumed they still maintained their traditional stake in the system.[77]

By mid-January 1850 a Pittsburgh newspaper was estimating that between twelve hundred and fifteen hundred men had stopped work. While the men went on strike to preserve a place in the decision-making process, the manufacturers rejected this position out of hand by closing their mills and importing replacement workers from the East Coast, where unemployment was high. By February 15, 1850, forty-nine puddlers had been imported, but, upon discovering that they were replacing strikers, many either returned home or joined the Pittsburgh puddlers. The imported puddlers informed their Pittsburgh comrades that the owners had deceived them by claiming that they wanted to employ American rather than English and Welsh puddlers. They also claimed that the Welsh and English puddlers' refusal to work was denying American men the right to work.[78]

As the strike dragged on, however, some of the imported workers decided to remain and take jobs in the mills. More decisive action seemed to be called for, so on February 16 and 18 several hundred puddlers, led by bands with banners flying, paraded through the downtown streets. It was clear that tensions were rising between the puddlers, the strikebreakers, and the owners.[79] On March 1, 1850, a group of women estimated to number between sixty and one hundred met at the rolling mill of Graff, Lindsay and Company, and a crowd of men and boys sympathetic to the cause soon joined them. Armed with sticks and stones, the women entered the mill, drove off all the replacement hands, and then ruined the day's run of iron by throwing coal and dirt into the furnaces. One report stated that the last worker in the mill was seized by the women and allowed to escape only after promising to leave Pittsburgh. The crowd then marched to the Shoenberger mill. There they were confronted by the sheriff and the mayor, whose attempt to disperse the crowd was met with a chorus of boos. No further incidents occurred that day; however, the "mob" had entered and damaged private property, thereby putting officials on alert.[80]

The next day, March 2, an even larger crowd of men, women, and children gathered at the Bailey, Brown and Company mill. This time the crowd proved more difficult, and the police were incapable of handling them. The owners closed the gates, but the rowdy throng made a forced entry. After chasing off the men at work, they took over the mill, removed the grates from the furnaces, and threw dirt and rocks into the iron. Once again, the sheriff and mayor attempted to disperse the rioters, but they were ignored. Only after one of the strike leaders urged them to comply did the angry crowd break up. Several of the more unruly rioters were arrested and convicted of inciting to riot. During the trial that followed, two men were fined and sentenced to eighteen months in the penitentiary, while five women were sentenced to thirty days in jail and fined fifty dollars each.[81]

The puddlers remained on strike following the trial, but their determination began to wane after four months without work and no tangible results. Consequently, when the mill owners offered to "compromise" on the wage reduction, the workers accepted. Because the owners refused to discharge the imported workers, the striking men were forced to wait until demand called for an increase in production before they were rehired at the reduced rate. Many of the strikers were not recalled to their jobs at all.

Thus ended the Pittsburgh iron strike of 1850, which has been called "the first great labor demonstration in the entire iron industry."[82] With the seeds planted and the lesson learned, the puddlers realized that they needed a national organization. When that time came, Welsh puddlers would be at the forefront of labor's cause.

4

The Age of Steel Begins

During the last half of the nineteenth century, the "Iron Valley" was transformed into the "Steel Valley" as steel replaced iron as the industry's principal product, thus launching a cascade of profound changes in the industry, the Pittsburgh region, and ultimately American society. Until after the Civil War, steel was produced in small quantities by the crucible process, a very labor-intensive method that involved mixing wrought iron and a substance high in carbon content in a crucible and then heating the mixture to a very high temperature. The steel produced was either very expensive or of poor quality. That changed when the Bessemer process for producing steel was adopted in the United States in 1864. Patented by Sir Henry Bessemer in England in 1855 and perfected at his Sheffield steel works by 1858, the Bessemer process forced air directly through a chamber containing molten iron. At a certain temperature, most of the silicon and carbon would be burned off. At the end of the "blow," an alloy of iron and manganese was added, thus supplying the carbon necessary to give the steel its strength. The Bessemer process was much cheaper than the blast furnace, so it was readily embraced for certain products, particularly steel rails.[1]

Whereas the Bessemer process produced massive quantities of steel very economically, crucible steel resembled the slow, arduous labor required for puddling, and, like puddling, the crucible process was not readily mechanized. Also like puddling, crucible steel was more art than science, and speed only diminished quality. Crucible furnaces produced far less steel than rolling mills were capable of processing; therefore, there was no economic incentive for managers of either the steel mills or the rolling mills to attempt to become more efficient by increasing speed or output.[2]

During the post–Civil War decades, the transition from iron to steel accelerated dramatically. In 1867, 98 percent of all rolled products were made of puddled, or wrought, iron. By 1897, that figure had fallen to 21 percent of all rolled products and to only 11 percent by 1907.[3] However, even though there was a decline in iron production relative to steel, the absolute amount actually increased during this period. Iron's decline, both relative and absolute, began in the 1890s and the first decade of the twentieth century. Many manufacturers produced both puddled iron and steel. Carnegie Steel and Jones & Laughlin did not close down their puddling furnaces until 1892, at what one historian aptly calls the "symbolic end of the era of iron in America." Thereafter, iron production went into a precipitous decline.[4]

As Bessemer steel increasingly dominated the markets, makers of wrought iron were forced to develop a higher-quality steel at a competitive price. Their response was to convert to the Siemens-Martin, or open-hearth, process of steel production, which had been developed in Wales and introduced in the United States a few years after the Bessemer process. An open-hearth furnace had brick chambers at either end of a reservoir, or hearth, of the furnace. These chambers were connected by flues through which heated gases would pass over the reservoir at a very high temperature. At the back of the furnace was a ladle that held all the molten steel in the furnace.[5]

Manufacturers were slow to embrace the open-hearth process because it took longer and was more expensive than the Bessemer process. The open-hearth furnace was much like a puddling furnace, so wrought iron and crucible steel manufacturers readily adopted the new method. Unlike the Bessemer converter set-up process, setting up for open-hearth steel production did not require extensive alterations to the plant, and the new process depended more on chemical engineering than the judgment of a highly skilled worker at the furnace. This was significant because it shifted decision-making from the worker to the company, transferred control over the production process to company managers, and enabled iron and steel manufacturers to eliminate certain classes of skilled labor. In 1884 only four plants made open-hearth steel in Pittsburgh; ten years later there were eighteen open-hearth operations in the city.[6]

The Age of Steel came into its own in the 1880s, with Pittsburgh and upper Ohio valley cities in the vanguard and the United States producing an increasing percentage of the world's steel. As recently as 1873 British steelmakers had regarded the United States as a "dumping ground" for its surplus of steel too inferior to be used at home, and "American rails" were made specifically for use by railroads expanding westward. That situation had begun to change by 1875. With the Lake Superior ore fields effectively incorporated into the production supply chain, American companies produced ever higher quality steel, utilized primarily for railroad construction. Nearly all of this business went to Andrew Carnegie and a few other steelmasters during this period, while British makers gradually lost their US market for iron rail.[7]

Steel production surpassed that of iron in the United States for the first time between 1880 and 1890, jumping from just 29 percent of the total output in 1880 to 61 percent just a decade later. By 1894 Carnegie had installed open-hearth furnaces at his massive Edgar Thomson plant, and they were capable of producing 180,000 tons of steel per year. That same year, Pittsburgh had eighteen additional open-hearth operations that varied widely in scale and production. By 1904 open-hearth steel had come to dominate the market, accounting for 72 percent of the iron and steel output in the United States.[8] The vast increase in the scale of operating plants, the substitution of machinery-driven equipment for manual labor, and the growing reliance on technology and economic rationalization also dramatically increased productivity in rolling mills, from 25.2 tons per worker to 42.1 tons. Achieving these efficiencies required large outlays of capital that led to a concentration of ownership as well as other characteristics that define modern industrial organizations. Driven by the growth of the iron and steel industry, by 1870 Pittsburgh and Allegheny City (annexed by Pittsburgh in 1907) had emerged as a major urban-industrial center with a population of 137,000, and that figure had reached 235,000 by 1880 and exceeded 340,000 by 1890. The city was the hub of an industrial hinterland with a radius of sixty miles.[9]

Formation of the Amalgamated Association of Iron and Steel Workers

The great expansion of the iron and steel industry during the late nineteenth century, with its associated technological improvements, organizational concentration, centralized control, and the massive scale of firms, fundamentally altered the relations between capital and labor. Nevertheless, iron- and steelworkers would not have an industry-wide union until August 1876, when the Amalgamated Association of Iron and Steel Workers of the United States (AAISW) was organized in Pittsburgh from the consolidation of three craft unions.

A large percentage of the most able founders, organizers, and executives of the largest American labor organizations, such as the United Mine Workers of America and its antecedents, the National Labor Union, and the Knights of Labor, were from the British Isles. One scholar has determined that, as a group, they were young men when they came to the United States, usually between twenty-one and thirty-five, but they came with a wealth of experience in British mines and mills, where they had begun working at a very early age. They also "retained an unquenchable interest" in developments in Britain, and some of them retained their affiliation with their old unions after emigrating, maintained an active correspondence with union men back home, and communicated through labor publications in the homeland. Some made return trips to visit family and old friends. These open channels between British working men at home and abroad made it possible for organizers in the United States to draw upon the vast experience of labor organizers in Britain.[10]

Although business and the press often portrayed them as dangerous radicals, they were overwhelmingly moderate men who, as one scholar described them, "deplored strikes, worked constantly for arbitration and conciliation, and without fatally compromising labor's objectives, urging harmony between capital and labor." While the economic climate in America encouraged their conservatism, it was lessons learned at home from the collapse of Chartism and the rise of "new model" unionism in Britain that shaped their attitudes on issues involving capital and labor. They retained the "same sense of propriety, the same self-discipline, diligence, stability, and the desire for 'respectability' often associated with the terms 'Victorian' and 'bourgeois.'" In short, they tended to reflect the values of the British middle class, or the "Protestant bourgeoisie," to which they aspired before emigration. These same values motivated them to cross the ocean with hope of improving their fortunes, and after immigrating they found nothing incompatible with becoming petty capitalists as well as labor leaders.[11]

Fig. 4.1. Puddler, Youngstown Sheet and Tube Puddling Mill, ca. 1920. Reproduced by permission from Mahoning Valley Historical Society, Youngstown, Ohio.

Men from the British Isles played an important role in organizing workers in the heavy industries, particularly coal mining and the iron and steel industry, where thousands of their compatriots labored. The important industrial state of Pennsylvania counted 22,422 ironworkers in 1880, of whom 7,947 were natives of the British Isles.[12] The first of the metal trades unions to merge with the AAISW, the United Sons of Vulcan, had been formed on August 17, 1858, by a small group of Pittsburgh puddlers who had met at an old hotel on Saturday evenings to discuss poor industry conditions and low wages resulting from the panic of 1857. The August 17 meeting was shrouded in secrecy for fear of retribution from their employers, and as a result of their secrecy the Vulcans experienced little growth during the group's formative years. Circumstances changed with the economic stimulus provided by the Civil War, and in September 1862 the puddlers met in a national convention in Pittsburgh to create the Grand Forge of the United States.[13]

Growth continued to be slow, and in 1868 the Vulcans reported fewer than 600 members. Their strategic roles within the production process greatly magnified the puddlers' influence, however, and by 1873 the group had grown to 3,331 dues-paying members in eighty-three lodges in twelve states. A milestone in the existence of the Sons of Vulcan was reached in 1867. The manufacturers proposed a reduction of wages in December 1866, and when the workers refused to accept the new terms, the mill operators locked them out. Following negotiations, an agreement was reached in July 1867; there would be a sliding scale for wages based on the price of the product they produced. This was probably the first sliding scale in the industry, a mechanism that prevailed for the rest of the century. More significantly, employers recognized the puddlers' union by bargaining with them.[14]

The second union that merged into the AAISW was the Associated Brotherhood of Iron and Steel Heaters, Rollers, and Roughers of the United States, founded in August 1872. For the most part, its membership consisted of workers in charge of furnaces and rolls in the mills concentrated principally in Pittsburgh and other mill towns of the upper Ohio River region west of the Allegheny Mountains, and to a lesser extent in midwestern cities like Chicago. Their leader was Thomas P. Jones. A native of Glamorganshire, South Wales, Jones entered the rolling mills as a youth, and in 1846 he went to work in the rolling mills near Glasgow, Scotland, where he immediately set about organizing his fellow workers. In 1862, during one of the frequent periods when work was slow, he left for America and found employment in the North Chicago Rolling Mills. Once again Jones resumed his organizing efforts, bringing swift retribution from his employers, who fired and "blackballed" him. Two years later he surreptitiously reentered the North Chicago mills and discreetly organized the first union lodge of the iron and steel rail heaters. A national convention of rollers and heaters met in Chicago in 1872 and reorganized as the National Association of Iron and Steel Heaters, with Thomas P. Jones as its first president.[15]

The third labor organization incorporated into the AAISW was the Iron and Steel Roll Hands of the United States, founded on June 2, 1873, with headquarters in Columbus, Ohio. The union admitted all hands who worked around the rolls—rollers, roughers, catchers, hookers, straighteners, and buggymen. The United Nailers, which was concentrated in the upper Ohio valley region, consisted of a few lodges and had no national organization but was admitted to membership in the Amalgamated Association nonetheless.[16]

Fig. 4.2. Rolling mill, Homestead Steel Works, 1907. Library of Congress.

Rampant speculation, as well as the collapse of the international investment house of Jay Cooke and Company in September 1873, destabilized the national credit markets and ushered in the panic of 1873. Heavy consumers of iron and steel, such as the railroads, suffered serious financial damage, and thousands of ironworkers in the rail mills found themselves unemployed during the ensuing depression, which lasted from 1873 to 1879. The *Bulletin of the American Iron and Steel Association* painted a dreary picture of its effects on the city of Pittsburgh: "Idle men by the scores were to be seen on every street, and the city wore a listless and woe-begone look. Men, women and children beg from house to house and besiege the doors of relief societies for the commonest necessaries of life."[17] To reduce their labor costs and thus stem their financial losses, ironmasters launched a new assault on organized labor. Technological improvements became the new weapon in their arsenal, and the 1870s was, as historian Paul Krause has observed, the "takeoff decade for Bessemer steel," a process that eliminated the well-paid puddler.[18]

The ironmasters and the Sons of Vulcan held a conference in November 1874 to discuss the sliding scale. At the meeting, the ironmasters notified the union that they intended to terminate the agreement of 1867 and reduce the puddlers' earnings, which were tied to the selling price of the iron they produced. The last meeting between the two parties was in December 1874, and when the union refused to agree to the wage reduction, the ironmasters locked out forty thousand workers. The immediate cause of the lockout was the decline in the price of iron, which triggered a downward adjustment in the sliding scale. The lockout continued until April 1875, when the ironmasters and the puddlers agreed to resume operations at the previously agreed upon scale. In its larger historical context, according to one authority, the lockout was "a debate over the place of labor in the American Republic and the nature of the Republic itself." More immediately, however, the lockout of 1874–1875 triggered the formation of the Amalgamated Association of Iron and Steel Workers.[19]

On August 1, 1876, the three ironworker unions gathered at different locations in Pittsburgh, and two days later the heaters and rollers and the roll hands adjourned to join the Sons of Vulcan in a joint convention at Emerald Hall. They were joined by representatives of the United Nailers, and the joint convention voted to form themselves into the Amalgamated Association of Iron and Steel Workers of the United States. The Sons of Vulcans, which had more than 3,000 members in 1873, contributed more than 85 percent of the original membership of approximately 3,755. In comparison, at the height of its power in 1891 the AAISW membership reached 24,068 taxable members in 292 sublodges. The puddlers became the driving force in the AAISW, and they provided the first three presidents of the new organization.[20]

Even though a disproportionately large number of the most highly skilled ironworkers, such as the puddlers, heaters, and rollers, were Welsh and other natives of the British Isles, it would be nearly impossible to determine the ethnicity of either the membership or the leadership of the AAISW from the available sources. Although the Welsh have relatively few distinctive surnames suggestive of national origin—and those names are liberally scattered throughout the list of national forge officers in the *National Labor Tribune*—those names do not provide conclusive evidence of national origin or place of birth. Most of the national leadership must have been born in the United States, but the ethnicity of the early leaders of this movement has been lost to time. During its first few years, the Sons of Vulcan kept no records and was largely a secret organization for fear of reprisals from their employers. The economic stimulus induced by the Civil War created more favorable working conditions, and the Sons of Vulcan then adopted the practices of a more formal organization.[21]

The Vulcans chose Miles S. Humphreys as their first grand master in 1862. He was born in Richmond, Virginia, in 1837 to parents who had emigrated from North Wales. It is likely that his father was an ironworker in Richmond's Tredegar Iron Works, which employed numerous Welsh ironworkers. Most likely Miles began work there, learning the puddling trade from his father. The family moved to Pittsburgh sometime in the mid-1840s, when Tredegar's Welsh and American ironworkers fiercely resisted attempts by ironmaster Joseph Reid Anderson to replace puddlers with enslaved apprentices.[22]

Humphreys headed the organization until 1866, in a period during which the organization grew in strength and expanded in Pennsylvania and seven other states. Perhaps his most noteworthy accomplishment was his successful negotiation with the manufacturer Benjamin F. Jones, of the Jones & Laughlin Iron Works, to implement the sliding scale, which became the cornerstone for establishing wages for decades. Humphreys also was active in the Labor Reform Party in Pittsburgh and was elected as a Republican to the Pennsylvania House of Representatives (1867–1871) and to the state Senate (1872–1874). He also served as Pittsburgh's fire chief and as director of the Pennsylvania Bureau of Labor Statistics from 1879 to 1882. Humphreys maintained a strong Welsh identity and was an active leader of the Pittsburgh St. David's Society.[23]

Succeeding Humphreys as head of the Vulcans was another Welshman, John O. Edwards. He had had organizing experience in England before heading the Vulcans between August 1868 and August 1871. Chicagoan Hugh McLaughlin, who was Irish, served as the third grand master, from 1871 to 1873, and was succeeded by David Harris of Pittsburgh. Little is known of these individuals, but it is likely that Jones and Harris were at least of Welsh descent. Thomas P. Jones, a Welsh expatriate in Chicago, was elected the first grand sire of the Associated Brotherhood of Iron and Steel Heaters, Rollers, and Roughers in 1872. This is all that we know about the ethnic identity of these very early national leaders of the iron- and steelworkers.[24]

THE CAMBRIAN

Now, go write it before them in a table, and note it in a book, that it may be for the time to come for ever and ever.

VOL. IX.	·MARCH, 1889.	No. 3.

MR. JOHN JARRETT, PITTSBURGH, PA..

SECRETARY OF THE TIN PLATE ASSOCIATION.

Fig. 4.3. John Jarrett, head of the Amalgamated Association of Iron and Steel Workers. *The Cambrian*, March 1889.

With the formation of the Amalgamated Association of Iron and Steel Workers, the national leadership of the early movement becomes clearer. The new organization had only four presidents. The first president, Joseph Bishop, was an American-born puddler. The second president, John Jarrett, held office from August 1880 to August 1883. Born in 1848 in Ebbw Vale, South Wales, Jarrett entered the mills at the age of twelve when he was orphaned, and by the age of eighteen he had become a puddler. In 1861 he immigrated to America, where he plied his trade in the mills, first at

Duncansville, Pennsylvania, and then the Lochiel Mills near Harrisburg. At this point he had no trade union experience, but in 1867 he returned to England when a relative left him property in a bequest. Jarrett remained there for the next four years, working as a puddler and being tutored in the principles of unionism by John Kane, "the foremost unionist in the English iron industry," as one authority has characterized him. Jarrett learned his lessons well, and before returning to the United States in 1872 he had organized a local ironworkers' union.[25]

Jarrett's father had been a Chartist miner, so the young puddler's conversion to unionism probably did not require a dramatic change of mind. Back in the United States, Jarrett took up his trade in the tinplate mill at Sharon, Pennsylvania, and became active in the Sons of Vulcan, serving one year as district deputy and then as a representative on the joint consolidation committee working out the details for the amalgamation. Prior to assuming the mantle of leadership of the AAISW in 1880, Jarrett also held the position of district vice president for two years. During the 1880s, Jarrett became one of the nation's high-profile labor leaders. President Chester A. Arthur nominated him to become the first federal commissioner of labor, although the post went to someone else. Regaining momentum in his rise to labor prominence, Jarrett assumed leadership of the National Federation of Trades and Labor Unions, a forerunner of the American Federation of Labor.[26]

John Jarrett fit the pattern of most British labor leaders in America. He was an adherent to the cult of self-improvement and overcame his lack of formal education through dedicated application. Also like his British counterparts, he was cautious when taking a stand on issues confronting capital and labor. A moral reformer, he insisted that workers could improve their lives dramatically by following the path of temperance and the golden rule of "do unto others as you would have others do unto you." Contemporary capitalists and employers justifiably regarded Jarrett as more conservative than the men he led. As if to underscore his commitment to a judicious approach to economic affairs, Jarrett lent full support to the manufacturers' advocacy of protective tariffs to safeguard the industry from less expensive imports.[27]

The third president of the Amalgamated Association, William Weihe, was an American-born puddler and served in the post from 1883 to 1892. The fourth president, another American, W. M. Garland, was a heater by trade. Other AAISW officers whose ethnicity can be identified as British were the first secretary, William Martin (roller) of Scotland; the second and third secretaries, Stephen Madden (puddler) and John Kilgallan (puddler), respectively, were both from Ireland. All four presidents of the AAISW were of British origin, reflecting the skilled workers they led, and that was the case with the vice presidents as well. As late as 1909, more than twenty-five years after Jarrett had stepped down from the AAISW presidency, all thirteen vice presidents were of British descent. They were also disproportionately Welsh; six of the thirteen were either born in Wales or were first-generation Welsh Americans.[28]

Some of the most skilled Welsh American steelworkers rose into the ranks of management, and others became technical experts such as engineers. Before World War I, few working men found career opportunities within organized labor, but union officials developed leadership skills that proved valuable in politics or management. Primed with the ideology of progress and success, the Welsh were strategically positioned within the industry and the union to benefit when opportunity knocked, as well as to shape the direction of the labor movement.

In his study of union leadership in the United States between 1870 and 1920, Warren R. Van Tine examined the careers of 350 unionists, breaking them into two distinctive leadership models: traditional "reform unionism" and, increasingly after the mid-1890s, the new "business unionism." By the 1890s, the reform-minded Knights of Labor (K of L) had failed in its effort to unite producers into one big union and to replace the wage system with cooperative associations as a way of elevating the condition of all workers. The American Federation of Labor (AFL) replaced the K of L, and, with the acceptance of industrial capitalism, the AFL abandoned the reformist vision of turning workers into owners to concentrate instead on the "bread and butter" issues of improving conditions, hours, and wages. Of the old-school leaders, nearly one-half were foreign born, with the "vast majority" originating in the British Isles. Similarly, the "new school" leaders were either second generation or immigrants (42 percent), mostly of British Isles origin. Although the number of foreign-born leaders declined over time, their places were taken by their American-born sons, who were raised in families and communities that esteemed unionism.[29]

Van Tine found that the traditional labor leader in the period before 1920 typically began his work life at fourteen, joined the union, rose through the ranks quickly to become a national officer by thirty-five, remained in office a few years, and then returned to the rank-and-file in his previous occupation. Relatively few traditional union officials escaped labor by entering business, politics, or the professions after leaving office. By 1920, a major shift in this pattern had occurred, as a new generation of leaders gained social advancement by becoming "corporate executives within the union structure." The differences between the two groups evolved not from their sociological origins but rather from "the institutionalization of the union, and the simultaneous professionalization of union leadership." Adapting to modernization transformed their organizations from a loose confederation of semiautonomous locals into centralized organizations with managerial subdivisions.[30]

Unions struggled against powerful national trends restructuring the late nineteenth-century American economy. The emergence of the national market system dissolved local labor markets, severe competition undermined wages and conditions, and large industries demanded control over their own workforces. Against these pressures, labor unions were forced to organize nationally in order to erect a countervailing resistance and to standardize labor conditions. Centralization, standardization, and increasing bureaucratization of organized labor inevitably resulted in a growing distance between the leaders and their members. By 1920 the role of the national labor leader had changed dramatically, from one that was largely informal, reflecting the decentralized nature of unionism, to one requiring the skills of a chief executive officer of a corporation. Reformers and radicals, like the socialist Eugene V. Debs and communist William Z. Foster, denounced the new business unionists for succumbing to capitalist "embourgeoisement" by embracing middle-class values, social striving, and the acquisition of property and wealth. The rank-and-file themselves, however, generally regarded the advancement of their leaders to prominent positions in government and industry favorably, because it reinforced the American myth that ordinary members of the workforce could still achieve success through determination and hard work.[31]

Like other craft unions of the era, the Amalgamated Association of Iron and Steel Workers emerged as a regional union with a fledgling national headquarters exerting limited central power and part-time leadership. Leadership in the centralizing AAISW sought to maintain order, discourage rank-and-file spontaneity, negate local control, and proceed cautiously in matters of politics. These developments often encountered opposition from local and district officers whose resistance had to be overcome. Centralization, however weak, did make the AAISW less democratic but also eventually led to a qualified acceptance of career unionists.[32] Full bureaucratization of the steelworkers' union awaited the successful organization of the United Steel Workers of America in the 1930s, an industry-wide organization that represented all who worked in and around the mills. John Jarrett and his colleagues in the AAISW were limited by the loyalties of workers to their locals and their crafts. As AAISW president between 1880 and 1883, Jarrett was a pragmatic organization man in a reformist era, a hybrid leader whose time had not yet arrived. Even so, he learned the leadership skills that were interchangeable whether he was employed on behalf of the union or the company.

Welsh union men occupied pivotal positions at strategic moments and thus had a profound impact on the evolution of the national union among American steelworkers. Many skilled Welsh steelworkers became managers by dint of their mastery of the industrial process. Jarrett's father-in-law, John R. Davies, immigrated with his family from Aberdare, Wales, to the United States in 1866. A highly skilled rolling mill worker, Davies served as superintendent at several steel mills, and in 1888 he moved to Duquesne, in Allegheny County, Pennsylvania, to oversee operations at the Allegheny Bessemer Steel Company, a position he held until his retirement in 1904. Jarrett married Davies's daughter Jennie, and they settled near her parents in Duquesne. Whereas Davies used his skills to climb the company ladder, his son-in-law settled conflicts between labor and management as he climbed the union hierarchy, thus developing skills vital to both company and union in the new era of industrial capitalism.[33]

It is likely that Welsh puddlers, heaters, and rollers were deeply involved in union affairs at the local and district levels during the 1870s and 1880s, although, again, there are no systematic assessments of their engagement during this period. An illustration is found in the ironworker community of Woods Run, which became the ninth ward of Allegheny City (annexed by Pittsburgh in 1907). The construction of several mills between 1864 and 1882 attracted ironworkers, including a significant number of Welsh, Irish, and German immigrants, nearly all of whom were skilled ironworkers.[34]

One of the most prominent leaders in the Woods Run district was John J. Morgan, a Welsh puddler and organizer for the Sons of Vulcan and then the AAISW. He also had served as a delegate for western Pennsylvania and

Ohio districts at conventions of the Sons of Vulcan and AAISW between 1870 and 1882, including the founding convention of the latter organization. Morgan held numerous local union offices and in 1883–1884 served as vice president of the national Amalgamated Association of Iron and Steel Workers. Like many prominent union leaders, Morgan had the knowledge and experience to become a supervisor, and in 1886 he joined his Woods Run colleague and former Sons of Vulcan president, John O. Edwards, as an overseer at the Elba Iron Works in Frankstown, Pennsylvania.[35] Another Welsh puddler, William R. Reese, was one of the earliest union leaders in Woods Run; he served as corresponding representative for the Allegheny Forge of the Sons of Vulcan and then the Allegheny Lodge of the AAISW.[36]

Skills like negotiating with employers, public speaking, and organizing were acquired at the local and district levels, and some Welsh union leaders leveraged these skills to elevate their personal careers outside of the union. James J. Davis offers an excellent illustration. He was born in 1873 in Tredegar, Wales, and came to America with his family in 1881. His father taught him the iron puddler's trade. A confirmed "bread and butter" unionist, Davis joined the AAISW, and, at the tin mills of Elwood, Indiana, Davis learned the art of maintaining harmony in labor-management relations. He also discovered a talent for speaking and organizing. Both served him well in elected office, as supreme organizer of the Loyal Order of Moose and then as the "Great Conciliator" while serving as secretary of labor in the administrations of Presidents Warren Harding (1921–1923) and Calvin Coolidge (1923–1929).[37]

Contract Labor and the Foran Act

The mid-1870s was not a propitious time to organize a national union, since the country was in the middle of an economic depression. The initiative behind the movement for national union representation came from the urgency to protect the wages of the three major crafts from the ironmasters' attempts to reduce labor costs. Emigration of Welsh iron- and steelworkers ground to a halt during the depression, but with the first hint of economic revival Welsh ironworkers again boarded ships for America. Some puddlers and rollers came under contract with American companies, but most came upon receiving a green light from friends and relatives, who reported improved conditions. Reflecting the industry's chronic boom-and-bust economic cycle, recovery in the iron trades responded quickly to the economic upturn in the early 1880s. By 1884, however, the iron trades had once again plunged back into depression and again immigration from Britain all but ceased. At the urging of AAISW leaders, Congress passed a bill in 1885 forbidding the importation of contract labor.[38]

The American version of the Industrial Revolution drew heavily on the British experience, and the latter's skilled workers became the aristocracy of the American labor force. Early on, however, American manufacturers were ambivalent about their reliance on these independent and mobile workers. Nevertheless, the most serious opposition to the recruitment of skilled British workers came from British rather than American manufacturers. When business was sluggish in the Welsh iron industry, employers urged their skilled workers to find work elsewhere in Britain until the trade picked up again. A Welsh representative for the iron industry declared that employers were "not opposed to emigration as a general principle, but that when a skilled workman emigrated he could not be replaced by importing unskilled Irish workmen."[39]

An increasingly broad range of media outlets for the exchange of information became available to British workers during the late nineteenth century. Trade unions and labor journals in Britain and the United States shared information regarding the state of the labor market. Welsh workers inclined to try their luck in the States typically relied on the informal networks of family and friends in America to verify information about wages and the cost of living. As American industrial development accelerated after the Civil War, employers also relied on these networks for recruiting skilled British workers. Industrialists also were convinced that tariffs would guarantee the supply of skilled immigrants attracted by the higher wages they could offer because of those import duties.[40]

The contract labor system, which had thrived during the first half of the nineteenth century, diminished in significance during the last half of the century despite the great demand for skilled labor in the iron and steel industry. According to one authority, misunderstandings over the terms of contracts, as well as the growing strength of trade unions, increasingly inhibited the efforts of American industrialists to obtain contract laborers. Moreover, skilled workers could easily leave an unsatisfactory contract for jobs elsewhere, and, with their higher wages, they had readily available cash to pay for passage home to Britain if they were dissatisfied, and many did. A trustee of the large Dowlais works in South Wales stated in 1867 that "it was the skilled workers who most frequently came back from America because they were able to get the means to do so."[41]

One of the contract labor agencies, the American Emigrant Company, circulated its newspaper, the *American Reporter*, in Britain, and the Sons of Vulcan commissioned an "Address to the Iron Workers of Great Britain" to counter any potential impact the publication might have on Welsh iron-workers. The "Address" declared that skilled ironworkers, such as puddlers, boilers, hammermen, and rollers were not needed in America and that wages printed in the newspaper were inaccurate.[42] The Sons of Vulcan and the Iron Moulders Union counterattacked the recruiting efforts in Britain by sending copies of the Moulders' journal condemning the American Emigrant Company to the *Merthyr Telegraph* newspaper in Merthyr Tydfil, the major center of iron production in Wales, as well as to British labor journals.[43] The Cleveland local of the Sons of Vulcan appointed a committee to warn British workers against American Emigrant Company contracts and urged workers to come only if assured of a job by a friend in the United States.[44]

In 1881, the Amalgamated Association of Iron and Steel Workers used the same means to thwart the efforts of manufacturers in Cincinnati to bring in British strikebreakers. On learning of the plan, union president John Jarrett and secretary William Martin sent a cablegram to "the Iron and Steel Workers of England, Scotland and Wales" informing them that the ironworkers in Cincinnati and several other cities had been on strike for sixteen weeks and that the employers had sent agents to recruit strike-breakers. They urged workers "not to be induced by the plausible tales of the employers' agents to come to this country and aid in our defeat."[45] The general secretary of the Iron and Steel Workers of England, Scotland and Wales replied and enclosed a copy of a circular that had been distributed among the workers of the iron districts; the secretary promised to "do all in my power to counteract the attempts of unprincipled agents who desire to induce workmen to cross the Atlantic for the purpose of blacklegging."[46]

Before 1882 the responsibility for rejecting immigrants or safeguarding their welfare fell to the individual states. As the rebound following the panic of 1873 lost steam in the early 1880s, however, the mood for immigration restriction set in among members of Congress. In 1882 federal intervention first took the form of prohibiting the importation of convicts, "lunatics," "idiots," persons affected by certain diseases, paupers, and Chinese. Then, in 1885, Congress passed the Foran Act, which prohibited the importation of contract labor. On the one hand, these federal laws also required the states to prove that immigrants were unlikely to become a public burden. On the other hand, the immigrants had signed a contract with an American employer that would have made this eventuality unlikely. The contradictory impulses embedded in this approach to immigration policy generated anxiety among immigrants for decades.[47]

Organized labor, particularly the AAISW and the Knights of Labor, were quick to pick up the call for immigration control. Martin Foran, the Ohio congressional representative who introduced the bill prohibiting contract labor importation, had been the president of the Coopers International Union and editor of its journal from 1870 until 1874, when he was admitted to the bar. Foran introduced the bill in the House of Representatives in January 1884. After the addition of three amendments that exempted new industries, allowed assistance to immigrating relatives, and permitted contracts made with foreign immigrants after they arrived, both the House and Senate approved the measure on February 18, 1885.[48]

The Foran Act prompted organized labor to join with industrialists in an effort to convince Congress that tariffs would protect American labor. During the 1880s some labor leaders were losing faith in the belief that tariff protection would also protect higher wages for workers, pointing to the fact that the tariff did not prevent employers from importing European strikebreakers and doing so without paying duties. AAISW president Jarrett and the union as a whole remained convinced, however, that the protective tariff bolstered the industry's growth. The reasoning behind this position was based on the conviction that Americans should not buy from abroad what they could produce at home. Otherwise, workers would have less work, which would depress wages. From their perspective, the tariff was to protect labor's market position by strengthening industry. For the same reason, Jarrett and the AAISW supported the Foran Act and other restrictions on imported labor. When arguments to protect American labor by restricting foreign workers were being presented to a Senate committee in 1883, Jarrett reported to his members that a circular had been sent by the AAISW's executive board urging union locals to hold pro-tariff meetings and to pressure their representatives for passage of the Foran bill.[49]

The growing recession in 1884 saw nearly half of the iron furnaces in the nation shut down, and the AAISW's *Bulletin* declared that it was time to

THE EDGAR THOMSON STEEL WORKS, BRADDOCK, PA.

THE HOMESTEAD STEEL WORKS, MUNHALL, PA.

THE DUQUESNE STEEL WORKS, DUQUESNE, PA.

Fig. 4.4. Edgar G. Thomson Works, Homestead Works, and Duquesne Works. From Bridge, *Inside History of the Carnegie Steel Company.*

stop importing foreign laborers. Notwithstanding all the noise and political posturing, it seems no one noticed that the Foran bill was passed into law without appropriating money for enforcement, such as inspection and investigation.[50]

The Foran Act adopted by the Senate in a 50-to-9 vote declared it illegal to prepay the transportation or in any way assist or encourage the importation or migration of aliens into the United States under a contract made previous to their importation. Among its exemptions were companies that engaged contract labor for an infant industry not established in the United States if skilled labor was not otherwise available.[51] This exception left the newly emerging American tinplate industry, a segment of the iron and steel industry that would grow exponentially during the 1890s, free to hire British skilled workers as long as tinplating was defined as an "infant" industry. Even with its subsequent revisions, the Foran Act did not protect the skilled unionists, as they had hoped, for the vast majority of the workers flowing into the United States by the 1890s were unskilled migrants from southern and eastern Europe.

The Emergence of Big Steel

The emergence of the great steel mills during the 1870s and 1880s was both cause and effect of the installation of the latest labor-saving machinery and organizational innovations, as well as a determined antiunion posture by the steel corporations. This "great leap forward" of the industry precipitated bitter conflicts between capital and labor, not the least of which occurred at Andrew Carnegie's Pittsburgh Bessemer Steel Works at Homestead. Carnegie's experience at his Homestead Steel Works, which had been completed in 1881, illustrated why he became so antiunion. According to James Howard Bridge, who was a close confidant of Carnegie, Homestead works superintendent William Clark was unable to unify the "conflicting racial elements employed at the new works. The rail-mill was controlled by the Welsh; and if a desirable post became vacant, it was not filled by the next man, but by some newly imported friend of the Welsh foreman." Similarly, "the Irish were supreme in the converting works; and in the blooming-mill yet a third nationality was in power." To make matters worse, Bridge declared, Clark's "unreasonable and arbitrary management" soon resulted in "open conflict with the workmen."[52]

When Carnegie's company announced that employees would have to sign an agreement not to join a labor union before January 1882 or leave the company's employment, unionists rejected the order and went out on strike. The company dropped the "ironclad oath" and replaced it with a new announcement that wages would be lowered. Again the men refused to sign, and in the summer of 1882 a national strike was called against the iron mills. AAISW members overruled their president, John Jarrett, who opposed the strike because he believed economic conditions rendered the union's bargaining position too weak to win in a showdown. Prior to the strike, most of the iron manufacturers west of the Alleghenies met in Pittsburgh to form an organization to fight the Amalgamated Association. At stake for both labor and management, in the words of one historian, was "who would control the Homestead mill and moreover the entire Bessemer industry, labor or management."[53]

Superintendent William Clark evicted strikers from company houses and charged them with conspiracy. He also started the mill with strikebreakers and hired armed guards to protect them. The police lent their support, and when the strikers fought back, fights and shootings ensued.

AAISW strikers were led by the Welsh-born John Elias Jones who, with full support from the community, arranged to have twenty-four AAISW men sworn in as municipal police officers (they called themselves "pickets") to seal off Homestead. He and other local union leaders also organized an advisory committee to coordinate measures taken to maintain civil order. The company was still dependent upon the skilled men to operate the mill, and when they could not fill orders, the company was forced to negotiate a conclusion to the conflict in September 1882. They agreed to recognize the AAISW, a win of sorts, but the men returned to work at the old wage scale, and not all of the strikers were rehired.[54]

The AAISW had won the important principle of recognition as the bargaining agent for the skilled workers. On the other hand, the 1882 strike also exposed the underlying divisions within the Amalgamated Association, as the strike erupted into fratricidal hostilities—the puddlers versus the rollers and heaters—with both groups considering reconstituting their former unions. The puddlers claimed that association president John Jarrett had betrayed them by encouraging the rollers and heaters to leave the AAISW. The criticism prompted Jarrett to resign from office at the group's convention in 1883, and membership among the demoralized workforce fell from about 16,000 in 1882 to 5,700 in 1885. The miners of Pittsburgh District Assembly 135 (Knights of Labor), led by their Welsh-born president, David R. Jones, who walked out in sympathy with the steelworkers, also failed to achieve their strike goals. Jones subsequently resigned his post as district president and became a lawyer.[55]

The issues at the center of the 1882 conflict foreshadowed subsequent battles that culminated in the violent Homestead lockout of 1892, the last general strike in the iron and steel industry. These struggles would be concentrated in the steel mills of Andrew Carnegie, who was determined not only to bring an end to unionism in his mills but also to introduce labor-saving mechanical improvements that would enable Carnegie to eliminate the high-wage puddlers, heaters, and rollers who controlled the production process.

Captain Bill Jones, general superintendent of the Edgar Thomson plant in Braddock, was instrumental in implementing Carnegie's plan to embrace technologies that would reduce the company's reliance on skilled (union) workers. In December 1884, the general superintendent posted a notice that the works would close; when the plant reopened, those workers who were

THE CAMBRIAN

Now, go write it before them in a table, and note it in a book, that it may be for the time to come for ever and ever.

Vol. X.	APRIL, 1890.	No. 4.

THE LATE CAPTAIN WILLIAM R. JONES.

GENERAL SUPERINTENDENT OF THE EDGAR THOMSON STEEL WORKS, BRADDOCK, PA.

Fig. 4.5. Captain William R. Jones. *The Cambrian*, April 1890.

welcome to return to work would be notified. Those who were not should consider their employment terminated; this drastic measure put sixteen hundred men out on the street. Reprising 1882, the company once again proposed a reduction in the wage scale. The notice also announced a return to the traditional twelve-hour turn, thus eliminating the eight-hour shift Jones had implemented. Consequently, one full crew out of three would be eliminated—a reduction of no fewer than three hundred employees. Fearing discharge, many of the workers quit the union and in February 1885 accepted the company's terms of employment and signed individual contracts.[56]

A clear pattern had begun to emerge by 1887. After a new rail mill was installed at the Edgar Thomson plant, the company again announced that the mill would be closed in December for repairs, and those employees who were not notified to return had been discharged. The Knights of Labor attempted to negotiate with Carnegie, but after restating his demands for a reduction in wages and requiring that the men sign an agreement that they would not belong to a union, Carnegie refused to meet with them again. Desperate after an entire winter without work, the men accepted Carnegie's terms and returned to work.[57] Although Bill Jones wanted his men paid well, he brooked no interference from any quarter that affected the efficient operation of his plant, and he therefore fully supported the efforts of Carnegie and Frick to rid the works of union labor. Finally, in the struggle for control of the Braddock mill, Carnegie and his general superintendent had rid themselves of interference by labor unions and had a free hand to maximize their drive for efficiency through technology.[58]

Captain William R. "Bill" Jones

Captain Bill Jones was one of the leading Bessemer steelmasters in a day when writers described the emerging industry as a grand heroic adventure. The English inventor of the process, Henry Bessemer, declared that Captain Jones knew more about steel than any man in the United States, and Andrew Carnegie claimed Jones was the "most remarkable character" he had ever employed. He was "Jones the Peerless" and "the mechanical genius," according to Carnegie business associate James Howard Bridge.[59] By all accounts there was good reason for the admiration, for most writers have agreed with one biographer who claimed that "until Captain Jones took the [Bessemer] converter under his wing, its possibilities were unknown; he for the first time demonstrated its worth, transforming it from a great mechanical toy into an engine that changed the physical face of the world."[60]

William R. Jones was born in Luzerne County, Pennsylvania, on February 23, 1839. His father, the Reverend John C. Jones, was born in Brecon, Powys, and his wife, Magdalene, in Ystradgynlais in West Glamorgan, Wales. They immigrated to America with their two children in 1832, settling first in Pittsburgh, then in Scranton, Hazleton, and finally Catasauqua. Reverend Jones preached in the local Welsh Baptist church and worked as a pattern-maker for David Thomas, the venerable Welsh ironmaster and acclaimed "father of anthracite iron," at the Lehigh Crane Iron Works. It is likely that John Jones had been employed at Thomas's ironworks near Ystradgynlais prior to the family's immigration to the United States. Reverend Jones was known as the intellectual and religious leader of his community, with the largest personal library in the town of Catasauqua.

John and Magdalene Jones had eight children, but Magdalene died in the late 1840s, and John was in poor health for several years before passing away in 1853. Under these circumstances, young William attended primary school until age ten, when in 1849 he was apprenticed in the Lehigh Crane machine shops under the supervision of the Welsh machinist Hopkin Thomas. By 1853, at fourteen, William was already receiving the wages of a journeyman. Among his fellow apprentices learning the iron trade under Hopkin Thomas was the latter's son, James Thomas. He and William became close, lifelong friends. At age twenty William decided to seek his fortune elsewhere. Accompanied by James, William left Catasauqua to work at a machine shop in Philadelphia, where, with the help of Hopkin Thomas, they became machinists in the shops of I. P. Morris & Company. There they worked on two large blast engines for the Lehigh Crane Iron Works and were sent to Catasauqua to help erect them. Jones returned to Philadelphia when the job was finished, but James chose to remain in the Lehigh Valley.[61]

In the spring of 1859, Jones moved on to Johnstown, Pennsylvania, where he found employment as a machinist at the Cambria Iron Company under general superintendent John Fritz. After three months, Jones was offered the position of master mechanic by Giles Edwards, another Welshman with whom he was connected through the Catasauqua network. Edwards had been engaged to build a blast furnace in Chattanooga, Tennessee; it became the Bluff Furnace, the first to be fired by coke in that state.[62] The Edwards family had known Bill Jones since he was an apprentice at the Lehigh Crane Iron Company in Catasauqua. It was at the Edwards's home that Jones met Harriet Lloyd, the visiting daughter of another Welsh friend of the Edwards family, and the two were married in Chattanooga.[63]

When the Civil War broke out in 1861, Bill Jones, who was an ardent Unionist, like most Welsh Americans, left Chattanooga and returned to the Cambria Iron works in Johnstown as a machinist. He enlisted in the Union Army as a private in 1862, and when the war was over, he mustered out as a captain. It was a title he was proud of and retained the rest of his life. At the invitation of Cambria works general superintendent George Fritz (who had succeeded his brother John), Captain Jones returned there to become his chief assistant.[64]

It was the Catasauqua-Welsh network that gave Captain Bill Jones his start, but it was his fortuitous meeting with Alexander L. Holley that provided the springboard for his ascent into the ranks of the elite among steelmakers. Holley has been described as "the greatest authority on Bessemer steel mills in America, if not in the world," by one biographer. He signed an agreement with Henry Bessemer for the exclusive rights to the process in the United States after having already constructed Bessemer converters in Troy, New York; Joliet, Illinois; Philadelphia, Bethlehem, Pittsburgh, and, most significantly for Captain Jones, at the Cambria Iron works, Johnstown, Pennsylvania. It was Jones who assisted Holley when he instituted the Bessemer process at the Cambria works, and Jones's ability made a lasting impression on the steelmaster.[65]

The supervisors of the Cambria works, general manager Daniel J. Morrell and general superintendent George Fritz, sharply disagreed over the question of wages, and the supervisors under them split into representative camps. Morrell wanted to cut costs by reducing wages, while Fritz insisted that wages must be kept high, with the costs offset by higher production per worker. Morrell was forced to concede to Fritz on the matter, but in the spring of 1873 Fritz died. As Fritz's chief assistant, Captain Jones expected to replace him, but he was too closely associated with Fritz. Instead, Morrell lost no time in hiring Daniel Jones, one of Bill Jones's friends and a fellow apprentice from the Catasauqua-Welsh network, as the new general superintendent. Captain Jones promptly resigned his position but was immediately taken on by Alexander Holley, who was planning the Edgar Thomson Bessemer mill for Andrew Carnegie. Holley took Bill Jones with him to Braddock as his chief assistant, and when the new plant was completed, Holley recommended that Carnegie hire Bill Jones as general superintendent. Taking his advice, Carnegie appointed Captain Jones to the position in 1872. Carnegie was ever grateful for having made that decision, declaring in later years that "much of the success of the Edgar Thomson Works belongs to this man."[66]

In the absence of Fritz and Bill Jones, the Cambria Iron Works was without effective leadership to oppose Morrell's wage-cutting policies, which included supervisors' wages. Jones knew the workers and supervisors well, and he singled out the most able among them to recruit. More than two hundred left Cambria to join Captain Jones at the Edgar Thomson Steel Works, including highly experienced department superintendents. Several years later, while touring the "ET" works, Carnegie asked Morrell what he thought of the plant. Morrell replied, "I can see that I promoted the wrong Jones."[67]

Captain Jones's insistence upon paying his workers well earned him the respect and loyalty of his employees, but on this one issue he disagreed with Carnegie, who was obsessed with cutting costs, including wages. For example, in 1878 Carnegie wanted a sharp reduction in wages, but Jones successfully opposed the move, arguing that "low wages does not always imply cheap labor. Good wages and good workmen I know to be cheap labor." Jones worked his men hard, but believed that they should be paid and treated well, and he generally prevailed as long as he was general superintendent of the Edgar Thomson plant—at least until Henry C. Frick became a partner in the firm in 1882.[68]

Bill Jones also convinced Carnegie to abandon the practice of having two twelve-hour turns a day, which was nearly universal throughout the industry in America, and institute three eight-hour shifts a day, which was common practice in Wales and Britain. Probably from personal experience, Jones believed that working men would be more productive when well rested than those who were tired and careless. Fewer accidents, less breakage, and less absenteeism would more than offset the one-third higher cost of labor. Jones expressed this conviction unequivocally in an address before the British Iron and Steel Institute in London in May 1881, when explaining the production record set by the Edgar Thomson works. "In increasing the output of these works," he declared, "I soon discovered it was entirely out of the question to expect human flesh and blood to labor incessantly for twelve hours." Therefore, he decided "to put on three turns, reducing the hours of labor to eight." This step was advantageous for the company as well as the workers, as production increased, and the workers now earned "more in eight hours than they formerly did in twelve hours, while the men can work harder constantly for eight hours, having sixteen hours for rest."[69]

In a general discussion of production costs, Captain Jones expanded on his approach to labor in a letter to Carnegie's partner, E. V. McCandless, dated February 25, 1875. "Now I will give you my views as to the proper way of conducting these works," he began. First, "we must be careful of what class of men we collect." He advised steering clear of workers from mills to the west, because they were accustomed to "infernal high wages," and "Englishmen[,] who are great sticklers for high wages, small production and strikes." From experience Jones believed that "Germans and Irish, Swedes and what I denominate 'Buckwheats'—young American country boys, ju-diciously mixed, make the most effective and tractable force you can find. Scotsmen do very well, are honest and faithful. Welsh can be used in limited numbers. But mark me, Englishmen have been the worst class of men I have had anything to do with; and this is the opinion of Mr. [Alexander] Holley, and George and John Fritz." Second, the secret of reducing the cost of wages, Jones added, was to "keep the works running steadily." Year in and year out, steady work would produce low wages. Third, the company "should endeavor to make the cost of living as low as possible." Summarizing the "salient points," Jones asserted that "the men should be made to feel that the company are interested in their welfare. Make the works a pleasant place for them. I have always found it best to treat men well, and I find that my men are anxious to retain my good will by working steadily and honestly, and instead of dodging are anxious to show me what a good day's work they have done. All haughty and disdainful treatment of men has a very decided and bad effect on them."[70]

Carnegie gave Jones a free hand with the working men until 1882, when Henry Clay Frick became a new partner in the firm. Carnegie acquired a large interest in the H. C. Frick Coke Company in 1882 and then a con-trolling interest in 1886. Frick and Carnegie were united in their obsession with reducing costs wherever that was possible, and that included wages and working hours. Frick gradually brought Carnegie over to the hard-boiled side. A new sliding scale that reduced wages and a return to the twelve-hour turn had been instituted at the ET works as part of the 1887 strike settle-ment, but in 1889 attempts to initiate the same sliding scale and two-turn system at the Homestead works ratcheted up tensions among the workers. The Homestead men were paid on a flat tonnage basis, and with the new mechanical innovations their incomes had increased significantly. Plant em-ployees suspected that a sliding scale would result in a wage reduction for the skilled tonnage workers among Homestead's workforce of 3,800. The men were preparing for a walkout when the contract expired in June 1889. The plant's general superintendent, William L. Abbott, brought in strikebreak-ers under the protection of the sheriff and 125 deputies. When they were confronted by some 2,000 workers blocking the gates and the Edgar Thom-son workers threatened to come out in sympathy with the Homestead men, the sheriff and the strikebreakers withdrew. Abbott lost his determination and capitulated in a compromise in which the Amalgamated Association accepted the sliding scale and the company recognized the union as the bargaining agent for the Homestead plant.[71]

It is apparent that by the 1880s Frick had influenced Carnegie to follow his hard-line approach to the labor question, rather than that of Bill Jones, but dissent ended on the night of September 26, 1889, when a newly constructed blast furnace at the Edgar Thomson plant exploded without warning. Jones was standing close to the furnace. When he jumped back to avoid the blast, he fell and struck his head on the side of an ore car, and he died two days later.[72] Frick and Carnegie were outraged by Abbott's capitulation and more determined than ever to rid the Carnegie mills of the interfering unions. Without Captain Bill Jones to mediate between the owners and the workers, the combustible materials were in place for an explosive confrontation when the union agreement ended in 1892.

Jones was one of the great inventors of the Bessemer steel industry, with more patents registered and pending than any individual in the history of steelmaking, and patent rights for a dozen more inventions were found in his desk after his death. Some fourteen years later, Carnegie associate James Howard Bridge wrote that Captain Jones was "probably the greatest mechanical genius that ever entered the Carnegie shops," and his inventions "added enormously to the profits of the firm every year of his life, and long after."[73] Perhaps the most famous invention was the "Jones Mixer," which he first installed in the Edgar Thomson works and subsequently in every Bessemer department throughout Carnegie's vast steel empire. It was described as "a huge iron chest capable of holding 250 tons of liquid pig metal from many different blast furnaces," and it revolutionized the steel-making process by "dispensing with the re-melting of pig iron in the converter's cupola." Jones also made innumerable equipment improvements that were not noticeable individually, but their cumulative effect contributed to the Edgar Thomson shop's record-breaking performance.[74]

Bill Jones famously turned down an interest in Carnegie's firm that, according to Carnegie, would have made him a millionaire: "'No,' he [Jones] said, 'I don't want to have my thoughts running on business. I have enough trouble looking after these works. Just give me a h—l of a salary if you think I'm worth it.' 'All right, Captain, the salary of the President of the United States is yours.' 'That's the talk,' said the little Welshman."[75]

The career of William R. Jones was a larger-than-life reflection of the trajectory of many skilled Welsh workers in the iron and steel industry of the period. Although Captain Jones's career was a singularly unique case, he, like many others to varying degrees, was brought up within the supportive network of Welsh artisans whose links with ethnic colleagues in other American iron- and steel-producing centers provided connections that facilitated that same freedom of movement and upward mobility that benefited Captain Jones. At some point, of course, they would have to compete with the best of whomever rose to the top of their trade. At that point, again as in Bill Jones's case, they all became enmeshed within a smaller, exclusive network of elite experts governed by management imperatives based on performance rather than ethnic identity.

Like Captain Jones, successful Welsh supervisors did not necessarily relinquish their Cymric identity so much as compartmentalize it as they prioritized their identity as managers over their Welshness. Still, Jones's Welsh heritage was important to him and a life-long feature of how he understood himself. Although Jones was raised in a Welsh-speaking household, English was the language of the successful in America, and speaking fluent Welsh carried an ever-declining value to the Welsh who made the United States their permanent home. Therefore, without persistent reinforcement, Bill Jones's fluency in Welsh declined over the years. His contributions to Welsh causes, however, only increased. It was estimated that Bill Jones donated more than $10,000 a year to various causes, not the least of which was that highest form of Welsh expression in the Welsh language, the National Eisteddfod. He gave liberally to fund eisteddfodic literary and musical prizes, encouraged competitors, and served on committees, finding the details of the eisteddfod and its planning "fascinating." After his death there was a growing desire among Welsh Americans to "perpetuate the memory" of William R. Jones. His biographical sketch in the 1913 eisteddfod program (see fig. 2.1) stated that "Captain Jones was a son of the Eisteddfod, and an ardent lover and supporter of eisteddfodic traditions and customs, and the Memorial Eisteddfod was a fitting tribute to this worthy Welsh patriot and genius."[76]

Praise denied in life may become praise lavished in death, but this was not the case with Captain Jones. In 1885, *The Cambrian*, a Welsh American magazine, published a biographical sketch declaring that he was "a patriotic Welshman in every sense of the word" and that no man was ever "readier to help a countryman in word and deed." And, even though Jones was not a member of a Welsh church, he always "contributed liberally to their support."[77] The funeral of Captain Jones on October 2, 1889, was attended by approximately ten thousand workers and their families. Some of the most prominent steel manufacturers in the industry also attended, including John and David H. Thomas, George Davies, James Thomas, and John Fritz. The casket was carried by honorary pallbearers Andrew Carnegie, Henry C. Frick, Robert W. Hunt, Owen Leibert, Andrew Hamilton, and James Thomas.[78]

It is likely that Carnegie's association with Bill Jones prompted the steel tycoon to think about how important Welsh workers had been to his industrial success. Carnegie was famously proud of his Scottish birth, and he rebuilt a castle (Skibo) in Scotland, where he spent his summers and entertained influential British politicians and business leaders. Much less known are Carnegie's connections with Wales. In the late 1870s, following the advice of Bill Jones, Carnegie purchased the patent of Sidney Gilchrist Thomas's Bessemer converter, which had been invented at Blaenavon and Dowlais. Thomas formed warm bonds with both steelmakers, and in 1881 he visited Carnegie and Bill Jones in America. Afterward, the tycoon praised Thomas as a "genius" who had done more for Britain than all the kings and queens put together, and he declared Jones a talent of the first order. Carnegie also cultivated friendships with Liberal members of Parliament, particularly William E. Gladstone, who lived in Flintshire, and David Lloyd George of Caernarvon. When the 1902 Welsh National Eisteddfod at Caernarvon was being organized, George probably suggested that Carnegie be invited to serve as president. The steel man accepted, but he withdrew at the last minute because his young daughter had become seriously ill. As for Welsh learning, Carnegie established thirty-five Carnegie libraries in Wales alone and located them primarily in industrial towns to elevate the education of all classes in society.[79]

Homestead Lockout, 1892

By 1889, Carnegie's Homestead Steel Works had become the industry's last union stronghold in Pittsburgh. The city's other mills, such as the large Jones & Laughlin plant, had followed Carnegie's lead in adopting an antiunion labor policy, so there was little prospect that the AAISW could succeed in organizing them. The steel magnate had purchased the Homestead plant in 1887 and presented the AAISW with a proposal for a sliding scale that

Fig. 4.6. Homestead Steel Works, Homestead, Pennsylvania, ca. 1900–1910. Library of Congress.

reduced wages by about 25 percent. He had also announced a return to the twelve-hour day, that all positions would become vacant on June 1, 1889, and that workers who were called back would be required to sign individual three-year ironclad, or "yellow-dog," contracts.[80]

Carnegie was committed to, and invested heavily in, technological innovations to make the mill as productive as possible. Therefore, he readily invested in the new Siemens-Martin, or open-hearth, process, which turned massive quantities of pig iron into a malleable and durable steel. Sidney Gilchrist-Thomas modified the basic method of steel production in the United States to create open-hearth steel, which made it feasible for manufacturers to use cheap, high-phosphorus ores found in the Great Lakes region. With an eye to tapping this vast reserve of iron ore, Carnegie decided in April 1886 to construct the nation's first open-hearth furnace at the Homestead works. These furnaces required large crews, but the overall skill level required was far lower than for puddling furnaces.[81] The Homestead

Steel Works, therefore, was at the cutting edge of steelmaking in 1889, and Carnegie was ready for a final showdown with the AAISW.

Homestead steelworkers met in June 1889 and unanimously rejected Carnegie's proposal over the objections of the more cautious AAISW national leadership. Recognizing that their major problem was preventing replacement workers from entering the mill, the steelworkers sealed off the town and set up an advisory committee, as they had done in 1882. A trainload of replacement workers escorted by the county sheriff was sent to Homestead, but a crowd of 2,000 strikers blocked their approach to the mill. A few days later the sheriff returned with 125 newly deputized men and a court order prohibiting the strikers from gathering on company property. This time the strikebreakers were met by an even larger crowd of perhaps 3,000 men, women, and boys, who once again succeeded in turning back the scabs. By the end of the day all of the deputies had boarded the trains and returned to Pittsburgh.[82]

At this juncture the company met with a committee of workers to bring the impasse to an end. The final agreement recognized the AAISW and guaranteed reinstatement of all the workers, but it also accepted Carnegie's sliding scale that reduced wages as much as 30 percent for some skilled workers.[83] The skilled workers saw the strike of 1889 as a success in maintaining control of their crafts, but it was also a partial victory for Carnegie. When the contract expired in three years' time, however, Carnegie would be prepared to finally achieve his goal of total control.

That contract ended in July 1892, a year when there was a glut in the steel market, making it a perfect time for Carnegie to finally rid his Homestead plant of unionism once and for all. Following his previous plan of attack, Carnegie closed his Homestead plant on July 1, 1892, and vowed it would never again be opened to union labor. Union men had good reason to expect that this time the lockout would be more difficult, since Henry C. Frick, well known as an inveterate foe of organized labor, was now head of the Carnegie Steel Company, and he assumed command of the lockout in Homestead. For the workers the lockout was a continuation of the decade-long assault on unionism and for control of the shop floor.[84] Any remaining question of Carnegie's motivation was removed when Carnegie himself ordered that all thirty-eight puddling furnaces at the Twenty-Ninth Street mill be dismantled, thereby eliminating the jobs of two hundred puddlers. Rumors circulated that the same fate was to befall the puddlers at the Thirty-Third Street mill. It seemed at the time that puddlers faced extinction in all Pittsburgh mills when Jones & Laughlin also closed thirty-five puddling furnaces and dismissed the puddlers.[85]

The AAISW was handicapped from the start by internal divisions. By 1892, Homestead locals had attempted to strengthen their base by organizing unskilled workers, but the national policy of the AAISW craft union leadership still barred admission to unskilled labor. Moreover, the metal product manufacturers had pivoted decidedly toward replacing iron with steel, so the old divide between ironworkers and steelworkers had turned into a gulf. At the same time, the ironworkers, particularly the puddlers, still dominated leadership of the 24,068-member union. At the convention that year the steelworkers openly complained that the ironworkers were unable to appreciate their concerns. To make matters worse, the heaters and rollers were convinced that they could no longer rely on the AAISW to support them, and they again began agitating for their own union.[86] On the eve of the Homestead lockout, therefore, the national AAISW was weakened by dissension from within at the same time it was under attack from without by the steel manufacturers. Nevertheless, the steelworkers, like the ironworkers, insisted that, whatever the dictums of the marketplace, they had a right to a fair wage just like the puddlers, heaters, and rollers.

Carnegie's determination to replace union representation with individual contracts was carried out by Frick as chairman of the board of Carnegie Steel. Carnegie was out of the country in Scotland at the time, so negotiations with the union became Frick's responsibility. That the assault on the AAISW was planned well in advance was demonstrated by the hiring of the Pinkerton National Detective Agency to secure the works. Moreover, in testimony before a congressional investigating committee on July 12, 1892, Frick himself was emphatic. Asked if he had intended to hire non-union replacement workers, Frick replied, "We did not care whether they were union or non-union, but we wanted men with whom we could deal individually. We did not propose to deal with the Amalgamated Association after that date [June 24], as we had plainly told them."[87]

The Homestead Lockout of 1892 is one of the most widely known and written about episodes in the history of American labor, so only a cursory recapitulation is necessary here. Well over three thousand were employed at the Homestead works; about eight hundred were skilled men, all but twenty of whom were AAISW members. Even though the vast majority of the workers were excluded from the AAISW, they nevertheless voted overwhelmingly to join the strike when the union failed to come to terms with Carnegie Steel. As during the 1889 strike, an advisory committee was organized to direct the walkout and, with the full support of Homestead's elected officials, controlled much of the city itself. Frick refused to negotiate. Instead, he had a tall board fence topped with barbed wire constructed around the mill, which the workers quickly dubbed "Fort Frick." The men hung effigies of Frick and the mill superintendent on company property, and when Frick ordered some hired hands to pull them down, they were thwarted by strikers, who turned water hoses on them. Frick then locked out the workers and ordered in three hundred Pinkerton agents to guard company property.

The Pinkertons arrived on July 6 but were met by ten thousand strikers. Both sides were well armed, and after an all-day battle the Pinkertons surrendered and were forced to walk a gauntlet through an abusive crowd. During the battle, nine strikers and seven Pinkertons were killed, and many more on both sides were wounded. Unable to recruit local residents as deputies, the county sheriff sought help from the Pennsylvania governor, who complied by sending in eight thousand militia members on July 12. Public opinion turned against the strikers when an anarchist, who had virtually no connection with the union, attempted to assassinate Frick in his office on July 23. Under protection from the militia, Carnegie's Homestead plant reopened on July 27 with a thousand new non-union workers. More than one hundred strikers were arrested on various charges, including murder, although they were never convicted. Defeated in this defensive effort, the AAISW called off the strike on November 20, 1892. Thereafter, all of Carnegie's steel mills operated with non-union labor, and the AAISW was all but destroyed.[88]

The Story of John Morris, the First to Die

In the early morning hours of July 6, 1892, barges with Pinkerton agents on board plied their way up the Monongahela River and docked at the Homestead plant's wharf. They had been called in to enforce the lockout of striking steelworkers and remove them from company property. The steelworkers had an elaborate surveillance system, however, and the Pinkertons

▶ Fig. 4.7. Homestead strikers assail the Pinkertons, 1892. Library of Congress.

FRANK LESLIE'S
ILLUSTRATED
HOMESTEAD TROUBLES.
WEEKLY

NEW YORK, JULY 14, 1892.

[PRICE, 10 CENTS.

THE LABOR TROUBLES AT HOMESTEAD, PENNSYLVANIA—ATTACK OF THE STRIKERS AND THEIR SYMPATHIZERS ON THE SURRENDERED
PINKERTON MEN.—DRAWN BY MISS G. A. DAVIS, FROM A SKETCH BY C. UPHAM.—[SEE PAGE 47.]

had been spotted. About 4:30 a.m. a crowd of locked-out workers, their families, and other interested parties from the community gathered at the riverbank to intercept the Pinkertons and prevent them from debarking and taking over the plant. When a gangplank was lowered to the shore, the agents were met by several strikers. Martin Murray, a Welsh immigrant, was one of them. A skilled heater and union leader who had worked at the mill for a decade, Murray was also a member of the advisory committee. The Pinkerton in charge of the agents declared his intention of reclaiming company property, and when the workers refused to move, he charged ahead. A volley of shots was fired into the large crowd of workers that had gathered, and the workers leveled their own barrage at the Pinkertons. Men fell on both sides during this initial engagement. Martin Murray fell wounded, and when his comrade Joseph Sotak, a leader of the Slavic workers, attempted to rescue Murray, he too was shot.[89]

The Pinkertons retreated to the safety of the barge, but just before 8:00 a.m. the captain of the Pinkertons informed the workers standing closest to the gangplank that his men would be coming ashore. A shot was fired, and the major gunfight of the Homestead rebellion that ensued lasted most of the day. The first to fall during this assault was John E. Morris, a twenty-eight-year-old Welsh immigrant and skilled worker in the blooming mill. His position atop the pump house from which he had been firing into the barge apparently had been spotted by a Pinkerton sharpshooter. During a lull in the battle, a comrade reported that Morris lifted his head to see what was happening, and in that split second a bullet pierced his forehead and knocked him from his perch to the ground sixty feet below. Morris's death and the sight of the mourning crowd conveying his body home to his widow "seemed to craze the people, and men, women, and children ran through the streets crying for revenge."[90]

Five resisters, including Morris and Sotak, were killed in this bloody encounter, and a number were wounded. They represented the ethnic groups who had come together under labor's banner to stop Carnegie Steel from imposing its will on them by force: Silas Wain, a recent immigrant from England; Henry Striegel, a German teamster; and Peter Fares, a Slovak immigrant. Along with the seriously wounded, such as William Foy, an immigrant from England, and George Rutter, a native-born American, the casualties suffered among the workers represented a cross section of the population of Homestead.[91]

Scholars who document the history of the working class often have difficulty tracing even an outline of their subjects' lives. In John Morris's case, the numerous newspaper accounts of those tragic hours in Homestead were all that was known of the man for more than a century. Nearly 130 years after his death, a Morris descendant shared his personal family history. These new details clarify some of the misinformation printed in the news reports and provide a sharper profile of a Welsh immigrant steelworker whose life probably was not so different from that of many other immigrant steelworkers.

According to the family historian, John Edmund Morris was born in 1864 in the tinplate town of Cwmavon, South Wales, the oldest son of eight children born to Jane Evans and John Morris Sr., a furnace worker at a local tinplate mill. His grandfather had been killed in the coal mines. Employment options were few, but John and his oldest sister managed to land jobs with their father at the tinplate mill.

In 1882 Pennsylvania mills were recruiting workers from Wales, and John leaped at the opportunity to work at the Homestead plant. He sailed from Liverpool, England, for New York in April 1882, an eighteen-year-old with little money and nothing but the clothes on his back. He did have considerable experience, however, having worked as a "behinder" in the sheet mill at Cwmavon since the age of fifteen. Because he was bilingual, John was able to land a skilled job almost immediately upon arrival at Homestead. Three years later he purchased a small cottage near the mill, and a year later, in 1886, he married Hannah Richards, another Welsh immigrant.

Tragedy struck the family in 1887 when Morris's father died at age forty-nine, leaving his wife alone to raise six children. Like so many of the working poor of that time, the children were forced to leave school to help support the family. John's three youngest brothers, ages five, six, and ten, all found places in the coal mines, while his three sisters, ages twenty, seventeen, and eight, went into domestic service. John sent home as much money as he could afford, but it was never enough. His two oldest sisters soon married, which alleviated some of the pressure. Meanwhile, John became a naturalized US citizen. Now qualified to sponsor his family's immigration to America, he purchased passage for his mother, Jane, and her four youngest children, who arrived at Philadelphia in June 1888. Upon their arrival in Homestead, they all crowded into John and Hannah's small cottage. The following year John's oldest sister, Rachel, her husband, and their baby daughter emigrated from Wales to New Castle, Pennsylvania, where the husband found employment at a tinplate mill.[92]

In an interview with a reporter from the *Pittsburgh Dispatch*, Hannah declared that the couple had just paid for their little house when her husband lost his life to the Pinkerton sharpshooter. Having a premonition of danger, she had tried to talk John out of joining the thousands of workers who had gathered at the pump house, but he felt it was his duty to be there, saying, "I would rather die defending you and my job than to live and be called a black sheep." So he kissed her, and "with his gun on his shoulder he ran out to his death." Hours later, John's body was brought back home to be prepared for burial. The onerous task was left to John's distraught wife, mother, and sisters, who dressed him in his Sunday suit and a clean white shirt.

The International Order of Odd Fellows, of which Morris had been a member, took charge of his funeral, paying for the coffin and gravesite and planning for the massive procession, which was extensively covered in the *Pittsburgh Times* and other newspapers. The procession was led by a plumed hearse drawn by two black horses, followed by thirteen carriages and two bands playing hymns and dirges. Members of the AAISW and two hundred Odd Fellows followed in two columns to the Methodist church on Fourth Avenue. The church was filled to capacity, and the overflow crowd spilled out into the street. During the service, the minister delivered a stout denunciation of the company for its inhumane policies and actions. Outside, three hundred AAISW men and two hundred members of the Knights of Pythias (Morris had been a member of that fraternal order as well) led by a band fell in behind the procession, and hundreds of people filled the streets leading to the cemetery. Two other casualties, Peter Fares and Silas Wain, were buried on the same day. Fares was buried in the Catholic cemetery. Wain was laid to rest in a gravesite near John Morris's, his procession arriving just as those in Morris's were leaving for home. The other three men were buried the following day.[93]

Tragedies at work beget tragedies at home, as working families were all too well aware. The following January tragedy struck again with the death of Hannah's baby. John's mother could not bear to remain in Homestead, so she and the children moved to New Castle to live with her oldest daughter and her husband. The widowed Hannah remained in Homestead to be near her brother. Unable to pay her debts, she was forced to sell the house and all of her possessions; after that, all documented traces of her life come to an end. John's other sister in America married, and his younger brothers began work in the New Castle tinplate mill. Eventually, John's mother returned to Wales to rejoin her two oldest daughters there.[94]

Welsh newspapers followed events in the mill and mine towns of America with great interest. The detailed reports of the Homestead events in 1892 were picked up by the South Wales newspapers, and they often added their own stories and comments to these accounts. Welsh families and friends of immigrants in America were always eager for news, and letters of interest to iron- and steelworkers or coal miners were often published in the local newspapers. Another Welsh immigrant working at the Homestead mill, David Jackson, experienced the same events that cost John Morris his life. The *Western Mail* in Cardiff received a copy of Jackson's letter to his father about the Pinkertons' assault and tagged it to the end of the story about the death and funeral of Morris from the July 8, 1892, issue of the *Pittsburgh Times*.

In the letter, Jackson described the "deadly conflict with our employers" and said he was thankful that he had escaped without a scratch, thank God. "Dear parents," he wrote, "I told you in my previous letter that I thought there would be trouble, and so it came to pass. The company employed about 300 men to shoot us down like dogs, and we were prepared." The Pinkertons came up the river on boats, "but we would not let them land. Then the shooting commenced. . . . They surrendered to us and we got all their guns. So we are well prepared for them when they come next time. . . . I have got one of the Pinkerton's guns; it is a sixteen-shooter 45 bullet, and a repeater rifle. . . . We are watching the mills day and night. The women were bringing coffee and food to us in the mills as we could not leave our posts of deadly duty. . . . The women were with us night and day, and when the Pinkerton men gave up, they had it badly with the women," a reference to the beating the Pinkertons received from the women as the agents were made to run the gauntlet after their surrender following the first gun battle.[95]

Coming as it did on the cusp of America's transition to a corporate economy, with economic power concentrated in the hands of fewer and fewer trusts, the Homestead Lockout of 1892 crystallized the issues inherent in the shift in power from the "labor republicanism" of the nineteenth century to the corporate domination of the twentieth. The Homestead workers' advisory committee issued "An Address to the Public" to state its position on the underlying issues of the lockout. "The most evident characteristic of our time and country is the phenomenon of industrial centralization," it stated, "which is putting the control of each of our great national industries into the hands of one or a few men and giving these men an enormous and despotic power over the lives and the fortunes of their employees and subordinates—the great mass of the people. . . . The right of employers to manage their business to suit themselves" had become nothing less than "a right to manage the country to suit themselves."[96]

At a more personal level, many workers were blacklisted and no longer able to find employment at their craft. Welshman John P. Edwards, a local leader of the AAISW and member of the advisory committee at Homestead, was blacklisted after the 1892 lockout. His experience was not unique, even if his survival strategy was—he formed the "Edwards Family," a small orchestra composed of now "Professor" Edwards and his five musically talented children.[97] So many Welsh were among the blacklisted that by 1898 David Davies, the "special correspondent" for the *Western Mail* newspaper of Cardiff, was surprised to find so few of his compatriots left in Homestead following "the fight to the finish" between capitalism and labor. Instead, Davies found Homestead, a city of about ten thousand, filled with former strikebreakers, mostly "Polocks, Italians, and Hungarians." Davies had supposed he would find a large number of Welsh in Homestead, but he was disappointed. "The great majority of those once employed at Carnegie's had disappeared in the dispersal caused by the strike." After the lockout they "found the gates closed to them," and they had gone elsewhere. On inquiring about certain individuals, he was repeatedly informed, "'He was one who did not come back after the strike.' In the whole of Homestead now there are probably not more than a hundred Welsh families. The whole community was disintegrated by that struggle . . . it ended one era and began another."[98]

After the Homestead Lockout of 1892, the AAISW entered a long decline in membership as skilled workers were replaced by technological advancements and mechanization and as smaller companies were consolidated into large corporations that dominated the industry. As the adoption of the Bessemer technology increased, there was a corresponding decrease in the demand for skilled puddlers, heaters, and rollers, among whom the Welsh were disproportionately represented.[99] With the declining demand for skilled labor, the immigration of Welsh iron- and steelworkers subsided once again, but the establishment of the American tinplate industry during the 1890s launched one last surge of Welsh immigration to the "land of opportunity."

5

Welsh Tinplate and the McKinley Tariff

Tinplate was emerging as a widely used commodity in the years following the Civil War. The demand for tinplate as a roofing material increased every year, and the use of tinned cans for food preservation and petroleum containers in particular also expanded rapidly during these years. In 1870 some ninety-seven American canneries were in operation; by 1890 that number had risen to 1,808, and the value of their products had risen from $5.5 million to $56.5 million.[1] Even with this explosive growth in the use and value of tinplate products, the United States still relied almost exclusively on Wales for its supply of tinplate until the late 1890s. Economic conditions changed dramatically after passage of the McKinley tariff in 1891, which levied a heavy duty on imported tinplate and triggered a new wave of Welsh tinplate expert immigration to America.

Pioneers of American Tinplate

Efforts were made to stimulate the manufacture of tinplate in the United States during the decades following the Civil War, but they faltered before numerous obstacles. In fact, the early history of the US industry was a struggle for survival. In 1868 the Cambria Iron Company of Johnstown,

Pennsylvania, sent an experienced metallurgist and ironworker to Europe to learn the process of making tinplate. Shortly thereafter, James Park Jr., founder of Black Diamond Steel, a major producer of crucible steel in Pittsburgh, sent another expert abroad to discover the secrets of the trade. During their quest both men visited works in England and Wales. Upon returning, they reported that even though the United States had the facilities and resources to manufacture tinplate, it would be impossible to compete with these countries because skilled mill workers in America received double the wages of their British counterparts. The only way American manufacturers could compete, therefore, was if their product was protected by a federal tariff on imported tinplate. Consequently, the business owners abandoned the idea of building a tinplate works.[2]

Even though tariff protection would not be forthcoming until the last decade of the century, several pioneering attempts at tinplate manufacture were undertaken in the United States between 1870 and the 1890s with the aid of skilled Welsh masters. Knowledge of Welsh tinplaters' involvement in the fledgling industry across the "herring pond" was widespread in Wales from the inception. Charles Wilkins, a contemporary Welsh observer writing in 1903, noted that by this time Wales had been the "smithy of the world" for a century and had contributed "industrial teachers" to other nations besides the United States. The Americans first mastered the details of blackplate (iron or steel sheet rolled, pickled, and annealed but not coated with tin) with assistance from Welsh workers who had chosen to immigrate there in the early days. Welsh expertise was wedded with American energy, he wrote, and Welsh workers were settling there in steadily increasing numbers until it seemed that Pennsylvania was "worthy of being called the Greater Wales." The actions of Welsh tinplaters who served as "teachers of the Americans" were noteworthy, he commented, but "played into American hands." Once the Americans had learned the skills of manufacturing tinplate they would no longer need their Welsh teachers.[3]

During the winter of 1871 and 1872, two Welshmen, William Oak Davies and another man known only as Davis, arrived in Pittsburgh. They claimed to have invented a new tinplating process that would enable the Americans to best the Welsh manufacturers. To demonstrate the efficacy of their process, Davies and Davis established in Leechburg, Pennsylvania, a small tin-coating facility using blackplate from a mill operated by

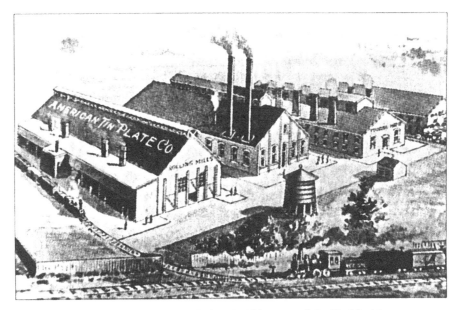

Fig. 5.1. American Tinplate Works, Wellsville, Ohio, 1873. After Paul Jenkins, *"Twenty by Fourteen."*

another Welshman, William Rogers, who operated the only mill in the United States capable of producing the cold-rolled, pickled bar and sheet iron suitable for making tinplate. Davies and Davis (the anglicized version of the name Davies) soon parted company. In early 1873 Davies organized the U.S. Iron and Tinplate Company and built a plant near what is now the city of McKeesport, outside Pittsburgh, while Davis established the American Tinplate Company down the Ohio River from Pittsburgh at Wellsville, Ohio. Both of these works confronted not only the difficulties inherent to establishing a new business but also the serious financial depression ushered in by the panic of 1873.[4]

Encouraged by these efforts, however, several other new companies began operations. The most effective of these was the United States Iron and Tin Plate Manufacturing Company established at Demmler Station (McKeesport) near Pittsburgh. Born in Germany in 1810, John Henry Demmler became an apprentice tinsmith prior to immigrating to the United States in 1834. Demmler migrated westward to Pittsburgh, where he found employment with a local ironworks and subsequently opened his own tinsmithing shop. J. D. Strouse, a Pittsburgh real estate developer and banker, bought the patent for William Oak Davies's tinplate-making process and chartered the U.S. Iron & Tin Plate Company, and he hired Davies to supervise the works. Demmler bought stock in the new company. In August 1874, Strouse and Demmler learned that Davies's machinery produced tinplate of poor quality, and when the workers went out on strike over Davies's abusive treatment, he was forced to resign as superintendent. In the reorganized company, Demmler was appointed president.[5] The reorganized U.S. Iron and Tin Plate Manufacturing Company remained in operation continuously from February 1875 to July 1882, when once again it was reorganized. A fire destroyed the mill in 1883, but it was rebuilt and resumed operation. With no demand for tinplate, however, the operators were only able to continue operations by producing sheet iron.[6]

Highly skilled labor was required in tinplating, and practically no one with those skills was available in the United States. For the pioneer operators, Wales was the world's leading producer of tinplate, supplying well over 70 percent of the product used in the United States. Naturally, the American operators turned to Wales for the skilled workers and technical experts required to establish their start-up plants. One chronicler of the early years, steel executive Roy Rutherford, related an oft-repeated story from the period: "A herd of 'goat' tin-workers descended on the country and scattered out to the towns where tin-mills were being built—in Pennsylvania, Ohio, West Virginia, and Indiana. Veterans tell of Welsh tin-rollers hurrying down the gangplank of a steamer in New York and excitedly hailing the first passerby: 'Hoy, Mister! Show me the way to Niles, America!'" Because this was such an often told story, the name of any number of cities might be substituted. These Welsh immigrants were the backbone of America's infant tinplate industry, he observed. Rutherford also repeated the frequent characterization of Welsh tinplaters as "intensely clannish" and the notion that they shrouded their trade secrets in mystery so that "for years the making of tin plate was considered to be something of a black art, something not amenable to the ordinary laws of chemistry and mechanics." Americans believed the Welsh used "secret powders" in their tinpots and performed certain of their operations only behind closed doors. Because of their "clannish" nature, the Welsh passed their crafts down from father to son and usually "did their best to make a Welsh monopoly out of the industry."[7] This behavior is explained less by innate Welsh traits, however, than family and occupational security through craft protection.

On the whole, Rutherford affirmed that the Welsh did know their business and were "the key men in the early American mills. Some of them developed into executives and capitalists. When you think of tin and tin plate, you think of Wales and its people. They dominated this field for a long period," and it was from them "we secured the knowledge which we enlarged greatly."[8] Rutherford observed that "the Welsh looked upon operating the hot rolls as "real abracadabra," and as late as 1927 a roll-turner had "grasped his sledge hammer and chased a young engineer, fresh from college, who had the temerity to be snooping around with a micrometer."[9] Again, more practical concerns undoubtedly animated this roll-turner, such as job protection rather than "abracadabra."

The Tinplate Industry of Alcania

Wales held a near global monopoly on the tinplate trade and production skills for a century prior to the first attempts to establish the industry in the United States. Therefore, it is essential to understand the background of the industry, manufacturing processes, and expertise that the Americans imported. William Lewis (Lewys Afan), a leader of the Independent Association of Tinplate Makers, founded in 1871, coined the term "Alcania" to refer to the areas of South Wales where tinplate production was concentrated. It was derived from the Welsh word *alcan* or *alcam* for tin. Tinplate had been manufactured in South Wales since the eighteenth century, but by the late nineteenth century Alcania had become centered on the two original "tinopolises" of Llanelli, in Carmarthenshire, and the Morriston-Swansea Valley, in West Glamorganshire. The large communities of Welsh tinplaters in the States were creating a "Greater Alcania," one expert observed in 1903.[10]

The use of tin to coat corrosion-prone metals and to produce alloys such as bronze and pewter has been known since ancient times. Cornwall is the only region of Great Britain where tin ore is available, and mining and smelting began in that region sometime between 1,000 and 600 BCE. Pewter (tin containing lead) for domestic wares, such as dishes, plates, and bowls, has been used since Roman times. From at least the fourteenth century, ferrous metals were coated with tin to prevent them from rusting. The burgeoning demand for tinplate since World War I has been driven by the food-canning industry, which, in turn, was instrumental in the social revolution in the human diet, as well as in food preparation and distribution.[11]

In modern times, however, the industry has passed through three phases, each dominated by a different nation using different production techniques. During the first phase, lasting until about 1750, tinplate manufacture was centered in Germany, specifically the Upper Palatinate and then Saxony. The second phase, from about 1750 to 1930, was dominated by Britain. During these two periods each nation held a virtual trade monopoly. During the third phase, from about 1930 on, the United States dominated, through new production methods and technology.[12]

Britain's domination of the tinplate industry was built on the development of the rolling mill for the production of plates for tinning during the 1690s by John Hanbury of Pontypool, in South Wales. A Welsh traveler reported in 1697 that "'one Major Hanbury of this Pont-y-Pool shew'd us an excellent invention of his own, for driving hot iron (by the help of a Rolling Engin mov'd by water [power]) into as thin plates as tin.'"[13] The rolling mill replaced the traditional method of using a trip hammer to make iron plates. By 1720 the Hanburys had established a tinplating works and were tinning iron plates in Pontypool. Thanks to that mechanical improvement, by 1750 the British tinplate industry had begun its rise to dominance.[14]

The tinplate industry became concentrated in South Wales because within this region was found an abundance of the required resources: cheap fuel, skilled labor, and the ready availability of tin ore from Cornwall. Most important, however, was the proximity to abundant supplies of iron plate, as well as water for the cleaning process and for driving the rolling mills. Water was also the primary means for transporting raw materials to the mills and shipping the finished product to market. Although Cornwall had an abundance of tin ore, it possessed no coal. Therefore, tinplate mills were usually erected in the South Wales coal and iron district near the iron forges located in the river valleys. By the late eighteenth century a small-scale tinplate industry, one that was a subsidiary to the iron industry, had been securely established in South Wales, and the new rolling process made its tinplate cheaper. As a result, Wales soon captured the home market and then the European and American markets as well.[15]

Tinplate had become a major segment of the iron and steel industry by the late nineteenth century. Few people are familiar with the processes by which tinplate was produced before the industry was fully mechanized, which had been accomplished by the mid-twentieth century. Therefore, the brief description that follows is adapted primarily from the economist

Fig. 5.2. Trefforest Tin Works, 1840. Artwork by Josias Appleby. National Library of Wales.

Donald E. Dunbar's summary of a report prepared in 1888 by Britain's inspector of factories for Wales. It describes the Welsh industry at its prosperous height after two hundred years of growth and development and on the eve of the shift of industry dominance to the United States.[16]

Coating a thin sheet of iron or steel with tin strengthens and renders the inner metal rust resistant. Manufacture of tinplate began with cutting the iron or steel sheet into bars approximately six to ten inches wide. The bar was cut into slabs twenty inches long then transported on trucks to the hot mill. A mill consisted of two stands of rolls twenty-six inches long and nineteen inches in diameter, plus the roughing stand and the finishing stand. Opposite the rolls were two furnaces, one for each stand of rolls. The mill crew comprised four workers: the rollerman, the furnaceman or heater, the doubler, and the behinder or catcher, generally a youth. The slabs were heated and rolled in five stages.

The slabs were piled in the roughing furnace and withdrawn in pairs when they reached red-hot condition and then passed through the roughing rolls. The two pieces were passed alternately, four or five times, until rolled into thin sheets 0.1520 inch thick. Then they were returned to the furnace for reheating. The slabs were withdrawn from the furnace singly and passed twice through the roughing rolls, which further reduced the slab to 0.0785 inch. The sheet was doubled over on itself by the doubler and returned to the finishing furnace for reheating. The slabs were doubled and redoubled until they had been rolled into eight twenty-by-fourteen-inch sheets cut into twenty-four sheets. The rolling of the sheet bar into a pack of thin sheets was a laborious task requiring a high degree of skill. The temperature in the hot mills was very high, and the mills were worked continuously, for three shifts of eight hours each.[17]

When the rolled packs cooled, they passed to the shearman to be cut to the desired size. The shears were driven by gearing from the main shaft of the hot mills. Thus, the shears were always in operation and uncontrolled by the shearman, who had to be well trained to synchronize his movements with those of the machine. In the process of rolling, the doubled and redoubled sheets became somewhat welded together, so after they were sheared to size they passed to the openers' bench. There, women and girls broke apart the laminated sheets with a piece of metal or a heavy knife.[18]

Once separated, the sheets passed to the pickling process to clear them of iron oxide. The black pickling bath consisted of immersion in sulfuric acid, followed by immersion in water. The pickling department was an unwholesome place where workers were exposed to wet floors, acid fumes, and general humidity due to vapors from the pickling vats. The sheets were then conveyed to the annealing furnaces, where the heat is so intense that annealers had to be conditioned to endure the high temperature. The plates remained in the annealing furnace from ten to twelve hours under an intense heat that rendered them tough.

The sheets were then passed through cold rolls to give them a smooth surface. The cold rolls were similar to those in the hot mills, but they operated at a much faster speed and subjected the sheets to very high pressure. Workers sat on benches in front of the rolls and fed the sheets one by one into the rolls. As sheets accumulated on the other side of the stand of rolls, workers gathered them and carried them back to the cold-roller's bench to be passed through again. The cold rolls make the sheets brittle again, so they

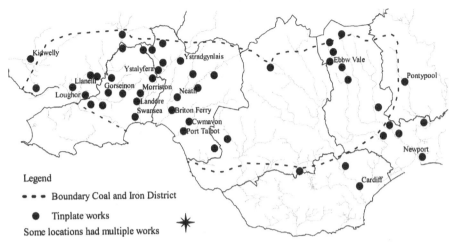

Map 4. Tinplate works in South Wales, 1700–1956. Cartography by Caroline Welter, Regional Research Institute, West Virginia University, Morgantown.

were given another, briefer annealing at lower heat. Following the so-called "white annealing" stage, the sheets underwent another pickling.[19]

This complicated process was to prepare the sheets, or "blackplate," for tinning, in five separate pots, or troughs, heated by fires from below. The first pot contained boiling palm oil to clean the surface of impurities and make it absorbent. The second pot held molten tin, which became part of the surface of the blackplate. The third pot also contained tin, but hotter and purer. Hemp brushes removed the excess tin from the plate, and then the plate was immersed into the fourth pot, which contained the purest tin. The sheets were then immersed in the boiling grease of the fifth pot. In the tin house the workers engaged in coating the sheets were all skilled because the process must be done in a very specific manner. Finally, the tin plates were removed from the grease pot and passed through an absorbent cleaning material to remove the grease. While the tin plates were still hot, they were hand-polished with sheepskin, and the product was then ready to be sorted and packed.[20]

South Wales tinplate works were spread over two districts: the western district, in the coastal belt between Port Talbot and Carmarthen, and the eastern district, in the hinterland of Newport and Cardiff and particularly around Merthyr Tydfil, the center of the Welsh iron industry. Between 1800 and 1891 the industry expanded because of the demand abroad, discovery of new uses for tinplate, and improvements in the canning of food.[21] In 1850,

25 of the 35 tinplate works in Great Britain were located in South Wales, but by 1891 they had concentrated even more in South Wales, with 90 of 98 located there. In 1891, 502 out of the 525 mills operating in the British tinplate industry were located in South Wales (each works had multiple mills). By the mid-nineteenth century, the principal center of tinplate production in South Wales had shifted from the eastern to the western district, where a large number of "tinplate towns" had developed. Llanelli, known as "Tinopolis," was the largest among them, with 6 tinplate works in operation in 1880. Tinplate was even more important to the life of numerous smaller, one-industry towns, such as Pontarddulais, Morriston, and Briton Ferry, each with 5 works; Port Talbot with 4; and Neath, Pontardawe, and Gorseinon with 3 works.[22]

This shift in the concentration of tinplate works to the western district of South Wales resulted from the abundance of resources, such as coal, limestone, and sulfuric acid; water power from the Avon, Neath, Tawe, and Amman Rivers; and the ports along the coastline, particularly Swansea, useful for both importing ores and exporting the finished products. Moreover, there were fewer employment options in the western district, so tinplate manufacturers were able to recruit labor directly from the copper industry, which was in rapid decline by the mid-nineteenth century.[23]

Tinplate makers had experimented with steel made by both the Bessemer and the open-hearth processes and determined that Bessemer was unsuitable for making tinplate. By the early 1880s, open-hearth steel had been embraced for its higher quality, and open-hearth steelworks had been built to supply the tinplate industry in western Wales. William Siemens developed his process at the Landore Siemens Steel Company in Swansea between 1868 and 1875. Unable to compete in rail manufacture with the major ironworks at the northern outcrop of the South Wales coal basin, the Landore works turned to the production of steel bars for tinplate. Moreover, the Siemens process was readily adapted to small-scale works because it took less time to produce steel than the Bessemer process, and it did not require the extensive capital outlay for machinery and construction. Tinplate makers in the district, therefore, were quick to adopt open-hearth steel. Nearly all of the Siemens steelworks erected in western Wales were built by firms already engaged in tinplate manufacture to replace their iron forges. The result was a radical reorganization of the industry with the separation of the iron bar industry from tinplate manufacture.[24]

Over the course of the nineteenth century, the Welsh tinplate industry became increasingly dependent on the export trade, particularly trade with the United States, which tied the industry to the boom-and-bust cycle of foreign markets. A booming export trade brought higher prices and encouraged the expansion of tinplate works. Overproduction inevitably led to an economic downturn, with prices and profits falling, and tinplate works were forced to close or remain idle until demand returned. This boom-and-bust cycle outlines much of the industry's history throughout the nineteenth century and up to World War I. The boom of 1879 and 1880 brought about the most rapid phase of expansion in the history of the industry in Wales, with 100 new mills constructed in 1879 alone. Despite a period of declining prices during the 1880s, there were 401 mills in 1885, and the number had risen to 525 mills by the end of the decade. The late 1880s was the last period of rapid expansion during the Welsh monopoly on tinplate.[25]

As the industry expanded, so did the number of tinplate workers, from about 1,000 in 1800 to 5,200 in 1851, 9,200 in 1871, 15,500 in 1880, and about 25,000 by 1891. After recovery from the depression of the 1890s, a peak of between 28,000 and 29,000 workers was reached in 1913. Tinplate wages were higher than in coal mining and there were few other local employment opportunities, so unemployed tinplaters seeking work in their trades moved to other mills or districts or immigrated to the United States. When conditions improved at home, migrants often returned. During the depression of the 1890s, however, numerous workers left the industry permanently to seek greater employment security.[26]

The composition of the Welsh labor force changed over the years, with the proportion of adult males increasing significantly in conjunction with a corresponding decrease in the proportion of women and children. In 1886 adult males were slightly more than one-half of the total number of workers, but by 1906 that figure had reached two-thirds. Boys made up more than 24 percent of the total in 1886, but that fraction had slipped modestly to less than 20 percent in 1906. The percentage of women also declined, from 17.5 percent in 1886 to 11 percent in 1906, while the figure for girls dropped from about 6 percent to 3 percent during the same period.[27]

The workforce required to operate an eighteen-mill plant, according to industry historian Paul Jenkins, was 584 male adults and 66 female adults, 161 male "young persons" (meaning under seventeen), and 42 female "young persons," for a total of 853. A smaller six-mill plant, Jenkins estimated, required 191 male adults, 29 female adults, and 39 male and 31 female "young persons," for a total of 290 employees. In addition, a manager, a few foremen, and several office workers were employed, totaling no more than 12 for an eighteen-mill plant and 6 for a six-mill plant.[28]

Welsh tinplate works recruited their labor locally for the most part, but the competition for managers, rollermen, and tinmen could be fierce. Managers likely to bring prized workers along with them to a new works enhanced their prospects with prospective owners, but skilled workers rarely moved far from home. The proportion of skilled workers in the labor force was relatively high, about 25 percent of the total, but not as high as the 30 to 40 percent in the large integrated ironworks.[29]

Traditionally, whole families worked at the trade in Wales. Consequently, changes that adversely affected one group were opposed by all of the workers. The introduction of new machinery, for example, such as tinning or cleaning and polishing machines, met with great resistance in Wales. This collective resistance to the introduction of labor-saving machinery has prompted many observers to conclude that Welsh tinplaters were conservative by nature and opposed anything that was different from past practice.[30] A contemporary scholar of the industry, economist Donald E. Dunbar, observed in 1912 that "even today they oppose innovations and sometimes refuse to cooperate with them, until manufacturers have to return to old methods." By way of illustration, he declared that "at Briton Ferry a manufacturer installed gas furnaces, but had to remove them owing to the opposition of the workmen."[31] Worker resistance to innovation is discussed further in chapter 6, but what many viewed as conservatism may well have been influenced as much by the tradition of family employment and the notions of a "family wage" and a "living wage" that evolved within tinplate work culture. Nevertheless, as will be seen in chapter 7, the tradition of employing young girls, boys, and women did not survive the migration of Welsh tinplaters to America.

Individual wages were considerably lower in Wales than in the United States. Welsh rollers earned the equivalent of fifteen to twenty dollars a week, whereas in America they earned forty to fifty. Doublers earned the equivalent of twelve to fifteen dollars a week in Wales, compared to about thirty in America. The gap was smaller in the tinhouse, where the Welsh tin worker earned the equivalent of about eleven dollars a week, and American counterparts earned fifteen to eighteen. Although hot-mill wages in the United States were about twice those in Wales, the US cost of labor per unit was lower than in Wales because American mills utilized more labor-saving machinery and therefore achieved greater productivity. It is difficult to make direct comparisons between standards of living in the two countries, but in Wales prices for the basic necessities were lower even as tinplate families earned the equivalent of twenty-five to thirty dollars per week, a comfortable family income. Although American firms paid skilled workers double the tonnage wages paid by Welsh firms, the actual per-unit labor cost was practically the same in both countries.[32]

In 1912, each American mill employed seven men and turned out from 120 to 130 boxes per shift, an output about three times greater than the typical Welsh mill. The standard box of tinplate contained 112 sheets of 20 inches by 14 inches, or 31,360 square inches. Twenty boxes of tinplate weighed about one ton.[33] This traditional Welsh measurement of production was carried over to the American industry and continued in use well into the twentieth century, even after it had lost its original meaning. Welsh workers understood that with mechanical improvements in the production process, their expected output would increase. In 1870, output was 30 boxes per eight-hour shift, which was the universal turn, or shift, in Wales. By 1890, the accepted output was 36 boxes per eight-hour shift. There was a consensus among workers and employers that this was a "fair day's work" and sufficient to provide a "living wage." Wages did vary between works in different districts, with wages tending to be lower in western Wales than in eastern areas, in part because there were fewer opportunities for alternative employment.[34] These differences disappeared in the late nineteenth century with the establishment of trade unionism.

Until late in the nineteenth century, employers followed relatively paternalistic policies toward workers and their families, often providing them with cottages, schools, reading rooms, and a benefits club for those injured or killed on the job, as well as encouraging gardens and workers' bands. Wages were negotiated individually between employers and employees within established customs accepted by both sides. Monthly wages encouraged the "truck system" of credit extended at the company shops instead of cash and some of its well-documented abuses. Due to the relative lack of mobility when disputes arose, both owner and employee preferred to quickly resolve grievances. Since many of the owners and managers of tinplate works typically were born and bred in South Wales, they probably understood the aspirations of their workers even if they did not always accommodate them.[35]

Prior to the amalgamation of the British steel industry after World War I, most owners of tinplate works lived within the local communities. As one historian has noted, unlike American steel magnates such as Andrew Carnegie, Welsh owners were "content with earning a good return on their investment rather than acquire immense wealth and power."[36] Also unlike American owners, Welsh tinplate masters generally upheld an earlier standard of Christian social ideals and supported the construction of churches in their districts. These owners embraced Victorian values, and "as hard-working moralists they imposed a stern discipline on the work-force and demanded acknowledgement of their status."[37] In that context, discourtesy could result in the dismissal and blacklisting of an employee. On the other hand, the code also required that the owners tend to the educational needs of their employees' families by building community libraries, reading rooms, and schools for the children, although the quality of these schools occasionally was substandard.[38]

Some owners made efforts to improve life in the workers' communities, but very few measures were taken to relieve conditions in the dark, drafty, poorly ventilated, unsanitary, and excessively hot tinplate works. Workers were paid solely on the basis of their output, there were no unemployment benefits, and no work simply meant no money for food or rent. Moreover, laboring in tinplate works prior to World War I was detrimental to the physical well-being of workers. In 1912 a comprehensive survey undertaken by medical inspector E. L. Collis and factory inspector J. Hilditch determined that the average age at death for tinplate workers was forty-five, forty-six for tinhouse workers, forty-three for mill workers, and forty-seven for others, compared with fifty-one for coal miners and fifty-nine for carpenters.[39]

Mill workers exposed to the constant heat suffered disproportionately from rheumatism and related maladies, as well as cancer. The shorter life span among the twenty-three thousand tinplaters was indicated by the age distribution among workers with a bias toward young workers: 46.5 percent of the workforce was under twenty-five and only a little more than 17 percent of the group exceeded forty-four years of age. By the age of fifty, Paul Jenkins concludes, the majority of tinplate workers had either left the industry to seek less arduous employment or, as is more likely, had labored themselves into a premature grave.[40]

Legislation restricting the age at which children could start employment began to appear in the second decade of the twentieth century. Before that time, children, who often started employment at age nine or ten, were severely affected by the hazardous nature of their labor. Cuts from the sharp-edged tinplate sheets were a common occurrence. In addition, women employed in the pickling department confronted dense clouds of acid vapor that permeated the atmosphere, causing irritation or lesions of the skin, especially around the nostrils and mouth, and teeth to blacken and decay. The debilitating nature of the work undertaken by women in the tinplate works was unique within the metal-working trades. Not surprisingly, therefore, the number of women in the industry peaked at a little more than forty-three hundred (14 percent of all employees) in 1923 and then declined when less demanding employment opportunities opened up in other industries in South Wales.[41]

British ironworkers who immigrated to the United States brought a rich tradition of trade unionism with them, but this was much less the case with tinplate immigrants. A decade into the twentieth century, nearly 100 percent of the South Wales tinplaters were unionized, but organized labor had been slow to develop in the late nineteenth century. A contemporary economist of the industry in Wales, J. H. Jones, described the average tinplate worker as "highly intelligent and a keen politician. Many of his class read widely, and are enthusiastic book collectors." They also formed "the largest group of Welshmen employed in manufacture—for the industry is still mainly in the hands of bi-lingual descendants of natives."[42] But organization was difficult for several reasons. The division of the industry into western and eastern sections, as well as the parochial nature of tinplate works, made cooperation difficult. Moreover, the nonconformist churches exerted powerful influence within the communities, and they opposed unions. Also, Welsh was the language of the western division, while English prevailed in the eastern division. The language difference alone formed a significant communications barrier for unionism within Wales and England. And, like owners in the United States, employers in Wales were determined to operate their works without interference from organized labor. Finally, some of the highly paid skilled tinplate workers, who controlled the production process, possessed a status not significantly inferior to that of their employers and often blurred the division between skilled employees and employers.[43] The divisions among workers were further complicated by the contract system, whereby the skilled mill or tin workers generally made an agreement with the employer to produce a certain amount during a given month. The skilled workers were like contractors who hired their own crews and, at the end of the period, paid their crews the agreed amount.[44] Welsh tinplaters transferred this system to the United States when they were called upon to establish the industry there.

Tinplate workers in eastern Wales formed the Independent Association of Tinplate Makers in 1871. Because iron and tinplate manufacturing were so closely linked, some ironworkers also joined the new union. Led by Jenkyn Thomas and William Lewis (Lewys Afan), the new union had accumulated a membership of four thousand by 1874. Early that year, it attempted to unify the tinplate workers by demanding that the same wages be paid to tinplaters in both western and eastern Wales. The employers refused and locked out the tinplate workers, shutting down nearly all of the works in the west. The union was not in a financial position to withstand a long stoppage, so it withdrew the demand for equal wages and returned to work. The employers did, however, agree to negotiate the establishment in the western district of a uniform scale of wages known as the "1874 List."[45] Welsh tinplaters on both sides of the Atlantic were in close communication about establishing a wage scale that would provide a mechanism for negotiations between labor and owners, as evidenced by the Welsh leader of the Sons of Vulcan, Miles Humphreys, who negotiated a similar scale with Pittsburgh iron manufacturer Jones & Laughlin that same year.[46]

The depressed economy during the years following the 1874 lockout undermined the Independent Association of Tinplate Makers. The weakened bargaining position of the workers induced apathy among tinplaters, and they simply ignored the union. Industrial disputes brought the workers back to the union, but when the difficulties were settled they once again lost interest, leaving it too weak to enforce the wage settlements as the price of tinplate fell. The 1880s was a period of falling tinplate prices, and by 1886 the ideal behind the 1874 List had been abandoned. Wages subsequently were reduced by up to 30 percent. Similarly, the traditional methods of restricting output during periods of overproduction failed to alter the situation.[47]

The union, now poor and weak, was powerless to stop wage reductions during the 1880s, and it all but disintegrated. In 1886, however, tinplate employees in the eastern district of Wales refused to accept another reduction of wages, and the employers locked them out. Tinplate workers in western Wales raised money to support the unemployed eastern district workers, marking the first occasion when tinplate workers in both districts demonstrated solidarity. Representatives from both districts came together in 1887, and, in recognition of their common problems and interests, they formed the new Tinplate Workers' Union.[48]

The Tinplate Workers' Union was stronger than its predecessor because only tinplaters were members. The primary objectives of the new union were restoration of the 1874 List and the thirty-six box per eight-hour shift output limit. Employers unwilling to undergo a work stoppage during that rare prosperous year agreed in 1889 to arbitrate the issues with their workers. The improved economy of the late 1880s also helped to stimulate the union's growth. By 1889 it had branches in seventy-six of the eighty-five tinplate works in South Wales, and in 1892 it claimed ten thousand members among the twenty-five thousand employed in the South Wales industry.[49]

Unfortunately, the Tinplate Workers' Union, like its predecessor, was not equipped to handle the economic depression ushered in by the McKinley tariff on Welsh tinplate in 1891 (discussed below). By 1895, ten thousand tinplate workers were out of work, most of them long-term unemployed. By 1898, only sixteen thousand still claimed to be tinplate workers. During the depression of the 1890s, when prices plummeted and employers demanded wage reductions, the union exercised little influence over events. When tinplate works closed during the depression, employers took the opportunity to install new labor-saving machines in their mills, a move the union had resisted.[50] The union also opposed the export of blackplate to the United States for tinning, taking the position that this trade gave direct assistance to the Americans' efforts to establish a competing industry. The mill workers ignored the concerns of the tinhouse employees, a division that also affected the tinplaters' union in the United States. Other issues divided the mill workers and the tinhouse employees, and relations became so strained that in 1899 they joined different organizations. The Tinplate Workers' Union ceased to exist in 1898, and, from that time on, tinplate workers enrolled in other unions that were indirectly related to their trades.[51]

Welsh Monopoly, American Tariff

The history of the tinplate industry in Wales and the United States during the last quarter of the nineteenth century can be divided into two periods: the Welsh monopoly to 1890 and, after a brief transition during the middle years of the 1890s, a period of competition with the rising American industry. The pivotal year was 1890, when the McKinley Tariff Act imposed a heavy protective duty on tinplate imported into the United States. After a brief struggle, South Wales manufacturers were forced to withdraw from the field as US imports of Welsh tinplate went into a precipitous decline. By 1897, the industry in Wales had slid into a depression, mills had closed, and unemployment persisted until new foreign markets were found. On the other hand, in the United States the number of mills grew steadily until by 1897 mills were producing enough tinplate to satisfy American demand.[52]

Limited legislation intended to encourage the manufacture of tinplate had been enacted in the United States before 1890. Congress accidentally imposed some protection on all metal products imported into the country in 1861 under the Morrill Tariff Act. The framers of the legislation had intended to encourage domestic production of tinplate, but the phrasing of the act apparently led to an erroneous interpretation by the Treasury Department. The provision stated that "on tin-plates, and iron galvanized or coated with any metal by electric batteries or otherwise 2½ c per pound" was levied. Even though the intent was clear, Secretary of the Treasury William P. Fessenden did not seem to understand that tinplate was not pure tin but rather plates of iron coated with tin. Therefore, he determined that there was an error of punctuation in the text and that a clerk had made the error. According to Fessenden, "If the comma which is inserted after the word plates be omitted and a comma placed after the word 'iron' the true sense will be had which unquestionably is that tinplate as well as the iron must be galvanized or coated with any metal by electric batteries, or otherwise, in order to bring them within the provision."[53]

The American tinplate industry found an extraordinarily valuable proponent in William C. Cronemeyer, who almost single-handedly led the fight for tariff protection in Washington, DC. Fortunately, he left a thorough account of the campaign to protect the "infant industry." Born in Germany in 1847, Cronemeyer immigrated to western Pennsylvania at the age of twenty-two, found employment with the U.S. Tin Plate Company in 1873, and was appointed secretary of that pioneering firm owned by John Demmler. With Welsh tinplate dominating the market, he found his major role in the industry as a lobbyist when pressing the Pennsylvania congressional delegation to revise Treasury secretary Fessenden's misinterpretation of the tariff.[54] Between 1875 and 1881, the free-trade Democratic Party held the majority in the House of Representatives, but when Republican Rutherford B. Hayes became president in 1877, the tinplate proponents went to Washington to plead their case, and Cronemeyer launched his illustrious lobbying career.[55]

With Republican James A. Garfield's election to the presidency in 1880 and his party's return to majority status in the House of Representatives, the lobbying campaign intensified between Republicans who advocated tariffs for the protection of domestic industry and Democrats who insisted they be for revenue only. In 1881, Cronemeyer went to Washington and called on William McKinley, a newly elected member of Congress from Canton, Ohio, where new iron and steel mills were opening. In McKinley, Cronemeyer found his political champion. Now aware that it would take a strong organization to overcome the political opposition to tariff revision, Cronemeyer called a meeting of leading tinplate executives in June 1883 to organize the American Tinned Plate Association. Cronemeyer was elected secretary, but with his workload increasing, he appointed John Jarrett, the former head of the Amalgamated Association of Iron and Steel Workers, to manage the association.[56]

Jarrett was uniquely qualified for the position. The Welshman's experience as head of the AAISW had brought him into contact with national industry and political leaders, and his practical knowledge as a former puddler gave him an understanding of the industry that accentuated his credibility as a lobbyist. According to Cronemeyer, he and Jarrett worked together effectively in the campaign for higher tariffs and in defending "ourselves against bitter attacks which were made on us by our opponents."[57]

Jarrett found an opportunity to demonstrate his skills as a political operative during the congressional election of 1886, when he was dispatched to Missouri to help whip up workers' support for a key Republican pro-tariff candidate.[58] His candidate won and, according to Cronemeyer, Jarrett's services as "a public speaker and political worker remained much in demand by Republican leaders."[59] He also improved his Republican bona fides during the 1886 campaign by visiting the district of Democratic representative John G. Carlisle of Kentucky, then Speaker of the House, who used his strategic position to block protectionist legislation. Details of Jarrett's visit to Carlisle's district remain unknown, but the Republicans succeeded in defeating the powerful Speaker at the polls.[60] Once again Jarrett reinforced his credentials as a Republican operative during the presidential campaign of 1888, when Senator Matthew S. Quay, the Pennsylvania political boss and chair of the Republican National Executive Committee, enlisted Jarrett's services to bring Pennsylvania's working men in line behind Benjamin Harrison. Once in office, Harrison rewarded Jarrett by appointing him consul at Birmingham, England, a post he held from 1889 to 1892.[61]

With the White House, Senate, and House of Representatives controlled by Republicans following the election of 1888, the tinplate lobbyists believed their time had come. After a decade of proselytizing, Cronemeyer finally found the opportunity to carry out his crusade when Representative William McKinley of Ohio became chair of the House Ways and Means Committee. He already supported a protective tariff on tinplate, as well as products of other branches of the iron and steel industries.[62]

Opponents of the tinplate tariff contended that the United States had neither the natural resources nor the skilled labor required to manufacture tinplate. The degree to which this view was believed or was a product of propaganda is uncertain, but there was a widespread conviction both in the United States as well as in Wales that American workers could never master the "mysteries" of tinplate production. Tinplate had been made in Wales for so long that, as one opponent declared, "even the children seem to acquire the art by instinct."[63] Therefore, opponents concluded, the importation of skilled workers from Wales, England, or Germany would be required to successfully launch the industry in the United States. Antitariff Democrats, however, also opposed the importation of foreign labor into the United States, insisting that American workers would be displaced, an argument to which working-class voters were receptive. This fear was coupled with a deeper anxiety over the many "un-American" southern and eastern European immigrants arriving at US ports. As William McAdoo, a future secretary of the Treasury Department, asserted in 1891, "a very high or substantially prohibitory tariff in the United States is bound to force, in spite of all mere restrictive measures, a large, unhealthy, undesirable, abnormal immigration," contrary to the best interests of the United States.[64]

Despite the political opposition, insecurity over American abilities, and the blatant xenophobia that characterized the era, the champions of protection were finally in a strong position to achieve their goal of imposing a tariff to protect the infant tinplate industry.[65] With William McKinley installed as chair of the Committee on Ways and Means, a protectionist bill was reported to the floor of the House of Representatives. Speaking for the bill, McKinley made one of his many impassioned speeches supporting the tariff on May 7, 1890, laying out the basic argument of the protectionists for passage of the bill. McKinley asserted that the Welsh manufacturers were manipulating the price of tinplate to preserve their monopoly. The pioneer American mills had launched their operations in the early 1870s, when prices stood at $12 per box, but then the Welsh overproduced until the price collapsed to $4.50. At this price US manufacturers could not survive if they continued to pay the usual wages, and the mills were forced to shut down. No sooner had the Welsh manufacturers driven Americans from the market than they increased the price of tinplate. High prices again stimulated the market for tinplate in 1879, and American mills began to reopen, only to face falling prices once again, "under a flood of foreign importations."[66]

It was at that moment, McKinley declared, that the Welsh manufacturers "determined to strike a final and death blow" to the nascent American industry. To that end, representatives of the Welsh mills announced to American customers that, no matter what the price of the American product might be, they would sell for the equivalent of twenty-five cents less. Welsh tinplate makers, the Ohio member of Congress declared, had not forgotten the instruction of Lord Brougham before Parliament that the British manufacturer "can well afford to sell his product in the American market at a loss for a while, that he may thereby stifle American industries in their cradle."[67]

McKinley's argument for imposing a tariff to protect the infant tinplate industry was grounded more in nationalism and the demands of the manufacturers than sound economic theory. In the continuous struggle between the forces of protection and free trade, economists have generally sided with the free trade position that tariffs hurt rather than benefit the nation imposing them.[68] The impact of the McKinley tariff could only be determined by answering what economist Douglas A. Irwin refers to as "a counterfactual question about how an industry would have developed in absence of the tariff." Irwin's analysis, coming 110 years after the passage of the tariff, led him to conclude that "domestic tinplate production would have arisen about a decade later as U.S. iron and steel prices converged with those in Britain. Although the tariff accelerated the industry's development," Irwin argues, welfare calculations suggest that protection did not pass the cost-benefit test.[69]

Nevertheless, protectionists were in control, and the McKinley tariff bill passed the House and then the Senate with the assistance of a powerful ally, Senator Nelson W. Aldrich, a Republican leader and stalwart protectionist.

In arguing for passage of the bill in the Senate, Aldrich declared, "It is claimed that the Welsh people have such a peculiar aptitude for, or knowledge of, this manufacture as to make successful production elsewhere impossible. The imposition of this duty will transfer this industry from Wales to the United States, and furnish us with better and cheaper tin plate."[70] Voting along party lines, Congress approved the McKinley tariff in October 1890, and under the president's signature it went into effect on July 1, 1891. The clause relating to tinplate established a tariff of 2.2 cents per pound, but with a probationary period ending on October 1, 1897. By this date, US production must "equal one third the amount of such plates imported and entered for consumption during any fiscal year after the passage of this act and prior to October 1, 1897"; otherwise, tin plates would be admitted duty-free, a concession primarily to the American canning industry.[71]

At the end of the six-year probationary period established by the McKinley tariff of 1890, the United States was producing enough to meet nearly all of the domestic demand, and "the period of tutelage for the iron and steel industry was over," as the prominent contemporary economist Frank Taussig observed. "The extraordinary development of this industry during the period between 1870 and 1895," he wrote, "is one of the most remarkable chapters in the remarkable economic history of our century." The discovery of the vast Lake Superior iron ore range, the "feverish" development of coal deposits in Appalachia and the Midwest, and the rapid improvements in the nation's transportation system "revolutionized the conditions of production." Therefore, "among the forces which were at work in these industries, protective duties probably counted for much less than is often supposed," he wrote.[72]

By the mid-1890s the tinplate industry had taken firm root in the United States. The depression of 1893 lasted for several years and strained the infant American industry but did not significantly alter its trajectory of expansion. Ira Ayer's special reports to the US secretary of treasury for the fiscal year ending in June 1896 listed 74 firms engaged in the manufacture of tin- and terneplate. An additional 188 hot mills for rolling blackplate were either in operation or under construction, and the number of tinning sets in operation or under construction stood at 460.[73] The introduction of automatic machinery revolutionized the canning industry by improving production speed and safety, thereby increasing the demand for tinplate dramatically. Thereafter, investors and manufacturers of tin products became confident that the future would bring a major reduction in the costs of production.[74]

Impact of the McKinley Tariff in South Wales

Already entering a period of recession because of a domestic economic decline, the Welsh tinplate industry suffered a serious blow when the US Congress passed the McKinley tariff. The duty placed on US imports of Welsh tinplate increased its market price by 70 percent, forcing Welsh manufacturers to slash prices if they hoped to sell any of their product in the United States. By 1893 the price had fallen 27 percent from pre-tariff levels, and companies whose operations were inefficient, or on a weak financial foundation, became insolvent.[75]

Believing that this was just another temporary downturn in the cycle, tinplate manufacturers in Wales responded to the McKinley tariff by increasing production to build up the inventories of products for the American market during the nine months before the tinplate schedule went into effect. Then they closed their mills, and twenty thousand Welsh workers lost employment. A British trade journal reported that "the Americans have duly anticipated the state of things which has come about," and "their agents are now busily engaged in Wales in picking up good workmen, as well as in exporting machinery and appliances for tin-plate making."[76]

Welsh tinplate manufacturers, workers, and interested parties such as the press followed these developments in the United States with keen interest, and the Welsh newspapers were filled with letters, reports, and analyses of the American tinplate market. "The seven years following the imposition of the McKinley duty was one of intense and almost unrelieved depression in the tinplate industry" in Wales, wrote the contemporary economist J. H. Jones. However, he cautioned against the misimpression that the tariff sent the industry into an immediate tailspin or that the American industry "suddenly sprang into being." Only by the end of this period were Welsh manufacturers eliminated from its major market in America. Meanwhile, new markets increasingly opened to Welsh tinplate, gradually compensating for the loss of American buyers.[77]

Although the McKinley duty contributed to the depression in Wales, the intensity of that downturn also resulted from more general economic conditions affecting the industry. American demand for Welsh plates surged before the tariff went into effect in 1891, causing a natural drop in demand the following year. Manufacturers anticipated the decline and closed their plants to clear their inventory as prices fell. Also, the boom years had encouraged

Welsh tinplate manufacturers to overexpand by adding new mills and more employees. Demand and prices were slow to bounce back in the face of this overcapacity, and at least half of the workforce was idled. In response to an 1895 government inquiry into the causes of the depression, the mayor of Swansea, a principal center of the steel and tinplate trade in South Wales, explained that the industry was "at a perfect standstill, resulting in no less than 4,450 being out of employment; 2,000 labourers and hauliers are also out of employment by reason of the stoppage of the different works."[78] A significant consequence of this prolonged slowdown was the emigration of thousands of unemployed tinplaters to the United States, where they hoped to find a secure place in an expanding tinplate industry, an industry hyperstimulated in 1898 by vast orders for canned goods to feed troops during the Spanish-American War.[79]

As American confidence grew, Welsh self-confidence declined in equal measure. A Swansea newspaper declared in 1898 that the Welsh response to the American upstarts had been totally inadequate. While Wales bemoaned the decrease in the export of tinplate and the number of idle mills, the Americans continued to erect new mills and increase their production capacity, the writer complained, stating, "The only satisfaction we have, if such indeed it be, is that American mills are manned almost exclusively with Welsh workmen, among whom are many of the very best workmen ever brought up in Wales." In July 1898, the annual production of tinplate in the United States was estimated at 6.2 million boxes, and the average total consumption was 7 million boxes a year. Consequently, by the end of that year American production of tinplate would exceed consumption, "and therein lays [sic] a further danger to the Welsh trade." Once filling domestic demand, the Americans might begin exporting tinplate and trying "to elbow us out of markets that are now completely our own."[80]

When the Americans first began to manufacture tinplate, "it was prophesied in Wales that they would be a long time" in learning the secrets of the trade, the *Llanelly Mercury* observed. However, "that prophecy has been falsified to a remarkable degree, for it is now generally accepted in America that with improvements in machinery and methods" the cost of producing tinplate had been greatly reduced. In fact, the report continued, "the genius of the American people" was in designing improvements of this kind, and "it would not be in the least surprising in the near future to see an American tinplate manufactory established in Wales." It is certain, however, that "American tinplate makers have a great deal more to teach Welsh makers than they can possibly learn in any tinplate works in Wales."[81]

The timely and continuous communication between Welsh and American publications interested in the tinplate industry reveals the transnational nature of "Greater Alcania." For example, the *American Artisan*, a labor publication based in Chicago, carried a special column in which pertinent information from the British tinplate industry was shared with readers. The *American Artisan* reprinted an item in 1895 from the *British Trade Journal* complaining that "a great distress exists throughout South Wales," and the cause was not difficult to ascertain. "Factory after factory is closed" because the American trade had fallen off substantially, and America "threatens ultimately to do without the famous Welsh product" entirely. The only salvation for tinplate production in Wales was to develop new markets.[82] The next issue of the *American Artisan* carried an article from a special correspondent of Cardiff's *Weekly Mail* declaring that in 1891 between 500 and 600 mills were operating in Wales, but by mid-1895 that number had been reduced to 247. The correspondent blamed Welsh manufacturers for lacking a unified response to the American threat.[83]

Similarly, and again demonstrating the binary community of interests between Wales and America, the *American Manufacturer* carried a report on the iron and steel industry prepared by a regular British correspondent. The Pittsburgh-based *National Labor Tribune* occasionally reprinted his pieces if they were judged to be of interest to American readers. In February 1895, the British correspondent reported that the Welsh tinplate industry was getting worse by the day, and massive unemployment was "leading to a great deal of distress." Desperate workers were prepared to "break up their homes" and leave for America. The correspondent wrote that in that very week "in the Llanelli district alone 50 operatives will shortly take passage." He too was convinced that the Welsh makers would have to look to new markets, such as Canada, Australia, and France, although these markets "cut but a sorry figure in the aggregate when placed side by side in the United States."[84] The Llanelli newspaper warned in 1897 that "the Americans are hitting us harder than we expected. . . . Already our supremacy is affected, and worse is in store."[85]

Even though some tinplate interests in Wales recognized the disagreeable fact that they were being driven from the American market, many—probably most—persistently dismissed the prospect that neither the tariff nor American tinplate presented a direct threat to Welsh dominance of the trade. Most believed the cost of establishing plants would be prohibitive. As one Welsh commentator put it, "the difference between the cost of works and plant will be enormously against the Yankee and in favour of the Cymro."[86] Similarly, a Welsh newspaper received articles from the *Pittsburgh Dispatch* and the *Pittsburgh Leader* in the fall of 1890 providing an account of "some of our Swansea men in the States" visiting iron- and steelmasters in Pittsburgh to investigate the progress of the infant tinplate industry. At their hotel the delegation met with a "crowd of men" who had worked for them prior to immigrating to Pittsburgh. William Williams, one of the largest tinplate manufacturers of Swansea, received the most visitors. The question of the McKinley bill immediately arose, with a specific inquiry as to whether it would impact the tinplate makers in Wales, to which Williams responded that "it would not affect them in the least." The other Welsh masters were convinced the new tariff would not provide enough of a competitive advantage for the Americans. Williams and his colleagues were in complete agreement that tinplate could not be profitably made in America with a protective tariff of less than four cents a pound because the Americans lacked experience and confronted much higher costs for capital, raw materials, rents, and wages than their Welsh counterparts did.[87]

Ernest Trubshaw, president of the Llanelli Chamber of Commerce and managing partner of the Western Tin-Plate Works, was one of the Welsh masters visiting Pittsburgh with William Williams. Speaking at a meeting of the chamber, Trubshaw asserted that there was little evidence that reports of progress in American tinplate-making were trustworthy. Republican newspapers carried glowing reports of progress, he declared, "but they were not worthy of credence, as they were only manufactured for electioneering purposes." Trubshaw concluded that the Americans would attempt to make tinplate with more or less success, but he was convinced that "even if the duty was not repealed, Welsh manufacturers would resume their usual business with America." Trubshaw's closing remarks elicited a rousing chorus of cheers.[88]

J. H. Rogers, the managing partner in the firm of E. Morewood and Company, tinplate manufacturers of Llanelli, Swansea, and Gas City, Indiana, personified the transnational nature of the American-Welsh tinplate community. He returned to his country estate of Glyncoed near Llanelli in June 1895, and, when queried by a Llanelli reporter, he offered a more measured viewpoint, claiming that "it was too late to overtake the American market." On the other hand, Rogers also cautioned that it was "premature to say that any serious injury so far has been done to the tinplate trade in Wales by the progress of the industry in the States." He also doubted that the Americans had built enough capacity to meet all their needs and believed such claims were "enormously exaggerated," for a large proportion of tinplate used in America still came from Wales. The best course for Welsh manufacturers was to develop new markets abroad and, most important, to keep production and labor costs lower than in the United States.[89]

By 1897 the mood in the Welsh tinplate centers had turned more jaundiced. One South Wales observer laid the loss of the American trade directly at the door of corrupt Yankee politicians—an easy target in the Gilded Age. America's industrial, financial, and governmental foundations were "rotten to the core," he proclaimed. The great majority of legislators held "their seats by the most degrading form of bribery ever devised, and they have prostituted government into a machine that rules by black-mail."[90]

Emigration, Immigration, Repatriation

As the tinplate industry in Wales went into a serious decline, open letters to unemployed tinplaters who were waiting for their plants to reopen appeared in local newspapers, advising them to leave the industry. "Silurian" declared that "many years must elapse" before the industry would return to its former health, and the number of skilled men far exceeded the available positions. Therefore, it would be better "for some of the younger men to clear out and seek other occupations, even at lower wages, for it is better to have regular work at a smaller wage than a good wage one week and starvation the next."[91]

And leave they did, but most did not abandon the industry. Instead, they chose to go to the United States. The official organ of the tinplaters' union, the *Industrial World*, published in Swansea, reported in August 1895 a farewell meeting in Ammonford for two rollers. There was no need to state where the two men were heading because Welsh tinplaters (in Welsh, *Alcanwyr*) were "teeming towards the land of the West like cockles teem on Penclawdd beach." Most were leaving to find employment, but they had other motives as well. Some were going to teach their trade to the "Yankees," while others took their patents for new machinery that would produce tinplate cheaper and, "alas, show them the easiest way to steal the chief trade of South Wales."[92]

South Wales newspapers serving tinplate communities during the 1890s were filled with notices of Welsh tinplaters heading for the United States.[93] The Cunard Line agent for the Swansea district stated that he had booked "between 30 and 40 passages from this locality during August" 1898. A group of twelve, including women and children, left the Swansea train station for Liverpool, where they would embark for America, "owing to the depressed state of the tinplate trade." As the train pulled alongside the platform, the Swansea Cymmrodorion Male Voice Glee Society sang "Comrades in Arms."[94]

The editor of the *Industrial World* warned union members against immigrating to the United States. One of the more revealing of such cautionary articles published, it expressed alarm in May 1895 at seeing "the departure of sturdy, sober and industrious tinplaters" to either find employment or escape unfair labor conditions. "Scarcely a week passes without a group of friends being seen at various stations bidding good-bye to men who leave Wales to seek a better home in America," the editor wrote. These were not "the ne'er do wells that leave us, but the very cream of the tinplate industry." The only party that would benefit from "superfluous labor at tinplate mills and tinhouses will be the capitalist," that is, the same class in both America and Wales, who were "only concerned in grinding down the privileges and wages of their men." The editor wondered why skilled Welsh tinplaters would fall into this trap.[95] Warnings failed to stem the flow, however, and departures continued to the end of the decade.

South Wales newspapers also carried letters from Welsh in America warning their compatriots to stay at home. "Will you please oblige a good many Welshmen here (Ellwood, Indiana), and also at other places, by publishing in your well-known daily this warning note to tinplaters intending to come out here expecting to find work anywhere and everywhere they may go to in the States, or places where there are tinplate works?" pleaded a "Tinplater Who Knows" in Cardiff's *Western Mail* in October 1898. Tinplate works in the United States were "overcrowded," he reported, and winter in the States was much colder than in Wales, "so it will be better for them to suffer in Wales in winter than here." The writer also declared that, even though tinplate workers could earn higher wages, it was also true that it cost a good deal more to live in the States than in Wales, and the work was much harder than in the old country.[96]

The official organ of the Welsh tinplaters' union published a letter from a Welsh emigrant lamenting his failure to heed the union's advice not to "take his chances" in America. "From time to time we have done what we could to keep Welsh tinplaters from breaking up their homes on the chance of getting employment in the United States," the editor commented. "A number of men have left our shores whose friends and relatives in America had secured positions for them upon their arrival there." However, even these men did not find America "the land of happiness they had pictured to themselves." As for those who had emigrated and taken their chances on finding employment, "many of them today would only be too glad to get back to the old country if they had the means."[97]

Welsh tinplaters who failed to find work or conditions in America that suited their expectations often returned to Wales, although it is impossible to establish a firm number for repatriation. A major American strike began in October 1894 when American manufacturers announced a wage reduction of 25 to 30 percent. The news that plants would operate with non-union labor set the wheels in motion for those who would make the decision to return. As one Welsh worker observed, the idea that motivated the Welsh workers was "to make money and go home." If that goal was not achievable, then there was no reason to stay.[98] This suggests that a sizable percentage loosely referred to as immigrants were sojourners who came to America to earn money but had no intention of remaining permanently.

When the American manufacturers declared their intention to impose a steep reduction in wages in 1894, one worker identified only as "Alcan" concluded that the reduction was so sweeping that the inducements motivating Welsh to immigrate to the States had been removed, and he anticipated "a speedy return to this country" would be the result.[99] Other Welsh commentators echoed the sentiments of "Alcan."[100]

A Llanelli tinplater, James Evans, who had recently returned to Wales from America in January 1899, informed a reporter that he had returned because of the "bad state of trade" in the United States. Evans advised all tinplaters to stay at home or risk joining the "hundreds of tinplaters in America on the verge of starvation." Asked if he would return, Evans replied in the negative. In Pittsburgh, where he had been employed, he had met "several Llanellyites who used to live in nice, comfortable houses at home, but were now roughing it in veritable hovels and slums, and having to work with all sorts of conditions and people."[101] Evans's observation supports Matthew Carter's description of Welsh mill workers in Pittsburgh, where technology was displacing skilled men, who were then forced to compete with the unskilled southern and eastern Europeans for employment in Pittsburgh's steel industry.[102]

A Welsh correspondent for an Aberdare newspaper who had recently visited the United States declared that many tinplaters who had immigrated to America subsequently returned. He claimed the newly formed American Tin

Plate Company trust had stopped some works in order to operate others more cheaply. The workers were warned, he reminded his readers, not to rush to America "without assurances from friends of work. I feel sure by now it would have been a blessing for many of them, had they listened to this advice."[103]

Tinplate manufacturers in Wales, as well as the newspapers in the tinplate centers, attempted to entice Welsh sojourners back to Wales as early as 1894 by offering them inducements. "It has been known for some time that a very large proportion of tinplate workers in America, not finding the promises under which they were lured there realized, have been desirous of returning to the 'Old Country,'" reported a Cardiff newspaper. The article urged workers to come back home. Several of the Welsh employers reportedly offered "to provide preference places for any of the men who should return from America." The returnees would be committing a patriotic act by withdrawing their skills from the American competitors and putting them to good use in Wales to save their nation's principal industry.[104] The Welsh owners reasoned that it took a long time to train essential skilled workers, so, if a significant number of them returned to Wales, the American works would be "paralyzed."[105]

American employers were aware of these tactics their Welsh competitors employed to encourage the repatriation of Welsh tinplaters. They were also aware of their Welsh counterparts' hopes that America's ability to produce tinplate would thereby be crippled. Conversely, Americans insisted that skilled labor was no longer "entirely essential" to the successful operation of their mills because they believed skilled union men could be replaced with non-union unskilled workers. This had been the case in Pittsburgh in 1894, when unskilled men were trained and put to work as rollers, heaters, doublers, and shearers. Therefore, even though imported skilled workers played an important role in establishing the industry, American makers were no longer convinced that hiring skilled men was "an absolute necessity in tinplate manufacture."[106] The attitude of American manufacturers was confirmed by returning Welsh workers. As one of them remarked, "It's all nonsense to doubt whether the Americans will be able to manufacture their own tinplate or not in the future. They are doing so now, and what is more, their machinery is more modern than ours, and far better in every respect."[107]

David Davies of Morriston, who had been sojourning in America for three years, took issue with a report circulating in the city that claimed Morriston tinplaters had returned from America with "woeful tales" about the working conditions. The only object of that report, he declared, was to "create a false

Fig. 5.3. American eagle (representative of the US tinplate industry) vanquishing the British lion. Rutherford, *Romancing in Tin Plate*, 59.

impression in the minds of workmen in this country. All I can say is that I am very glad now that I left this country for America, and I may tell you that I am going back next Friday." Moreover, he continued, the only difference in the work was that in America they worked ten hours a day and in Wales they worked eight hours. "No, my opinion is that American workmen have no cause to grumble," he stated.[108] Nevertheless, it is likely that one-quarter to one-third of the Welsh who went out to America returned because they encountered difficulty in finding employment they considered acceptable.[109]

Despite the punitive effect of the McKinley tariff, the creation of new markets and the rapid expansion of the food-canning industry during the early twentieth century reversed the downward trend in the demand for Welsh tinplate. In 1905, 396 mills were in operation, but enhanced market opportunities boosted that number to 472 in 1912 and to 550 in 1914.[110] In 1890 Welsh mills produced approximately 700,000 tons of tinplate with 29,000 workers. By 1913 Welsh mills had managed to achieve the same level of production with only 21,000 workers, probably as the result of weeding out inefficient mills. Most of this new production capacity was for export.[111] The still-expanding demand for tinplate in Europe, the British West Indies, Australia, and other countries accelerated the industry's rebound in Wales after the loss of its American monopoly.

During this period there were twice as many producing firms in Wales as there were in the United States. In the States the trend was toward consolidation of production into fewer and fewer larger, more efficient plants, whereas in Wales the scattered and localized nature of the tinplate firms made it difficult to form large combinations. In both Wales and in the United

Fig. 5.4. "The 'British Despot' Beaten Again." Artwork by John S. Pughe, 1897.
Library of Congress.

States the quantities of tinplate manufactured were about the same in 1907, at slightly more than 500,000 tons, but the United States produced a similar quantity with 229 operating hot mills versus 390 in Wales. Welsh firms employed 20,000 employees compared with 18,000 in the United States. In 1912, the difference between the Welsh and the American industry was even more apparent. That year Wales produced 700,000 tons of tinplate in 466 hot mills whereas the United States produced 962,000 tons from 270 operating hot mills, even though both countries employed about 21,000 tinplate workers.[112]

The end of the Welsh tinplate monopoly and the brief period of competition for the American market ended with the American eagle vanquishing the British lion. However, Wales was able to reclaim its position as a dominant producer of iron, steel, and tinplate because Welsh metal products became more diversified and their distribution more global. With recovery of the home industry, there was little pressure on Welsh tinplaters to leave Wales for America, and the surge of exiting metalworkers came to an end.

6

The Rise of the Trusts and Decline of Greater Alcania

The decade of the 1890s marked the end of the Welsh tinplate monopoly as American manufacturers took control of the domestic market. In 1890 the United States was importing virtually its entire consumption of tinplate from Wales. A decade later, American producers had effectively driven the Welsh product from the US market.[1] To achieve this impressive reversal, manufacturers embraced new technology and labor-saving innovations, displaced high-cost skilled workers, and trained Americans or European immigrants to perform the less skilled work that remained.[2] The larger, technologically sophisticated plants required not only greater capital investment but also new organization and management structures conducive to the formation of the first corporations and behemoth trusts. Organized labor presented a final obstacle to these trends, and the trusts waged a relentless war against the Amalgamated Association of Iron, Steel, and Tinplate Workers, one that ended in 1910 with the union's demise. The ensuing non-union era in the steel industry eliminated the one last magnet attracting Welsh industrial workers to the United States and closed the final chapter on "Greater Alcania."

Welsh Methods, American Innovations

Almost immediately after the tinplate industry was established, Americans began to make changes to the processes and techniques imported from Wales. Most of these changes were intended to improve efficiency and, as was the case throughout the iron and steel industry, mechanize the processes previously controlled by skilled workers. In this way labor costs were reduced, and control of production was shifted to management. Americans developed few innovations in the tinplating process, but the cumulative result replaced the Welsh methods and put a distinctively American stamp on the production of tinplate. For example, in Wales blackplates would be rolled through two stands of hot rolls, one for roughing and another for finishing. In the United States one of these stands was eliminated, and each bar was rolled in a single stand. The rolls themselves were made larger and heavier to place greater pressure on the plates, which allowed manufacturers to dispense with the skilled tinners. Strong unions in Wales successfully opposed the introduction of these machines, but in America the tinners were not strong enough to resist the move.[3]

One tinplate manufacturer informed Ira Ayer, a special agent compiling a report on the industry for the Treasury Department in 1892, that his firm was "departing very largely from the beaten path of the Welsh manufacturers in the direction of improved machinery in the various operations of tin-plate making." W. C. Cronemeyer, president of the United States Iron and Tin Plate Manufacturing Company in Demmler, Pennsylvania, informed Ayer that the "inventive genius" of Americans had been unleashed by the McKinley tariff. As a consequence, he stated, within the next months machines would be constructed "which will facilitate the work to such an extent that very little skilled labor will be required to do the work." The result would free the American industry "of foreign labor, and will enable us to carry forward this industry without the necessity of importing skilled workmen from other countries," an obvious reference to the Welsh.[4] Some of these American innovations resulted from efforts of transplanted Welsh workers and managers. For example, a major advancement in the tinplating process was invented by a Welshman in Pittsburgh who "devised a new process of giving a uniform coating to tin-plates" by dipping a rack of plates into the tinning pot rather than using rollers.[5]

Similarly, the Welsh method connected the rolling mill with the doubling shear to double the packs of sheets so that the mill was continuously in operation. This system required a highly skilled shearer to insert the pack at exactly the right time. The American plan rearranged this process and powered the shear by a separate electric motor, which sidelined the doubling shear when not actually in operation and therefore did not require a highly skilled worker. Americans also sought to improve on older Welsh methods by initiating labor-saving techniques already in use by other manufacturers. The old method of placing boxes of plates in the annealing furnace on carts with roller-wheels required several workers but left them idle between charges. American managers improved this process and reduced labor costs by using cars on tracks, a method long employed in iron mills to reduce the number of workers required.[6]

Another form of change the Americans brought to the Welsh methods was simply to rearrange the process to be more efficient. For example, all machines were powered by one steam engine in Wales, but the Americans achieved greater flexibility by installing a separate power source for each phase of the production process. Sometimes machines were rearranged to avoid wasting time, labor, and materials or to initiate a system of "automatic continuous work."[7]

Redistributing the labor force was another adaptation of American manufacturers to achieve greater efficiency and production. This did not always mean a reduction in labor. For example, the hot-mill heater and doubler each were given an unskilled helper to do much of the routine labor; even with the extra men, output per worker increased.[8] As machines became larger and faster, workers with lesser skills could be employed to operate and maintain them even as worker productivity increased. Tinplate manufacturer William C. Cronemeyer testified that "the only result of the improved machinery has been to enable a man to produce perhaps 10 per cent more work than he did before we had the machinery."[9]

Some Welsh observers expressed resentment that Americans claimed innovations first made in Wales, but there is little doubt that innovations were more quickly accepted and efficiently used in the United States.[10] As one scholar has noted, "A Welsh emigrant would have recognized the machinery of an American mill in 1900, but he would have been a stranger to its arrangement and operation. Therein lay the contribution of American industrial technology to the manufacture of tin plate."[11]

American manufacturers no longer needed the Welsh workers, and

Fig. 6.1. LaBelle Nail Works, Wheeling, West Virginia, 1906. Reproduced by permission from Ohio County Public Library, Wheeling, West Virginia.

Cronemeyer even expressed dissatisfaction with the ones in his mills. "They know their business," he admitted, "but when you ask why they do a thing in a certain way they say, 'because my father did it, and my grandfather before him,' and therefore they think they have to do it the same way.'"[12] One company declared that "it was only a matter of honor on their part that they kept the Welshmen, as they got them for the purpose of starting the thing, but the American workmen were producing more from each mill."[13]

In the 1890s, when cut nails, manufactured primarily in the Wheeling, West Virginia, district, were quickly being displaced in the market by wire nail, iron mills shifted to tinplate manufacture. In 1893, the Aetna Standard Iron & Steel Company of Bridgeport, Ohio, across the river from Wheeling, became the first light-gauge sheet mill in the district to add tinning equipment. The LaBelle Iron Works of Wheeling erected a tin mill in 1895, the Laughlin Nail Company of Martins Ferry, Ohio, began to erect a new tin mill in 1894, and the Wheeling Corrugating Company in 1895 installed four stacks for tinning blackplate supplied by Whitaker Iron Company of Wheeling. Unlike newly built tinmill plants, former cut-nail works that converted to tinplate production tended to retain their former employees, so few Welsh were recruited to run these mills.[14]

The number of tinplate mills constructed during the 1890s increased steadily, but they were individual plants, not part of a geographic concentration such as those in the greater tristate district of the upper Ohio valley region. The first tinplate works built in the gas-belt district of Indiana, northeast of Indianapolis, tapped the seemingly limitless supply of natural gas to fire the furnaces of the Morewood Tin-Plate Manufacturing Company. This firm was owned by Edmund Morewood, a native of Wales who had invented the patent rolling of tin plates as they left the tinning pot. This innovative method submerged a pair of revolving rollers in a pot of hot grease, which spread the tin more evenly over the plates. This new system led to major improvements in the production process.[15] The McKinley tariff, as well as the precipitous decline of prices, placed the Welsh industry in the crosshairs of bankers, who refused financial assistance to firms in what they considered a fading industry. As a result, by 1898 many tinplate works had been forced to close, including Morewood's plant in Llanelli.[16] Perhaps Morewood anticipated the closures, because by 1892 he had already established the Morewood Tin-Plate Manufacturing Company in Elizabeth Port, New Jersey, and that same year had begun erecting another tinplate works, E. Morewood and Company, at Gas City, Indiana. Morewood decided that all foremen at his Gas City plant were to be Welsh, but, unlike other new plants in the district, all the other workers were to be Americans. [17]A general rumbling of disapproval ran through Llanelli when J. H. Rogers, Morewood's managing partner in Wales, permitted a "personal friend" of Representative McKinley to inspect the company's tinplate works, and some machines were removed for use in America.[18]

Morewood was soon joined in the gas belt by another Welsh owner, Jenkin W. Stanford, from Loughor, near Llanelli. He and his father had come to Elwood in 1891 to erect the first plant in the gas belt, and they were "among the first of that flood of tinplaters who have since invaded the States." In 1892, Stanford was president of the Indiana-Ohio Tin-Plate Manufacturing Company, which broke ground at Atlanta and Middletown, Indiana, for what was described as "the largest tin works in the United States."[19]

By 1895, J. Rhys Samuel, a skilled tinplater from Llanelli who was sojourning in the Welsh tinplate colonies of the United States, paused his travels for a time to work in the gas belt. Not only was he a skilled worker, he also authored *A Short History of Tin and the Tin Plate Trade*. Under his bardic name "Ut Prosim" (That I may serve), Samuel penned a series of articles about his visit for the major daily newspaper of Swansea. He found five tinplate works operating in the gas belt: Middleton (six mills), Montpelier (four mills), Gas City (eight mills), Elwood (sixteen mills), and Anderson (four mills). All of these plants were located within a radius of forty miles and connected by rail. Therefore, most of the Welsh employees of each works were acquainted with one another. Because of the reputation of Edmund Morewood among them, Gas City was considered the primary colony of the district's Welsh workers.[20] Samuel found many former acquaintances among the millworkers, but he provided no solid numbers for those who lived in these "Welsh colonies." Apparently, he never took a count, but he did observe that Elwood, where he took up residence and worked, contained "40 to 50 families, and is second only to Gas City as the American home of Welshmen."[21]

Rise of the Trusts

Almost from the inception of the industry, tinplate plants became captives of a large trust. The 1890s marked the dramatic ascent of corporate trusts, often portrayed by political cartoonists as corpulent men in frock coats and silk hats, pockets stuffed with money, and a foot on the neck of the common man. The cartoons summed up the way many thought about the trusts, but, according to a Wheeling steel producer and historian, the industrialists who organized the trusts regarded them quite differently. "The trust was American industry's answer to the problem of destructive competition," wrote Henry Dickerson Scott, relating that "American business had been a war to the death, marked by alternate periods of dizzy prosperity and of violent depression." Competition had been ruthless and fought with "a reckless disregard for ethics." Standard Oil of Ohio, organized by John D. Rockefeller in 1870, is generally recognized as the first combination of companies created with the intent to dominate an industry. Other industrialists looked to Standard Oil as the model for managing large business organizations, and other combinations began to appear, such as the Carnegie iron and steel interests. In 1900 Andrew Carnegie created the Carnegie Steel Company. This was not a general merger of competing firms but the consolidation of cooperating subsidiary companies into one large firm. It was a vertically integrated enterprise that acquired auxiliary facilities, from ore fields and coal and coke properties to railroads. By becoming completely self-sufficient and able to produce at lower costs than its competitors, the combination could gain a monopoly.[22]

The true trust, however, emerged as "competitors coming together in a friendly way and combining their interests while all were yet solvent."[23] The period of monopoly may be said to have begun in 1898, when the American Tin-Plate Company was formed. It dominated the industry until 1901, when it was absorbed into the United States Steel Corporation.[24] The 1890s marked the zenith of the much-reviled "trusts." This was a period of cut-throat competition in American business, and, in the interest of lowing costs, firms sought to become self-contained by acquiring other firms. Although many large firms were called trusts, actual trusts resulted when one company absorbed like firms in order to exert a dominant influence on the market. Such was the case with the American Tin-Plate Company, the "tinplate trust."

The nucleus of the nascent tinplate trust was the American Tin Plate Company of Elwood, Indiana, not to be confused with the short-lived company of that name established at Wellsville, Ohio, in 1873. With nineteen hot mills and forty-five tinning stacks fired by natural gas, it was one of the most important tinplate mills in the United States during this period. Some of the plant itself was physically shipped from Wales and set up in Elwood, and Welsh superintendent William Banfield assembled a group of compatriots to staff the works. The plant was completed in 1891, and the company held a huge McKinley Day celebration, with William McKinley himself the guest of honor. A group photograph showing "nine of the original old time Welsh boys" is preserved in Roy Rutherford's history of American tinplate.[25] Rutherford identified Banfield as a Cornishman, but "Cochfarf," a Cardiff city council member who knew Banfield, visited him when he was superintendent of the Follansbee Tin-Plate Works near Wheeling, West Virginia, and reported that Banfield was from Abertillery, Wales, and was "the father of the American tinplate trade." Cochfarf also noted that Banfield employed "about 200 Llanelly and Port Talbot men" at the works.[26] By 1898, the American Tin-Plate Company at Elwood was the most important tinplate plant in the country. A large number of Welsh worked at the operation, and all of the department heads were Welsh.[27]

Ferocious competition among American tinplate manufacturers in the late 1890s had resulted in cripplingly low prices, so two company owners, Daniel G. Reid and William B. Leeds, contacted "Judge" William H. Moore, who, in collaboration with his brother James H. Moore, had been the principal movers behind the organization of the National Biscuit Company and the Diamond Match Company. Together Reid, Leeds, and Judge Moore developed a plan to acquire the entire tinplate capacity in the country. Their strategy was to take a cash option on a plant. When negotiations were nearing completion, they suggested instead that payment be made in preferred stock of the new company with an incentive bonus of 100 percent in common stock.[28] The plan succeeded because confidence in the future of the tinplate industry and in the management of the new American Tin-Plate Company was very high. The first meeting of the original thirty-eight-firm combine took place on December 15, 1898 (see appendix 1).[29]

The American Tin-Plate Company was interested in acquiring only other tinplate mills, but Judge Moore and his associates next turned their attention to the steel mills that furnished the raw materials. Few of the earlier tinplate mills produced their own supply of sheet-bar. Consequently, in 1899 the National Steel Company was established using the same strategy and organization as American Tin-Plate by merging independent steelworks and bar mills. With the exception of the Carnegie interests and the Federal Steel Company, which had been organized in 1898 by Elbert H. Gary and financed by J. P. Morgan, National Steel acquired almost every important steelworks that manufactured semifinished steel products, such as slabs, billets, and sheet-bars. That same year, Moore and his associates put together the American Steel Hoop Company, a consolidation of nine firms that specialized in the manufacture of merchant bars, hoops, bands, cotton-bale ties, and small skelp—products that had become obsolete by the 1920s because of the development of the continuous strip mill.[30]

In 1900 Judge Moore also organized the American Sheet Steel Company by consolidating firms that operated 164 sheet mills producing blackplate and galvanized sheets. This company was subsequently combined with the American Sheet and Tin-Plate Company in 1903, following the creation of United States Steel Corporation in 1901. Other industrialists also caught the trust fever and were busy consolidating steel plants. John W. Gates organized the American Steel & Wire Company and bought most of the firms making rods, wire, wire fencing, and wire nails. With the financial backing of J. P. Morgan, E. C. Converse in 1899 promoted the consolidation of thirteen tube mills into the National Tube Company. Other major consolidations in the steel industry were the American Bridge Company and the Lake Superior Consolidated Iron Mines.[31]

The American steel industry was consolidated into ten large companies, each with scores of subsidiaries. They each exercised a near monopoly in their field of specialization, and yet each cooperated in order to gain the benefits of that monopoly. A conflict among these giant organizations would have been catastrophic. As long as no increase in steel-making capacity occurred, equilibrium was maintained, but that balance was disrupted when J. P. Morgan's National Tube Company decided to discontinue purchasing its steel and skelp from Carnegie and instead to establish its own mills. Carnegie then decided that if National Tube could produce semifinished steel, he would manufacture tubes and let it be known that he intended to build the largest tube mill in the world.[32]

A struggle between these two giants of the industry would have inflicted considerable damage on the steel business, so Morgan and Carnegie found a mutually advantageous solution in having Morgan buy the Carnegie Steel Company. Having added Carnegie Steel to his holdings in National Tube and Federal Steel Company, Morgan decided to go all in and acquire the seven other steel companies that remained. On February 25, 1901, Morgan consolidated these ten firms into the United States Steel Corporation, the largest corporation in the world (see appendix 2). Directed from afar by men with little knowledge or interest in the communities in which the plants were located, these new US Steel subsidiaries lost their local character. As Wheeling steel producer Henry Dickerson Scott observed, the local companies "became cogs in a big machine, a machine in which the cogs have to justify their existence by cold figures."[33]

In 1897 a new machine was introduced that automatically sealed and crimped the ends of a can to its body in a double seam. The new can, known as the "sanitary," or "double seamed" can, was more sanitary than its predecessors because it was soldered on the outside.[34] The improvements to the tin can brought a revolution in the preservation and distribution of food and dramatically increased the demand for tinplate. By this time food packers were abandoning the manufacture of their own cans, finding it cheaper and more efficient to purchase containers from a specialized manufacturer. This growing demand for tinned cans motivated the "big three," or the "tinplate kings"—Daniel G. Reid, William B. Leeds, and William H. "Judge" Moore, who had formed the American Tin-Plate Company—to consolidate one hundred producers into the American Can Company in 1901. A few years later, in 1904, the Continental Can Company was formed to pool management and equipment into fewer, larger companies. As in other segments of the steel industry, this amalgamation was organized in order to manage cut-throat competition that was undermining prices and profits.[35]

The period from 1908 to America's entry into World War I was one of expansion for tinplate producers generally, but the American Sheet and Tin-Plate Company experienced a decline in market share from 71 percent in 1908, to 50 percent in 1913, and to about 40 percent on the eve of the war. Nevertheless, business was growing fast enough to support reasonable profits for all, and, while there was still sometimes fierce competition, it was not ruinous, as it had been in the 1890s. Some large steel producers erected tinplate mills to enlarge the finished steel phase of their business. For example, Jones & Laughlin Steel Company, a large independent producer, erected a tin mill at its Aliquippa, Pennsylvania, works in 1909–1910, and a number of other steel companies soon followed suit.[36]

Tinplate production in the United States surpassed the million-ton mark in 1912. During World War I the primary concern American tinplate producers confronted was acquiring enough steel to roll and being able to import tin from overseas. Military uses of canned food for troops in Europe accelerated growth in the food-processing industry; "Food Will Win the War" became one of the slogans of the day. Tinplate production, including that of blackplate, reached an all-time high in 1917 of 1,958,000 net tons, and war demand pushed prices up from $3.20 per base box in December 1914 to $15.00 per base box or higher during the war years.[37]

Demise of the AAISTW

Following the Homestead Lockout of 1892, the Amalgamated Association of Iron and Steel Workers entered a long decline in membership as skilled workers were replaced by mechanization and other technological advancements and as smaller companies were consolidated into large corporations that dominated the industry. The union recognized that it could not win in a direct struggle with the US Steel Corporation, which was formed in

1901, so the union focused its attention away from basic steel to the less technologically advanced sheet and tinplate mills. Sheet steel and tinplate manufacturers still relied on skilled workers in the hot mills, as well as semiskilled labor in the tinhouse, and these workers were primarily Americans and immigrants from Wales and Great Britain. Although mechanical improvements were brought to the tinplate shops, these changes did not radically alter the processes already in use.[38]

The Welsh immigrants who established sheet and tinplate mills in the United States brought with them firmly entrenched work cultures. The heater, or furnaceman, needed to have an extensive knowledge of the heat treatment of metals, and the roller needed an extended period of learning and experience to make steel sheets a uniform thickness.[39] But the work processes in the tinhouse, where sheet steel received a tin coating, were more readily mechanized. In the 1890s, coating tin required the skills of an experienced worker, but a decade later the machine that passed tinned sheets through revolving rolls replaced not only the skilled hands but all hand labor other than for the initial feeding.[40]

The unskilled and semiskilled workers in the tinhouse remained unorganized. As their employment conditions declined, they met in Columbus, Ohio, in 1899, to organize the Tin Plate Workers' International Protective Association of America (TPWIPA). The AAISW had always been reserved for the skilled workers in the hot mills, specifically the puddlers, boilers, heaters, roll hands, nailers, hammermen, and helpers, but in 1877 the AAISW constitution had been written to include tinmen from the hot mills, as well as picklers, annealers, washmen, hot and cold straighteners, and shearmen. For unknown reasons, "tin" was not incorporated into the Amalgamated Association's full name until 1897.[41]

After the sheet and tinplate trusts merged into US Steel in 1901, the world's largest corporation continued to pressure the Amalgamated Association of Iron, Steel, and Tinplate Workers (AAISTW). Union officials tried to bring the companies into uniform contract compliance, but, when negotiations failed in July 1901, the sheet and tinplate workers went out on strike against US Steel. It did not last long.[42] The strike was brief, lasting only from August 10 to September 14, 1901. US Steel brought the union to its knees by sending contracts to non-union affiliates and by closing other plants until the workers signed individual, or "yellow-dog," contracts guaranteeing that they would not join the union. The final settlement forced upon the Amalgamated Association was one from which, according to historian David Brody, "the union never recovered." The AAISTW had grossly miscalculated the degree to which US Steel relied on skilled labor, as well as the corporation's "willingness to spend millions teaching greenhorns to become efficient steelworkers."[43]

The AAISTW lost the strike, but it had also lost representation at fifteen mills. Now there were ninety-six non-union mills and only seventy-one union mills. The Amalgamated Association's treasury was empty, and it had agreed that it would not even attempt to organize any of US Steel's plants that were non-union.[44] The future did not look promising. The workers also complained that the trust was extending the "Monessen system" of tinplate production to other plants. The Monessen tinplate plant opened in 1898 along the Monongahela River just outside Pittsburgh. Almost a year later it was acquired by the American Tin Plate Company, which installed the new design of continuous production of thin plates in hot rollers. Workers disliked the new system and complained that it resulted in a major reduction in wages, a decrease in the number of skilled rollers by one-half, and increases in the number of unskilled men employed in the plant.[45]

The Amalgamated Association continued to lose ground during the decade. It suffered another major blow in 1904, when the American Tin Plate Company and the American Sheet Steel Company merged to become the American Sheet and Tin-Plate Company and nearly the entire finishing side of the industry fell under one management. All of the tube works became non-union in 1907 and 1908.[46] Through it all the Amalgamated Association remained an exclusive craft union even as its crafts were in a death spiral. With the finishers from the steel mills now dominant in the union, it was the remaining puddlers who became frustrated with the inattention to their concerns. They broke away from the Amalgamated Association to reestablish the Sons of Vulcan.[47]

Financier J. P. Morgan and his US Steel associates fiercely resisted coming to terms with the AAISTW. "Big Steel's" strategy was to crush weak unions and accommodate strong ones.[48] US Steel made a strategic advance in its campaign against the Amalgamated Association on June 1, 1909, when it decided the union was weak enough that it could be crushed. Therefore, the corporation announced that after June 30 the remaining unionized tinplate mills would operate as open shops. In response, the Amalgamated Association's advisory board met in Pittsburgh on June 7. Walter Larkin,

Fig. 6.2. Amalgamated Association of Iron, Steel and Tinplate Workers of America officers, 1909. *Amalgamated Journal*, May 6, 1909.

the Welsh-born vice president of the tin division, and Llewellyn Lewis, the Welsh American vice president of the sheet division, were among those who attended. Upon their recommendation the Amalgamated Association met in convention in Pittsburgh on June 14 and concluded that the union's only recourse was to stop work after June 30, 1909.[49]

About 60 percent of members in the AAISTW tinplate division were organized, and they all complied with the strike order. The largest tinplate plants—those in Elwood, Indiana; New Castle and Sharon, Pennsylvania; Martins Ferry, Ohio; and Wheeling, West Virginia—stopped work on July 1; the tinplate strike was conducted for the most part in these mill towns. About one-third of the sheet steel mills were still union and they responded to the call, but two-thirds of them had been non-union since the strike of 1901. A total of about five thousand workers, approximately three thousand of them members of the TPWIPA (a third of those were women), were on strike out of the twenty-five thousand employed by the American Sheet and Tin-Plate Company.[50]

These events were followed closely in South Wales, and newspapers denounced the Welsh who did not support the strike. One union man in Swansea expressed regret that "a few of the old workers from South Wales were "traitors of their fellow-men in the strike" convulsing America.[51] Writing in the *Amalgamated Journal*, "Optimist" of Wheeling lamented those Welsh who were "arrayed against us their brothers" by aligning with the manufacturers in what he called a "war of extermination." Appealing to the "inherent characteristic love of the Cambrian for liberty," Optimist wondered what "true Welshman" did not feel "his blood surge up within him, and did not feel the shades of his ancestors come upon him and instill in him the old warlike spirit" when learning of the "tyrannical ultimatum" issued by US Steel.[52]

The giant US Steel Corporation set industry standards, and most of the independents, some of them very large firms such as Jones & Laughlin, joined the union-busting campaign by refusing to negotiate with the Amalgamated Association.[53] Consequently, the union declared a national organizing drive throughout all departments of the industry. P. J. McArdle, head of the AAISTW, urged all workers to join forces to create "a powerful organization for their mutual protection and welfare." He urged them "to forget that you are English, Irish, Welsh, Slavish, Polish, German, Croatian, Italian, or Hungarian" and to remember instead that they were all workers "with interests in common with, and inseparable from, those of all other workingmen."[54]

At the top of the list targeted for union organization were the mills at Apollo and Vandergrift, Pennsylvania, located along the Kiskiminetas River in Allegheny County, northeast of Pittsburgh. William Rogers, an English immigrant, purchased a local rolling mill in 1872 and converted it into a tinplate mill. In 1886, J. J. Vandergrift and several other investors joined forces to create the Apollo Iron and Steel Company. George McMurtry became managing partner in the firm. An Irish immigrant, McMurtry had been an executive with the Jones & Laughlin Company in Pittsburgh before going into the iron business for himself in 1880. He initiated plans for the expansion of the Apollo mill by replacing the iron puddling furnaces with two open-hearth furnaces to create a fully integrated steel mill. After passage of the McKinley tariff in 1890, McMurtry further increased the company's production capacity by building another plant just a few miles away at a new town called Vandergrift. With more than twenty-nine mills, Apollo Iron and Steel in Vandergrift became the largest sheet steel plant in the nation.[55] McMurtry sold the Apollo Iron and Steel Company to the American Tin-Plate Company in 1899. He then sold the new steel works in Vandergrift to the American Sheet Steel Company and became its first president. The latter company merged with the American Tin-Plate Company in 1903, and McMurtry became the first president of the new American Sheet and Tin-Plate Company, a subsidiary of US Steel, after 1901.[56]

In the early years, Apollo's owners relied on Welsh and English skilled workers. In 1880 there were twenty-one puddlers and rollers at the Apollo mill, slightly more than 80 percent of whom were Welsh or English immigrants who had arrived in the early 1870s. Like superintendents John Fritz of the Cambria Iron Works in Johnstown and Captain Bill Jones of the Edgar Thomson works in Braddock, Pennsylvania, McMurtry preferred to hire and train more malleable teenage farm boys from the surrounding countryside. Therefore, during the early years of tinplate production, English, Welsh, and native Pennsylvanians accounted for almost the entire workforce, but as the company expanded into Vandergrift and became an integrated steel plant, the composition changed. The open hearths depended on large numbers of unskilled laborers, and the new immigrants, particularly Greeks, Italians, and Russian-Lithuanians, filled the bill. As the number of Europeans swelled at Apollo Iron and Steel, the number of British workers shrank, although they continued to maintain their grip on the skilled positions. In 1910, more than half of the British immigrants in Vandergrift were skilled craft workers, compared to less than 10 percent of the new immigrants. Conversely, only 3 percent of the British worked as laborers, compared to 74 percent of Italians and 84 percent of Russian-Lithuanians.[57]

Llewellyn Lewis, of Martins Ferry, Ohio, was appointed to lead the AA-ISTW's organization of Apollo and Vandergrift. By 1909 Lewis had gained considerable experience as a union leader. He had served as an organizer by 1903, was active in the Ohio Valley Trade and Labor Assembly, and had been president of the Ohio Federation of Labor. Lewis, only thirty-four years of age during the 1909 strike, was vice president of the sheet division of the AAISTW. Lewis also had family with prominent connections to organized labor. His parents had emigrated from the Dowlais district of Wales in 1866, first to Pennsylvania and then to the Hocking Valley coalfield of southeastern Ohio. The oldest son, William T. Lewis, was born in Dowlais, entered the coal breaker at six, and went underground at nine. He was twenty-three in 1879 when his father died and he became the family's chief breadwinner. An ardent unionist, W.T. soon rose to become grand master of the Knights of Labor's National Trade Assembly 135 (coal miners). A trade unionist rather than a reformer, he led NTA 135 into a merger with the National Progressive Union of Miners and Mine Laborers (NPU) in an effort to organize all miners into one union. His action prompted some of his colleagues to mistrust him, so he left the NPU to facilitate the formation of the United Mine Workers of America (UMWA) in 1890. A self-educated man, W.T. studied law and took up that profession after his resignation. In 1892 Governor William McKinley appointed him Ohio labor commissioner, and he was reappointed in 1908.[58]

Thomas Llewellyn Lewis, W.T.'s younger brother by five years, also became a prominent leader of the coal miners. Born in Pennsylvania in 1866 shortly after his parents arrived from Wales, he entered the coal breaker in Luzerne County at age seven, and his father took him underground at age eleven. When the family moved to Ohio, he worked in the mine by day and attended school at night. T.L. also read law at night. He imbibed unionism from his father and older brother and served as a delegate to the founding convention of the UMWA in 1890. He rose through the ranks of union leadership and was elected UMWA president in 1909, a position he held until 1912. Like many union leaders of the period, T. L. Lewis went to work for industry when his tenure in office came to an end.[59]

Lesser known than older brothers William, Thomas, and Llewellyn, Isaac "Ike" Lewis became mayor of the city of Martins Ferry in 1909. After nearly two years in office, however, he abruptly resigned to "go back to the mill." During the 1910 steel strike, Ike Lewis and eight other Aetna mill strikers were arrested and indicted for attacking strikebreakers and "shooting with intent to kill." The court reduced the charges, and the defendants pleaded guilty to assault and battery and were fined fifty dollars each plus court costs.[60]

Llewellyn Lewis was therefore from a Welsh family that was a blend of reformist, bureaucratic, and radical convictions. When he arrived at

Vandergrift on July 9 to organize the workers, Llewellyn was met by several other union organizers who had been sent to assist George Evans, George Bender, and William Hilton with the drive. Initially, the workers were receptive to the organizers' overtures and eager to talk about joining the union, but when management threatened them with losing their jobs, they backed away from participating in the campaign. Fearing retaliation from the American Sheet and Tin-Plate Company, which had acquired the plant from Laughlin in 1899, property owners in Vandergrift would not rent the organizers a hall in which to hold meetings. The four organizers were also confronted by a mob led by two company security officers, named Steele and Dunn. According to an affidavit filed by Llewellyn Lewis, he "tried to point out to them that we were there for the purpose of discussing the question of organization, when I was struck alongside the head with a broom handle in the hands of Mr. Steele, Mr. Dunn smashing my glasses at the same time." Other members of the mob then assaulted the union organizers, and they were unceremoniously ushered to the train depot and ordered to leave town and never return.[61]

Robert Edwards, one of three Welsh-born brothers from Martins Ferry who served as organizers during the strike, remained in Vandergrift. Two weeks later, while Edwards was distributing union circulars, one of the company foremen confronted him. He was quickly surrounded and squired to the depot, where he was ordered to leave town on the next train and warned that if he returned he would be "taken out in a box."[62] Edwards went down the line as far as Apollo, where he managed to rent a vacant lot for a meeting on July 31, 1909. When the lot owner learned that Edwards intended to hold a union meeting, however, he attempted to return the rental fee. The organizer persisted, however, and went to the Apollo chief of police to request protection. Llewellyn Lewis presided over the meeting, apparently the first held in Apollo in fifteen years. The meeting went off without any serious problems, but back at the hotel the organizers received a visit from Oscar Lindquist, superintendent of the Vandergrift plant. He asked their business, and, when they replied that they were representatives of the AAISTW, Lindquist ordered them to leave within the hour or he would "burn the hotel down." A crowd of about two hundred had gathered outside, and the burgess of Apollo informed the organizers that he could not control the crowd if it turned into a mob. In order to avoid bloodshed, the organizers left town, their mission scuttled.[63]

Despite this setback, Llewellyn Lewis claimed there was a way to secure better treatment in the towns and cities where the union was trying to organize.[64] The plan called for recruiting 150 union men from Martins Ferry to parade through the streets of Vandergrift on Labor Day to demonstrate that they were not troublemakers, but the burgess of Vandergrift refused to grant a parade permit.[65]

The Tin Plate Workers' International Protective Association's contract expired on July 15, 1909, and they too joined the strike. Plants at Chester, West Virginia, and New Kensington and Demmler, Pennsylvania, where the AAISTW had no lodges, were brought to a standstill. Plants in New Castle and Sharon, Pennsylvania, in Elwood, Indiana, and three plants in the Wheeling district also walked out. A total of approximately three thousand tinhouse workers, or 90 percent of the TPWIPA membership, joined the stoppage.[66] The American Tinplate Company reported that 68 percent of its tinplate mills and 80 percent of its sheet mills were operating in October, but there had been "several brawls" and "shooting affrays" in New Castle.[67] Welsh newspapers still following the strike in February 1910 reported that twenty-six "Welsh-American women[,] mostly wives and relatives of tinplaters," had recently been arrested at New Castle, Pennsylvania, for their actions during the tinplate strike. "A number hail from Llanelli, Morriston, Aberavon, and Monmouthshire," *The Cambrian* reported. The women were charged with violating an injunction "by scaring and intimidating persons employed in the plants of the American Steel and Tinplate Co. The evidence given was to the effect that some of them threw snowballs at 'strikebreakers'" and "hustled them off the pavement."[68] Another Welsh newspaper reported that "many Llanelly men and women had been sent to prison because they dared to fight for the right to combine."[69]

In the industrial heartland of the upper Ohio watershed, New Castle, Pennsylvania, lay in the Shenango River valley about twenty miles east of Youngstown, Ohio, and forty miles north of Pittsburgh. That location was advantageous for the iron and steel industry. Limestone and clay deposits were nearby, and heavy transportation was readily available over the Baltimore and Ohio Railroad and the Erie and Ashtabula Division of the Pennsylvania Railroad, which intersected at New Castle. In 1880 it was a small manufacturing city of about 10,000 inhabitants dependent on four blast furnaces, two rolling mills, a wire-rod-and-nail mill, and two window-glass factories. Driven by growth of the tinplate industry, the population of New

Castle grew exponentially, by 244 percent, over the next two decades, catapulting to 36,280 in 1910.[70]

George Greer, a local businessman and farmer, took advantage of the McKinley tariff of 1890 to organize the New Castle Steel and Tin Plate Company, which went into production in 1893. Greer expanded his plant over several years, from eight mills to twenty. Each mill was a complete manufacturing unit within the plant complex. It employed fifteen hundred workers at peak production. Taking a cue from Greer, in 1898 the Shenango Valley Steel Company began production with a thirty-mill tinplate plant in New Castle that employed two thousand workers when operating at capacity. With fifty tinplate mills and thirty-five hundred employees, New Castle had the greatest concentration of tinplate production in the world and boasted that it was the "Tin Plate Capital of the World."[71]

Between 1890 and 1910, New Castle's workforce grew dramatically alongside tinplate production. The city had a mixed manufacturing economy, but metals dominated. The male workforce numbered 12,717, according to the 1910 census, with 7,309 (57 percent) of them employed in manufacturing and nearly 6,000 of them in some segment of the metal industries. By 1900 the 1,447 Welsh living in New Castle had become the city's largest ethnic group. The next largest group comprised 861 immigrants from England.[72]

By 1900, the steel trust had gained control of the tinplate plants. Three-quarters of the tinplate industry workforce was American-born, and one-quarter were foreign-born immigrants, most of whom were from Britain. Bart Richards's parents were born in Wales, and upon emigrating from their native land they initially settled in Pittsburgh, where Bart was born in 1893. His father was a heater "in any kind of a mill—sheet mill, bar mill, tin mill." When Bart was six years old, his father moved the family to New Castle and went to work at George Greer's Shenango Valley Steel plant, which became part of the American Sheet and Tin-Plate Company. Bart Richards grew up New Castle and remained there the rest of his life. As a youth he worked at the American Can Company plant during the summers. In 1920 he began his career as a reporter and editor with the *New Castle News* and, along the way, served in the 1928, 1929, and 1931 sessions of the Pennsylvania legislature. Historically conscious, Bart left an oral history interview that provides a valuable internal perspective on the local Welsh community and the strike of 1909–1910.[73]

Richards confirms some of the commonly accepted assertions about the Welsh migrants, observing that when the tinplate industry began in America, employers brought in Welsh workers to open and operate their new plants, and New Castle was no exception.[74] Also, these Welsh tinplaters were "pretty rock-headed" and "egotistical," Richards observed, and they thought "nobody but a Welshman could make tinplate," which he dismissed as a "silly idea." Like most Welsh migrants, those who came to New Castle chose to cluster together. Preferring to live near the plant, they settled together mostly on the south side. This part of the city became recognized as the Welsh community because "many were not too fluent in English," and they could attend one of the two Welsh churches where the sermons were delivered in the Welsh language.[75]

The native- and foreign-born population of New Castle was overwhelmingly of British origin in 1900, but, according to Richards, the following decade witnessed a change as southern and eastern European immigrants began to arrive. While the skilled Welsh clustered in the better, middle-class neighborhoods, the new immigrants congregated in the poorest neighborhoods, with Russians and Hungarians living in the Eighth Ward, while Italians lived in the Fifth Ward. Historian John Bodnar found that by 1900 two-thirds of the laborers in the mills were Italian, and a decade later 2,397 resident Italians constituted the city's largest ethnic group, followed closely by the Austrians, with 1,263. The 1,108 Welsh now comprised the third-largest ethnic group, followed by the English with 834, Russians with 719, Hungarians with 505, Germans with 491, and Irish with 449.[76]

The core of the workforce at the New Castle mills consisted, as elsewhere, of the skilled rollers, doublers, and heaters who controlled the process of tinplating steel until the 1930s, when the mills were finally fully mechanized. Therefore, the skilled men who originally held a near monopoly on these jobs bore surnames such as Llewellyn, Thomas, Jones, Richards, Williams, Jenkins, Lewis, Prichard, Hopkins, Davis, Price, and other "Welsh and Cymric names." According to Richards, the Welsh hot-mill workers brought with them "the traditions of strongly organized labor," and once in the United States they soon formed a branch of the Amalgamated Association.[77]

Bart Richards's perspective on the 1909–1910 strike is interesting because of his Welsh family connections. His father was a staunch union man. "I was raised in a union family," he reminisced, and in 1909 his father went out on strike. Although his father, for health reasons, was working in the blacksmith shop at the time rather than the hot mill, he went out on strike anyway because, as he said, "'I never scabbed in my life, and I'm not going to do it now.'"[78] Moreover, Walter Larkin, the AAISTW vice president in charge of the strike, was married to the sister of Richards's mother. "Uncle Larkin" was a millworker in Martins Ferry, Ohio, "a little short fellow," and "a typical Welshman." Richards also described Larkin as an "aggressive fellow" who had been engaged in union work long before 1909.[79]

Both of New Castle's Amalgamated Association locals had survived the 1901 strike, but by 1909 they had greatly diminished membership, with fewer than 30 percent of the workers having paid dues. Therefore, the AAISTW was woefully unprepared for a major showdown with the trust when the 1909 strike began. Nevertheless, on July 1, 1909, all but one of the fourteen hundred skilled workers scheduled for shifts in the hot mill walked out. Since the Tin Plate Workers' International Protective Association contract expired on July 15, the tinhouse workers also joined the walkout, bringing the total to three thousand New Castle tinplaters out on strike.[80] Nearly all of the three thousand national members of the TPWIPA joined the strike in July 1909; a thousand of them plied their trade in New Castle, one of the union's most redoubtable fortresses.[81]

During the struggle, the AAISTW's New Castle locals counterintuitively formed alliances with the Socialist Party and the Industrial Workers of the World (IWW), an unusual arrangement for a craft union, a left-wing political party, and a radical industrial union.[82] While the IWW and the Socialists were no more effective in countering the steel trust than the Amalgamated Association, the convergence of political radicals, the critique of capitalism, and loss of the strike had a powerful effect on local politics. "Some of the greatest radicals in the world" came to New Castle, Bart Richards recollected, and he was impressed with the ideas the Socialist Party representatives brought with them, as "most Welsh people were." "Big Bill" Haywood of the International Workers of the World, the Socialist Party's Eugene V. Debs, Kate Richards O'Hare, and Mother Jones (Mary Harris Jones) all came to New Castle.[83] Richards was proud that Welsh people, as a rule, were for "good reform." They were "not aggressive particularly," but "a lot of them" were "enamored of the socialist doctrine." Bart was uncertain whether his father was a socialist, but he did subscribe to radical publications, such as the *Appeal to Reason* and *Wilshire's Magazine*.[84]

The IWW coordinated the strike through the Pittsburgh–New Castle

Industrial Council. The plants were able to reopen, however, because an injunction prohibited strikers from interfering with the strikebreakers, because union leaders and pickets were jailed, and because too many of the skilled workers deserted the cause. Following the IWW's withdrawal, the Amalgamated Association conceded that the strike was effectively lost. The city elected a socialist mayor in 1911, and ten of the twenty-six city council members were socialist as well. The Socialist Party candidate for president in 1912, Eugene V. Debs, found considerable support in New Castle, as well as in other steel towns of the greater Pittsburgh district. However, the Socialist Party's political power was undercut by the national trend toward corporate economic and political dominance, and its ability to retain those early political gains evaporated.[85]

The AAISTW encountered similar problems when it attempted to prevent the American Sheet and Tin-Plate Company from restarting the large Aetna Standard mill in Aetnaville (Martins Ferry), Ohio. On December 1, 1909, the day shift came out of the plant and were met by a crowd of two hundred men protesting their decision to work on a non-union basis. The following night, about seven hundred people assembled near the plant, and when a trainload of non-union workers arrived, several shots were fired. That same night seven company guards disembarking from another train were met by hostile strikers, and further violence erupted. By December 4, three company guards and one striker had been wounded. Llewellyn Lewis charged the company guards with instigating the trouble.[86]

Meanwhile, the Belmont County sheriff wired the Ohio governor claiming that there were several hundred well-armed strikers picketing the plant, and there had been shooting. In the face of this challenge, the sheriff declared that he could no longer control the situation, and he urged the governor to send a thousand National Guard troops at once. The governor promptly complied, and the National Guard arrived in Martins Ferry on December 5. They immediately established machine-gun positions covering every street leading to the plant in order to prevent strikers from approaching the plant gates, but they encountered no disorderly conduct. Half of the troops were sent home on December 7 due to lack of activity, and on December 16, when the remaining guards pulled out of town, they donated their leftover rations to the strikers. The company also sent home the hired guards and once again closed the plant gates.[87] The county grand jury issued twenty-four indictments against strikers. Llewellyn Lewis, Walter Larkin, and David Jenkins, all of them Welsh, were indicted on felony counts of shooting with intent to kill or wound. They were acquitted, as were the others who were charged with assault and battery and rioting.[88]

The struggle in Martins Ferry produced a local martyr when, on March 14, 1910, Solomon "Sol" Edwards, a Welsh American picket, was shot by non-union bricklayer Emanuel Robinson, who lived in Martins Ferry and was returning from his job at the LaBelle works, located upriver in Steubenville. When Edwards and several other pickets confronted Robinson, he pulled a pistol and fatally wounded Edwards. He was rushed to the hospital, but he died two days later. Some five thousand people attended Edwards's funeral, including several Amalgamated Association officers. At the cemetery service Llewellyn Lewis eulogized Edwards as "a champion and defender of the rights of his fellowmen."[89] For his service in the British army in the Boer War, Sol Edwards had been awarded the Victoria Cross for valor. In death, the thirty-year-old martyr became a local hero of the labor movement. A monument was erected in the city's Riverview Cemetery bearing this inscription: "If I die, it will be fighting for a good cause. Greater love hath no man than this, he gave his life for his brother."[90] At his trial, Robinson testified that Edwards and the pickets had attacked him and that he had been struck by a blackjack before he pulled his pistol and fired. On his deathbed Edwards had verified Robinson's testimony, so the shooter was acquitted on grounds of self-defense.[91]

Sol was one of three Edwards brothers active as organizers among steelworkers during the 1909–1910 strike. Robert, as previously mentioned, was born in 1870, William R. "Bill" in 1875, and Sol in 1879. They and their siblings were all born in Neath, Glamorganshire, Wales, where their father, Robert, worked as an iron puddler. He immigrated to the United States in 1879, landed a job in the local mill in Martins Ferry, and brought over his wife and children in 1881. The Edwards boys were industrial unionists (they were members of the Industrial Ironworkers of America), but they formed an uneasy alliance with the Lewis brothers—Isaac "Ike" and Llewellyn, also of Martins Ferry—who were leaders in the craft-oriented AAISTW. All of the Edwards boys were radical union men. Bill Edwards spent years organizing steelworkers, and his son, Robert, became a union professional. According to Bill's son, the family lived in a house across the street from the Aetna Standard mill during the 1909 strike, and from their rooftop the strikers sniped at the guards and strikebreakers. Luckier than his brother

Sol, Bill escaped death at the hands of company guards while trying to organize workers at the Weirton Steel Corporation plant in Clarksburg, West Virginia. According to an eyewitness, Bill Edwards was captured and made to stand on a box with a noose around his neck. He pleaded with his captors for one last request, reportedly stating, "I want to see Old Glory up in front of me when I die." Bill declared that he had tried to enlist during the Spanish-American War but was told he had too many children. The company men decided that someone so patriotic should not be killed, however errant his ways. They released Bill but ordered him to get out of town. He still had to stay one step ahead of the law, however. A derby with his name inside the hatband was found with the body of a dead strike-breaker, presumably planted there by company guards, and Bill was forced to "skip" to Canada to avoid incarceration. Upon learning of Sol's death, Bill returned and was immediately apprehended but subsequently acquitted of the charges against him. When the International Workers of the World organizers arrived during the steel strike of 1919, Bill Edwards readily agreed to work with them, but the strike failed and the company blacklisted him, thus ending for good the labor organizing career of William R. Edwards.[92]

The American Federation of Labor (AFL) entered into the struggle on January 1, 1910, initially raising the strikers' morale, but the policy of both the AFL and the AAISTW to organize only skilled workers was counterproductive at a time when mechanization was transforming skilled into unskilled and semiskilled labor. Adhering strictly to the principles of craft unionism eliminated a large reservoir of potential reinforcements to the struggle, such as the members of the TPWIPA. Moreover, clinging to American racial norms, the AAISTW generally barred African Americans from membership by both rule and practice. Although the number of Black workers in the steel industry remained small until World War I, AAISTW policies restricted another potentially important source of support. In the final analysis, the Amalgamated Association was too weak to withstand the assault of the US Steel Corporation, which used all of the power at its disposal to force its employees back to work.[93]

It was clear by the spring of 1910 that support for the strike was losing steam. In April, US Steel granted a wage scale that was higher than the scale demanded by the Amalgamated Association.[94] Under increasing pressure, the AAISTW took a nationwide vote of its members on whether to continue the strike. By a vote of 942 to 548, workers cast their ballots to continue the strike, but slightly more than half of the vote to continue came from just one location—Elwood, Indiana. The lodges in Aetnaville, Martins Ferry, Sharon, and New Castle voted to end the strike, while the Wheeling lodge voted to continue the stoppage. The fact that only 1,490 members cast ballots indicated how few AAISTW members had remained steadfast and how many had gone to work at non-union mills.[95]

Recognizing defeat, the Amalgamated Association's executive board officially ended the strike on August 27, 1910. The AAISTW was a craft union founded primarily by Welsh and English puddlers and rollers during the heyday of the iron industry, but the importance of the iron crafts in the mechanized world of steelmaking had been seriously diminished. The iron craftsmen harkened back to the world of the artisan from which they had emerged, whereas the manufacture of steel that replaced iron looked toward the future world of industry driven by technology and scientific management. At the time of the 1909–1910 strike, US Steel employed close to 120,000 workers, and fewer than 8,000 of them were union members.[96] The AAISTW hoped to gain members from the tin and sheet mills, which still relied on skilled labor in some strategic positions, but US Steel was organized with the clear intention of eliminating skilled labor through technology and labor-saving machinery, an outcome the AAISTW was powerless to prevent. The end of the strike ushered in the non-union era in the steel industry, and the Amalgamated Association became a national union in name only. Conditions would not change until the depression of the 1930s, when powerful industry-wide unions, such as the United Steel Workers of America, were organized.

Leaders of the Amalgamated Association were late in realizing the extent to which the rise of steel had altered labor-management relations in the industry. Instead of organizing all who worked in and about the mills, as the industrial unions would, they clung to organization by craft to the very end. Llewellyn Lewis, vice president of the AAISTW's sheet division, became disillusioned as the craft unionists failed workers in a changing industry. "When officials of a great corporation are permitted to lead mobs against honest citizens; . . . when the state is so rotten under the control of the money power; when in all the space between abject submission and rebellion no place is given for appeal, argument or protest, what is the remedy?" Lewis asked. The answer was trade unionism and labor's political engagement in public policy making.[97] Lewis resigned from the AAISTW shortly after the strike, blaming both the union as well as the AFL for the failure of the 1909–1910 organizing drive and the strike. In parting, he declared that the AFL's policies were "antiquated and unfit for application to present day conditions. The policies of 25 years ago won't do for today. The world is moving and we must move onward with it or be left far behind."[98]

With the demise of the AAISTW and the displacement of skilled workers by technology, mechanical innovations, and scientific management, the iron and steel industry in the United States no longer offered much of a magnet for Welsh immigrants. Meanwhile, the recovery of the tinplate industry in Wales once again offered Welsh workers secure employment at home. The migration had been driven by the push of unemployment in Wales and the pull of a more secure economic future in the United States. With those forces neutralized, there was little reason for Welsh workers to pull up stakes and start anew in America.

7

Gender, Transnational Work Culture, and the Hetty Williams Affair

The domestic life of women in Pittsburgh's iron- and steelworker households was difficult at best. Childbearing and childrearing, cleaning house, washing clothes, and cooking meals in crowded, dirty mill neighborhoods while husbands worked up to eighty hours a week meant a life of endless drudgery. Women often compounded their burdens by taking in single mill workers as boarders to supplement the family income. Women very seldom found paid employment outside the home in Pittsburgh because, as social worker Margaret Byington observed in 1907, the production of steel was the principal employment in the city, and the industry "cannot use the work of women and children." In 1880 about 4 percent of the employed women did work for the steel mill companies, but they did so in menial, nonproduction jobs. Pittsburgh women employed outside of the home were most commonly working as servants (44 percent) and dressmakers (12 percent).[1]

Hetty Williams was an exception. A close examination of her personal story not only opens a window of understanding into the lives of Welsh women in the steel industry, as well as the broader transnational work culture of "Greater Alcania," but also, and most important, provides a rare private view of the central role of family in that experience.

Hetty Williams's Background

Hetty Williams reportedly was the first woman to gain employment in an American tinplate mill when she was hired as a sorter, or opener of tinplates, at Pittsburgh's Monongahela Tin Plate Works in April 1895. A Welsh immigrant, Williams had already gained considerable experience sorting tinplates in the Lewiston mill near Swansea, Wales, and the Monongahela works hired her to train other women. The chorus of opposition that arose from recently arrived Welsh tinplaters, even though they were accustomed to women being employed in the tinplate mills back in Wales, reveals the class and gender fault lines that fragmented the transnational culture created by the Welsh tinplate workers.

"Hatty" Williams, the name given her by a newspaper reporter and repeated by other newspapers thereafter, was born Hetty Ellen Evans (1864–1950) in New Quay, Cardiganshire, Wales, a fishing village that had become a shipbuilding community by the mid-nineteenth century. In 1871 she lived in a house overlooking the harbor along with her parents and ten siblings. Her father was a master tailor. By then, however, New Quay's shipbuilding days had come to an end, and by 1881 the family had migrated to Llangyfelach, near Morriston, where her father continued his trade as a tailor. Hetty, two sisters, and their brother Joshua were still living at home; the three girls were employed as sorters in the tinworks, while Joshua worked there as a "bundler."[2]

In 1883 Hetty married William Jenkins, a doubler in the tinworks, and in 1887 she gave birth to a son, David Richard Jenkins. Little is known about Hetty's first husband, but he died on January 6, 1891, at Parc Gwyllt, the Glamorgan Lunatic Asylum in Bridgend.[3] Why Hetty then left the security of home and family is unknown, but her decision was precipitous, for she and her son were aboard the RMS *Umbria* on their way to the United States on February 21, 1891. They arrived in New York on March 2, 1891, and, probably with the help of Welsh boarding and travel agents, made their way to Pittsburgh.[4] Again, the reason Hetty chose Pittsburgh is lost to us, but her brother Jenkin, a tailor like his father, had immigrated to Pittsburgh in 1886. Like most Welsh immigrants, Hetty would have relied on her brother to provide her with refuge while she reestablished her life in a new world. Her brother Joshua subsequently followed Jenkin and Hetty, immigrating in 1894 to become a roller in a Pittsburgh mill. One year later, in 1895, Hetty married Thomas Edward Williams (1861–1928), a "day laborer" who had crossed the Atlantic in 1881. Thomas was asthmatic and returned to Wales in 1895 to recover his health, according to newspaper accounts. His departure was the apparent reason Hetty returned to her earlier occupation of sorter in 1895, setting off a commotion among the tinplaters of Greater Alcania.[5]

Male resistance to Hetty's employment was anchored in the nineteenth-century ethos of female domesticity, the male breadwinner, and the family wage, but there were structural reasons as well. During the dramatic restructuring that accompanied the Industrial Revolution in Britain, new or radically reorganized and mechanized industries, such as railroading, deep mining, and basic iron- and steelworks, denied employment to women. The manufacture of tinplate, however, continued to rely on skilled hand-labor and did not undergo "modernization" until after the Great War. Women had been part of that workforce in Wales from an early period, although in strictly subordinate positions, and the pattern was continued without significant interruption into the twentieth century.[6]

When the tinplate industry was established in the United States during the 1890s, the Welsh immigrants recruited to operate the new mills found an opportunity to radically reconstruct the new workplace in accord with "modern" ideas about the proper roles for women. Therefore, the Hetty Williams episode offers an opportune moment for exploring the role of gender within the dynamics of tradition and change in a transnational industrial community. It demonstrates how gender ideologies and economic self-interest among tinplaters were bound together in the work culture the Welsh transplanted in the United States.

A Transnational Work Culture

The infant American tinplate industry was inextricably bound to its counterpart in Wales through transatlantic labor migrations, which ebbed and flowed with the boom-and-bust cycles of the British and American economies.[7] The US Industrial Commission reported in 1910 that three-quarters of Welsh-born iron- and steelworkers in the country had held jobs in that industry prior to immigration. Correspondingly, British historians have documented a pattern of migration and remigration between Wales and the United States paralleling the economic cycles of the tinplate industry, with Welsh workers leaving during hard times and returning when conditions improved.[8]

The broader transnational identity of "Greater Alcania" being forged by the labor migrations took root in Wales and the United States and became a common frame of reference.[9] *Industrial World*, the official organ of the South Wales Tinplate Workers' Union, reported that "the burning question in the ranks of Alcania today was emigration."[10] The concern was not just about the loss of workers. In 1903, an expert on the steel industry in Wales claimed that "Welshmen, with women and girls well trained," were migrating in large numbers to tinplate communities in Pennsylvania, where they were teaching the trade to Americans.[11] The Welsh tinplate families who immigrated to the United States represented an industry in which the social relations of production had been evolving for more than two hundred years. A firm control over craft knowledge and labor organization had become an established tradition among them. One authority observed that the strength of the industry in Wales "was due in great measure to the inherited skill of a tin-plate community."[12]

In Wales, women traditionally played a far more significant role in the industry than in the United States even though the line between male and female work was clearly defined and women were limited to jobs that required the lowest level of skill and paid the worst wages. Approximately 20 to 25 percent of the twenty-five thousand workers employed in the Welsh tinplate industry in 1890 were women. They formed the largest group of females in any industrial occupation in Wales in the late nineteenth and early twentieth centuries, and yet they have not been the focus of detailed study.[13] In Llanelli, known as "Tinopolis" at the turn of the twentieth century, women generally worked six days a week, from 6:00 a.m. to 2:00 p.m. The local economy was dominated by a multitude of small tinplate works, resulting in few employment alternatives beyond domestic service. Working-class girls were brought into the industry at about age fourteen. Although the tin mill offered an escape from the drudgery and isolation of the home, many women were less than thrilled with the prospect of life in a difficult job with low social status. Women who had worked in the tin mills during the 1930s left oral work histories similar to those of their mothers' generation. "Once you started as a tin-worker," one woman observed, "it was very difficult to get out because you were then sort of branded. . . . You had to remain one." Another female worker commented, "Slaver, they called us; another word for slave." Yet another declared that "tin working girls were looked down on." The class dimensions of this discrimination were readily

Fig. 7.1. Women workers, Kidwelly Tinplate Works, Wales, 1900. People's Collection, National Museum of Wales.

Fig. 7.2. Women workers, boxing department, Kidwelly Tinplate Works, 1930. People's Collection, National Museum of Wales.

apparent, but the women were also aware that their sex was another source of discrimination.[14]

During the Great War, the tin industry fell under the jurisdiction of Sir Edgar R. Jones, who served as controller of the Priority Department. He subsequently published a history of the tin industry in which he described women openers as "a vigorous class of their own." The work was hard, but attempts by social reformers to remove women from factories met with fierce resistance because generally there was no other employment for them in the villages.[15]

Although some felt socially stigmatized by their jobs in the industry, women tinplate workers emigrated from Britain only at the insistence of their husbands or out of dire necessity because otherwise they stood to become isolated and to lose the independence and camaraderie women found at work.[16] As a group, Welsh women were among the least likely to participate in Pittsburgh's labor force. Among Pittsburgh's eight major ethnic groups in 1880, Welsh women were sixth on that list, with a participation rate of 9.5 percent. Only the Italian (6.7 percent) and German (7.3 percent) women had lower rates. Interestingly, English women had the highest rate of participation, at 26.8 percent, followed by African American women (25.3 percent) and Irish women (17 percent). American women stood at 15.3 percent.[17] The most striking comparison is the labor-force participation rate of Welsh-born women in the United States (8.3 percent) in 1880 and Welsh-born women working in Wales (32.9 percent) in 1881. In Wales nearly 17 percent, or 3,984 of the 23,576 total tinplate workforce, were women sixteen and older. An additional 2,666, or 11.31 percent of the workers, were children under sixteen years of age; neither group was employed in Pittsburgh's steel mills.[18] This is an interesting distinction that reflects how work culture in the same industry in the United States evolved away from the older traditional norms in Wales and the United Kingdom.

There were also major differences in employment patterns in Wales and the United States at the turn of the twentieth century. Samples from both the 1861 and 1891 censuses of Morriston, where Hetty Williams lived and worked during her first marriage, support existing oral testimony that the vast majority of females in the Welsh tin mills were between the ages of fourteen and twenty-two (this age cohort typically left the mills after marriage); a small minority were older, single, or widowed women. The census returns do not record the workplaces of the girls or their fathers, but anecdotal evidence suggests they probably were not employed in the same mills as their daughters. The full implications of this pattern are worthy of further research but beyond the scope of this project.[19]

The introduction of new machinery, such as tinning and polishing machines to replace the women who performed these jobs by hand, met with great resistance not just from the women but also from the men. In his history of the industry, Donald E. Dunbar declared that this resulted from the fact that tinplate workers were "by nature conservative and oppose anything that savours of novelty. Even today [1915], they oppose innovations and sometimes refuse to cooperate with them, until manufacturers have to return to old methods."[20] But Dunbar missed an important point. The men were organized by skill, and they opposed the introduction of machinery that would have eliminated the unskilled jobs held by women as the thin edge of a wedge that threatened their control of the production process. On the other hand, manufacturers were too small, disorganized, and undercapitalized to challenge the workers' unions.

There were also structural reasons for the relatively conservative work relations within the Welsh tinplate industry. A major scholar of British tinplate claimed that well into the twentieth century tinplating exhibited the features of an "immature" industry: workers were engaged and paid monthly; wages were determined by custom and individual bargaining; some wages were paid in kind; conditions of employment varied from one workplace to another; and the relationship between owners and workers generally was personal and paternal. Ellen Jordan and others have shown that once work practices become industrial traditions, it is very difficult to change them. This seems to have been the case in Welsh tinplate.[21] Therefore, the employment of women in Wales continued because male workers and owners were reluctant to initiate changes they could not control.

By contrast, women and children played a far less significant role in the new US tinplate industry that the Welsh helped to create. Only 63 women and 308 children were employed in the US blackplate (unfinished) branch of the industry in 1899, and 625 women and 32 children were employed in dipping. Together, those workers represented less than 7 percent of the industry's total workforce. In finished tinplate, in whose manufacture female workers were common in Wales, their relative number and percentages in the United States quickly declined from 625 (17 percent) in 1899 to 495 (9.2 percent) in 1909. Whereas tinplate workers resisted attempts by mill owners in Wales to mechanize the least skilled processes of tinning, cleaning, and polishing, US manufacturers actively curtailed the influence of the Amalgamated Association of Iron, Steel, and Tin Workers on labor policy. The union had gained strength with the arrival of Welsh tinplaters in the 1890s, but it was greatly diminished after losing major strikes between 1892 and 1910. According to Dunbar, it was the attempt of the Welsh "to restrict output and to define working conditions" (i.e., to transplant their work culture from Wales) "that prejudiced American manufacturers against them."[22] W. E. Minchinton and Rowland Tappan Berthoff show that by the late 1890s American owners regarded Welsh workers as too troublesome because of their traditions.[23] American mill owners, therefore, were quick to substitute machinery for labor in these less skilled positions where women were concentrated. The few women who remained in 1910 generally worked in the packing room.[24]

In Wales, skilled tin mill operatives lacked the power to exclude women, but in the United States it was a different story. Wage rates were generally two to three times higher in American mills than in Wales even though the tinplaters lacked negotiating power with the owners. American manufacturers were willing to pay much higher wages because they were not hampered by the labor customs of Wales, which gave control to the key men in the production process, and because the productivity of American mills was so much higher as a result of the willingness of owners to adopt the most modern technology, which US tinplate workers were powerless to resist. Consequently, experts on the tinplate industry estimated that the American mills were about three times more productive than their Welsh counterparts even though labor costs were higher.[25]

Skilled Welsh tinplaters in the United States often realized their dream of rising into the middle class and could therefore afford to exclude women from the workforce—one of the key demarcation lines between the working class and the middle class. With the elevation in socioeconomic status came the concomitant social anxieties generated by the Victorian concern for "respectability," particularly regarding gender roles. Like other class-conscious Victorians, Welsh immigrants fretted over a "deterioration" of moral standards and the "awful danger" presented by the "tendency in today's women to neglect and despise the office that belongs to them especially, that of keeping house," one commentator wrote. Participation in the public sphere could only be countenanced, he declared, where women's work was of the most impeccably respectable nature. In the Welsh American press, which dogmatically espoused respectability and the cult of domesticity, the employment of women in the South Wales tinplate industry was cited as evidence of the moral and social chaos into which the fatherland had descended.[26] A group of British ironmasters visiting the United States in 1890 observed that many upright Welsh Americans were distressed by "their womenfolk's novel forwardness." Gone were the days when Welsh women were content to wait for their men "outside about the windows of the hotel [pub] nursing in shawls their rosy Cymric offspring in the true Cymric fashion," lamented one of their informants.[27] It is not surprising then that the hiring of Hetty Williams would prove so distasteful to Welsh men.

Gender Segmentation and Hetty's "Shame"

The Monongahela Tin Plate Company, which hired Hetty Williams, was chartered in 1894 by Henry William Oliver, who, after Andrew Carnegie and Benjamin F. Jones of Jones & Laughlin Company, was the third most powerful iron and steel manufacturer in Pittsburgh. It was an inauspicious time to go into the tinplate business. The McKinley tariff of 1890 stimulated the American tinplate industry, but the economy suffered a sharp downturn during the depression of 1893 to 1897.[28] Confronted with the depression and his ill-timed investment, Oliver must have been under intense pressure to reduce costs when he hired Hetty to train women for the mill's sorting department. Oliver was already accustomed to using women workers; one-third of the employees at the Oliver Iron and Steel Company's nut-and-bolt factory, located next to the tinplate mill, were women. Primarily Poles and Hungarians, they worked at machines, their clothing dripping with grease and lubricating fluid. Oliver's son, David B., was rebuked in the *Pittsburgh Leader* in 1912 for his part in amassing the family fortune on the "bent backs, [of] sickly children, [and] suffering mothers" and women who were "cut down when they should have been enjoying the glories of young womanhood."[29]

Although women had toiled in difficult and dirty jobs in Pittsburgh before Hetty Williams appeared on the scene in 1895, they had not been employed in the American tinplate industry. The social conventions being flouted by Hetty Williams were embedded in the headlines of the *Pittsburgh Commercial Gazette*, the daily newspaper that broke the story: "Women in Mills. Strange Innovation at the Monongahela Tin Plate Plant. Welsh Custom Introduced. Mrs. Williams Took Her Husband's Place at Work. Now She Is Teaching Girls." The article stated that women were "employed by the hundreds in the tin plate mills of Wales, and it is the intention of the operators to introduce the same custom in this country[;] . . . the male employees fear they will soon be supplanted entirely."[30]

The *Pittsburgh Commercial Gazette*'s interview with Hetty Williams provided most of what little was known about her for a long time. From his personal contact with his interview subject, the reporter described her as "a young Welsh woman" and "the first woman in America" to be employed in the tinplate industry. "She is short, heavy set, rather good looking and looks capable of taking care of herself," he wrote. Although Hetty and her husband had been in the United States for some time, she had not worked outside of the home. Her husband was described as a laborer earning $1.20 a day, "when he is able to toil." Because Hetty's husband was frequently unemployed and earned a very low wage when he did find work, their savings apparently were too meager to support Hetty during her husband's return to Wales. Her motive for entering the Monongahela Tin Plate Works was practical in nature: "I worked ten years in a tin plate mill in Lewistown, near Swansea, Wales, and can do any work they put me at in the mill. My husband is sick with asthma, and he is soon going to Wales for his health." Since she could not accompany him, she decided to take a job in his absence. Therefore, "I went to Mr. Thompson, the foreman, two weeks ago, and asked him to give me a position and he did so."[31]

Williams was proud of her skills and the importance of teaching the occupation to other women. "The boys who had been engaged at the work were not doing it right," she asserted, and as a result a large number of plates had been spoiled. "My work is to open the plates," she declared. "I have five girls under my instruction at present, and will put three more to work next week." When asked how much the women were paid and how many of the iron plates they handled each day, she replied, "We work piece work and are paid .83 cents a turn. I could do three turns a day, but am kept busy part of the day teaching the new girls, so I am only doing about two turns. We work on an average eight hours a day. None of the girls are working at night." Regarding the reporter's question about the fate of the young men "whose positions you took," she replied, "They were put at other work, as there is a great demand for experienced men in the mill. The men were angry at me for doing the work, but I did not care, as long as the work is honest. I do not intend to work at the business long, probably for a year." Asked to compare American women with Welsh women in learning the work, she observed, "Each turn runs about 5,200 to 6,000 pounds. We have to pound the plates and use two hangers to open the plates, and the work is very heavy. Only a small percentage of the girls who apply are capable of doing the work. American women are not as strong as Welsh women." Nevertheless, she declared, "American girls are very bright and accommodating, and they do anything I tell them to. Girls will be put to work to do all the opening as soon as we can teach them."[32]

Hetty Williams was keenly aware of her newfound notoriety and told the reporter, "When I started to work[,] hundreds of people gathered around me to see me as it was quite a curiosity to see a woman in a tin plate mill." Like the parliamentary commissioners in nineteenth-century Britain who investigated the conditions of industrial employment for women and children, the *Pittsburgh Commercial Gazette* reporter expressed surprise upon visiting her home and discovering that she still found the time "to attend to her household duties" in addition to working in the mill. He proclaimed that "the neatness of the home proved that this part of her work was not neglected." The *Commercial Gazette* also reported an interview with several of the male employees at the mill, one of whom expressed his belief that "the tinplate mill is no place for women to work, even though they do it in Wales," and, while there was "no organized movement to stop this encroachment yet, trouble can be looked for when the attempt is made to introduce women wholesale into the mill."[33]

"Trouble" was averted because no such attempt was ever made, but even the prospect of women entering into the American steel mills stirred up a storm of controversy. The transnational culture of the American tinplate industry in the 1890s is evident in how integrated the reactions were among male tinplaters in the United States and Wales that mill work degraded women. *The Bulletin* newspaper in Philadelphia exclaimed that the employment of women in the metal industries "has always been one of the deepest disgraces of England's industrial policy. If it is to be adopted here we shall be paying a very heavy price for our manufacturing supremacy. We cannot afford the moral and social degeneracy which accompanies the degradation of women."[34]

The editor of the *National Labor Tribune*, the official organ of the Amalgamated Association of Iron, Steel, and Tin Workers, noted that numerous American newspapers had expressed "condemnation in no qualified terms of the introduction of what is considered to be a deplorable Welsh custom into America."[35] One correspondent, "Populist," found his sense of decency assaulted when he witnessed girls wearing the coarse canvas aprons and leather gloves of the sorters and polishers while "toiling in a stifling heat under the same roof . . . and in the midst of two or three hundred men in an atmosphere that was reeking with smoke, gas and profanity, with none of the privacy, that we could see, that is so essential to the delicacy of womanhood."[36] An editorial in Philadelphia's *Public Ledger* newspaper postulated that "we had much better import our tin than import the European custom of reducing women to the unwomanly work of the tin plate mills."[37]

The most frequently expressed fear among the male correspondents was the potential for losing jobs to women. A reporter from the *Pittsburgh Commercial Gazette* who interviewed workers at the Monongahela Tin Plate Works found that all of them expressed the opinion that the employment of female workers would soon lead to a cut in wages because "women cannot resist their employers like men."[38]

Commentators decried the company's policy as one motivated solely by greed. They were convinced that the company would force women to work for less than men and use them to drive down wages throughout the industry. Writing in the *National Labor Tribune*, "Populist" opined that workers' minds become callused by the "constant turmoil and strife going on between rich and poor," but the prospect of employing women in the tin mills "ought to spur on every man with [a] love of justice in his heart . . . to vote down a system that drives women to work in a rolling mill. This is a damnable blot on civilization, a fitting analogy to the overshadowing curse—monopoly—that stops at nothing to satisfy its insatiable greed."[39]

At the other end of Pennsylvania, Philadelphia's *Public Ledger* acquiesced in the general view that the introduction of women into the mills would not only degrade women but also lead to "a reduction of wages as it is almost the universal rule that the woman worker is paid less than the man for doing the same task."[40] A correspondent writing to the *National Labor Tribune* called the employment of women the "entering wedge" for the industry as a whole because employers were "too ruthlessly engaged in competition for dirty dollars" to miss the opportunity to cut the workers' wages. The writer noted that women were not in the skilled jobs yet, but he believed that time was not long in coming.[41] Another correspondent observed that Hetty Williams was not to blame so much as the girls she was training as sorters. She "only took the place of a boy, and earns the wages of a boy, but those girl 'assorters' take the place of a man and work for the wages of a boy—one dollar per day. Talk about scabs, why those girl 'sorters' are the scabs of the scabs."[42]

The most vituperative condemnation was written by a Welsh tinplate worker in Pittsburgh using the pen name "Vox Populi." Although he did not declare himself to be Welsh, internal evidence demonstrates otherwise. Vox Populi's commentary was written in Welsh and published in *Y Drych*, the prominent Welsh-American newspaper. The article was headlined, "A Shame on Our Nation. Women in the Tin Plate Mills. Dirty Work Regarding Tin Plate Manufacturing in Pittsburgh. Welsh Tin Platers Being Deceived—Too Many of Them in the Country Already."[43] Vox Populi's broadest recrimination against Hetty Williams is signaled in the article's primary headline, "A Shame on Our Nation" (i.e., the Welsh nation); he condemns her for being the first person to commit the "unworthy act" of introducing "old customs" from the "land of our fathers that do not reflect much honour on us as a nation."[44] Further, "Vox Populi" charged that, while poverty and a lack of opportunity justified female labor in the tinplate mills of Wales, conditions in American industry did not justify the employment of women. Voicing the nearly universal male opinion of the day, he declared that if Hetty Williams needed to work outside the home, Pittsburgh offered plenty of jobs that were more "compatible with [her] sex, and fully honourable in the eyes of the world."[45] Finally, like his coworkers, the author feared that other women would soon follow Hetty Williams's lead not just into the Monongahela works but into other tinplate mills as well. The substitution of women for men would result in lower wages throughout the industry, and the result was certain to be disastrous for the industry's male workforce.[46]

The transnational culture binding Welsh and Welsh American tinplate workers is illustrated in the extensive exchange of information about the trade and its workers through informal correspondence between family and friends, as well as ethnic communication networks maintained by newspapers and periodicals. But tinplaters, like other workers, found it difficult to maintain a transnational work culture in the United States, and the Welsh response to the Hetty Williams affair illustrates the lines of fragmentation within that culture when issues of economic self-interest and gender arose. The market for tinplate declined during the depression of the mid-1890s, for example, and the Welsh tinplaters did their level best to discourage their Welsh comrades from emigrating (see chapter 5). If the sentiments expressed by the editors and correspondents published in the labor newspapers is any guide,

Welsh-born tinplate workers in the United States joined their native-born colleagues in supporting a high tariff on imported tinplate even as workers in Wales supported free trade and the elimination of the high tariffs that so negatively impacted their industry. Although Welsh nationalists might have abhorred this apostasy, Welsh industrial migrants in America were, as Welsh historian Dai Smith has suggested, busy surviving in the daily world of work rather than upholding the purity of their Welsh identity.[47]

Like their colleagues in the United States, tinplaters in Wales voiced nearly unanimous opposition to the employment of women in the American tinplate mills. The controversy ignited by Hetty Williams refocused the attention of Welshmen on the working conditions of women in the mills of South Wales and their ineffective unionizing efforts. Earlier attempts to exclude women had failed. For example, in 1890, the male Welsh workers at the Yspitty tinworks near Loughor went on strike demanding the dismissal of six newly hired female "assorters." The company refused, and the stoppage dragged on until 1891, when the works closed.[48] Reexamining the issue, however, resulted in the reaffirmation of the Welsh tinplaters' commitment to at least the ideal of female domesticity. The *Industrial World* clearly revealed this ideological commitment in regular columns such as "Home and Household" and "Domestic Hints," which were devoted to advising housewives on such topics as cooking, marriage, and hygiene. One column advised women that "it is not expedient to kill a husband with daily reports on domestic troubles" after he comes home from a hard day's work in the mill.[49] Rarely did anything else appear in the pages of the *Industrial World* relating to women and certainly not anything written by women.

Tinplaters of "Greater Alcania" expressed general agreement with a correspondent to the *Industrial World* who asserted that low wages were an excuse for using women in the industrial plants of Wales but not in American ones.[50] Another writer declared that in Wales tin men were indifferent to "girl labor," but it was in "the true interest of workers to remove them altogether."[51] Another Swansea newspaper, the *South Wales Daily Post*, announced that, since "it is the ambition of every trade in America to rise above their level in Great Britain and Europe generally," Hetty Williams's action was "a serious step towards lowering that trade to the lowest depths."[52] This sentiment was freely repeated in the community in numerous newspapers throughout Greater Alcania that picked up the Hetty Williams story.[53]

The views expressed in the labor newspapers disproportionately represented those of the skilled Welsh tinplaters, and no doubt their attitude toward women in the mills represented an ideal that some unskilled tinplate families who depended on the contribution of girls and women could ill afford. As one article in the *Industrial World* reported, "These girls are generally sisters and daughters of tinplaters, and though they may be rather ready with a flippant answer, they keep themselves in a most respectable manner."[54] Men may have regarded conditions in the Welsh mills, such as inadequate sanitation and eating facilities, as degrading to women, but they did little to change them. Occasionally the women went on strike, but the unions did not come to their aid, and women remained unorganized.[55]

Economic self-interest was scarcely concealed in the male response to Hetty Williams's so-called "treachery." One Welsh tinplater in Pittsburgh painted in light tones the darker fears of an ultimate role reversal that he believed was threatening the very foundation of the male workers' identity. His poem, which was printed in the *Industrial World* out of Swansea "through the courtesy of a valued correspondent," is a parody of the Welsh song "All through the Night." The following is an excerpt:

Girl Labour at American Tin-Plate Works

Pretty maids from the Vale of Swansea,
All through the day,
Down at Oliver's new tin factory,
All through the day,
Toil 'mid din of rolls and spindles,
Sorting tin in sheets like shingles
And surprise most all the peoples,
All through the day. . . .

Wife in the tin mill among the grease pots,
All through the day,
Husband home among the cook pots,
All through the day
Baby yelling, almost frantic,
For a dose of paregoric,
Or something to cure the colic,
All through the day.

"Hush-a-bye-baby, hush-a-bye-baby,"
All through the day,
Sings the faithful, loving daddy
All through the day;
But he is in great dilemma,
Because the "kid" shouts for its mamma,
And won't heed the voice of papa,
All through the day.[56]

The "Male Breadwinner" and "Family Wage" Ethos

Although job protection was the most obvious motive behind tinplaters' opposition to the employment of women at the Monongahela Tin Plate Company works, these male workers expressed their displeasure in overtly sexist terms. Both Welsh and American male tinplate workers defined Hetty Williams's employment as a gender issue rather than a working-class issue. By the 1890s it had already become conventional in Britain to think of these gender divisions as an old tradition when in fact they represented a new "tradition" rooted in the Victorian cult of domesticity and in two powerful and interrelated working-class ideals: the "male breadwinner" and the "living" or "family" wage.[57] The dramatic growth of industrial capitalism with its concentration of capital and production into ever larger-scale facilities dissolved the old household and cottage industry economy in which women had played a central role as producers. As the nineteenth century unfolded, the definition of a "producer" evolved into one who left the home and family unit to work in a factory for wages.[58] The male breadwinner and family wage ideals established as a middle-class standard that the earnings of male workers should be sufficient to support a dependent wife and children. This ideology and its applications have been thoroughly studied in Britain. It is sufficient here to reiterate that the ideology legitimized the division of labor along gender lines by recasting female labor as supplemental, rather than central to the family economy, and thereby justifying unequal wage rates and gender segregation in the labor market.

British emigrant workers, disproportionately from the skilled trades, were instrumental in transplanting these ideas to the United States.[59] Fearing the erosion of customary craft traditions, a decline in the status of workers, and decreasing wages, male workers in the United States agreed that, if they, as the male breadwinner of the household, could not earn a living wage, poverty and disintegration of the family would be the inevitable outcome.[60] Mary H. Blewett's studies of English shoe and textile families who migrated en masse to New England during the nineteenth century demonstrate how British working-class definitions of masculinity and femininity were encoded within "vital traditions of radical politics" that they transplanted to industrializing America.[61] By the turn of the twentieth century, American Federation of Labor president Samuel Gompers had unambiguously adopted the male breadwinner ideology when he declared that a "minimum wage" was one "sufficient to maintain [workers] and those dependent upon them in a manner consistent with their responsibilities as *husbands, fathers, men* and *citizens*."[62] Although the AFL declared its intention to organize working women, there is no evidence that it followed through on this promise.[63]

Historians Ileen A. DeVault and Susan J. Kleinberg have ably demonstrated the degree to which women in Pittsburgh, during the period when Hetty Williams entered Oliver's tinplate mill, faced a labor market that, as was the case elsewhere in America, was "highly segregated by sex." Also, male workers in Pittsburgh shared a powerful historical commitment to gender divisions in the workforce, and it was this tradition that Hetty Williams confronted in 1895 when she agreed to train women for work at the Monongahela Tin Plate Works.[64] Far from showing any evidence of the hundreds of women tinplaters that "Vox Populi" had predicted would soon displace the men, reformer Elizabeth Beardsley Butler's 1908 social survey of Pittsburgh estimated that the Monongahela tinplate mill normally employed only twenty women. In the end, the Welsh tinplaters' anxiety was for naught. Instead of Welsh or American women, mill owners reserved this hard, physical labor for Polish immigrant women because of their perceived strength and willingness to work for the lowest wages.[65]

The Hetty Williams episode demonstrates how tinplate workers in the United States and Wales were bound together in an occupational culture and community that spanned the Atlantic Ocean. The gender ideologies the Welsh brought with them were readily embraced by their American colleagues. Welsh tinplaters were accustomed to single women being marginalized in unskilled jobs, and they expected married women to work only in the home. With their high wages, the support of organized labor, and the fluid class structure of America, Welsh tinplaters who came to the United States hoped to further their gender and class aspirations by excluding women from mill work entirely. Many of their colleagues in Wales agreed with the ideal but were bound by work customs and the need for single women to earn a livelihood where few alternatives were available.

Like their Welsh colleagues, the American steelworkers' response to Hetty's hiring expressed their particular construction of masculinity. The new technologies and management techniques that undermined the steel-workers' ability to control production and command high wages also threat-ened their ideal of manhood. As Louis Martin has explained, their loss of control over the conditions of labor and inability to earn a family wage sufficient to support their wives and children constituted a direct assault on their masculine identity.[66] If, as feminist scholars generally argue, women's work can be understood only by first analyzing the political struggles within the household and the family economy, then the Hetty Williams story casts a ray of light into that private world.[67] Male Welsh tinplaters may have transported their gender ideologies with them in their migration to Amer-ica, but Hetty Williams showed no remorse in ignoring them and, not so incidentally, neither did the mill owners. Despite the uproar, women found no lasting foothold in the American tinplate industry. As unskilled labor, they were among the first to be replaced by mechanization. Theirs was a fate that foretold what would happen to the skilled men of "Greater Alcania" who so vociferously opposed Hetty Williams's effort to train women.

When and under what circumstances Hetty Williams left the mill is unknown, but by 1900 she, her husband (Thomas Williams), and their son (David) had moved to South Connellsville, Fayette County, Pennsylvania, where Thomas once again found employment as a "day laborer." The census that year reveals the repeated tragedies that befell Hetty, who gave birth to ten children, only one of whom survived. This profound series of losses was confirmed (although the numbers of children do not quite match) by the 1910 census, in which she is recorded as having given birth to a second son in 1908, with the additional note that only two of her eleven children had survived. Undoubtedly Hetty endured unrelenting waves of grief over the loss of her children, the death of her first husband, the wrenching change of adapting to life in a new country, and the absence of her sick husband at the very time the American and Welsh press were attacking her for taking a job in a tinplate mill.[68]

Hetty, Thomas, and their youngest son still resided at the same South Connellsville location in 1920, and they had taken in a lodger, a Welsh coal miner named Hopkins. Thomas was now a security guard at a glassworks. Hetty's brothers, Jenkin and Joshua Evans, were living within a block of Hetty in Connellsville when her husband died in 1928, and Jenkin then moved in with his sister. In 1940 Hetty was living with her son Charles, a plumber, and his wife, Marguerite. Hetty passed away at eighty-seven on July 23, 1950, as the result of a cerebral hemorrhage. In the United States she had always been a "housewife" except for that brief stint as a sorter at the Monongahela Tin Plate Works.[69]

The courage, and perhaps desperation, that drove Hetty Williams to immigrate to America was momentous, particularly for the widowed mother of a child. Standing up to the onslaught of hostile metalworkers both in person and in the press required a character and constitution of steel.[70] Her story also is suggestive of the survival strategies pursued by Welsh working men and women who immigrated to American mill towns during this period, and it demonstrates how family was the keystone to success in that life-changing transition.

8

Republicanism and the Search for Success

The industrial migration to the United States began in earnest during the 1850s, and the Welsh migrants who crossed the sea entered a society that was already familiar to them as a result of almost continuous migration from Britain for well over a century. Therefore, native-born Americans, most of whom were of British extraction, did not regard these newcomers as unwanted foreigners so much as "cousins" joining the kinfolk who had preceded them and made the United States part of the Anglo world. In an essay poignantly titled "A Prospect of Paradise?," the Welsh historian Glanmor Williams argues that the century between 1815 and 1914 represented "a unique chapter in Welsh-American relationships, the like of which can never be repeated. Wales gave America a host of her sons and daughters; America offered them a haven, opportunity and a future. The two countries shared in a religious, political, moral and cultural connexion [*sic*], which brimmed over with a spirit of confidence and optimism."[1]

The numerous tracts written by Welsh immigration promoters emphasized these themes over and over again. Benjamin Chidlaw, one of the most influential promoters in the early nineteenth century, claimed that it was hearing his father talk of America as a "free and virtuous country, with neither monarchy nor tithe and where poor people could buy farms," that had prompted him to migrate to the United States. Wisconsin immigrant Henry Davies declared that the "feeling of equality" was stronger in America than Wales, and "snobbery and servility were far less evident." Captain David Evans, of Talsarnau, Wales, who found himself seated next to President Ulysses S. Grant in the Metropolitan Methodist Church in Washington, observed that "it does one good to see the chief magistrate of a great nation like another human being, not putting on some artificials to endeavour to make him something above human."[2] On the other hand, letters to Wales often forewarned compatriots that "America is not all paradise." The level of satisfaction was generally determined by the location and experience of the individual worker, but most probably agreed with David Morgan in Minersville, Ohio, who wrote, "I like the country and the work famously; I wish I had been wise enough to come here years ago."[3]

Much of what has been written about the Welsh abroad has been influenced by the writings of self-appointed ethnic leaders overly conscious of convincing Americans that Welsh immigrants were worthy citizens. The scholar Prys Morgan observed that, from the 1840s on, nonconformist journalists, preachers, and radical politicians created a national image of the Welsh as the most virtuous, hardworking, most God-fearing Sabbath observers, most abstemious, and most devoted to educational improvement and matters of the mind of all Europeans.[4] Conceptually, the idea of a homogeneous Welsh identity is itself a problem, but Welsh boosters promoted these values as innate to both the Welsh and to the American dream of success. The qualities advanced as innately Welsh were just those qualities that made the Welsh admirable American citizens. As historian Robert Tyler points out, "central to this image was the idea that the Welsh aspired to socioeconomic upward mobility in every area in which they made their presence felt," and they possessed "an innate ability" to succeed in America because of these attributes.[5] That many did achieve their aspirations is beyond question, but by whose measurement—that of the immigrants or of the middle-class boosters? That is a fundamental question with which scholars of Welsh immigration must come to terms.

The American Ideal and Labor Republicanism

The republicanism of nineteenth-century skilled craft workers was less an ideology and more of an economic and political strategy for success and one the Welsh were predisposed to embrace. "All the struggles they have ever had in their native land were but struggles to fit them to be Republicans in America," a Welsh American politician proclaimed in 1890 before a crowd of his compatriots in Scranton. Historian Roland Berthoff astutely implied that this predisposition toward republicanism had an even deeper cultural wellspring. "For the party that had appropriated the traditional name 'Republican,'" he observed, "it was a happy if minor circumstance that the Welsh word for republic is *gweriniaeth*: government by the *gwerin*, the people, the folk, the peasantry. To immigrant Welshmen the Republicans were *Gwerinwyr* or *Plaid Werinol*," that is, the folk or people's party. Many Welsh Americans had been agrarians who migrated off the land to take jobs in the South Wales coal mines and ironworks. Therefore, their life experience rooted them in the *gwerin* even though they had become members of the permanent wage-earning proletariat. In the transition from the land to industry, they substituted customary claims to land with the ideology of labor republicanism, which had grown out of the Industrial Revolution. Welsh industrial immigrants, overwhelmingly coal miners and ironworkers were therefore predisposed to be "Republican" in politics and "republican" in economic outlook.[6]

Belief in the dignity of labor has been one of the cultural underpinnings of American society from the beginning, and by the time of the Civil War it was an affirmation of the North's "free labor" social system in contrast to slavery in the South. Capitalist values were anchored in the so-called "Protestant ethic," which, as a product of the Reformation, emphasized the notion that all individuals had a calling for which they were created by God. Achieving success in this calling was therefore a religious duty, and the personal qualities of honesty, frugality, diligence, punctuality, and sobriety required for success were also religious obligations.[7] Welsh Nonconformism embraced these tenets and, in a manner of speaking, predestined the Welsh for success in the United States so long as it was an open society governed by a free people.

The economic goal of the "labor republicanism" embraced by Welsh and American workers was not great wealth but rather the middle-class desire for economic security and independence. In the republican ideal, all classes benefited from an expanding economy. Therefore, class conflict worked against the interests of capital and labor alike because it obstructed the equal opportunity that generated upward mobility for all. Instead, it was cooperation between labor and capital that produced long-term upward mobility for laborers.[8]

Republicans were suspicious of corporations and financial concentration because they limited upward mobility, and an individual's success or failure was largely attributable to one's personal character. The republican notion that labor created all value (the labor theory of value) evolved prior to the Civil War in a nation dominated by yeoman farmers, artisans, and privately owned shops and factories but one already being eclipsed by large-scale corporate enterprise. Historian David Montgomery estimated that by 1860 more than half of American workers were dependent upon employers for wages.[9]

Even though republicanism continued to be a driving force into the postwar decades and workers could expect a rising standard of living and upward mobility in an expanding economy, self-employment and economic independence became increasingly unattainable with the emergence of corporate capitalism. In late nineteenth-century America, "labor republicanism" increasingly became an outdated roadmap to success, and "free labor" degenerated into the "cult of the self-made man," a mythology that justified the excesses of the "robber barons" and proclaimed personal wealth to be the measure of moral worth.[10] The opinion-makers of the Welsh American press and pulpit were therefore propagating an image of the Welsh as ready to be full Americans by espousing the values of a socioeconomic situation that no longer materially existed.

As the United States marched into the twentieth century, it seemed obvious that the producing classes could no longer realistically hope to restrain corporate power, and republicanism died the death of spent movements.[11] Social historian Herbert Gutman observed that believers in republicanism lamented the loss of "Old America" in the post–Civil War years but persisted nonetheless in clinging to a vision of the United States as a nation of independent male workers. By the 1890s, such workers feared for their future in a country where working-class status would be permanent.[12] Ohio Knights of Labor official William A. Davis declared in 1880 that the United States and organized labor had to break away from capitalists who, like the "monarchical governments of Europe," opposed freedom for the working man, arguing that "the Creator never intended that one man should ride in his gold-mounted carriage with his six in hand, and another to walk barefooted through the mud and mire." Instead of embarking on class warfare, however, Davis argued that the old virtues of republicanism should be resuscitated because they were more "in accordance with the laws of nature."[13]

Welsh workers had their own troubadours of labor republicanism in sympathetic nonconformist ministers who turned evangelical religion against the capitalist traducers of traditional democratic ideals and the individualistic materialism of institutional Protestantism. By the early twentieth century, activist ministers had transformed the optimistic individualism of early Welsh Nonconformism into the humanistic socialism of Keir Hardie, the first to lead the Labour Party in Parliament (1906). Welsh immigrants would have readily recognized these driving ideas in the Social Gospel movement in the United States. Both movements sought a broader application of religious doctrine to real life, as well as improvement in the human condition, by translating "socialist ethics" into imagery of evangelical Nonconformism.[14]

Socially conscious Welsh American ministers often supported labor's cause from their pulpits, fusing the democratic ideas of evangelical religion, Welsh nonconformity, and American labor republicanism. In an article entitled "Trusts and Trade Unions," Reverend W. R. Evans expressed the Welsh reform ministers' application of moral law to material conditions. "Can any act that affect[s] my neighbor inimically, be legally right when the same is morally wrong?" he asked. Capitalists claimed the right to manage their property as they please, but there are some laws are greater than the law of nations, he insisted—"I mean the law of God." Reverend Evans questioned whether it was "a greater crime to starve a man to death than to freeze him to death." Altruism, he concluded, "is not a mere sentiment, but a fundamental law—a basic principle upon which rests civics as well as ethics."[15]

Tensions produced by the loss of traditional republican ideals informed artisan and working-class protest and reform from nativism to labor activism. Gutman claimed that Gilded Age workers coined the pejorative phrase "robber baron" because it encapsulated their concerns about proletarianization. In America, declared the *National Labor Tribune* in 1874, "we have realized the ideal of republican government at least in form." America was "the star of the political Bethlehem which shone radiantly out in the dark night of political misrule in Europe. The masses of the old world gazed upon her as their escape." Men in America could be "their own rulers," and "no one could or should become their masters." But industrialization had created instead a nightmare in which "the working people of this country . . . suddenly find capital as rigid as an absolute monarchy."[16]

Rags to Riches?

It was a matter of existential importance to Welsh industrial immigrants whether American capitalists intended to impose a new set of class limitations upon them that would simply replace those they had hoped to leave behind in Great Britain. Certainly the lure of "America" was in large part due to the widespread belief that working people were going to a land of opportunity. That hope, perhaps more than the substance, was expressed in the "rags to riches" myth that the ordinary man could, through discipline and hard work, elevate his status from poverty to wealth. The relatively open economy and class structure presumably rewarded the deserving.

Herbert Gutman explored in his now classic essay, "The Reality of the Rags-to-Riches 'Myth,'" on the social origins of the iron, machinery, and locomotive manufacturers of Paterson, New Jersey, between 1830 and 1880. His findings demonstrated that most of the successful proprietors began their careers as apprentices in a skilled trade, often as a machinist, and then opened their own shops and factories. A few became "manufacturers of great wealth," but most acquired modest wealth. Nearly all of them were British immigrants who came from working-class backgrounds. Gutman concluded that, at least in the case of Paterson, the "rags-to-riches" myth was not a myth at all. Gutman claimed that newly developing industries offered those who were skilled in a craft or mechanics some exceptional opportunities for advancement in the early phases of American industrialization.[17]

Scholars in the 1950s who examined the social origins of elite manufacturers found that between 86 and 90 percent of them were native born, white, and predominantly Anglo-Saxon Protestants, from mostly upper-class families, and their fathers engaged in business.[18] Because these studies were based on selected national samples, little upward mobility was detected. Gutman's more focused study of Paterson, New Jersey, however, revealed the emergence of numerous "local elites." The only full study examining the efficacy of the "rags to riches" myth for the iron and steel tycoons of the late nineteenth century came a decade after Gutman's essay first appeared. John Ingham's *The Iron Barons*, published in 1978, which examined 696 iron and steel manufacturers in selected iron and steel cities, replicated the patterns the earlier studies had revealed. Not only were 88 percent of the metal barons native born but nearly two-thirds of their families had been in America since the seventeenth and eighteenth centuries. Nearly three-quarters of them were from wealthy families of the mercantile, manufacturing, or banking elite. Only 12 percent were foreign born.[19]

Herbert Casson's *Romance of Steel*, published in 1907, is frequently cited in studies of Pittsburgh during this period as a source for the "rags to riches" rise of the iron and steel industrialists. Casson declared that "Pittsburgh has about one hundred shirt-sleeve millionaires and a very few silk hat ones. Without a single exception, the steel kings and coal barons of today were the bare-footed boys of yesterday." In this respect, he asserted, no other American city was "as genuinely republican, as thoroughly American as Pittsburgh. Its motto might be 'From Rags to Riches.'" Casson's explanation for Pittsburgh's uniqueness was that it was a city where "even yet 'all men are born free and equal'—where the ladder of opportunity has rungs that reach to the bottom."[20]

Casson's description of the leading iron and steel center is an exemplary product of the "pageant of American steel" style of mythologizing. Conversely, John Ingham's examination of 360 iron- and steelmakers shows them as hardly unique. Only 12 percent of Pittsburgh's steel magnates were immigrants, and only 19 percent were the sons of immigrants. And, like other elite manufacturers, 70 percent of the iron and steel manufacturers in Pittsburgh were the sons of men of business, and another 14 percent were sons of professionals, all from the upper class and upper middle class.[21] Only 4 percent of the city's iron and steel elites emanated from immigrant working-class origins, although they did possess skills that were vital to the industry. Andrew Carnegie is often considered the archetype of the Pittsburgh steel magnates who rose from "rags to riches," but only five of them could be characterized as immigrants from poor families. Two of them were Andrew and his brother Tom Carnegie from Scotland, the other three being H. W. Borntrager, a German; William R. Jones, Welsh; and Henry Phipps, English. In short, less than 1 percent came from poor immigrant backgrounds, and all five worked in Carnegie's mills. Ingham concluded, therefore, that "outside of this establishment in Pittsburgh, the poor-immigrant-to-steel-mill-owner syndrome never occurred."[22]

Welsh immigrants would not have found this reality encouraging, if becoming wealthy elites had been their motivation for immigrating. They left Wales to improve their chances for a better life, but individuals rarely expressed themselves publicly regarding what actually constituted a "better life." If we judge their success by the standards of labor republicanism, that is, achieving economic security and maintaining an open social class structure, then the definition of success should incorporate not just those who became wealthy but also a broader representation of the communities the immigrants created. The common bonds forged in the mines and mills of Great Britain were strengthened in the United States by the need to construct new communities. Social barriers to upward mobility were much weaker in the United States than in Britain, thus opening opportunities to those with the skills required to become small shopkeepers, barbers, insurance agents, undertakers, and similar occupations in an economy expanding in all directions.[23]

Such declarations are not uncommon in the literature, but attempts to actually quantify social mobility among Welsh Americans have been rare. Anne Kelly Knowles's study of the Welsh in antebellum Ohio's rural-industrial counties of Gallia and Jackson employs a collective biography approach to measure geographic and upward mobility. What she found reinforces the accepted view that the Welsh, like other British immigrants, achieved success with a minimum of difficulty because of the skills they brought with them to a labor-scarce, expanding economy.[24] I employed the collective biography approach in coming to similar conclusions in my study of Welsh coal miners in nineteenth-century America.[25]

John E. Bodnar measured upward mobility among Welsh and Irish coal miners in Scranton, Pennsylvania, using 1880 census data to demonstrate the role of ethnicity in achieving economic security and upward mobility. The Welsh had worked in mines in Wales and were similarly employed in skilled and semiskilled occupations in Scranton, whereas the Irish came from agricultural backgrounds and lacked the skills that experience in the mines conferred. Consequently, for the most part the Irish worked in the unskilled jobs in and about the mines. Moreover, the children of Welsh miners gained early and direct access to the experience that would allow them to enter the skilled ranks. The sons of Irish mine workers lacked that opportunity and instead generally followed their fathers into the ranks of the unskilled. In other words, Bodnar found that the socialization of Welsh boys provided greater exposure to adult occupations, thus teaching them valuable industrial skills and facilitating a generational continuity into the better-paying skilled positions.[26]

It is reasonable to assume that a similar dynamic could be found among Welsh iron- and steelworkers, although a major comparative ethnic study would be required to demonstrate that claim conclusively. Nevertheless, the preponderance of evidence suggests that the same kind of occupational socialization occurred within Welsh American mill communities as a strategy for success.

Fig. 8.1. Book cover, *Pittsburgh the Powerful*, 1907. University of Pittsburgh Library, Historic Pittsburgh Digital Collection.

Native-born Americans and Welsh immigrants alike frequently commented on the proclivity of the industrial Welsh to "cluster" within mill towns when they came to the United States. Clustering together was a clear example of community maintenance, especially for the first generation and their children, as well as a successful adjustment strategy. Earning a secure place in the economy enabled them to exercise some control over their own lives. The vast majority of them might not have risen from "rags to riches," but then there is little evidence that gaining significant wealth was their motivation for immigrating. Until the master quantitative study appears, however, the outward signs signifying the degree to which they achieved their own American dream must suffice. These signs are found in data of upward mobility, the maintenance of culture and community, and individual biographies. A sizable number who were not economically successful nonetheless regarded settling in America to have been in itself a measure of success because they and their children had escaped the class barriers that constrained social and economic mobility in Great Britain.

Welsh American Communities

Iron and steel industries arose in a number of American cities, both large and small, and attracted significant communities of Welsh immigrants. The greater Pittsburgh and the upper Ohio valley region constituted the foremost iron and steel-producing region in the United States. Therefore, the focus here is on the producing centers of Pittsburgh, Martins Ferry, Ohio; Sharon, Pennsylvania; and Youngstown, Ohio, and their environs.

Pittsburgh

Congregational minister Robert D. Thomas visited Pittsburgh during his travels to Welsh communities in the United States, and in his 1872 book *Hanes Cymru America/A History of the Welsh in America* he described it as "a large and well-populated old city" containing "a large number of people from various nations" who worked in the numerous iron and glass manufactories. There were also collieries "in which thousands of men work and make a good living." However, he regarded Pittsburgh as an unhealthy place to live because the city was located in river valleys that trapped the river mists and factory smoke, made the air dense, and blocked the light.

Nevertheless, "the Welsh began to populate Pittsburgh over 30 years ago," he wrote, "and miners, craftsmen and firemen have continued to immigrate here over the years. There are now over three thousand Welsh here," served by three Welsh churches. In his estimate Thomas included Allegheny City, located on the north side of the Allegheny River and later absorbed into Pittsburgh.[27]

David Davies, another Welsh traveler visiting the Welsh American tinplate communities in 1898, offered an even less flattering description of Pittsburgh in an article for readers back in Cardiff. Much had changed during the twenty-six years since Reverend Thomas's visit, with Pittsburgh transitioning from the "iron city" to the "steel city," a shift marked by the massive growth in industrial scale, which only magnified the problems alluded to by the Reverend Thomas. Pittsburgh, Davies observed, was "Hell with its lid off," a city where the smoke hung heavy "like a London fog." The Welsh had settled primarily on the south side (left bank) of the Monongahela River, Davies wrote, which was "an unlovely locality in close touch with the many works, large and small, distributed over the banks of the river." He estimated the Welsh numbered between 4,000 and 5,000 of the city's 250,000 inhabitants. They were served by seven Welsh churches, but, according to Davies, fewer than 1,000 of those Welsh residents were regular chapel-goers. He believed that the city had "a larger proportion of poor and thriftless than is usually found in the Welsh settlements of the States." It was here in Pittsburgh where Davies "heard for the first time disparaging remarks respecting the Welsh."[28]

Moving beyond the always colorful descriptions of fin de siècle Pittsburgh, historian Matthew Carter provides a much more pointed analysis of the Welsh in Pittsburgh, which he developed after mining decennial census data from 1850 through 1880.[29] His findings offer a much more detailed statistical profile of Welsh American iron- and steelworkers than has been available for any American mill city to date. Some of his conclusions confirm while others counter the general characterizations of Welsh ironworkers in the United States as primarily skilled, economically secure, and religiously devout.

The largest immigrant groups in Pittsburgh between 1850 and 1880 were the Irish, Germans, English, Welsh, and Scottish, in that order. They represented 96 percent of all immigrants in Pittsburgh up to 1880. Most of the Welsh-born residents in Pittsburgh were blue-collar workers and did

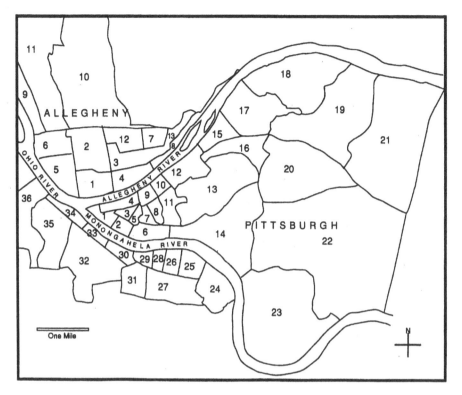

Map 5. Pittsburgh ward map, 1900. The Welsh were concentrated in the Twenty-Fifth and Fourteenth Wards. Based on Sanborn maps.

not own their own homes or work at high-status jobs. While other scholars generally focus on the high percentage of Welsh who were skilled workers, Carter reveals that more than two-thirds of Welsh workers were either unskilled, semiskilled, or unemployed.[30]

While the Irish were scattered throughout the city, the Welsh tended to cluster together in neighborhoods near the iron and steel mills, particularly the Twenty-Fifth Ward on the South Side, and the Fourteenth Ward, located north of the Monongahela River in the Soho neighborhood of South Oakland. The Fourteenth Ward included the site of Carnegie's Eliza furnaces and the Jones & Laughlin steel mill. No other immigrant group was as concentrated as the Welsh. The Welsh-born in Pittsburgh engaged in the well-documented practice of following friends and relatives to familiar locations where other Welsh had already settled.[31]

The Pittsburgh Welsh were not only overwhelmingly employed in the iron and steel industries; they also preferred to remain blue-collar workers rather than move out of the industry into new lines of employment. With the rise of steel, the trend toward de-skilling became evident between 1850 and 1880 in the decline of Welsh skilled workers, from 40.2 to 30.7 percent. On a percentage basis, however, Welsh skilled labor represented a consistently higher percentage by several percentage points than for Pittsburgh workers as a whole. The preference for blue-collar occupations is also seen in the low percentage of the Welsh workers found in white-collar occupations, which accounted for only 3.4 percent in 1850 and rose to a mere 5.69 percent in 1880, generally three to four times lower than average for the city.[32]

Carter found that the lives of most Welsh Americans differed very little from other mill workers in Pittsburgh throughout the 1850–1880 period. Most Welsh residents were unskilled mill workers who lived in crowded dwellings located in the neighborhoods close to the mills where they were employed, and the vast majority declared no wealth at all. Living conditions were undesirable, with dense crowding, ever-present smoke and dirt from the mills, and high levels of poverty, disease, and mortality. Under these conditions lived an overwhelming majority of the Welsh in Pittsburgh.[33]

The idea that Welsh workers in America were significantly "better off" than other iron- and steelworkers is contested by Carter's data for Pittsburgh, and those workers' status appears to have deteriorated in the decades following 1880. That conditions were less than desirable is reinforced by the testimony of some of the immigrants who returned to Wales. An interview with one tinplater, twenty-two-year-old James Evans, who returned to Llanelli in 1899 after a sojourn in Pittsburgh, was printed in the *Llanelly Mercury* and reprinted in the *National Labor Tribune*, published in Pittsburgh. He believed he had been forced to return home because of the "overflooding of the labor market" by European immigrants. His experience had been disappointing, and he advised his fellow Welsh to remain at home because "there are hundreds of tinplaters in America on the verge of starvation." Evans had worked at Henry W. Oliver's Monongahela Tin Plate Works in Pittsburgh, and he considered the city's living conditions intolerably worse than in Wales. In addition to the high cost of living, working men were forced to "live among all sorts and conditions of people—Jews, Italians, Chinese, etc. etc." Evans had met several former residents of Llanelli "who used to live in nice comfortable houses at home, but who were 'roughing' it and living in veritable slums and hovels out there. The appearance alone of these dens was enough to shock a respectable man's constitution. No more America for me!"[34]

As with the population as a whole, wealth among the Pittsburgh Welsh was disproportionately concentrated among a select few. Thus, in 1870 the top 1 percent of the Pittsburgh Welsh owned 60 percent of the total wealth of the group, the top 5 percent owned a little more than 90 percent, and the top 10 percent owned 99 percent of the group's wealth. This wealth disparity was not substantially different for the city as a whole, but a more equitable distribution of wealth prevailed among those born in Ireland, England, and Germany.[35]

One way the Pittsburgh Welsh dealt with these trying conditions was simply to move elsewhere. This they did in uncommonly large numbers. In fact, 84 percent of the Welsh-born who lived in Pittsburgh in 1870 did not reside there in 1880. Thirty-four percent of those who left Pittsburgh during that decade lived elsewhere in the United States in 1880, and just about 39 percent of them had returned to their homeland.[36] The limited number of Welsh surnames makes family history research grievously difficult, so accepting the accuracy of such claims requires caution, but Carter does confront the almost impossible challenge of tracking the movements of these notoriously peripatetic workers.

Pittsburgh served as a leavening oven for iron- and steelworkers who stayed for a time and then moved on to new opportunities. Unskilled and skilled workers, as well as those who became managers and owners, came to Pittsburgh and then followed the meandering path of opportunity that led them to a growing multitude of mill towns. Joseph Corns serves as an example. Born in Tredegar, he immigrated to the United States with his parents in 1830 as a youth. His father was a rolling mill heater who changed locations often, and Joseph followed his father into the mill. The family arrived in Pittsburgh in 1837, and Joseph struck out on his own in rolling mills and nail works. In 1847 Corns moved to Buffalo, New York, where he built the Buffalo Iron and Nail Works. He moved to Akron, Ohio, to become general manager of the Akron Iron Company works in 1869, and in 1878 he and Evan Morris reopened the Girard Mill in Girard, Ohio. Two years later, in 1880, Corns leased the Massillon Rolling Mill, which he purchased in 1883.[37]

As the leading coal and iron district in the United States by the Civil War and the emerging center of the American steel industry in the last half

THE CAMBRIAN

Now, go write it before them in a table, and note it in a book, that it may be for the time to come for ever and ever.

VOL. XI.	OCTOBER, 1891.	No. 10.

THOS. REES MORGAN, Sr., Esq.

PRESIDENT AND TREASURER OF THE MORGAN ENGINEERING CO., ALLIANCE, O.

Fig. 8.2. Thomas Rees Morgan. *The Cambrian*, October 1891.

of the nineteenth century, Pittsburgh attracted large numbers of workers from Britain during these years. Among the most talented was Thomas Rees Morgan Sr., who was recognized as one of the most capable mechanical engineers of his time. Born into humble beginnings in 1834 in

Merthyr Tydfil, Wales, he was taken from school at age eight and went underground first as a door boy and then as a teamster with his father, who was a coal-mining contractor. When he was ten, Morgan was caught between loaded coal cars, causing him to lose his left leg below the knee. His employer, the Penydarren Iron and Mining Company, for which his father had worked nearly forty years, urged Thomas's parents to give their son a higher education and promised to aid in that endeavor. Morgan showed a special gift for mathematics and mechanics, so when he was fourteen his parents reluctantly permitted him to become an apprentice machinist at the Penydarren Iron Works.[38]

Following his five years of training at Penydarren, Morgan spent the better part of a decade at his trade in various South Wales ironworks, including Dowlais Iron Works in Merthyr Tydfil. While at Dowlais he assisted Henry Bessemer in preparing machinery for his first trials of the new Bessemer converter. Attracted by the larger stage of opportunity offered by the expanding iron and steel industry in the United States, Morgan and his young family set sail for America in April 1865. After stops at the Lackawanna Railroad shops in Pittston and the Cambria Iron Works in Johnstown, Pennsylvania, Morgan arrived in Pittsburgh to hold positions as machine shop supervisor for several local companies.[39]

In 1868 Morgan went into business for himself, manufacturing steam hammers and other special lines of heavy machinery in Pittsburgh, but in 1871 he relocated the plant to Alliance, Ohio, and expanded the business significantly. From this beginning arose the Morgan Engineering Company, a leading manufacturer of steam hammers, punching and shearing machinery, railroad cranes, and electric overhead traveling cranes. "Nearly all of the great traveling cranes in use by the Carnegie Steel Company and all of the rolling mills of Pittsburgh were designed and built by Morgan," crowed a Welsh American magazine. He was the first to construct electric cranes, and he held patents on most of the machinery he produced. Morgan also solved the problem of shaping armor plates for US battleships and built the massive armor-plate bending machines used at the Carnegie Steel plant in Homestead. He also built shears for cutting steel plates "on a scale never before attempted."[40]

A large number of American, English, German, Welsh, and other nationalities were employed by Morgan Engineering. Morgan reportedly employed "a large number of Welsh mechanics to whom he gives special attention by contributing in aid of their churches and other movements which tend to advance their welfare as American citizens," it was reported. His Welsh workforce were all "sober men of good habits" who lived in a section of Alliance known as "Goat Hill." T. R. Morgan died in 1897, and Thomas Rees Morgan Jr. replaced his father as head of the firm.[41]

Metalworkers were naturally drawn to nineteenth-century Pittsburgh, the expanding iron- and steel-producing center of the United States, but moving on and up was not the only reason for the turnover of Welsh in Pittsburgh. David Davies, editor of the *South Wales Daily Post*, stopped at Pittsburgh in late 1899 during his extended tour of Welsh communities in the United States. An exceptionally astute observer with deep knowledge of the industry, Davies reported that there was "no appreciable influx of Welsh to Pittsburgh now; newcomers and the younger people among the old settlers are drifting steadily to the westward."[42] Like the more fortunate Joseph Corns and Thomas Morgan, innumerable skilled and nonskilled workers also migrated to smaller mill towns like Martins Ferry, Ohio, New Castle and Sharon, Pennsylvania, and Ellwood, Indiana, to improve their odds in achieving the better life they all sought.

Being strong union men, Welsh iron- and steelworkers also found themselves displaced by the labor-management conflicts resulting from the drive for efficiency in the industry. David Davies found that the great majority of the Welsh who had been employed at the Homestead works dispersed for parts unknown. The entire Welsh community had disintegrated, and "not more than a hundred Welsh families" remained.[43]

The high level of geographic mobility, or low retention rate, among Welsh workers tends to support those studies grounded in anecdotal sources asserting that the Welsh migrated frequently in search of better working conditions and economic opportunities and underscores their primary motivation for crossing the Atlantic in the first place. If Matthew Carter's estimate that about 40 percent returned to Wales is even close to the actual number, many Welsh migrants in Pittsburgh were transnational migrants or sojourners (rather than immigrants) who readily moved from one place to another, including back to Wales.[44] This transitory migration between the United States and Wales was part of the transatlantic coal, iron, and steel business cycle. As discussed in chapter 1, the rapid industrialization of Wales and the United States during the last half of the nineteenth century kept Welsh coal and metalworkers home when the industry in America was depressed and attracted them when it was expanding.[45]

The decision of Welsh steelworkers to return to Wales was not unique. Between 1908 and 1910, 45 percent of all immigrants who arrived in Pittsburgh returned home. "We came here hoping to find better conditions; we are going back home because we believe we were better off there," one man declared. "We could not stand the work here very much longer." One historian suggested that such sentiments explain why only 20 percent of all eligible immigrant steelworkers actually chose to become naturalized citizens.[46]

As the Pittsburgh economy transitioned from iron to steel during the late nineteenth century, the new technology became decreasingly reliant on skilled labor and shifted manufacturers' preferences to massive numbers of unskilled laborers. Nevertheless, adult male Welsh migration to the city grew by more than 200 percent between 1870 and 1880.[47] Through informal and other networks, Welsh migrants would have been aware of the growing demand for unskilled labor in Pittsburgh but may still have believed the possibility for economic improvement in Pittsburgh was more attractive than remaining in Wales. If their dreams were unfulfilled, they could always return home or move to another American mill town. This is the likely explanation for the large influx of Welsh migrants to Pittsburgh during an era when the demand for skilled labor was in decline. This pattern probably was unique to the dynamic between Pittsburgh's power to attract metalworkers on the one hand and its being at the center of the mechanization movement on the other. Moreover, the growth of the American tinplate industry in the 1890s brought in a different occupational group than basic iron- and steelworkers. A comparative study of mill towns is required to determine how unique this pattern was to Pittsburgh.

Just over 70 percent of Pittsburgh's Welsh-born males eighteen and older were married in 1880, in a city where, among all men in this age range, only 48 percent were married.[48] This high percentage of married couples in an ethnic group was one of several reasons that education was a high priority among Welsh families in Pittsburgh, and they also sent a higher percentage of their children to school than any other major population group in the city. The 1880 attendance rate overall for Pittsburgh's boys and girls between the ages of six and eighteen was 33 percent, whereas the rate for children of the Welsh-born was 44 percent. The result was an increase for second-generation Welsh employed in skilled and white-collar jobs, a jump from 36 percent for the Welsh-born parents in these positions to more than 53 percent for their children. Third-generation American-born children achieved positions of even higher occupational status than their second-generation parents, thanks to their school attendance rate of 58.5 percent.[49]

The potential for upward social and occupational mobility for their children undoubtedly played a major role in attracting and retaining Welsh migrants, both skilled and unskilled, to Pittsburgh and other mill towns and motivated some to remain even as their prospects diminished. David Davies visited several Welsh families in Youngstown prior to his arrival in Pittsburgh in 1899. Among those he visited was that of David Edwards, a puddler who had lived in the United States for eighteen years. Like all iron- and steelworkers, he and his family had suffered during the depression of 1893, which "completely changed their circumstances." Davies asked Edwards if he would like to return to Wales, to which Edwards replied, "'I think I should for myself, but not for my children. Here my daughters can mix with the best—no one, however wealthy, looks down upon them—in Wales they couldn't do that; they would suffer because their father is only a workman.' In these few pregnant words one of the fascinations of America in the lowly-born stands revealed."[50]

Improving the status of their children was a fervent desire among Welsh immigrants, even though they might not have expressed it as eloquently as Edwards did. A Welsh tinplater from Elwood, Indiana, calling himself "Hen Undebwr" (Old Unionist) echoed this hope when he declared that American society was "healthier" than South Wales, where "the working-man is expected to bow and bend all he knows to win the attention of his employer." In the United States, on the other hand, at the last conference on wages, representatives of the men and masters were "practically on an equal footing," and tinplate works managers who "come over from the old country and fail to realise the difference . . . soon show themselves at a disadvantage because of it."[51]

Martins Ferry, Ohio, and Sharon, Pennsylvania

The experience of Welsh immigrants in Pittsburgh was different from that of their compatriots who lived in America's smaller mill towns. Pittsburgh was a large city with a massive and expanding iron and steel capacity during the late nineteenth century, and in that dense landscape Welsh and other

immigrants encountered an urban-industrial complex with a long-estab-
lished workforce hierarchy. Even though Welsh ironworkers settled together
in certain residential sections of the city, they had little control over their
community circumstances. In smaller mill cities as diverse as Martins Ferry,
Ohio; Sharon and New Castle, Pennsylvania; and Ellwood, Indiana, or
even in medium-sized cities like Youngstown, Ohio, the Welsh were able
to establish a community within the city, own their own houses, be served
by Welsh merchants and professionals, and still become fully integrated into
city life rather than ghettoized and proletarianized.

On the eve of his return to Wales following an extensive tour of America's Welsh communities in 1899, David Davies mused on "the future of
this great commonwealth." For two hundred years "the surplus population
of the earth has been intermittently pouring into it, each race losing a separate identity, but contributing to produce a strange amalgam, a new type
compounded of many." Americans were "a plebeian people," he wrote, "the
great majority of them, of lowly origin, who, until they reached America
scarcely knew they had a right to live." These "reunited races" were "working
the greatest experiment since the beginning of time," Davies concluded. In
the newer Welsh communities he visited, such as Gas City, Anderson, and
Elwood, Indiana, he found "bits of Gwalia superimposed upon American
soil too newly removed to have lost their distinctive old-world character."
On the other hand, the older and larger Welsh communities in cities such
as Cleveland and Pittsburgh had "swallowed up their Welsh element and
all but digested it."[52]

Martins Ferry, in Belmont County, Ohio, one of the newer tinplate towns
on the Ohio River, was first settled as early as 1779. Ebenezer Martin laid out
the town in 1835, and subsequently it was named for the ferry operated by his
father. Opened in 1785, the ferry connected the town with Wheeling, West
Virginia, and for decades was the only transportation link between the two
states. Arrival of the railroad in 1852 and the discovery of coal stimulated local
industrial growth, and by 1886 Martins Ferry was a thriving manufacturing
town. The tinplate industry, developed after passage of the McKinley tariff
in 1890, became the industrial mainstay of Martins Ferry, just as it was for
numerous mill towns on both sides of the Ohio River.[53]

The presence of abundant coal and iron ore reserves near Martins Ferry,
as well as its location on a wide floodplain of the Ohio River and its being served by a branch of the Pennsylvania Railroad, provided the town's

industry with access to the river and rail transportation required for getting raw materials and shipping iron and steel products to the national market. The first blast furnace in the upper Ohio valley was constructed in the city in 1857, and in 1903 it was still in operation, owned by the Wheeling Steel & Iron Company. The Laughlin Nail and Steel Company began operations in 1874 and expanded in 1878 from 50 to 192 nail machines, making it one of the largest cut-nail producers in the world. When the cut-nail industry shifted to tinplate manufacture in the 1890s, the Laughlin Tin Plate Company, which was acquired in 1903 by the American Tin Plate Company, employed 1,750 workers. A number of secondary metal manufacturers, as well as glass and lumber companies, employed another 5,600 of the city's workers.[54]

The growth of the tinplate industry attracted a dynamic influx of people and more than doubled the city's population between 1880 and 1890, from 3,819 to 7,760. Martins Ferry grew to 9,133 in 1910, reached 11,634 in 1920, and 14,524 in 1930. Initially, immigrant tinplate families from Wales, England, and Germany constituted nearly all of the influx from overseas, but after World War I immigrants from Hungary, Italy, and Poland took the lead. During the forty years between 1880 and 1920, however, the Welsh represented the city's major immigrant group, comprising nearly 10 percent of the city's population.[55]

Although the kind of detailed study provided by Matthew Carter for the Pittsburgh area does not exist for Martins Ferry, Robert Tyler, a historian of the Welsh diaspora, has analyzed this Welsh community. His analysis of local census data was designed to demonstrate the degree of cultural continuity and maintenance of the Welsh-born community from which we may reasonably conclude whether their personal standards of success had been satisfied. Tyler found that the Welsh community was sustained by services provided by a cross section of their compatriots, from minister to milk peddler, and physician to post office clerk. Most Welsh families lived in close proximity to one another, worked in the same mills, and worshiped in churches with Welsh-language services. Even though they represented a distinct cultural group, Tyler concludes that they were thoroughly integrated into city life.[56] The extensive representation of Welsh employees in the community services sector indicates that the standard avenues of social mobility were open to Welsh immigrants. In this new and expanding industrial town, the Welsh found it easier to preserve those cultural institutions that enhanced their transition in their adopted homeland.

Another element reinforcing the resiliency of Welsh ethnic community was their concentration in the metal-working industry. Of the 158 Welsh-born men in the city in 1900 whose occupations can be discerned, 80 percent of them were employed in metal manufacture, with 108 (68.3 percent) of them in the tinplate mills.[57] The percentage probably was higher because the workplace or skill level of many employed in the mills was not always identified in the census. Not much had changed by the 1910 census, which showed 60.1 percent of the 165 Welsh workers employed in the production of tinplate. A decade later, in 1920, the percentage of Welsh-born men working in the tinplate industry remained high, at 63.3 percent, or 88 of the 139 whose occupation could be determined. Unlike Carter's Pittsburgh, the "great majority" of them were in the skilled occupations.[58] This continuity of Welsh-born men employed in the metal trades, with a majority holding skilled jobs, is a strong indication that the Welsh community was stable and comfortably established over an extended period of time. In other words, they had found security and were consequently "successful" by their own reckoning.

That such a high percentage of the Welsh in Martins Ferry were concentrated in the metal industries, and overwhelmingly the tinplate mills, Tyler asserts, indicates that there is a powerful link between community maintenance, a vibrant local economy, and the Welsh achieving their own personal standard of success. The ability to replenish the supply of immigrants from Wales was just as crucial to maintaining the Welsh American community in Martins Ferry as it was elsewhere. Also, like other communities, Welsh Martins Ferry was being threatened by a general decline in Welsh immigration by the first decade of the twentieth century. The number of Welsh people in the city fell from 688, or about 8.2 percent of the population in 1910, to 475, or 2.2 percent of the total population, in 1930. The vast majority of Welsh residents in 1930, a little more than 82 percent of them, had arrived before 1910.[59]

Sharon, Pennsylvania, located two miles from the Ohio-Pennsylvania state line, about twenty miles east of Youngstown, Ohio, and sixty miles north of Pittsburgh, shared a similar experience as Martins Ferry. The Reverend R. D. Thomas, who visited many Welsh settlements in the United States in 1872, described Sharon as "a beautiful small town on the Shenango River on a narrow fertile plain between beautiful hills," an old place where "the Welsh began to settle in 1851." One of the first settlers was a native of St. Clairs, Carmarthenshire, South Wales. He and others had come from Pittsburgh to work in the rolling mill, Thomas reported, but after the ironworks failed most of the Welsh departed. In 1870 the ironworks was restarted, and subsequently a blast furnace and several new iron mills were erected in Sharon and another in nearby Wheatland, where many Welshmen also worked. The Welsh established Calvinistic Methodist, Congregationalist, and Welsh Baptist churches in Sharon and nearby Wheatland. Reverend Thomas estimated the Welsh population in Sharon and Wheatland to be three hundred.[60]

Robert Tyler analyzed occupational mobility within Sharon's Welsh community to measure the degree to which they achieved social and economic security. Among Tyler's sample of 121 individuals engaged in skilled blue-collar work in 1880, 97 (80.2 percent) were iron- and steelworkers, such as puddlers, boilers, rollers, heaters, roughers, and doublers. As late as 1920, 32 of the 56 (57.1 percent) were still skilled blue-collar workers. Like Martins Ferry, but unlike Pittsburgh, the majority of the Welsh workers continued to occupy the skilled positions in the mills between 1880 and 1920. Tyler concluded that the Welsh who arrived with industrial skills occupied a privileged position in the city's iron and steel industry, and that advantage persisted over the four decades between 1880 and 1920.[61]

Predictably, the members of the Welsh community of Sharon were overwhelmingly engaged in the iron and steel industries. In fact, in 1880, 73.3 percent were employed as blue-collar skilled workers, such as puddlers, rollers, heaters, and doublers. That percentage had declined by 1920 but remained high at 55.4 percent. Again unlike Pittsburgh, the number of Sharon's Welsh in white-collar occupations more than doubled over that same forty-year period, from 6 percent in 1880 to 15.8 percent in 1920. The employment pattern for blue-collar semiskilled workers and laborers in Sharon also diverged from that found by Carter in his Pittsburgh study, with the workforce in that category remaining relatively flat during this entire period, at 20.5 percent in 1880 and only slightly higher at 28.7 percent in 1920. Compared with other ethnic groups, the Welsh definitely occupied a privileged position in Sharon's economy. For example, the Irish occupied a high percentage of the unskilled positions in 1880 and only 22.7 percent of the blue-collar skilled workforce in 1880, and that figure had increased only modestly by 1920, to 27.5 percent. The combined categories showed that 70.4 percent of the Irish were blue-collar semiskilled workers or laborers (44 percent and 66 percent, respectively) in 1880, and by 1920 that figure was still relatively high at 49.4 percent (15.9 percent and 43.5 percent, respectively).[62]

There was no major movement of the Welsh out of blue-collar occupations in the steel mills in the 1880–1920 period. Tyler's data reconfirm the evidence that Welsh workers preferred to continue with their occupations, changing employers rather than industries. Although there was some upward movement from the blue-collar to the white-collar categories, "upward" would depend on the definition of the term, since puddlers or rollers would earn a greater income than lower-level white-collar workers. His data also demonstrate that the primary upward mobility of the second generation was from the semiskilled moving into the skilled jobs, and from unskilled labor to semiskilled occupations. With one-third of Tyler's sample falling into the unskilled or semiskilled occupations, the Sharon data reveal a much more secure position for the Welsh than in the large city of Pittsburgh, where 60 to 70 percent of Welsh metalworkers were found in those job categories.[63]

The Youngstown District

In the medium-sized Mahoning Valley industrial center of Youngstown, Ohio, built upon coal, iron, and railroads, the Welsh were far more numerous than in Martins Ferry or Sharon, and their numbers rivaled those of their counterparts in Pittsburgh. Although "rags to riches" does not describe the experience of most Welsh workers in either small towns or larger urban areas, the story of the Welsh in Youngstown and the greater Mahoning Valley district can be told through several Welsh ironmasters who rose in status and power along with that industrial region.

There are no detailed statistical studies of the Mahoning Valley Welsh beyond calculating their numbers in the census, but considerable anecdotal evidence indicates that they found fertile soil in which to set down roots. Unlike Pittsburgh, Youngstown provided ample opportunity for success on all levels of the social hierarchy when the Welsh entered the new and growing coal and iron district in eastern Ohio. Local historian Ewing Summers observed in 1903 that "no class of foreign-born citizens surpasses the Welsh in quick and appreciative adaptability to American institutions. They immediately enter upon the duties of citizenship with a keen, almost juvenile enthusiasm, insisting on their children having the best education that can be obtained, and rearing them to respect their adopted country and participate in its functions." His assessment was a bit over the top perhaps, but the qualities Summers attributed to the Welsh are exactly those that other Americans, as well as Welsh American leaders, promoted as essential for success.[64]

Fig. 8.3. Ohio Steel Works and Furnaces, Youngstown, Ohio, 1905. Library of Congress.

Some sense of the occupational and social advancement within the Welsh community may be gleaned from the biographies of several ironmasters who played leading roles in establishing the Mahoning Valley iron industry.

The first blast furnace in Youngstown, constructed specifically to use the bituminous coal mined in the Mahoning Valley, known as Brier Hill or block coal, was erected by William Philpot and several partners. Philpot emigrated from Wales to the United States in 1835 and found his way via Pittsburgh to northeastern Ohio and then Youngstown by 1846.[65] He arrived with a wealth of experience. In Wales he had entered the mines as a child, rose to the position of overseer, and then went into business for himself as a coal contractor. Philpot leased some property at Brier Hill and, while banking for coal, discovered a higher grade of iron ore than was currently being used locally. With several partners, he purchased the land and erected the Eagle Furnace along the north bank of the Pennsylvania and Ohio Canal, which was completed in 1835 and linked Akron, Youngstown, and Sharon, Pennsylvania. Once underway, Philpot's new enterprise, the Ohio Iron & Mining Company, proved that the locally mined block coal and iron ore could be profitably used to make iron.[66] The *Iron Trade Review* described Mahoning Valley block coal as a "peculiarly dry bituminous mineral, unlike Pittsburgh coal, which because of its tarry nature could not be used for furnace fuel until coked." The block coal and black-band iron ore lay in deposits under southern Trumbull County and northern Mahoning County and provided the minerals for the Mahoning Valley iron industry for more than three decades.[67]

By 1847 another blast furnace, the Brier Hill Furnace, erected by future governor David Tod, had been constructed in Youngstown and, together with the Maria Furnace in Niles and the Mahoning Furnace in Lowellville, brought the total number of furnaces in the Mahoning Valley to five. In 1841, two brothers from Staffordshire, England, James and William Ward, who became leading iron manufacturers in the valley, constructed the Falcon Iron Works. Their new rolling mill in Niles was the first attempt to produce finished iron in the valley. The Youngstown Iron Company also constructed a rolling mill in 1846, using local pig iron to make bar, hoops, sheet, nails, and spikes.[68]

Growth in pig iron production in the Mahoning Valley was stimulated by the dynamic expansion in the manufacture of finished iron products in Pittsburgh, where there were thirteen rolling mills employing twenty-five hundred workers in 1850. Supplying these mills with pig iron was profitable but also made the Mahoning ironmasters dependent on the success of the industry in Pittsburgh.[69] Three Welsh-born ironmasters became prominent leaders in the development of the Mahoning Valley, at least in part by using the expansion of Pittsburgh's iron and steel industry to their advantage.

Joseph H. Brown

Joseph H. Brown (1810–1886), a native of Glamorganshire, Wales, was exposed to the industry at an early age by his father and grandfather, both of whom were iron manufacturers. He immigrated to the United States with his parents around 1815, settling near Baltimore, Maryland, where Joseph's father and his two brothers-in-law erected and operated an iron mill. Joseph

Fig. 8.4. Joseph H. Brown. After J. Butler, *History of Youngstown and the Mahoning Valley*, 2:120.

worked alongside his father in the mill, gained valuable expertise in all phases of the industry, and at age twenty began his career as an ironworks supervisor. When Brown was called to New Castle, Mercer County, Pennsylvania, to assist in the construction of the Cosalo Iron Works rolling mill, his younger brother Richard joined him and went to work in the mill as a roll-turner. On his honeymoon in England and Wales a few years later, Richard took the opportunity to tour ironworks and thereby explore the latest technology and methods.[70]

In 1847 Joseph Brown joined with partners to build and operate the Orizaba Iron Works in New Castle. Joseph's youngest brother, Thomas, also became a partner, as did William Bonnell, an immigrant from Yorkshire, England, who had settled in as bookkeeper. According to one historian, the Orizaba works were among "the largest in the state," with all "the latest improvements in plant and machinery." Unfortunately, a fire destroyed the mill shortly after its construction, but it was rebuilt the following year. Brown remained in "full control of the mechanical departments," but financial control rested in the hands of his new partners, whose poor business decisions prompted Brown to sell his share in the company.[71]

Finding an opportunity to start over, Joseph Brown moved to Youngstown, where in 1855 he, his brothers Richard and Thomas, and William Bonnell were joined by James Westerman in establishing the Mahoning Rolling Mill. By 1856, the rolling mill contained nine puddling furnaces, three heating furnaces, three trains of rolls, and sixteen nail machines. The nails, spikes, and various sizes of finished iron were shipped to Cleveland, Chicago, and other Great Lakes cities. Located in proximity to his own iron furnaces, Brown's rolling mill was assured of a constant supply of pig iron, thus reducing their dependence on Pittsburgh as a source.[72]

Joseph H. Brown also entered into business with Jonathan Warner, a prime mover in the local iron and coal industries. The Civil War created a great demand for bar iron, prompting Brown, Bonnell, Westerman & Company to expand in 1863 by purchasing the Phoenix and Falcon blast furnaces, as well as a coal company that employed six hundred workers, to ensure a steady supply of block coal for its furnaces. In 1866, Brown, who was a very wealthy man by then, joined with Warner and two other investors to organize the Mineral Ridge Iron and Coal Company in neighboring Trumbull County.[73]

The iron industry in Youngstown slowed to a crawl following the war. In Pittsburgh, however, the number of rolling mills had grown rapidly, from thirteen in 1850 to thirty-two by war's end, along with nine small crucible steel mills and two copper mills. These mills consumed almost 380,000 tons of pig iron a year, and yet only three of the rolling mill companies owned their own blast furnaces. On the other hand, in 1868 two of the five Mahoning Valley rolling mill companies operated their own blast furnaces, and the other eight iron companies produced pig iron for Pittsburgh's six hundred puddling furnaces and forty foundries. This relationship was financially rewarding for the Mahoning ironmasters, but it locked them into a dependency upon the Pittsburgh market for the rest of the century.[74]

Brown, Bonnell, Westerman & Company survived the downturn after the war and was still the largest iron manufacturer in the Mahoning Valley in the early 1870s, employing some five hundred men in its rolling mill and blast furnaces, as well as several hundred more digging coal in its local mines. A large percentage of them were Welsh. Brown was intrigued by the experiments underway at the Cwm Celyn and Blaina Iron Company back in Monmouthshire, Wales, which used blast furnace gases to generate steam for puddling and rolling mills, and he adapted the technique to power his company's two rolling mills.[75] Joseph Brown also introduced into the Mahoning industry the closed-top stack, or "bell and hopper," another technological innovation used in Welsh ironworks that noticeably improved the efficiency of the iron furnaces.[76]

During the financial panic that began in 1873, a number of the Mahoning iron companies either failed or were reorganized, but Brown, Bonnell, Westerman & Company continued to operate until 1876, when the Chicago industrialist Herbert C. Ayer purchased Brown's stock. Several years later, Brown retired to a life of comfort in Youngstown.[77] Joseph H. Brown had played a pivotal role in the development of Youngstown and the Mahoning Valley as a major center of coal mining and iron manufacture and was instrumental in attracting several thousand Welsh immigrants to the district. According to one authority on the iron industry in the Mahoning Valley, "the arrival of the Browns and Bonnell in Youngstown was quite possibly one of the most significant events in the Valley's nineteenth-century industrial history."[78]

William Richards

David Tod, the prominent Mahoning Valley industrialist and former governor of Ohio (serving 1862–1864), consolidated his coal and iron interests in 1868 into the Brier Hill Iron and Coal Company. To build a modern blast furnace in Girard, Tod brought into the firm William Richards (1819–1876), who had previous experience managing several Youngstown blast furnaces. Richards was born near Merthyr Tydfil, Wales, home of Cyfarthfa and several other massive ironworks. Even though he grew up in a major British iron-producing center, Richards had been trained as a blacksmith and was not employed in the iron industry. Richards immigrated to the United States in 1840 with his mother and sister, settled in the Mahoning Valley, and eventually found employment at the James Ward & Company rolling mill in the late 1840s.[79]

Fellow Welshman William Philpot introduced Richards to the operation of the blast furnace at his Brier Hill furnace, and Philpot appointed Richards furnace manager in 1850. Philpot died in 1851, and, when Philpot's furnace returned to blast in 1853, Richards became superintendent. He also invested in a rolling mill in New Castle, Pennsylvania, which earned him a substantial fortune. While in Dowlais, Wales, for a visit in 1865, Richards studied the designs of newer Welsh iron furnaces at the request of several Youngstown iron manufacturers. Their plan was to erect a new pig iron furnace in Girard, and they placed Richards in charge of the new works upon its completion.[80]

William Richards left the Girard Iron Company in September 1867 to start his own iron company in Warren. Three years later Warren Packard sold his rolling mill to Richards and his two sons, who incorporated under the name William Richards & Sons. The new furnace that went into operation in September 1870 employed 26 men, and another 175, many of whom were Welsh, worked in the rolling mill. With the rolling mill, William Richards & Sons had the only fully integrated iron or steel works in Warren until after World War I.[81]

John Rhys Thomas

Like Richards, John Rhys Thomas (1834–1898) was not born into the industry. Born in the iron and tinplate center of Llanelli, Carmarthenshire, Wales, in 1834, he initially held jobs as a coal miner, brickyard worker, stonemason, and blacksmith. In October 1868 John and his wife immigrated with their three sons to the United States and settled in Youngstown.[82]

Thomas established the Niles Fire Brick Company in 1872, and the family moved to Niles the following year. Firebrick was invented in 1822 in the Neath Valley, Glamorganshire, and, having worked in a brickyard, Thomas was undoubtedly familiar with its uses in blast furnaces. His company filled an important local need by supplying firebrick to the Mahoning Valley's puddling, rolling mill, and blast furnaces. Thomas purchased a blast furnace in Niles, rebuilt the old stack with his firebrick, and put the works back into operation as the Thomas Furnace Company in 1879.[83]

All three of John R. Thomas's sons extended the family business interests well into the twentieth century. The Thomas Furnace was managed by the eldest son, John Morgan Thomas, and the firebrick company was managed by the second son, Thomas E. Thomas. The third son, William Aubrey Thomas, was educated in metallurgy, and he too was involved in the family's businesses. After serving in Congress from 1904 to 1911, however, William Aubrey moved to Talladega, Alabama, in 1918 and became president of Jenifer Iron Company.[84]

Scale and Success

The biographies of Joseph H. Brown, William Richards, and John R. Thomas present three Welsh-born men who rose to become local elites in the Mahoning Valley iron industry, although each followed a different path to achieve that status. Brown was born into the industry as the son and grandson of iron manufacturers. Richards grew up in the shadow of Cyfarthfa Ironworks but was a blacksmith by trade. Thomas was born in the iron and tinplate center of Llanelli but came to the industry later in life after working in a brickyard. These men from Wales were able to rise into the top tier of industrial society in the Mahoning Valley, and to establish family dynasties, because they entered the industry during the early years of development. By maximizing their individual abilities and Welsh connections, they succeeded in riding the crest of expansion. Although the number of Welsh workers they employed in their mines and ironworks cannot be determined, they definitely were instrumental in bringing thousands of Welsh immigrants to the Mahoning Valley, thus establishing one of the prominent Welsh American communities in the United States.

Just below them in socioeconomic status was a significant group of Welsh industry figures who joined mostly Americans at the head of the Mahoning Valley iron, steel, and tinplate businesses. Excluding the three elites and their families, thirty-one of them were found in the biographical sections of local histories that were so popular at the turn of the twentieth century. All of them came to the United States with their families, indicating that they viewed the move as permanent. This list is not exhaustive because managers and skilled workers constantly moved from one location to another for advancement, better conditions, or a variety of other reasons.[85]

Among this secondary group of Welsh industrialists in the region, three were ironmill owners (William Philpot, David Davies, and William Hutchings) and one (Daniel R. Jenkins) was described as an "international authority in the tinplate business." Fourteen others were superintendents at iron or steel mills, and thirteen were skilled workers, primarily puddlers, rollers, and heaters. Five of the superintendents had been skilled workers earlier in their careers. This sample suggests that a significant percentage of Welsh immigrants occupied higher-level positions in the workforce and that the occupational hierarchy was open to the Welsh. Of course, far more Welsh-born workers in the Mahoning Valley would have been skilled workers who did not supply biographies to the compilers, and a majority of Welsh residents would have remained undocumented unskilled or semiskilled workers.

Of the twelve Americans with Welsh-born fathers among these men with documented biographies, five moved up to superintendent or the equivalent in the industry and thus exceeded their fathers' occupational status. Four of them were skilled puddlers and molders. Three began their working careers in the iron or steel mills and then left the industry for other occupations. A molder became a dental surgeon, a blacksmith became a store owner, and a paymaster became Trumbull County treasurer. Examples of upward social and occupational mobility are easy to find among Welsh ironworkers, and the many anecdotal and quantitative data suggest that the Welsh were able to take advantage of a fluid class structure that privileged Welsh individuals over other nationalities.

As the heavily capitalized trusts consolidated companies in the steel industry at the turn of the twentieth century and as investment in mechanization increased, the demand for skilled ironworkers declined in the Mahoning Valley just as it did in other iron and steel communities. By World War I, the number of British-born residents in the Mahoning Valley had dropped dramatically. The Welsh had stopped coming, and only 1,103 Welsh-born people lived in the city of Youngstown. Their places were taken by southern and eastern European immigrants, who had come to dominate the foreign-born segment of the population.[86]

In Pittsburgh the industry was long established and already dominated by an old American elite. The lack of fluidity in the class structure there made it nearly impossible for Welsh immigrants, or those of any other nationality, to rise in the socioeconomic hierarchy. The Welsh benefited from arriving in the small- to mid-sized mill towns like Martins Ferry, Sharon, and Youngstown when the iron industry was in its infancy and Welsh expertise was in high demand. The Welsh were among the founders of the industry in these mill towns. Consequently, they found few structural barriers to either economic or social mobility, and they held positions in every occupational and social category within these communities. The Youngstown district was large enough to offer more opportunities than the small mill towns but not so large and established as Pittsburgh, where Welsh culture was diluted by the masses. Failure to achieve the republican ideal in Pittsburgh motivated the Welsh to move on to places where cultural maintenance reinforced Welsh American institutions, ethnic identity, and family security. By their own definition, therefore, these iron- and steelworkers probably regarded the outcome of their decision to immigrate as a "success."

Epilogue

The US economy expanded at an unprecedented rate during the last decades of the nineteenth century, as manufacturing doubled and production quadrupled. Advancements in travel by steamship fostered major changes in the British-American migration. A new migration pattern emerged as British workers entered the American labor market when it was to their advantage and returned home when working conditions became unfavorable. Thus, emigration from Britain rose and fell with the business cycles in the two nations. There are estimates that as many as 40 percent of all British emigrants returned to their native land between the late 1890s and 1914, although estimates for returning Welsh are considerably lower, at about 25 percent.[1]

The meteoric rise in manufacturing output was due in large part to mechanization, which accelerated in the 1880s and resulted in the replacement of skilled workers by machines. Mechanization eliminated skilled jobs but required more unskilled labor and, along with the great influx of European immigrants, increased the competition for those jobs the Welsh were not inclined to take. Therefore, when British emigration picked up again in the early twentieth century, Welsh workers looked beyond the United States to countries within the British Empire, particularly to Canada and Australia, where expanding economies offered opportunities for labor. World War I marked the end of the industrial migration to the United States. By then, American industry no longer required their skills at all. Skilled iron- and steelworkers remained at their jobs in Wales, where mechanization of the mills lagged significantly behind that of the United States. The unemployed were able to survive at home with assistance from the government dole, made available in 1920 with passage of the Unemployment Insurance Act.[2]

As mechanization of the mills proceeded, Welsh immigrants who made the passage tended to be less skilled and employed in trades other than coal, iron, and steel. Unlike most other immigrants, the Welsh were still able to take advantage of their "ethnic affinity" with most native-born Americans, an affinity rooted in the common ground of national origin, Protestantism, the English language, and their whiteness in a period when racism and xenophobia had a firm grip on the American mind. Restrictive immigration legislation barred some groups, such as the Chinese, and by the early 1920s quotas by nationality had restricted immigration of ethnic groups to their proportion of the population already in the United States. Naturally, the immigrants from Britain enjoyed the highest quotas, and those quotas were not closely observed.[3]

Although largely forgotten to history, Welsh immigrants in industrial America between the Civil War and World War I left a significant legacy, one manifested in the transfer of metalworking skills, industrial organization and technology, and a work culture that shaped the American Industrial Revolution and, ultimately, America's emergence as a global industrial power. Even in the earliest days of the antebellum American iron industry, the Welsh played a critical role in elevating the production of iron from an isolated and fragmented undertaking dependent on small charcoal furnaces into the next stage of technical development by introducing the "Welsh Plan." Following the organizational design found at the Cyfarthfa and Dowlais ironworks in Wales, each step of production from raw materials to shipping the final product was integrated into one linear process. In conjunction with Welshman David Thomas's discovery of how to burn anthracite coal in iron furnaces, the foundation was laid for large-scale coal and iron production and the Industrial Revolution, which transformed the United States between the Civil War and World War I.

The Welsh also were instrumental in moving the American iron and steel industry forward during the 1860s and 1870s with the development of the Bessemer process for the mass production of iron and then the

Siemens-Martin, or open-hearth process, which enabled the direct production of steel on a large scale. Both methods were perfected at ironworks in Wales, and these systems, along with the technical knowledge to operate them, were then transferred to the United States. The increasing reliance on technology, mechanization, and labor-saving innovations transferred control over the labor process from the artisans to management. This fundamental shift in labor-management relations sparked the rise of labor unions among the skilled ironworkers. Here again, the Welsh left a prominent legacy of leadership in the founding and organizational activities of ironworker unions, such as the Sons of Vulcan and the Amalgamated Association of Iron, Steel, and Tinplate Workers of America. Beyond their active engagement in union organization, administration, and labor action, the Welsh and their English colleagues transferred to the United States the fundamental principles of organized labor then current in Britain: organization by craft, accommodation with industry and new production technologies, and negotiation of grievances with management. These principles were not abandoned by iron- and steelworkers until the formation of industrial unions in the 1930s. This model was broken earlier, however, by the coal miners, when they formed the United Mine Workers of America in 1890 to organize not just the skilled but all those who worked in and about the mines—another labor organization shaped by Welsh and English workers.

Countering the decline in British metalworkers immigrating to the United States was the wave of tinplate workers who flocked aboard ships to cross the Atlantic in the 1890s. The tinplate industry had been overwhelmingly concentrated in Wales until it shifted to the United States during the 1890s. The McKinley protective tariff resulted in a "tinplate war" between Welsh makers and American pioneer manufacturers for control of the US market. By the end of the decade the Americans had won that struggle, and the production technologies and occasionally the physical plants themselves were transferred to the United States. The new American industry was another legacy of the skilled Welsh workers, managers, and the technical experts who transported their knowhow to the United States. Thousands of Welsh tinplaters came to America and created so many tinplate communities that they were conceptualized as "Greater Alcania," to reference the original concentration of tinplaters and their communities in South Wales. The self-descriptive name acknowledged a unique transnational community of interests within the Anglo-American world.

During the first decade of the twentieth century, powerful American trusts had horizontally consolidated most of the tinplate companies into one overarching corporation, eventually integrating them vertically as well. By then the trusts had gained control of the iron and steel industry and had successfully mechanized their plants. The Welsh lost their privileged position in the American industry and hence the incentive for migrating to the States. Their presence, and the influence they exerted in America's development as an industrial power, quickly faded into the past and was all but forgotten.

If upward mobility and acceptance by society are the primary measures of immigrant success, there is little question that Welsh immigrants were one of the more successful ethnic groups that came to the United States during its industrializing era. Their own definition of "success" involved upward mobility within the context of family security. By this standard, most first-generation Welsh iron- and steelworkers who remained were "successful." Therefore, part of their legacy was to reinforce the ideological belief structure of America as the promised land, free and untrammeled, where opportunity was open to all. Although the reality was quite different for most immigrants, Welsh leaders not only reinforced the American dream but loudly proclaimed themselves living proof of its vitality. The first generation considered themselves neither "Yankees" nor immigrants but as "valuable reinforcements to the British 'stock' that had built America." Like British immigrants generally, the first-generation Welsh thought of themselves as Welsh first, although the liberal society mirrored in American culture resonated powerfully with their own values. They clung to this bifurcated national identity even after becoming American citizens.[4]

Assimilation of Welsh immigrants came easily and without undue friction compared with most of the Europeans, but it did induce a deep sense of loss and longing for home, a sort of nostalgia that the Welsh called *hiraeth*. The Welsh became Americanized at what many of the first generation considered an alarming rate. Like other immigrants, first-generation Welsh Americans became painfully aware that they could not go home again. Without memories of the old country, however, second-generation Welsh Americans felt little sense of loss from Americanization or the decline of Welsh cultural institutions that had helped to ease their parents' transition to a new home. Welsh heritage did not present an obstacle to assimilation into American society, so there was no second "ill-adjusted" generation; they simply, and quickly, became Americans.[5]

Americanization proceeded with particular speed in Welsh-heavy iron and steel communities in the United States. Industrialization had advanced South Wales to the forefront of anglicization and modernity, so immigrants from this region did not share the same commitment to preserving Welsh culture as did the earlier rural agricultural migrants. If culture is defined as a fixed set of immutable traits, then Americanization was a tragic, irreversible loss. On the other hand, if culture is understood as a dynamic process of human adaptation to new circumstances and the abandonment of traditional ways that are no longer useful, then cultural change is a healthy sign of vitality. However "Welshness" is defined, the memory of Wales among the first generation began to fade almost immediately, and subsequent generations with no memory of Wales were proud of their Welsh ancestry but prouder still of being Americans.[6]

Economic and social mobility spurred the disintegration of Welsh community cohesiveness and a distinctive ethnic culture. Prosperity reduced the need for mutual support and cooperation and enabled even greater mobility among communities that were already widely dispersed over the vast American landscape. The signs of Welsh cultural decline in the immigrant communities had been present for decades, but Welsh community leaders disagreed on what if anything should be done about it. For many there could be no distinctive Welsh identity without the Welsh language, which was threatened almost from the time immigrants stepped off the boat. Welsh children may have heard Welsh spoken in the home, but as soon as they went out the door the dominant culture crowded them from all corners. School, play, work, and popular culture all were conducted in English. Consequently, a struggle for cultural hegemony often was waged day by day and household by household. In retrospect the outcome seems to have been inevitable.[7]

The identity of the second generation was a bifurcation of Welsh and American. "Welsh" offered an identity based on group continuity and solidarity, reinforced through family and Welsh-language social institutions. "American" identity offered new and exciting possibilities for material advancement and acceptance; its influence was exerted through education, work, recreation, and the media. The vitality of the Welsh language served as a weathervane of Americanization. So long as a steady inflow of immigrants arrived from Wales to provide a transfusion of traditional values from the homeland, their chapels, societies, and festivals remained

Welsh-language institutions. The tide turned when new arrivals from Wales came to a halt; within two or three decades, Welsh institutions faced a life-changing choice: shift to English or die.[8]

There is no precise way to measure language use before World War I, but the loss of native-language ability among the Welsh in America was significant throughout the nineteenth century and accelerated dramatically in the twentieth. Those unconcerned about the fate of the language responded that they had immigrated to America to improve their position in the world and not to preserve the Welsh language and culture. Many thought efforts to preserve the Welsh language were misplaced. As one proponent of Americanization declared in 1909, "the effort to perpetuate the Welsh language in this country is as useless as trying to stem the tide with a broom. It would be far better for those who wish to keep it to go back to Wales."[9] By the turn of the twentieth century, the "good old tongue" was seldom heard in the streets of Welsh American communities, even in the leading population centers like Scranton, Pittsburgh, and Youngstown. There seemed little regret, and the inability to speak Welsh was not, in historian William D. Jones's phrase, regarded as a "negation of Welsh identity."[10]

Welsh scholar Hazel Davies has perceptively observed that nineteenth-century United States was a nation of the uprooted with few restraining traditions. The American ethic was therefore to push forward; the "American dream" was about neither preserving nor opposing ethnic identities but rather about "endlessly becoming." There was little or no value in looking back. Most American immigrants navigated these turbulent cultural waters, and descendants measured their history by the ease with which their forebears were able to lay claim to their part of the dream. Like most immigrants, the Welsh looked ahead toward success in America, and only later did descendants take stock of what had been left behind in Wales.[11]

APPENDIX 1

Firms of the American Tin-Plate Company

American Tin Plate Company, Elwood, Indiana
New Castle Steel & Tin Plate Company, New Castle, Pennsylvania
United States Iron and Tin Plate Manufacturing Company, Demmler,
  Pennsylvania
Pittsburgh Tin Plate Works, New Kensington, Pennsylvania
Pennsylvania Tin Plate Company, New Kensington, Pennsylvania
Star Tin Plate Company, Pittsburgh, Pennsylvania
Humbert Tin Plate Company, Connellsville, Pennsylvania
Washington Steel & Tin Plate Mills, Washington, Pennsylvania
Crescent Sheet & Tin Plate Company, Cleveland, Ohio
Falcon Tin Plate & Sheet Company, Niles, Ohio
Beaver Tin Plate Company, Lisbon, Ohio
National Tin Plate Company, Anderson, Indiana
Irondale Steel & Iron Company, Middletown, Indiana
LaBelle Iron Works, Wheeling, West Virginia
Wallace Banfield & Company, Irondale, Ohio
Aetna Standard Iron & Steel Company, Bridgeport, Ohio
Atlanta Steel & Tin Plate Company, Atlanta, Indiana
Baltimore Tin Plate Company, Baltimore, Maryland
Blairsville Rolling Mill & Tin Plate Company, Blairsville, Pennsylvania
Cincinnati Rolling Mill & Tin Plate Company, Cincinnati, Ohio
Great Western Tin Plate Company, Joliet, Illinois
Ellwood Tin Plate Company, Ellwood City, Pennsylvania
Johnstown Tin Plate Company, Johnstown, Pennsylvania
Laughlin Nail Company, Martins Ferry, Ohio
Morewood Company, Gas City, Indiana
Neshannock Sheet & Tin Plate Company, New Castle, Pennsylvania
Ohio River Sheet & Tin Plate Company, Rochester, Pennsylvania
Hamilton & Company, West Newton, Pennsylvania
Marshall Brothers & Company, Philadelphia, Pennsylvania

Britton Rolling Mill Company, Cleveland, Ohio
Cumberland Steel & Tin Plate Company, Cumberland, Maryland
Reeves Iron Company, Canal Dover, Ohio
Somers Brothers, Brooklyn, New York
Canonsburg Iron & Steel Company, Canonsburg, Pennsylvania
Stickney Iron Company, Baltimore, Maryland

APPENDIX 2

Firms of the United States Steel Company

American Bridge Company
American Sheet Steel Company
American Steel Hoop Company
American Steel & Wire Company
American Tin-Plate Company
Carnegie Steel Company
Federal Steel Company
Lake Superior Consolidated Iron Mines
National Steel Company
National Tube Company

NOTES

Preface & Acknowledgments

1. Muller, "Metropolis and Region," 182–83.

2. Muller, "Metropolis and Region," 185–86, 189, 191 (quotation).

3. Faires, "Immigrants and Industry," 7.

4. For an evaluation of Welsh immigrant correspondence and its strengths and weaknesses as a historical source, see B. Jones, "Writing Back"; and W. D. Jones, "'Going into Print.'"

1. The Transplanted

1. Conway, *Welsh in America*, 5.

2. Wittke, *We Who Built America*.

3. Hansen, *Atlantic Migration*; Easterlin, *Population, Labor Force, and Long Swings in Economic Growth*; Vecoli, "Contadini in Chicago"; T. Smith, "Religion and Ethnicity in America."

4. Bodnar, *The Transplanted*; Higham, "Current Trends in the Study of Ethnicity in the United States."

5. Bukowczyk, "*The Transplanted*: Immigrants and Ethnics," 233–41.

6. O'Leary, "Power and Modernity," 33–35; Kenny, "Diaspora and Comparison," 134–35, 137.

7. Bryce, *American Commonwealth*, 2:360–61; Murdoch, *British Emigration*, 113.

8. Carnegie, *Triumphant Democracy*, 82–83; Murdoch, *British Emigration*, 114.

9. Erickson, *Invisible Immigrants*; Guglielmo, *White on Arrival*. See also Murdoch, *British Emigration*, 115–17, 125.

10. Hoerder, *Cultures in Contact*, 344–45; Fones-Wolf, "Transatlantic Craft Migrations and Transnational Spaces."

11. W. D. Jones, "Wales in America," xvii–iii.

12. Hartmann, *Americans from Wales*, 90–95; Van Vugt, *British Buckeyes*, 143–58; W. D. Jones, "Wales in America," 19–23.

13. W. D. Jones, "Wales in America," 6; Berthoff, *British Immigrants in Industrial America*, 5–10; G. A. Williams, *When Was Wales?*, 179.

14. B. Thomas, "Wales and the Atlantic Economy." See also B. Thomas, *Migration and Economic Growth*, particularly chapters 7 and 14; and B. Thomas, *Industrial Revolution and the Atlantic Economy*.

15. B. Thomas, "Wales and the Atlantic Economy." Brinley Thomas also argues that the Welsh language was saved by the redistribution resulting from industrialization because the absorptive power of the coal valleys allowed Wales to retain its native Welsh speakers. See also W. D. Jones, "Wales in America," 9; Knowles, *Calvinists Incorporated*, 6–10; Baines, *Migration in a Mature Economy*, 220–49, 266–82; and Conway, "Welsh Emigration to the United States," 265.

16. Berthoff, *British Immigrants in Industrial America*, 23, 28–29, citing *Eleventh Census of the United States* (1890), 2:484–89; US Congress, Senate, *Reports of the Immigration Commission*,

no. 633 (June 15, 1910), 6:44, 50; 8:41, 48; 10:73, 83, 665; 11:34, 37; 16:24, 27–28, 227, 230; 19:95, 104, 11 (respectively).

17. David Davies, "Wales and the American Tin Plate Trade," *South Wales Daily Post*, July 4, 1898, 2.

18. B. Thomas, *Welsh Economy*, 11–12 (table 4 and quotation on 11); Murdoch, *British Emigration*, 116.

19. Berthoff, *British Immigrants in Industrial America*, 28–29.

20. Harvey, *Best-Dressed Miners*, 20.

21. R. D. Thomas, *Hanes Cymry America*, 336–37; Glanmor Williams, *Religion, Language and Nationality in Wales*, 225–26.

22. Hartmann, *Americans from Wales*, 79–81; W. D. Jones, "Wales in America," 20, citing *Tarian y Gweithiwr*, August 22, 1879.

23. W. D. Jones, "Wales in America," 21, citing the *Llanelly and County Guardian*, June 5, 1890.

24. Rutherford, *Romancing in Tin Plate*, 98.

25. Rutherford, *Romancing in Tin Plate*, 99.

26. "Bill Davey Reminisces," reproduced in Rutherford, *Romancing in Tin Plate*, 100–103.

27. For a description of the process before and after the Morewood pot, see Dunbar, *Tin-Plate Industry*, 33, 44, respectively.

28. "Bill Davey Reminisces," in Rutherford, *Romancing in Tin Plate*, 100.

29. "Bill Davey Reminisces," in Rutherford, *Romancing in Tin Plate*, 101–2.

30. "Bill Davey Reminisces," in Rutherford, *Romancing in Tin Plate*, 102–3.

31. "Bill Davey Reminisces," in Rutherford, *Romancing in Tin Plate*, 103.

32. G. A. Williams, *When Was Wales?*, 180.

33. Conway, *Welsh in America*, 6, citing Stephens, *Madoc*. For a corrective view, see G. A. Williams, *Search for Beulah Land*; and David Williams, "John Evans' Strange Journey [parts 1 and 2]."

34. Quoted in "Another 'Nauseating' Writer from 'the Little Dependency of Wales'?," *NINNAU*, 17. See also Sanders, *Wales, the Welsh and the Making of America*.

35. Conway, "Welsh Emigration to the United States," 183–84.

36. Great Britain, Parliamentary Papers, *Reports of the Commissioners of Inquiry into the State of Education in Wales*, 1847, vol. 27, part 3, 3; Conway, "Welsh Emigration to the United States," 193.

37. Conway, "Welsh Emigration to the United States," 193; Great Britain, Parliamentary Papers, *Reports of the Commissioners of Inquiry into the State of Education in Wales*, vol. 27, part 3, 3.

38. Conway, "Welsh Emigration to the United States," 194–95. For similar circumstances in prefamine Ireland, see K. Miller, *Emigrants and Exiles*, 26–101.

39. Conway, "Welsh Emigration to the United States," 199–204; David Williams, *Rebecca Riots*, 251–52, 286–89.

40. Great Britain, Parliamentary Papers, *Reports of the Commissioners of Inquiry into the State of Education in Wales*, 1847, vol. 27. The reports were issued in blue bindings. The title was based on *Brad y Cyllyll Hirion* [Treachery of the long knives], an incident in the wars between the Welsh and Saxons. For a scholarly study, see Roberts, *Language of the Blue Books*, particularly 140–67, on female sexual morality, which was particularly insulting.

41. K. Morgan, *Wales in British Politics, 1868–1922*.

42. Shepperson, *British Emigration to North America*, 32–36; G. A. Williams, *Search for Beulah Land*; S. Williams, *Saga of Paddy's Run*, 18–28, 167–85; Knowles, *Calvinists Incorporated*, 18–22; Shepperson, *Samuel Roberts*; Conway, "Welsh Emigration to the United States,"

216–17; For Michael D. Jones and the Patagonian settlement, see Glyn Williams, *Desert and the Dream*; and Glyn Williams, *Welsh in Patagonia*.

43. Shepperson, *British Emigration to North America*, 80–84; W. D. Jones, "Wales in America," 5; Hartmann, *Americans from Wales*, 68–70; Conway, "Welsh Emigration to the United States," 226; Glanmor Williams, *Religion, Language and Nationality in Wales*, 225–26; Murdoch, *British Emigration*.

44. Davies, *Mormon Spirituality*, 48; Conway, "Welsh Emigration to the United States," 240; Hartmann, *Americans from Wales*, 73–75.

45. Dodd, *Industrial Revolution in North Wales*; John, *Industrial Development of South Wales*; B. Thomas, "Migration of Labour into the Glamorgan Coalfield," 275–94.

46. Morris, "Coal and Steel"; D. Smith, *Wales! Wales?*, 16, 18 (quotation).

47. Morris, "Coal and Steel," 177–84; John, *Industrial Development of South Wales*, 23–57; Walters, *Economic and Business History of the South Wales Steam Coal Industry*, chaps. 1–3. For the social changes that accompanied the industrial transition in South Wales, see N. Evans, "'As Rich as California'"; and B. Jones, "Banqueting at a Moveable Feast."

48. D. Smith, *Wales! Wales?*; Holmes, "South Wales Coal Industry, 1850–1914," esp. 163; G. A. Williams, *When Was Wales?*, 222; B. Thomas, "Growth of Industrial Towns," 2:186; D. Evans, *History of Wales, 1815–1906*, 186–89.

49. Philip Jenkins, *History of Modern Wales*; G. A. Williams, "Emergence of a Working-Class Movement," 2:142–43; G. A. Williams, *When Was Wales?*, 192.

50. G. A. Williams, "Emergence of a Working-Class Movement," 2:143–44. For a full account, see G. A. Williams, *Merthyr Rising*.

51. David Williams, *John Frost*; Wilks, *South Wales and the Rising of 1839*; David J. Jones, *Last Rising*; John Humphries, *Man from the Alamo*.

52. E. W. Evans, *Miners of South Wales*, 213–15.

53. E. W. Evans, *Miners of South Wales*, 216–21.

54. Morris and Williams, *South Wales Coal Industry*, 269–73, 282–84.

55. D. Evans, *History of Wales*, 76–77, 219.

56. D. Evans, *History of Wales*, 79–80.

57. D. Evans, *History of Wales*, 86–88, 94 (quotation), 133–36, 139–44.

58. E. Davies, *Religion in the Industrial Revolution in South Wales*, 76–82; D. Evans, *History of Wales*, 144–45, 166–67.

59. E. Davies, *Religion in the Industrial Revolution in South Wales*, 91; Gwyther, "Sidelights on Religion and Politics in the Rhondda Valley," 32; *The Druid*, December 19, 1912; *The Cambrian* 29 (September 1, 1909): 11; Hartmann, *Americans from Wales*, 135.

60. Conway, "Welshmen in the Union Armies," 143–74; R. W. Griffiths, "Welsh and the American Civil War," 231–74.

61. Conway, "Welsh Emigration to the United States," 250, citing *Merthyr Telegraph*, August 29, 1863.

62. Conway, "Welsh Emigration to the United States," 250, quoting *Merthyr Telegraph*, April 24, 1869.

63. B. Jones, "'We Will Give You Wings to Fly,'" 27, quoting *Merthyr Express*, May 16, 1868.

64. B. Jones, "Inspecting the Extraordinary Drain," 110–11. The press complained of this neglect by industrialists throughout the first half of the nineteenth century. See C. Evans, "*Labyrinth of Flames*," 145–77.

65. *Merthyr Express*, March 31, 1866; *Merthyr Telegraph*, March 2, 1861, May 2, 1863, April

30, 1869; B. Jones, "Inspecting the Extraordinary Drain," 112, citing *Merthyr Star*, August 15, 1863, February 4, 1864.

66. B. Jones, "'We Will Give You Wings to Fly,'" 29, citing *Merthyr Star*, March 17, 1868.

67. B. Jones, "'We Will Give You Wings to Fly,'" 30–34.

68. B. Jones, "'We Will Give You Wings to Fly,'" 36–41.

69. *The Times* (London), November 25, 1969, 7; A. Gottlieb, "Immigration of British Miners in the Civil War Decade," 369.

70. M. Jones, "Background to Emigration from Great Britain," 54–55; Van Vugt, *Britain to America*, 13; Johnston, "Welsh Diaspora," 56–57.

71. Van Vugt, *Britain to America*, 13; Baines, *Emigration from Europe, 1815–1930*, 41.

72. Van Vugt, *Britain to America*, 14–16; *Merthyr Express*, May 23, 1868; B. Jones, "Raising the Wind," 1.

73. B. Jones, "Raising the Wind," 20, citing *Baner ac Amserau Cymru*, October 20, 1869.

74. B. Jones, "Raising the Wind," 28–29, citing *Cardiff and Merthyr Guardian*, March 20, 1869, and *Baner ac Amserau Cymru*, March 31, 1869.

2. Transnational Institutions

1. Glanmor Williams, *Religion, Language and Nationality in Wales*, 226–27; D. Smith, *Wales! Wales?*, 42; M. Jones, "From the Old Country to the New," 89–90.

2. Berthoff, *British Immigrants in Industrial America*, 125 (quotation), 134, citing the *Pottsville* (PA) *Miners Journal*, May 26, June 30, August 18, 1855.

3. David Davies, "Wales and the American Tin Plate Trade," *South Wales Daily Post*, July 4, 1898, 2.

4. Berthoff, *British Immigrants in Industrial America*, 140; Wyman, *Round-Trip to America*, 11.

5. W. D. Jones, "Wales in America," 90; W. D. Jones, "Welsh Language and Welsh Identity in a Pennsylvania Community," 261–63, 266; R. Thomas, *Hanes Cymry America*, 38–51.

6. Hartmann, *Americans from Wales*, 176–81; R. Thomas, *Hanes Cymry America*, 117–27, 232–33, 254–60; Knowles, *Calvinists Incorporated*, esp. 225–58; D. J. Williams, *One Hundred Years of Welsh Calvinistic Methodism in America*, 126–29, 144–58, 232–36.

7. Van Vugt, *Britain to America*, 132–33.

8. Knowles, *Calvinists Incorporated*, 225–34; Van Vugt, *Britain to America*, 133–34.

9. Hartmann, *Americans from Wales*, 101–2; Berthoff, "The Welsh," 1014; R. Thomas, *Hanes Cymry America*, 345.

10. R. Thomas, *Hanes Cymry America*, 340–43, 345; Hartmann, *Americans from Wales*, 170–91.

11. Hartmann, *Americans from Wales*, 104, 107.

12. "American Notes," *Western Mail*, March 7, 1882, 3. Morien came to the United States as a correspondent of Cardiff's *Western Mail*. He became a well-known figure among Welsh Americans. *Western Mail*, November 1, 1890, 7. Where Morien made his home is unknown, but his work often carried a Pittsburgh dateline.

13. Berthoff, *British Immigrants to Industrial America*, 127; Hartmann, *Americans from Wales*, 106–7.

14. *The Druid*, February 18, 1909. In this context *hwyl* means a feeling and style of speaking specific to Welsh preaching.

15. William Roberts in *The Druid*, October 19, 1911.

16. *The Druid*, September 9, 1909.

17. Hartmann, *Americans from Wales*, 107–9. For Williams Pantycelyn (as he was often

known), see Hodges, *Flame in the Mountains*. For the Methodist Revival, see D. L. Morgan, *Great Awakening in Wales*.

18. K. Morgan, *Wales in British Politics, 1868–1922*, 12.

19. M. Jones, "From the Old Country to the New," 94; Berthoff, "The Welsh," 1015.

20. Van Vugt, *Britain to America*, 137–38.

21. W. D. Jones, "Wales in America," 204, citing *Y Drych*, July 28, 1870. See also "Welsh Settlers a Boon to America," *The Cambrian*, 7.

22. W. D. Jones, "Wales in America," 204–12. See, for example, four articles in one single issue of *The Druid*, January 11, 1914. See also David Jones, *Memorial Volume of the Welsh Congregationalists of Pennsylvania*, 353.

23. *The Druid*, June 17, 1909.

24. D. J. Williams, *One Hundred Years of Welsh Calvinistic Methodism*, 113–14.

25. Hartmann, *Americans from Wales*, 139–51; Berthoff, *British Immigrants in Industrial America*, 173–75.

26. Hartmann, *Americans from Wales*, 143.

27. Hartmann, *Americans from Wales*, 146–47.

28. W. D. Jones, "Wales in America," 99–100; *Scranton Republican*, March 11, 1871 (quotation).

29. Rhys, *Little Hero*, 4, 10–12; Rhys and Bott, *To Philadelphia and Back*, 24, 26–28.

30. The life and work of Joseph Parry is fully explored in his autobiography, edited by Rhys, *Little Hero*; and in works by Rhys and Bott, *To Philadelphia and Back*; E. K. Evans, *Cofiant Dr. Joseph Parry*; and "Joseph Parry," in John Davies et al., *Welsh Academy Encyclopaedia of Wales*, 652.

31. *Scranton Republican*, May 11 and June 10, 1875.

32. "Pittsburgh Eisteddfod," *The Cambrian*, 52–53.

33. "Pittsburgh Eisteddfod," *Evening Express* (Cardiff), May 27, 1903, 2.

34. W. D. Jones, "Wales in America," 179.

35. Carter, "Industrial, Industrious, and Diverse," 317; W. D. Jones, "Wales in America," 184, citing *Y Drych*, March 13, 20, 1919; *The Druid*, January 1, March 15, 1919 (quotation).

36. Hartmann, *Americans from Wales*, 151–52. See also W. M. Jones, "Gymanfa Ganu," 7–22, 28, 33.

37. Berthoff, *British Immigrants in Industrial America*, 172; *The Druid*, July 24, 1907 (quotation). See also W. M. Jones, "Gymanfa Ganu," 17.

38. Hartmann, *Americans from Wales*, 158–60; W. D. Jones, "Wales in America," 95; Van Buskirk, "History of the Philanthropic Order of True Ivorites," 20.

39. *The Druid*, February 13, 1908 (quotation); Hartmann, *Americans from Wales*, 156–57.

40. "Welshmen in America," *South Wales Daily News*, October 7, 1898, 4. This news was shared from a Pittsburgh newspaper.

41. *The Druid*, March 25, 1909.

42. *The Cambrian* 7 (April 1887): 123; "Thomas C. Jenkins," *The Cambrian*, 163. At the 1893 annual banquet, John Jarrett was the main speaker. *The Cambrian* 13 (April 1893): 128.

43. "Consul at Cardiff," *Evening Express*, June 6, 1894, 4.

44. *The Druid*, March 4, 1909.

45. *Youngstown Telegram*, marked August 1898, clipping in "Minute Book" of the Welsh Pioneers Society, Mahoning Historical Society, Youngstown, Ohio. See also clippings from the same newspaper marked August 1896, August 25, 1899, August 1900, and August 1901, in the same source. This collection has been microfilmed and is also available online from the National Library of Wales, Aberystwyth, Wales, https://journals.library.wales/home.

46. *The Druid*, February 13, 1908; Hartmann, *Americans from Wales*, 156–57.

47. *The Druid*, January 21, 1909.

48. *The Druid*, May 13, 1909. See also *The Druid*, May 27, 1909.

49. "Choir at Pittsburgh," *South Wales Daily News*, September 28, 1893, 4, reprinting an article from the *Commercial Gazette* (Pittsburgh), September 19, 1893.

50. "Llanelly Singers in America," *Llanelly Mercury*, November 11, 1909, 2.

51. *The Druid*, January 22, 1914, February 5, 1914.

52. *The Druid*, November 23, 1911, January 8, 1914.

53. *Merthyr Express* quoted in *The Cambrian* 33 (January 1, 1913): 4. For other examples, see *The Druid*, October 10, 1907, September 24, October 8, 1908, September 23, and December 23, 1909.

54. "Welsh Singer's Romance," *Evening Express* (Cardiff), December 21, 1909, 2.

55. "Welsh Singers in America," *Weekly Mail* (Cardiff), January 9, 1909, 10. See also *Evening Express*, January 2, 1909, 4; and *Glamorgan Gazette*, February 19, 1909, 8. The Gorsedd of Bards of Great Britain was an organization of highly talented writers and musicians with strong ties to the International Eisteddfod.

56. See, for example, *The Cambrian* 4 (October 1884): 271–72. See also *The Druid*, July 20, 1911, April 15, 1909; *Y Drych*, January 9, 1868, May 26, 1881, cited in A. Jones and B. Jones, *Welsh Reflections*, 59.

57. *The Druid*, August 3, 1911.

58. Hartmann, *Americans from Wales*, 127–30; A. Jones and B. Jones, "*Y Drych* and American Welsh Identities," 50, 54; B. Jones, "Ethnic Journalism and the Reconstruction of Identity."

59. A. Jones and B. Jones, *Welsh Reflections*, 56; Hartmann, *Americans from Wales*, 130–35.

60. Evans, "Census Reports of the Welsh Population in the United States from 1850–1890," 135.

61. See, for example, "Hustlers for the Druid," *The Druid*, February 15, 1912.

62. A. Jones and B. Jones, "*Y Drych* and American Welsh Identities," 54.

63. *Y Drych*, March 29, 1888, April 28, 1892, March 16, 1893, October 5, 1893, cited in A. Jones and B. Jones, "*Y Drych* and American Welsh Identities," 53.

64. *Y Drych*, August 10, 1893, cited in A. Jones and B. Jones, "*Y Drych* and American Welsh Identities," 55.

65. A. Jones and B. Jones, "*Y Drych* and American Welsh Identities," 55.

66. B. Jones, "Ethnic Journalism and the Reconstruction of Identity," citing *Y Drych*, July 4, 1895. "Gomer's race" is a reference to a common belief of the period that the Welsh had descended from Gomer of the Old Testament.

67. B. Jones, "Ethnic Journalism and the Reconstruction of Identity"; A. Jones and B. Jones, "*Y Drych* and American Welsh Identities," 57. For journalism and the press in Wales during this period, see A. Jones, *Press, Politics and Society*.

68. B. Jones, "Ethnic Journalism and the Reconstruction of Identity."

69. Murdoch, *British Immigration*, 104–06, 112 (quotations). See also K. Miller and Boling, "Golden Streets, Bitter Tears," 27.

70. Murdoch, *British Emigration*, 107, 116 (quotation). His quoted reference is to Charlotte Erickson's *Invisible Immigrants*.

71. Murdoch, *British Emigration*, 117.

3. Early American Iron and the Welsh Plan

1. Knowles, *Mastering Iron*, 7–8.

2. Knowles, *Mastering Iron*, 39–41; Gordon, *American Iron*, 28, 103.

3. Knowles, *Mastering Iron*, 82.

4. Knowles, *Mastering Iron*, 98–99.

5. Knowles, *Mastering Iron*, 100.

6. Knowles, *Mastering Iron*, 105–6; Brody, *In Labor's Cause*, 26–27. For the Chartist uprising in Wales, see G. A. Williams, *Merthyr Rising*; Wilks, *South Wales and the Rising of 1839*; and D. Jones, *Last Rising*.

7. Bining, *British Regulation of the Colonial Iron Industry*, 122, 134; Temin, *Iron and Steel in Nineteenth-Century America*, 14.

8. R. Lewis, *Coal, Iron, and Slaves*, 11–12; Robbins, "Principio Company," 55–56; K. Johnson, "Genesis of the Baltimore Ironworks," 177, 157, respectively.

9. R. Lewis, *Coal, Iron, and Slaves*, 12; Bining, *Pennsylvania Iron Manufacture in the Eighteenth Century*, 187–92.

10. R. Lewis, *Coal, Iron, and Slaves*, 17; Schubert, *History of the British Iron and Steel Industry*, 335; Ashton, *Iron and Steel in the Industrial Revolution*, 99; Temin, *Iron and Steel in Nineteenth-Century America*, 14–15.

11. R. Lewis, *Coal, Iron, and Slaves*, 17; Temin, *Iron and Steel in Nineteenth-Century America*, 16.

12. R. Lewis, *Coal, Iron, and Slaves*, 17–18; Temin, *Iron and Steel in Nineteenth-Century America*, 17, 52.

13. Temin, *Iron and Steel in Nineteenth-Century America*, 18; Scrivenor, *History of the Iron Trade*, 252–53; Bining, *Pennsylvania Iron Manufacture in the Eighteenth Century*, 73.

14. R. Lewis, *Coal, Iron, and Slaves*, 19; Robbins, *Maryland's Iron Industry during the Revolutionary War Era*, 12; Scrivenor, *History of the Iron Trade*, 84–86.

15. V. Clark, *History of Manufactures in the United States*, 1:285–86, 260–62, 452, and chap. 14; Bishop, *History of American Manufactures from 1608–1860*, 590–91; Swank, *History of the Manufacture of Iron in All Ages*, 256.

16. Cappon, "History of the Southern Iron Industry, 9, 107c, 107d, 107f; K. Johnson, "Genesis of the Baltimore Ironworks," 178–79.

17. Knowles, *Mastering Iron*, 188; R. Lewis, *Coal, Iron, and Slaves*, 20–35; Gordon, *American Iron*, 85; W. Lewis, *Sloss Furnaces and the Rise of the Birmingham District*, 484–89; Berlin and Gutman, "Natives and Immigrants, Free Men and Slaves."

18. Bruce, *Virginia Iron Manufacture in the Slave Era*, 151, 153, 224; Schechter, "Free and Slave Labor in the Old South"; Dew, *Ironmaker to the Confederacy*, 23–26; Knowles, *Mastering Iron*, 190; Knowles, "Labor, Race, and Technology in the Confederate Iron Industry," 18–20.

19. Berthoff, *British Immigrants in Industrial America*, 64; *The Druid*, August 19, 1909; Rule, Mellen, and Wooldridge, *Standard History of Knoxville, Tennessee*, 208–10; Goodspeed, *History of Tennessee, Knox County Edition*, 856–57; J. Clark, "History of the Knoxville Iron Company," 19–28. For biographical sketches of David Richards, see "Hon. David Richards," *Y Drych*, April 12, 1906; "Hon. David Richards," *The Cambrian*, 181–82; R. Thomas, *Hanes Cymry America*, 152–54.

20. J. Clark, "Knoxville Iron Company," 55, quoting *Knoxville Weekly Chronicle*, February 19, 1873.

21. J. Clark, "Knoxville Iron Company," 55, citing *Knoxville Daily Chronicle*, December 11, 1870. The company employed free labor at the mines until 1878, when it began leasing state convicts to work in the mines, precipitating what became known as the Coal Creek Mine War. See Shapiro, *New South Rebellion*.

22. J. Clark, "Knoxville Iron Company," 55, quoting *Knoxville Daily Press and Herald*, September 8, 1871.

23. Armes, *Story of Coal and Iron*, 174–75; Council, Honerkamp, and Will, *Industrial Technology of Antebellum Alabama*, 69, 74; Fritz, *Autobiography of John Fritz*, 108–15, 149–72.

24. Council, Honerkamp, and Will, *Industrial Technology of Antebellum Alabama*, 88; Knowles, *Mastering Iron*, 196–97; US Congress, *Report of the Committee of the Senate upon the Relations between Labor and Capital*, 4:383.

25. Armes, *Story of Coal and Iron*, 356; R. Lewis, *Welsh Americans*, 83.

26. Armes, *Story of Coal and Iron*, 230–31; Council, Honerkamp, and Will, *Industrial Technology of Antebellum Alabama*, 88; R. Lewis, *Welsh Americans*, 87.

27. For Edwards's testimony, see US Congress, *Reports of the Committee of the Senate upon the Relations between Labor and Capital*, 4:384–87.

28. R. Lewis, *Welsh Americans*, 87–90.

29. Knowles, *Calvinists Incorporated*, 131–32; W. H. Jones, "Welsh Settlements in Ohio"; S. Williams, *Saga of Paddy's Run*, 176.

30. Knowles, *Calvinists Incorporated*, 137–38.

31. Knowles, *Calvinists Incorporated*, 162–63. For the Hanging Rock iron district, see also Willard, *Standard History of the Hanging Rock Iron Region*; Keeler, "Economic History of the Jackson County Iron Industry," 132–44; and Swank, *History of the Manufacture of Iron in All Ages*, 304–8.

32. Knowles, *Calvinists Incorporated*, 168; Van Vugt, *British Buckeyes*, 170.

33. Knowles, *Calvinists Incorporated*, 165.

34. Knowles, *Calvinists Incorporated*, 178, 182–83; Willard, *Standard History of the Hanging Rock Iron Region*, 449; Keeler, "Economic History of Jackson County Iron Industry," 19; Van Vugt, *British Buckeyes*, 170–71.

35. Knowles, *Calvinists Incorporated*, 185, 190–91, 208–9; Keeler, "Economic History of Jackson County Iron Industry," 181; E. Davis, *Industrial History*, 29.

36. Knowles, *Calvinists Incorporated*, 210–13.

37. Knowles, *Mastering Iron*, 112; Vance, *North American Railroad*, 18–21; Yates, "Discovery of the Process for Making Anthracite Iron," 207–8; Hyde, *Technological Change and the British Iron Industry*, 60–63, 90–91; C. Evans, *"Labyrinth of Flames,"* 27–28.

38. C. Evans, *"Labyrinth of Flames,"* 28.

39. Knowles, *Mastering Iron*, 116–18 (quotations on 117).

40. Knowles, *Mastering Iron*, 119, 126, 128.

41. Knowles, *Mastering Iron*, 128.

42. Knowles, *Mastering Iron*, 129–37.

43. Knowles, *Mastering Iron*, 140–41, citing Harvey, *Lonaconing Journals*, part I, 67, part II, 7–10; Dilts, *Great Road*, 286n13 (quotation). See also French, *History of the Rise and Progress of the Iron Trade*, 58.

44. Knowles, *Mastering Iron*, 144–45; Harvey, *Best-Dressed Miners*, 377–78. For the problem of excessive drinking at early American ironworks, see, for example, Bezís-Selfa, *Forging America*, 190–223.

45. Knowles, *Mastering Iron*, 146–48.

46. Knowles, *Mastering Iron*, 152–53; Gordon, *American Iron*, 78, 162; Swank, *History of the Manufacture of Iron in All Ages*, 256; Bishop, *History of American Manufactures from 1608–1860*, 591; R. Lewis, *Coal, Iron, and Slaves*, 19; Allen, "Mount Savage Iron Works."

47. Temin, *Iron and Steel in Nineteenth-Century America*, 51–53, 61; Swank, *History of the Manufacture of Iron in All* Ages, 354–61; Firmstone, "Sketch of Early Anthracite Furnaces," 152–56; Gordon, *American Iron*, 155–58.

48. Wallace, *St. Clair*, 85–88; S. Thomas, "Reminiscences of the Early Anthracite-Iron Industry," 901–7; P. Williams, *David Thomas*, 1–10; Swank, *History of the Manufacture of Iron in All Ages*, 360–62; French, *History of the United States Iron Trade*, 57–59.

49. S. Thomas, "Reminiscences of the Early Anthracite-Iron Industry," 908–28; P. Williams, *David Thomas*, 11–18; Wallace, *St. Clair*, 88–89. See also Chandler, "Anthracite Coal and the Beginnings of the Industrial Revolution"; Yates, "Discovery of the Process for Making Anthracite Iron"; Stapleton, *Transfer of Early Industrial Technology to America*, 169–207; and Adams, *Old Dominion Industrial Commonwealth*.

50. Wallace, *St. Clair*, 89–90; Chandler, "Anthracite Coal and the Beginnings of the Industrial Revolution"; Swank, *History of the Manufacture of Iron in All Ages*, 359.

51. Knowles, *Mastering Iron*, 99–100, based on 1850 census data for Montour County. For Joseph Parry, see E. K. Evans, *Cofiant Dr. Joseph Parry*; and John Davies et al., *Welsh Academy Encyclopaedia of Wales*, 652.

52. R. Thomas, *Hanes Cymry America*, 39.

53. W. Lewis, "Early History of the Lackawanna Iron and Coal Company." For more on Cyfarthfa and Dowlais ironworks, see C. Evans, *"Labyrinth of Flames."*

54. Folsom, *Urban Capitalists*, 25.

55. Folsom, *Urban Capitalists*, 25; W. Lewis, "Early History of the Lackawanna Iron and Coal Company," 428–38; W. D. Jones, "Wales in America," 3–4.

56. W. D. Jones, "Wales in America," 14.

57. Folsom, *Urban Capitalists*, 25–28, 33; W. Lewis, "Early History of the Lackawanna and Coal Company," 440–66; W. D. Jones, "Wales in America," 4–5.

58. W. D. Jones, "Wales in America," 252; "The Pennsylvania Iron Industry: Furnace and Forge of America," Explore PA History, accessed June 29, 2021, explorepahistory.com/story. php?storyId=1-9-17&chapter=3.

59. R. Thomas, *Hanes Cymry America*, 44–45.

60. W. D. Jones, "Wales in America," 15–16.

61. Berthoff, *British Immigrants in Industrial America*, 64. See also Clapham, *Economic History of Modern Britain*, 1:149; and US Congress, *Reports of the Immigration Commission*, no. 633 (June 15, 1910), 8:389.

62. Berthoff, *British Immigrants in Industrial America*, 64, quoting *Miners' Journal*, April 11, 1857.

63. Ingham, *Making Iron and Steel*, 21–22; Wade, *Urban Frontier*, 10, 45.

64. Dieterich-Ward, *Beyond Rust*, 2; Ruminski, *Iron Valley*; Gruenwald, *River of Enterprise*.

65. Ingham, *Making Iron and Steel*, 22–23; Bining, "Rise of Iron Manufacture in Western Pennsylvania," 239; Sullivan, *Industrial Worker in Pennsylvania*, 13–14; Swank, *History of the Manufacture of Iron in All Ages*, 227–28; S. Jones, *Pittsburgh in the Year 1826*, 50–57.

66. Ingham, *Making Iron and Steel*, 26–27; Swank, *History of the Manufacture of Iron in All Ages*, 230–31.

67. Temin, *Iron and Steel in Nineteenth-Century America*, 53.

68. Temin, *Iron and Steel in Nineteenth-Century America*, 76–77, 79–80; Gordon, *American Iron*, 158–59.

69. Sheppard, *Cloud by Day*, 29–31; Eavenson, *First Century and a Quarter of American Coal*, 225–27.

70. Swank, *History of the Manufacture of Iron in All Ages*, 217; Samways, "Welshman Installs First Revolutionary New Process in America Iron Puddling and Bar Rolling," 22. For a technical explanation of puddling see, Gordon, *American Iron*, 153–54.

71. Ingham, *Making Iron and Steel*, 30–31; *Iron Age*, September 25, 1924, 795; Cushing, *History of Allegheny County*, 2:438–39.

72. "First Rolling of Iron Bars in America," *The Cambrian*, 328–29.

73. Sheppard, *Cloud by Day*, 32–36; Eavenson, *First Century and a Quarter of American Coal*, 178; Long, *Where the Sun Never Shines*, 116–25.

74. H. Evans, *Iron Pioneer*, 33; Ingham, *Making Iron and Steel*, 226–27; *Iron Age*, February 7, 1907.

75. Ingham, *Making Iron and Steel*, 31–33; Porter and Livesay, *Merchants and Manufacturers*, 58–67. For information on Benjamin F. Jones, whose paternal great-grandfather was from Wales, and the American Iron Works, which evolved into the Jones & Laughlin Company, see "Benjamin Franklin 'B.F.' Jones (1824–1903)," National Park Service, last updated April 8, 2017, https://www.nps.gov/jofl/learn/historyculture/benjamin-franklin-jones.htm; "Jones, Benjamin Franklin," *DAB*, 10:162–63; Fleming, *History of Pittsburgh and Environs*, 3:832; and Cushing, *History of Allegheny County*, 2:233.

76. Linaberger, "Rolling Mill Riots of 1850," 1–3.

77. Linaberger, "Rolling Mill Riots of 1850," 4–7; *Pittsburgh Daily Morning Post*, December 24, 1849, January 7, 1850.

78. Linaberger, "Rolling Mill Riots of 1850," 8–9; *Pittsburgh Daily Morning Post*, January 14, 22, February 12, 25, 1850.

79. Linaberger, "Rolling Mill Riots of 1850," 10–11; *Pittsburgh Daily Morning Post*, February 18, 19, 1850.

80. Linaberger, "Rolling Mill Riots of 1850," 10–12; *Pittsburgh Morning Daily Post*, March 2, 1850; *Pittsburgh Morning Chronicle*, March 2, 1850; *Pittsburgh Daily Gazette*, March 2, 1850.

81. Linaberger, "Rolling Mill Riots of 1850," 10–16; *Pittsburgh Morning Gazette*, March 4, 1850.

82. Linaberger, "Rolling Mill Riots of 1850," 17–18.

4. The Age of Steel Begins

1. Ingham, *Making Iron and Steel*, 49–50; Fitch, *Steel Workers*, 39–42. The literature on the Bessemer process is vast, and it is technical for the most part. For relatively recent studies that are more accessible to lay readers, see, for example, Kobus, *City of Steel*, 87–147; Misa, *Nation of Steel*, 5–43; Gordon, *American Iron*, 222–24; and Birch, *Economic History of the British Iron and Steel Industry*, 315, 319–25.

2. Ingham, *Making Iron and Steel*, 37–39. See also Tweedale, *Sheffield Steel and America*, 36–37, chap. 2; and Fitch, *Steel Workers*, 38–39.

3. Temin, *Iron and Steel in Nineteenth Century America*, app. C, table C.7, 276–77.

4. Ingham, *Making Iron and Steel*, 51 (quotation), 77. See also Mapes, "*Iron Age*: An Iron Manufacturer's Journal and the 'Labor Problem' in the Age of Enterprise," 6; *Bulletin of the American Iron and Steel Association*, February 24, 1892; Clark, *History of Manufactures in the United States*, 3:83.

5. Fitch, *Steel Workers*, 42–43.

6. Ingham, *Making Iron and Steel*, 85–87. See also American Iron and Steel Association, *Directory to the Iron and Steel Works*, 1884 and 1894; and Elbaum and Wilkinson, "Industrial Relations and Uneven Development," 281. For descriptions of the open-hearth process that

are accessible to lay readers, see Misa, *Nation of Steel*, 74–83; Kobus, *City of Steel*, 155–96; and Gordon, *American Iron*, 226–29.

7. Hendrick, *Life of Andrew Carnegie*, 308–9.

8. Ingham, *Making Iron and Steel*, 85, 87; US Bureau of the Census, *Twelfth Census of the United States: 1900*, vol. 10, *Manufactures*, pt. 4, 3–95; US Bureau of the Census, *Thirteenth Census of the United States, 1910*, vol. 10, *Manufactures*, 1909, "Reports for Principal Industries," 205–61.

9. Ingham, *Making Iron and Steel*, 50, 52; Mapes, "*Iron Age*: An Iron Manufacturer's Journal," 5–6.

10. Yearley, *Britons in American Labor*, 85–89.

11. Yearley, *Britons in American Labor*, 89–90.

12. Yearley, *Britons in American Labor*, 142; US Bureau of the Census, *Status of Population in the U. S. at the Tenth Census*, 1:731; US Congress, Senate, *Report of the Immigration Commission*, "Immigrants in the Iron and Steel Industries," Senate Doc. 633, vols. 8 and 9, 1910.

13. Wright, "Amalgamated Association of Iron and Steel Workers," 401–2; Jarrett, "Story of the Iron Workers," 171–77; Fitch, *Steel Workers*, 77.

14. Wright, "Amalgamated Association of Iron and Steel Workers," 405–7; Fitch, *Steel Workers*, 78–79; Jarrett, "Story of the Iron Workers," 272–73; Hogan, *Economic History of the Iron and Steel Industry*, 1:86–87.

15. Wright, "Amalgamated Association of Iron and Steel Workers," 411–12; Jarrett, "Story of the Iron Workers," 277–79; Fitch, *Steel Workers*, 81–82.

16. Wright, "Amalgamated Association of Iron and Steel Workers," 413; Jarrett, "Story of the Iron Workers," 279–81; Fitch, *Steel Workers*, 83; Yearley, *Britons in American Labor*, 145–46.

17. Krause, *Battle for Homestead*, 102, quoting the *Bulletin of the American Iron and Steel Association*, February 6, 1875.

18. Krause, *Battle for Homestead*, 103.

19. Wright, "Amalgamated Association of Iron and Steel Workers," 408; Krause, *Battle for Homestead*, 103–4 (quotation).

20. Wright, "Amalgamated Association of Iron and Steel Workers," 413–16; Jarrett, "Story of the Iron Workers," 281–83; Fitch, *Steel Workers*, 85–87; Hogan, *Economic History of the Iron and Steel Industry*, 1:88–90.

21. Jarrett, "Story of the Iron Workers," 271–73; "National Forge Officers," *National Labor Tribune*, July 8, 1876.

22. "Miles S. Humphreys," Pennsylvania State Senate Historical Biographies, accessed January 26, 2021, https://www.legis.state.pa.us/cfdocs/legis/BiosHistory/MemBio.cfm?ID=4793&body=S; Knowles, *Mastering Iron*, 189.

23. "Miles S. Humphreys," Pennsylvania State Senate Historical Biographies, accessed January 26, 2021, https://www.legis.state.pa.us/cfdocs/legis/BiosHistory/MemBio.cfm?ID=7469&body=H. For references to Humphreys's political career, see Krause, *Battle for Homestead*, 94, 97, 99, 100, 108, 135,136, 200; and Couvares, *Remaking of Pittsburgh*, 63, 64–65, 66, 68, 70. For his role in the St. David's Society, see, for example, *The Cambrian* 7 (April 1887): 123–24, and 13 (April 1893): 128.

24. Wright, "Amalgamated Association of Iron and Steel Workers," 410, 412; Jarrett, "Story of the Iron Workers," 175–76; Fitch, *Steel Workers*, 77.

25. Yearley, *Britons in American Labor*, 143; US Congress, Senate, *Report of the Committee of the Senate upon the Relations between Labor and Capital*, 48th Cong., 2nd sess., 1885, 1:1153, 1159.

26. Boston, *British Chartists in America*, 97; Yearley, *Britons in American Labor*, 144; *Report of the 1st Annual Session of the Federation of Organized Trades and Labor Unions of the United States and Canada, Pittsburg, Pennsylvania, Dec. 15–18, 1881*, 8, accessed at https://babel.hathitrust.org/cgi/pt?id=msu.31293010524464&view=1up&seq=33&skin=2021; US Congress, Senate, *Report of the Committee of the Senate upon the Relations between Labor and Capital*, 48th Cong., 2nd sess., 1885, 1:1118–69.

27. Yearley, *Britons in American Labor*, 89, 145; US Congress, Senate, *Report of the Committee of the Senate upon the Relations between Labor and Capital*, 48th Cong., 2nd sess., 1885, 1:1122, 1125, 1129, 1135, 1137. For Jarrett's Welsh background, see Boston, *British Chartists in America*, 97. For Jarrett's own assessment of his term as president and the circumstances of his departure, see Jarrett, "Story of the Iron Workers," 282–83, 285, 288–95. See also Robinson, *Amalgamated Association of Iron, Steel, and Tin Workers*, 145, 151.

28. Wright, "Amalgamated Association of Iron and Steel Workers," 416–18; Fitch, *Steel Workers*, 86. For the vice presidents, see *Amalgamated Journal* 10, no. 32 (May 6, 1909). The six Welsh vice presidents were Llewellyn Lewis, Ben I. Davis, Ben F. Jones, D. J. Davis, John William, and Walter Larkin.

29. Van Tine, *Making of the Labor Bureaucrat*, 1, 4–5, 10–11, 19–22.

30. Van Tine, *Making of the Labor Bureaucrat*, 17–18, 24–25, 28–30, 58, 61 (quotations, 25, 30).

31. Van Tine, *Making of the Labor Bureaucrat*, 84, 158–59, 176–77.

32. Van Tine, *Making of the Labor Bureaucrat*, 180–81.

33. For John R. Davies, see Jordan, *Genealogical and Personal History of Western Pennsylvania*, 2:29.

34. *The Cambrian* 2 (July–August 1882): 179–80; Bennett, "Iron Workers in Woods Run," 354.

35. Bennett, "Iron Workers in Woods Run," 315–16.

36. Bennett, "Iron Workers in Woods Run," 126; *National Labor Tribune*, November 21, 1885. See also *National Labor Tribune*, May 13, 1882, November 14, 1885, and May 5, 1888.

37. J. J. Davis, *Iron Puddler*, 173–94, 204–41; Zieger, "Career of James J. Davis," 67–89.

38. Berthoff, *British Immigrants in Industrial America*, 65. See also Great Britain, Parliamentary Papers, *Report of the Foreign Commerce of the United States of America*, 1880, vol. 72 (C. 2570), 176–78; *American Manufacturer*, September 19, 26, October 10, 31, 1879; Robinson, *Amalgamated Association of Iron, Steel, and Tin Workers*, 44.

39. Erickson, *American Industry and the European Immigrant*, 4–5, 21–22 (quotation), quoting testimony of George T. Clarke, trustee of Dowlais Works, in Great Britain, Parliamentary Papers, *Reports of the Trade Union Commissioners*, 1867–1868, 39:92.

40. Erickson, *American Industry and the European Immigrant*, 22–23, 33.

41. Erickson, *American Industry and the European Immigrant*, 46, 49 (quotation), quoting testimony of Clarke, in Great Britain, Parliamentary Papers, *Reports of the Trade Union Commissioners*, 1867–1868, 39:92–93.

42. Erickson, *American Industry and the European Immigrant*, 53; *Aberdare Times*, June 16, 1866, 4.

43. Erickson, *American Industry and the European Immigrant*, 57, citing *Fincher's Trades' Review*, September 30, 1865.

44. Erickson, *American Industry and the European Immigrant*, 57, citing letter from "Oblique," *Workingman's Advocate*, September 30, 1865, 6–7.

45. Erickson, *American Industry and the European Immigrant*, 57–58, quoting Jarrett and Martin, letter to the Iron and Steel Workers of England, Scotland and Wales, 856.

46. Erickson, *American Industry and the European Immigrant*, 58, quoting E. Trow, Darlington, to W. Martin, September 24, 1881, which appeared in the *Journal of the Proceedings of the Annual Convention of the Amalgamated Association of Iron, Steel, and Tin Workers* (1882) (hereafter, *AAISW Proceedings*, plus the relevant year).

47. Erikson, *American Industry and the European Immigrant*, 148–49; Hutchinson, *Legislative History of American Immigration Policy*, 83–84.

48. Erickson, *American Industry and the European Immigrant*, 155, 158.

49. Jarrett, "Story of the Iron Workers," 310–11; Erickson, *American Industry and the European Immigrant*, 159–60; Jarrett, AAISW President's Report (1883), 1105. See also Harris, *Welshmen and the United States*, 65; and *Iron and Coal Trades Review*, January 4, 1878.

50. Erickson, *American Industry and the European Immigrant*, 161–62; *American Iron and Steel Bulletin*, October 1, 29, 1884; *Congressional Record*, 48th Cong., 2nd sess., 1885, vol. 16, pt. 2, 1625–26.

51. Erickson, *American Industry and European Immigrant*, 164, quoting United States, *Statutes at Large*, 48th Cong., 2nd sess., 1885, vol. 23, 332–33. For the Foran Act, see also Hutchinson, *Legislative History of American Immigration Policy*, 87–89; and Garis, *Immigration Restriction*, 90–92.

52. Bridge, *Inside History of the Carnegie Steel Company*, 153.

53. Krause, *Battle for Homestead*, 178 (quotation); Jarrett, "Story of the Iron Workers," 293; Fitch, *Steel Workers*, 108–9.

54. Krause, *Battle for Homestead*, 178–79, 184, 190, 194; Fitch, *Steel Workers*, 110; *National Labor Tribune*, May 6, 1882; *AAISW Proceedings* (1882), 919, 806, respectively; *Pittsburgh Evening Telegraph*, March 6, 10, 1882; *Pittsburgh Times*, March 9, 1882.

55. Krause, *Battle for Homestead*, 200; *Pittsburgh Dispatch*, July 4, 1882; *AAISW Proceedings* (1882), 814–17, 967, (1884), 1084–87, 1112; Jarrett, "Iron Workers," 293–94; *National Labor Tribune*, April 1, October 28, 1882, January 6, 1883.

56. Fitch, *Steel Workers*, 112–13; *National Labor Tribune*, February 7, December 12, 1885; *Pittsburgh Chronicle-Telegraph*, December 18, 1884, January 2, February 5, 1885.

57. Fitch, *Steel Workers*, 114–15; *National Labor Tribune*, December 12, 1885, January 22, July 9, 1887, May 5, 1888.

58. Krause, *Battle for Homestead*, 235; *National Labor Tribune*, January 9, 16, April 24, 1886, April 14, 28, May 5, October 6, November 3, 1888.

59. Hendrick, *Life of Andrew Carnegie*, 205; Bridge, *Inside History of the Carnegie Steel Company*, 79, 104.

60. Hendrick, *Life of Andrew Carnegie*, 205.

61. "Hopkin Thomas Project," Catasauqua Public Library.

62. "Late Captain William R. Jones," *The Cambrian*, 98.

63. Armes, *Story of Coal and Iron in Alabama*, 176.

64. Kobus, *City of Steel*, 105; "Late Capt. W. R. Jones: Biographical Sketch and Crown Memorial Poems," 86–87.

65. Wall, *Andrew Carnegie*, 312–15. For Alexander Holley, see McHugh, *Alexander Holley and the Makers of Steel*. On Andrew Carnegie, I have relied on Joseph Wall's biography, but there are others. See, for example, Livesay, *Andrew Carnegie and the Rise of Big Business*; Krass, *Carnegie*; and Nasaw, *Andrew Carnegie*.

66. Kobus, *City of Steel*, 104; Wall, *Andrew Carnegie*, 315–16; Carnegie, *Autobiography of Andrew Carnegie*, 205 (quotation). For John Fritz, see Fritz, *Autobiography of John Fritz*.

67. Wall, *Andrew Carnegie*, 315–16 (quotation on 316). See also Casson, *Romance of Steel*, 27.

68. Wall, *Andrew Carnegie*, 344–45, 520 (quotation on 345).

69. Wall, *Andrew Carnegie*, 520–21 (quotation on 521).

70. W. R. Jones to E. V. McCandless, February 25, 1875, quoted in Bridge, *Inside History of the Carnegie Steel Company*, 81–82.

71. Wall, *Andrew Carnegie*, 529–30; Kobus, *City of Steel*, 108.

72. Wall, *Andrew Carnegie*, 532.

73. Bridge, *Inside History of the Carnegie Steel Company*, 79.

74. Wall, *Andrew Carnegie*, 532 (quotation); Bridge, *Inside History of the Carnegie Steel Company*, 80, 104. See also Kobus, *City of Steel*, 111–12. For an extended list of Jones's inventions, see "Late Capt. W. R. Jones," 88. See also Bridge, *Inside History of the Carnegie Steel Company*, 106, quoting Joseph D. Weeks in *American Manufacturer*, October 4, 1889.

75. Carnegie, *Autobiography*, 205. See also Hendrick, *Life of Andrew Carnegie*, 208.

76. "Late Capt. W. R. Jones," 85. See also "Late Captain William R. Jones," *The Cambrian*, 99; and "Captain William Richard Jones, Inventive Genius and Philanthropist," *The Druid*, December 19, 1912, 7.

77. "Captain William Richard Jones," *The Cambrian*, 264.

78. "Hopkin Thomas Project," Catasauqua Public Library.

79. R. A. Griffiths, *Free and Public*, 25, 27–28, 41, 43.

80. Krause, *Battle for Homestead*, 241; Fitch, *Steel Workers*, 119–20; *Pittsburgh Chronicle-Telegraph*, May 18,1889, July 11, 12, 15, 18, 1889; *Pittsburgh Commercial Gazette*, July 12, 13, 1889; *National Labor Tribune*, May 25, June 15, 1889; *AAISW Proceedings* (1890), 2962–64.

81. Krause, *Battle for Homestead*, 243–44; Fitch, *Steel Workers*, 42–44.

82. Krause, *Battle for Homestead*, 246–48; Fitch, *Steel Workers*, 121; *National Labor Tribune*, May 25, June 15, July 1, 1889; *Pittsburgh Chronicle-Telegraph*, May 15, 18, 20, 23, June 20, 21, July 15, 1889; *AAISW Proceedings* (1890), 2962.

83. Krause, *Battle for Homestead*, 248; Fitch, *Steel Workers*, 121. Full reports on the strike of 1889 are to be found in President Weihe's report, *AAISW Proceedings* (1890), 2962–77; and *National Labor Tribune*, May 25, June 15, July 13, July 20, 1889.

84. Fitch, *Steel Workers*, 124; Krause, *Battle for Homestead*, 287.

85. Krause, *Battle for Homestead*, 288; *Pittsburgh Chronicle-Telegraph*, January 22, 1890, April 22, 1892.

86. Krause, *Battle for Homestead*, 288–89; Holt, "Trade Unionism in the British and U.S. Steel Industries," 10, 11, 14, 26; *National Labor Tribune*, April 11, 1892.

87. Finch, *Steel Workers*, 125, quoting US Congress, House of Representatives, Misc. Doc. No. 335, 52nd Cong., 1st sess. (1892), 33; Hogan, *Economic History of the Iron and Steel Industry*, 1:231–32.

88. The outlines of the lockout are well known, but I have followed the events of the Homestead Lockout of 1892 from Krause, *Battle for Homestead*, 12–43. Other scholars have presented authoritative summaries as well. See, for example, Fitch, *Steel Workers*, 122–32; and Burgoyne, *Homestead Strike of 1892*. See also US Congress, House Committee on the Judiciary, *Report 2447: Investigation of the Homestead Troubles* (hereafter cited as US Congress, *Report 2447*).

89. Krause, *Battle for Homestead*, 17–21. For Martin Murray, see *Homestead Times*, August 5, 1882, April 21, 1883; *National Labor Tribune*, April 26, 1890; Burgoyne, *Homestead Strike of 1892*, 59–61, 67, 92–93, 197; *AAISW Proceedings* (1891), 3245; *Pittsburgh Commercial Gazette*, July 7, 1892; US Congress, *Report 2447*, 90–91; *Pittsburgh Commercial Gazette*, July 7, 1892; *Pittsburgh Dispatch*, July 7, 1892; and *Pittsburgh Press*, July 7, 1892.

90. Krause, *Battle for Homestead*, 22.

91. Krause, *Battle for Homestead*, 22–23; Burgoyne, *Homestead Strike of 1892*, 65–67, 93; *Pittsburgh Post*, July 7, 8, 1892; *Pittsburgh Dispatch*, July 7, 1892; US Congress, *Report 2447*, 12.

92. Forrester, "John E. Morris Story," 24; *Western Mail*, July 26, 1892, 5.

93. *Pittsburgh Times*, July 8, 1892. The story was picked up by the South Wales newspapers. See "Pittsburgh Labour War," *Western Mail*, July 26, 1892, 5.

94. Forrester, "John E. Morris Story," 25.

95. "Letter from Another Welsh Emigrant," *Western Mail*, July 26, 1892, 5.

96. The full text of the advisory committee's address can be found in the *National Labor Tribune*, July 30, 1892.

97. Krause, *Battle for Homestead*, 330; Burgoyne, *Homestead Strike of 1892*, 183, 297.

98. David Davies, "Carnegie's Great Works," *Western Mail*, December 27, 1898, 4.

99. Erickson, *American Industry and the European Immigrant*, 125–27; Fitch, *Steel Workers*, 27, 29, 33–34, 78, 87.

5. Welsh Tinplate and the McKinley Tariff

1. Arthur L. Lunt, "Canning and Preserving," in US Bureau of the Census, *Twelfth Census of the United States: 1900*, vol. 9, *Manufactures*, part 3, 464, 467. See also Pursell, "Tariff and Technology," 267–68. Tinplate used for roofing was usually called terneplate, which was a sheet of iron or steel coated with an alloy of lead and tin.

2. Ingham, *Making Iron and Steel*, 41l; Gilmer, "Birth of the American Crucible Steel Industry," 30–32; Rutherford, *Romancing in Tin Plate*, 53.

3. Wilkins, *History of the Iron, Steel, Tinplate Industry*, 420, 422 (quotation).

4. Cronemeyer, "Development of the Tin-Plate Industry [part I]," 29.

5. Jason Togyer, "The 'Tinplate Liar' of McKeesport," Tube City Online: Steel Heritage, 2007, accessed February 5, 2021, http://www.tubecityonline.com/steel/demmler_fr.html.

6. Pursell, "Tariff and Technology," 269; *Iron Age* 48 (December 31, 1891): 1166.

7. Rutherford, *Romancing in Tin Plate*, 58.

8. Rutherford, *Romancing in Tin Plate*, 59.

9. Rutherford, *Romancing in Tin Plate*, 66.

10. Samuel, *Short History of the Tin and Tinplate Trade*, 7, 65. For "Greater Alcania," see Wilkins, *History of the Iron, Steel, Tinplate, and Other Trades of Wales*, 422.

11. Paul Jenkins, *"Twenty by Fourteen,"* 9–13. See also J. Jones, *Tinplate Industry with Special Reference to Its Relations with the Iron and Steel Industries*, 1–7.

12. Minchinton, "Diffusion of Tinplate Manufacture," 349.

13. Quoted in Paul Jenkins, *"Twenty by Fourteen,"* 24.

14. Minchinton, "Diffusion of Tinplate Manufacture," 352; Minchinton, *British Tinplate Industry*, 10–11; Great Britain, Parliamentary Documents, Home Office, *Report on the Conditions of Employment in the Manufacture of Tinplates*, 3 (hereafter cited as Home Office, *Report on the Conditions*).

15. Paul Jenkins, *"Twenty by Fourteen,"* 24–27; Minchinton, *British Tinplate Industry*, 16–17, 19.

16. Dunbar, *Tin-Plate Industry*, 5–11. For the full report Dunbar used, see Great Britain, House of Commons, Parliamentary Documents, *Report of the Chief Inspector of Factories and Workshops*, 45–59. See also J. Jones, *Tinplate Industry with Special Reference to Its Relations with the Iron and Steel Industries*, 8–9. For the process in Wales versus that used in the United States, see "Comparison of American with Welsh Tinplate Making," *Industrial World*, September 11, 1896, 2.

17. Dunbar, *Tin-Plate Industry*, 1, 6–7. Only a few improvements had been made by 1912. For a similar description of the process twenty-four years after the 1888 report, see Home Office, *Report on the Conditions*, 5–9, 14–15. See also Samuel, *Short History of the Tin and the Tinplate Trade*, 51–54.

18. Dunbar, *Tin-Plate Industry*, 8. See also Home Office, *Report on the Conditions*, 6; and Samuel, *Short History of the Tin and the Tinplate Trade*, 54.

19. Dunbar, *Tin-Plate Industry*, 8–9. See also Home Office, *Report on the Conditions*, 6–8; and Samuel, *Short History of the Tin and the Tinplate Trade*, 54–55.

20. Dunbar, *Tin-Plate Industry*, 10–12. See also Home Office, *Report on the Conditions*, 8–10, 14–15; and Samuel, *Short History of the Tin and the Tinplate Trade*, 56–57.

21. Minchinton, *British Tinplate Industry*, 25–27, 29.

22. Paul Jenkins, *"Twenty by Fourteen,"* 28, 37; Samuel, *Short History of the Tin and the Tinplate Trade*, 65–86; Minchinton, *British Tinplate Industry*, 34–35.

23. Watts, "Changes in Location of the South Wales Iron and Steel Industry," 296, 298–99; Minchinton, *British Tinplate Industry*, 35–36.

24. Watts, "Changes in Location of the South Wales Iron and Steel Industry," 294, 300–304. See also J. Jones, *Tinplate Industry with Special Reference to Its Relations with the Iron and Steel Industries*, 45–48; and Minchinton, *British Tinplate Industry*, 37, 39.

25. Minchinton, *British Tinplate Industry*, 44–46, 52–53.

26. Minchinton, *British Tinplate Industry*, 108–9, 125.

27. Dunbar, *Tin-Plate Industry*, 66.

28. Paul Jenkins, *"Twenty by Fourteen,"* 161.

29. John, *Industrial Development of South Wales*, 59; Minchinton, *British Tinplate Industry*, 110.

30. Minchinton, *British Tinplate Industry*, 111.

31. Dunbar, *Tin-Plate Industry*, 71n1.

32. Dunbar, *Tin-Plate Industry*, 96, 71–72; J. Jones, *Tinplate Industry with Special Reference to Its Relations with the Iron and Steel Industries*, 26–27.

33. Dunbar, *Tin-Plate Industry*, 67–28; Paul Jenkins, *"Twenty by Fourteen,"* 40.

34. Minchinton, *British Tinplate Industry*, 113.

35. Minchinton, *British Tinplate Industry*, 112; Paul Jenkins, *"Twenty by Fourteen,"* 43–44.

36. Paul Jenkins, *"Twenty by Fourteen,"* 148.

37. Paul Jenkins, *"Twenty by Fourteen,"* 150.

38. Paul Jenkins, *"Twenty by Fourteen,"* 151–54.

39. Home Office, *Report on the Conditions*, 20; Paul Jenkins, *"Twenty by Fourteen,"* 156–57.

40. Paul Jenkins, *"Twenty by Fourteen,"* 158–60.

41. Home Office, *Report on the Conditions*, 7; Paul Jenkins, *"Twenty by Fourteen,"* 160–65, 171–72.

42. J. Jones, *Tinplate Industry with Special Reference to Its Relations with the Iron and Steel Industries*, xi.

43. Minchinton, *British Tinplate Industry*, 114. See also J. Jones, *Tinplate Industry with Special Reference to Its Relations with the Iron and Steel Industries*, x.

44. Paul Jenkins, *"Twenty by Fourteen,"* 175. For a personal perspective on the labor movement, see Pugh, *Men of Steel, by One of Them*.

45. J. Jones, *Tinplate Industry with Special Reference to Its Relations with the Iron and Steel Industries*, 30–39; Minchinton, *British Tinplate Industry*, 115–16.

46. Wright, "Amalgamated Association of Iron and Steel Workers," 408.

47. Minchinton, *British Tinplate Industry*, 118–19; Pugh, *Men of Steel, by One of Them*, 121; J. Jones, *Tinplate Industry with Special Reference to Its Relations with the Iron and Steel Industries*, 192.

48. Minchinton, *British Tinplate Industry*, 119–20; J. Jones, *Tinplate Industry with Special Reference to Its Relations with the Iron and Steel Industries*, 55–58.

49. Minchinton, *British Tinplate Industry*, 120. Membership numbers vary depending on the source consulted.

50. Minchinton, *British Tinplate Industry*, 123; *Industrial World*, October 11, 1895, 2.

51. Minchinton, *British Tinplate Industry*, 124–25. For an example of how the interests of mill workers differed from those of tinhouse employees in the United States, see the article bylined "Swansea Boy," "The Tinplate Business," *National Labor Tribune*, December 15, 1883,

52. J. Jones, *Tinplate Industry with Special Reference to Its Relations with the Iron and Steel Industries*, 59, 61.

53. Cronemeyer, "Development of the Tin-Plate Industry [part 1]," 26–27. See also James M. Swank, "An Important Issue," *National Labor Tribune*, January 5, 1889.

54. Togyer, "'Tinplate Liar' of McKeesport."

55. Cronemeyer, "Development of the Tin-Plate Industry [part 1]," 32–33.

56. Cronemeyer, "Development of the Tin-Plate Industry [part 1]," 35–36, 39.

57. Cronemeyer, "Development of the Tin-Plate Industry [part 1]," 39–40.

58. M. Summers, *Party Games*, 216–17 (quotation on 217). See also Skrabec, *William McKinley, Apostle of Protectionism*, 71–72.

59. Cronemeyer, "Development of the Tin-Plate Industry [part 1]," 41; "Mr. John Jarrett, Pittsburgh, Pa.," *The Cambrian*, 65–66.

60. M. Summers, *Party Games*, 218.

61. Cronemeyer, "Development of the Tin-Plate Industry [part 1]," 41–42; "Mr. John Jarrett," *The Cambrian*, 65–66.

62. Togyer, "'Tinplate Liar of McKeesport'"; Cronemeyer, "Development of the Tin-Plate Industry [part 1]," 41; H. Morgan, *William McKinley and His America*, 126; Skrabec, *William McKinley, Apostle of Protectionism*, 73; Merry, *President McKinley*, 79–82.

63. Pursell, "Tariff and Technology," 271, quoting US Congress, House Committee on Ways and Means, *Revision of the Tariff*, letter from A. B. Farquhar, March 21, 1890, 1217.

64. McAdoo, "Immigration and the Tariff," 405; Pursell, "Tariff and Technology," 271. See also Erickson, *American Industry and the European Immigrant*; and Reitano, *Tariff Question in the Gilded Age*.

65. H. Morgan, *William McKinley and His America*, 142–47.

66. "The Tariff of 1890," speech in the House of Representatives, May 7, 1890, in McKinley, *Speeches and Addresses*, 411.

67. Quoted in Rutherford, *Romancing in Tin Plate*, 55.

68. Speech delivered at Niles, Ohio, August 22, 1891, in McKinley, *Speeches and Addresses*, 554.

69. Irwin, "Did Late-Nineteenth-Century U.S. Tariffs Promote Infant Industries?," 335–60. For an examination of the free trade position, see Irwin, *Against the Tide*. For a brief discussion of free trade and protectionist thought, see Reitano, *Tariff Question in the Gilded Age*, 57–62.

70. Quoted in Rutherford, *Romancing in Tin Plate*, 55.

71. Dunbar, *Tin-Plate Industry*, 14; Brands, *American Colossus*, 539–40; "McKinley Act, October 1, 1890," in Proctor, *Tariff Acts Passed by the Congress of the United States*, 333 (quotation).

72. Taussig, *Tariff History of the United States*, 345 (quotation), 346–48. See also Taussig, "Iron Industry in the United States," 143, 175.

73. Cronemeyer, "Development of the Tinplate Industry [part 2]," 129, citing US Department of Treasury, Special Reports to the Secretary of Treasury, by Ira Ayer, June 30, 1894, and June 30, 1896.. See also "American Tin Plate Industry," *American Artisan* 29 (May 25, 1895): 17–25.

74. Dunbar, *Tin-Plate Industry*, 17; *Iron Age*, August 28, 1890, February 19, 1891, January 17, 1895.

75. Paul Jenkins, *"Twenty by Fourteen,"* 40–43.

76. Pursell, "Tariff and Technology," 273, quoting the *Ironmonger* from *Iron Age* 48 (July 16, 1891): 90.

77. J. Jones, *Tinplate Industry with Special Reference to Its Relations with the Iron and Steel Industries*, 100.

78. J. Jones, *Tinplate Industry with Special Reference to Its Relations with the Iron and Steel Industries*, 101–4, 107 (quotation).

79. "The American Tinplate Trade," *South Wales Daily Post*, September 3, 1898, 3.

80. "The Tinplate Trade, the Position of the Industry in America," *South Wales Daily News*, July 16, 1898, 6.

81. "The Tinplate Trade, Progress of the Industry in America," *Llanelly Mercury*, September 16, 1897, 3.

82. "Tin Plates Abroad," *American Artisan* 29 (May 11, 1895): 24.

83. "Welsh Mills Idle," *American Artisan* 29 (May 18, 1895): 29. For a fuller development of how Welsh mill operators responded to the crisis, see, for example, several articles all titled "Welsh Tinplate Trade," in the *National Labor Tribune*, February 21, 28, 1895, and April 18, 1895.

84. "Welsh Tinplate Trade," *National Labor Tribune*, February 21, 1895, 8, citing *American Manufacturer*, January 30, 1895.

85. "America and the Tinplate Trade," *Llanelly Mercury*, February 25, 1897, 5.

86. "Enormous Cost of Setting Up," *The Cambrian* (Swansea), December 26, 1890, 5. See also "America and the Tinplate Trade," *South Wales Daily Post*, February 28, 1891, 3.

87. "South Wales Tinplate Manufacturers in America," *The Cambrian* (Swansea), October 24, 1890, 8.

88. "Future of the Welsh Industry," *South Wales Daily News*, October 28, 1891, 6.

89. "Interesting Interview with Mr. J. H. Rogers," *South Wales Daily News*, June 12, 1895, 5.

90. "American Corruption," *The Cambrian* (Swansea), July 23, 1897, 4.

91. "Future of Tinplate Workers," *Llanelly Mercury*, August 26, 1897, 5.

92. "Ammanford and Its Circumstances," *Industrial World*, August 30, 1895, 5.

93. See, for example, *South Wales Daily News*, April 6, 1895, 5, August 31, 1895, 4; and *Evening Express* (Cardiff), September 21, 1895, 2.

94. "Morriston Workmen Off to America," *South Wales Daily News*, September 3, 1898, 4.

95. "Emigration," *Industrial World*, May 10, 1895, 9, reprinted in the *National Labor Tribune*, May 23, 1895. See also "Outlook in the States," *South Wales Daily News*, August 9, 1895, 4, citing the *Industrial World*.

96. "Warning to Welsh Tinplaters," *Western Mail*, October 17, 1898, 6.

97. "Warning to Welsh Tinplaters," *Industrial World*, September 27, 1895, 5.

98. "Interesting Message from a Welsh Workman," *South Wales Daily Post*, July 31, 1897, 3.

99. "Call to Welsh Tinplate Workers in America," *Evening Express*, October 2, 1894, 2.

100. "Dissatisfaction with America," *South Wales Daily Post*, September 7, 1895, 7.

101. "Welsh Tinplaters in America," *South Wales Daily Post*, January 12, 1899, 3, citing the *Llanelly Mercury*. See also *National Labor Tribune*, February 16, 1899.

102. See Carter, "Industrial, Industrious, and Diverse."

103. "Return of Tinplaters from America," *Tarian y Gweithiur* [The workman's shield], December 14, 1899, 4. Thanks to Bill Jones.

104. "Great Strike in America," *Cardiff Times*, October 6, 1894, 6.

105. "The Invitation to Welshmen to Come Home," *Western Mail*, November 15, 1894, 5.

106. "Tinplate Trade in America," *South Wales Echo*, October 17, 1894, 4.

107. "Welsh Tinplate Workmen in America," *South Wales Daily Post*, September 9, 1895, 3.

108. "Welsh Tinplate Workmen in America," *South Wales Daily Post*, September 9, 1895, 3.

109. "Tinplaters in the States," *South Wales Daily News*, November 28, 1895, 4.

110. Paul Jenkins, *"Twenty by Fourteen,"* 43.

111. Dunbar, *Tin-Plate Industry*, 25.

112. Dunbar, *Tin-Plate Industry*, 27.

6. The Rise of the Trusts and Decline of Greater Alcania

1. Pursell, "Tariff and Technology," 267.

2. Berthoff, *British Immigrants in Industrial America*, 65.

3. Pursell, "Tariff and Technology," 276–77.

4. US Department of Treasury, Special Report to the Secretary of the Treasury, by Ira Ayer, April 26, 1892, 35, 36, respectively.

5. "Tin-Working in America," *Evening Express* (Cardiff), November 17, 1892, 4, citing an article from the *Pittsburgh Dispatch*.

6. Pursell, "Tariff and Technology," 277–78.

7. Pursell, "Tariff and Technology," 277–78; Commonwealth of Pennsylvania, Secretary of Internal Affairs, *Annual Report* (1895), 14. See also *Iron Age* 47 (May 28, 1891): 1008–9.

8. Pursell, "Tariff and Technology," 279; US Congress, House, *Report of the Industrial Commission on the Relations and Conditions of Capital and Labor Employed in Manufactures and General Business*, testimony of John Schaffer, September 23, 1899, 7:389.

9. Pursell, "Tariff and Technology," 284; US Congress, House, *Tariff Hearings before the Committee on Ways and Means . . . 1896–1897*, testimony of W. C. Cronemeyer, January 9, 1897, 1:330 (quotation).

10. Dunbar, *Tin-Plate Industry*, 50.

11. Pursell, "Tariff and Technology," 280.

12. Pursell, "Tariff and Technology," 279–80; US Congress, House Committee on Ways and Means, *Revision of the Tariff: Hearings before the Committee on Ways and Means, 1889–90*, testimony of W. C. Cronemeyer, 99 (quotation).

13. Quoted in Berthoff, *British Immigrants in Industrial America*, 69.

14. Knox, *Development of the American Tin Plate Industry*, 19. See also Scott, *Iron and Steel in Wheeling*, 122–29; and Loveday, *Rise and Decline of the American Cut Nail Industry*, 141–43.

15. Dunbar, *Tin-Plate Industry*, 3–4, 44.

16. Minchinton, *British Tinplate Industry*, 75.

17. "Welsh Makers in America," *South Wales Daily News*, September 17, 1892, 6.

18. "Crisis in Tinplate Trade," *Evening Express*, October 13, 1892, 4.

19. "Erected First American Tinworks," *Cardiff Times*, April 16, 1910, 3; "Tin-Working in America," *Evening Express*, December 1, 1892, 4.

20. Ut Prosim, "Welshmen in America," *South Wales Daily Post*, December 28, 1895, 4.

21. Ut Prosim, "The Welsh in America," *South Wales Daily Post*, November 12, 1895, 2.

22. Scott, *Iron and Steel in Wheeling*, 133 (quotations), 141. For a comprehensive background

of the consolidation movement, see Hogan, *Economic History of the Iron and Steel Industry*, 1:235–302.

23. Scott, *Iron and Steel in Wheeling*, 133.

24. Dunbar, *Tin-Plate Industry*, 15.

25. Rutherford, *Romancing in Tin Plate*, 61. The "Welsh boys," all of whom had been born in Wales, included John Johns, Griffith Morgan, John Phillips, John Reese, William Morgan, William Williams, John Lloyd, and John Aurelius. At the time of their reunion photograph, their ages ranged from seventy-five to eighty-six. See also Scott, *Iron and Steel in Wheeling*, 133.

26. "Cochfarf" (Red Beard), *Evening Express*, January 2, 1909, 4; "Cochfarf," *Weekly Mail* (Cardiff), January 9, 1909, 10.

27. "Tin-Plate Towns of America," *Western Mail* (Cardiff), October 6, 1898, 5.

28. Rutherford, *Romancing in Tin Plate*, 62.

29. Knox, *Development of the American Tin Plate Industry*, 22; Rutherford, *Romancing in Tin Plate*, 63; Scott, *Iron and Steel in Wheeling*, 134. The hyphen was variously used in "tinplate," with some using it while others did not. Thus, the original American Tin Plate Company of Ellwood adopted the hyphen when it became a combination of firms: the American Tin-Plate Company.

30. Scott, *Iron and Steel in Wheeling*, 139–40.

31. Scott, *Iron and Steel in Wheeling*, 140–42; Knox, *Development of the American Tin Plate Industry*, 26.

32. Scott, *Iron and Steel in Wheeling*, 142.

33. Scott, *Iron and Steel in Wheeling*, 143 (quotation); Knox, *Development of the American Tin Plate Industry*, 25. See also Warren, *Big Steel*, 7–21; Hogan, *Economic History of the Iron and Steel Industry*, 2:463–73; and Lamoreaux, *Great Merger Movement*.

34. Busch, "Introduction to the Tin Can," 97–98; Hogan, *Economic History of the Iron and Steel Industry*, 2:646–47.

35. Knox, *Development of the American Tin Plate Industry*, 26–27; Hogan, *Economic History of the Iron and Steel Industry*, 2:646–52.

36. Knox, *Development of the American Tin Plate Industry*, 31–32; Hogan, *Economic History of the Iron and Steel Industry*, 2:757–62.

37. Knox, *Development of the American Tin Plate Industry*, 33–34.

38. Brody, *Steelworkers in America*, 119; Fitch, *Steel Workers*, 133; US Congress, Senate, *Report on the Conditions of Employment in the Iron and Steel Industry*, 3:516, 516–22.

39. US Congress, Senate, *Report on the Conditions of Employment in the Iron and Steel Industry*, 3:181, 184; Dunbar, *Tin-Plate Industry*, 53.

40. Dunbar, *Tin-Plate Industry*, 44–45.

41. Martin, "Causes and Consequences of the 1909–1910 Steel Strike," 23; Lawyer, "History of the Trade Unions," 841.

42. Nash, *Conflict and Accommodation*, 102–3.

43. Brody, *Steelworkers in America*, 68, 67 (quotations), respectively. For details of the negotiations, see *National Labor Tribune*, August 1, 8, 1901. See also *American Federationist* 8 (October 1901): 415–31.

44. "Tinplate Trade," *Cardiff Times*, October 5, 1901, 6; Brody, *Steelworkers in America*, 67; Robinson, *Amalgamated Association of Iron, Steel and Tin Workers*, 162; Nash, *Conflict and Accommodation*, 103.

45. *National Labor Tribune*, September 19, 26, 1901; Magda, *Monessen*, 5.

46. Brody, *Steelworkers in America*, 69.

47. Santos, "Between Hegemony and Autonomy," 399–423.

48. Nash, *Conflict and Accommodation*, 103. For a detailed assessment of the efforts of the steelmasters, particularly by Albert H. Gary, to reform this harsh position and to ameliorate the conditions of labor, see Eggert, *Steelmasters and Labor Reform*.

49. *Wheeling Intelligencer*, June 7, 8, 1909; *Amalgamated Journal*, June 17, 1909. Six of the vice presidents in 1909 were Welsh: Llewellyn Lewis, Ben I. Davis, Ben F. Jones, D. J. Davis, John William, and Walter Larkin. See *Amalgamated Journal* 10, no. 32 (May 6, 1909).

50. Martin, "Causes and Consequences of the 1909–1910 Steel Strike," 39, citing "Strike Against the Steel Trust," AFL National and International Union Correspondence and Jurisdictional Dispute Records, Amalgamated Association of Iron, Steel, and Tin Workers File, Reel 38-6, *AFL Proceedings* (1909), 203; *Wheeling Intelligencer*, July 2, 5, 28, 1909.

51. "Tinplate Strike in America," *South Wales Daily Post*, March 14, 1910, 5.

52. *Amalgamated Journal*, August 15, 1909.

53. Martin, "Causes and Consequences of the 1909–1910 Steel Strike," 40, 51.

54. P. Foner, *History of the Labor Movement in the United States*, 4:300–301; *Amalgamated Journal*, October 7, 1909 (quotations).

55. Martin, "Tin Plate Towns, 1890–1910," 495. For background on George Gibson McMurtry, see Mosher, *Capital's Utopia*, 43–45.

56. Mosher, *Capital's Utopia*, 165.

57. Martin, "Tin Plate Towns," 500; Mosher, *Capital's Utopia*, 48–49.

58. For more on William T. Lewis, see R. Lewis, *Welsh Americans*, 257–69.

59. For more on Thomas L. Lewis, see R. Lewis, *Welsh Americans*, 269–73.

60. R. Lewis, *Welsh Americans*, 273.

61. US Congress, House of Representatives, Committee on the Investigation of the United States Steel Corporation, *Hearings* (1912), 3142. See also Martin, "Tin Plate Towns," 513; US Congress, Senate, *Investigation of the Strike in the Steel Industries: Hearings before the Committee on Education and Labor* (1919), 3:124–25; *Amalgamated Journal*, July 15, 1909.

62. *Amalgamated Journal*, August 12, 1909.

63. Martin, "Tin Plate Towns," 514; *Amalgamated Journal*, July 15, 1909; *Wheeling Intelligencer*, August 6, 1909.

64. Martin, "Causes and Consequences of the 1909–1910 Steel Strike," 46; *Wheeling Intelligencer*, August 6, 1909.

65. Martin, "Tin Plate Towns," 514; Martin, "Causes and Consequences of the 1909–1910 Steel Strike," 46; *Wheeling Intelligencer*, September 3, 1909; US Congress, Senate, *Report on the Conditions of Employment in the Iron and Steel Industry*, vol. 3, *Working Conditions and the Relations of Employers and Employees*, app. E, 509.

66. Martin, "Causes and Consequences of the 1909–1910 Steel Strike," 50–51; *Wheeling Intelligencer*, July 15, 16, 22, 1909.

67. "American Tinplate Strike," *Cardiff Times*, October 2, 1909, 8.

68. "Welsh Tinplate Workers Wives," *The Cambrian* (Swansea), February 18, 1910, 4.

69. "Strife in the America Tinplate Trade," *Llanelly Mercury*, June 16, 1910, 8.

70. Kaltinick, "Socialist Municipal Administration," 174–75.

71. Kaltinick, "Socialist Municipal Administration," 174–75, 179, 183; Martin, "Tin Plate Towns," 493–94; B. Richards, *Lawrence County*. See also John J. Rocky, "New Castle as Viewed by the State Department of Interior," *New Castle News*, January 16, 1912.

72. Kaltinick, "Socialist Municipal Administration," 175; US Bureau of the Census, *Twelfth Census of the United States of America (1900)*, vol. 1, *Population*, part 1, 800–803.

73. Bart Richards, interview by Joe Uehlein, February 21, 1974.

74. B. Richards interview, 5.

75. B. Richards interview, 6, 13.

76. Kaltinick, "Socialist Municipal Administration," 176–79; Bodnar, "Italians and Slavs of New Castle," 269–78. See also Martin, "Tin Plate Towns," 498, 524n24. A small Alawi sect from Syria also settled in the city, as did some five hundred African Americans. Toth, "Syrian Community in New Castle," 269–78.

77. B. Richards, *Lawrence County*, 51 (quotation). See also Kaltinick, "Socialist Municipal Administration," 184.

78. B. Richards interview, 33.

79. B. Richards interview, 10–11, 30. Larkin died in 1912 or 1913.

80. Kaltinick, "Socialist Municipal Administration," 189–90; Pyle, *Pioneer History of the Tin Plate Industry at New Castle, Pennsylvania* (mimeographed pamphlet), 8; *Amalgamated Journal*, July 17, 1909, 1, and October 1909, 13.

81. Martin, "Tin Plate Towns," 516; Kaltinick, "Socialist Municipal Administration," 186, 189–90; *Iron Trade Review*, July 22, 1909.

82. Martin, "Tin Plate Towns," 515; Kaltinick, "Socialist Municipal Administration," 186, 190–91.

83. B. Richards interview, 17–18.

84. B. Richards interview, 27.

85. Nash, *Conflict and Accommodation*, 113–15.

86. *Amalgamated Journal*, December 9, 1909; *Wheeling Intelligencer*, December 10, 1909.

87. Martin, "Causes and Consequences of the 1909–1910 Steel Strike," 59; *Amalgamated Journal*, December 9, 16, 1909.

88. *Wheeling Majority*, January 27, 1910; *Wheeling Intelligencer*, January 21, May 4, 7, 14, 1910.

89. *Amalgamated Journal*, March 17, 24 (quotation), 1910.

90. Solomon "Sol" Edwards, Find a Grave, accessed June 13, 2022, https://www.findagrave.com/memorial/148448570/solomon-edwards.

91. *Amalgamated Journal*, April 7, 1910; Martin, "'So Nobly Struggling for Their Manhood,'" 438–39.

92. Robert "Bob" Edwards, interview by Keith Dix, October 10, 1974.

93. P. Foner, *History of the Labor Movement*, 4:303; *Amalgamated Journal*, December 9, March 17, 24, April 7, 1910; *Wheeling Intelligencer*, January 21, 22, 27, May 4, 7, 14, 1910. For more on Black Americans being denied union membership, see Dickerson, *Out of the Crucible*, 7–26.

94. *Wheeling Intelligencer*, April 22, 1910.

95. "Welshmen's Strike in America," *Cardiff Times*, August 27, 1910, 5; Martin, "Causes and Consequences of the 1909–1910 Steel Strike," 63; *Wheeling Majority*, August 11, 1910.

96. Robinson, *Amalgamated Association of Iron, Steel and Tin Workers*, 26n26; Martin, "Causes and Consequences of the 1909–1910 Steel Strike," 66; P. Foner, *History of the Labor Movement*, 4:281.

97. *Amalgamated Journal*, August 12, 1909.

98. Quoted in Martin, "Tin Plate Towns," 520; Martin, "'So Nobly Struggling for Their Manhood,'" 440; P. Foner, *History of the Labor Movement*, 3:192.

7. Gender, Transnational Work Culture, and the Hetty Williams Affair

1. Carter, "Industrial, Industrious, and Diverse," 267, 278–79; Byington, *Homestead*, 107 (quotation). For an earlier version of this chapter, see W. D. Jones and Lewis, "Gender and Transnationality."

2. Huw Davies, "Hattie Williams Affair of 1895," 166.

3. Huw Davies, "Hattie Williams Affair of 1895," 167.

4. Huw Davies, "Hattie Williams Affair of 1895," 168.

5. *Pittsburgh Commercial Gazette*, April 13, 1895; Huw Davies, "Hattie Williams Affair of 1895," 169.

6. E. Jordan, "Exclusion of Women from Industry."

7. Berthoff, *British Immigrants in Industrial America*, 20–21. See also Conway, "Welsh Emigration to the United States"; and M. Jones, "Background to Emigration from Great Britain," 3–92.

8. Berthoff, *British Immigrants in Industrial America*, 28–29. See also Conway, "Welsh Emigration to the United States"; and M. Jones, "Background to Emigration from Great Britain."

9. Samuel, *Short History of the Tin and Tinplate Trade*, 7.

10. *Industrial World*, June 29, 1894, 2; September 13, 1895, 3; March 26, 1897, 5.

11. Wilkins, *History of the Iron, Steel, Tinplate, and Other Trades of Wales*, 422.

12. Dunbar, *Tin-Plate Industry*, 11 (quotation), 68.

13. The only study that focuses solely on Welsh women tinplate workers is Owen-Jones, "Women in the Tinplate Industry," but it covers a later period than the one considered here. See Owen-Jones, "Women in the Tinplate Industry," 42–49; as well as Wilkins, *History of Iron, Steel, Tinplate, and Other Trades of Wales*, 404–7; Dunbar, *Tin-Plate Industry*, 53, 65; and National Museum of Wales, Museum of Welsh Life, transcripts of interviews with Cecil Frederick Lewis and Doris Rees.

14. Quotations from Owen-Jones, "Women in the Tinplate Industry," 44–45; Pollert, *Girls, Wives, Factory Lives*, 97.

15. E. Jones, *Toilers of the Hills*, 16–17.

16. Erickson, *Invisible Immigrants*, 65; Shergold, *Working-Class Life*, 71. Parr, *Gender of Breadwinners*, shows that English women recruited to Canadian hosiery mills had an esprit de corps because they were achieving financial and physical independence by migrating.

17. Carter, "Industrial, Industrious, and Diverse," 279. Rates include those women born to two parents who were born in another country.

18. Carter, "Industrial, Industrious, and Diverse," 279–81.

19. Great Britain, Enumerators' Books, 1861 Census for England and Wales, Swansea Registration District, RG 9/4098 Enumeration Districts 1 and 6; Great Britain, Enumerators' Books, 1891 Census for England and Wales, Swansea Registration District, RG 12/4473 E.E. 6 and E.D. 7. See also National Museum of Wales, Museum of Welsh Life, Cecil Frederick Lewis and Doris Rees interview transcripts.

20. Dunbar, *Tin-Plate Industry*, 71. He noted that "at Briton Ferry a manufacturer installed gas furnaces, but had to remove them owing to the opposition of the workmen" (71).

21. E. Jones, *Toilers of the Hills*, 16; Minchinton, *British Tinplate Industry*, 33, 55, 59, 108; E. Jordan, "Exclusion of Women from Industry."

22. Dunbar, *Tin-Plate Industry*, 52–53, 71.

23. Minchinton, *British Tinplate Industry*, 69; Berthoff, *British Immigrants in America*, 69.

24. Minchinton, *British Tinplate Industry*, 52, 71; Berthoff, *British Immigrants in America*, 94–95.

25. Minchinton, *British Tinplate Industry*, 69; Dunbar, *Tin-Plate Industry*, 68.

26. A. Jones and B. Jones, *Welsh Reflections*, 75, quoting *Y Drych*, August 24, 1899. See also *Y Drych* editorial, July 4, 1895.

27. Berthoff, *British Immigrants in Industrial America*, 182, quoting O. Morgan, *Souvenir of the Visit of the Iron and Steel Institutes*, 66–67.

28. H. Evans, *Iron Pioneer*, 84–85, 108; Ingham, *Making Iron and Steel*, 80–84; "Henry William Oliver," *DAB*, vol. 14, 19–20.

29. Shergold, *Working-Class Life*, 67, quoting *Pittsburgh Leader*, December 27, 1912.

30. *Pittsburgh Commercial Gazette*, April 13, 1895.

31. Quoted in *Pittsburgh Commercial Gazette*, April 13, 1895.

32. Quoted in *Pittsburgh Commercial Gazette*, April 13, 1895.

33. Quoted in *Pittsburgh Commercial Gazette*, April 13, 1895.

34. *The Bulletin* (Philadelphia), April 15, 1895.

35. *National Labor Tribune*, May 23, 1895.

36. *National Labor Tribune*, April 25, 1895.

37. Reprinted in *Industrial World*, May 10, 1895, 9.

38. *Pittsburgh Commercial Gazette*, April 13, 1895.

39. *Pittsburgh Commercial Gazette*, April 13, 1895.

40. Reprinted in *Industrial World*, May 10, 1895, 9.

41. *National Labor Tribune*, May 16, 1895.

42. *National Labor Tribune*, May 30, 1895.

43. *Y Drych* (Utica, NY), April 13, 1895.

44. For Welsh attitudes toward "respectability," see A. Jones and B. Jones, *Welsh Reflections*; and W. D. Jones, *Wales in America*.

45. Vox Populi, "A Shame on Our Nation," *Y Drych*, April 13, 1895.

46. Vox Populi, "A Shame on Our Nation," *Y Drych*, April 13, 1895.

47. D. Smith, *Wales*, 74.

48. "Female Assorters and Tin-Platers Union," *Carmarthen Journal and South Wales Weekly Advertiser*, September 26, 1890, 1; "Yspitty Tin-Plate Works," *South Wales Daily News*, October 27, 1890, 4.

49. *Industrial World*, May 14, 1897, 4 (quotation). See also *Industrial World*, February 24, June 5, and June 19, 1896; and May 14, 1897.

50. *Industrial World*, May 10, 1895, 9.

51. *Industrial World*, May 10, 1895, 4. The author identifies Hetty as being from Morriston and as having worked at the "Gorseinon tin plate works" (4).

52. *South Wales Daily Post* (Swansea), May 4, 1895, 3.

53. See, for example, *Western Mail* (Cardiff), May 3, 1895, 6; *Evening Express* (Cardiff), May 4, 1895, 4; and *South Wales Daily Post*, May 10, 1895, 5.

54. *Industrial World*, January 12, 1894, 2.

55. See, for example, *Industrial World*, January 12, August 3, 1894, 1; August 23, 30, 1895, 10; February 12, 1897, 2; and *Herald of Wales and Monmouthshire Recorder* (Swansea), February 13, 1897, 8.

56. Quoted in *Industrial World*, June 7, 1895, 2.

57. The literature on this topic for Great Britain is extensive. This discussion is drawn most heavily from Humphries, "Working-Class Family, Women's Liberation and Class Struggle," 25–42; May, "Bread before Roses," 2; Rose, "Gender at Work"; Lown, *Women and Industrialization*; Seccombe, "Patriarchy Stabilized"; and L. Downs, *Manufacturing Inequality*.

58. Seccombe, "Patriarchy Stabilized," 61–62; Humphries, "'Most Free from Objection,'" 935.

59. The evolution of the literature on women, work, and the family wage in the United States is extensive and growing. See, for example, Milkman, *Women, Work and Protest*, 1; May, "Bread before Roses," 2–21; Kessler-Harris, *Out to Work*, 75–107; and Levine, *Labor's True Woman*.

60. For the view that British immigrants were generally more skilled than most other nationalities, see Berthoff, *British Immigrants in Industrial America*, 28.

61. Blewett, "Deference and Defiance." For a full elaboration on the ideas presented in that article, see Blewett's major studies, *Constant Turmoil* and *Men, Women, and Work*. See also Yans-McLaughlin, *Immigration Reconsidered*; and Hoerder, *"Struggle a Hard Battle."* For a case study of two Canadian towns, see Parr's *Gender of Breadwinners* and "Skilled Emigrant and Her Kin."

62. May, "Bread before Roses," 8 (original emphasis), quoting American Federation of Labor, *History, Encyclopedia, Reference Book*, 7. See also Boyle, *Minimum Wage and Syndicalism*, 73.

63. Greenwald, introduction to *Women and the Trades*, xxii; May, "Bread before Roses," 9; Milkman, "Organizing the Sexual Division of Labor"; Gabaccia, *From the Other Side*, 86. For a study devoted to gender relations constructed by craft unions, see DeVault, *United Apart*, particularly 75–104 on the AFL. Similarly, skilled Belgian window-glass workers also adopted the American gender norms by excluding women from window-glass factories in the United States, something they did not do in Belgium. See Fones-Wolf, "Transatlantic Craft Migrations and Transnational Spaces," 306. See also Fones-Wolf's *Glass Towns*.

64. DeVault, "'Give the Boys a Trade'," 195; Kleinberg, "Technology and Women's Work."

65. Greenwald, introduction to *Women and the Trades*, xix; Butler, *Women and the Trades*, 227–28; DeVault, "'Give the Boys a Trade,'" 196.

66. Martin, "'So Nobly Struggling for Their Manhood,'" 429–30.

67. Gabaccia, "The Transplanted," 248–51.

68. Huw Davies, "Hattie Williams Affair of 1895," 169.

69. Huw Davies, "Hattie Williams Affair of 1895," 169–70.

70. Huw Davies, "Hattie Williams Affair of 1895," 170.

8. Republicanism and the Search for Success

1. Glanmor Williams, *Religion, Language and Nationality in Wales*, 235.

2. All quotations from Glanmor Williams, *Religion, Language and Nationality in Wales*, 221–22.

3. Quoted in Conway, *Welsh in America*, 178–79. See also Glanmor Williams, *Religion, Language and Nationality in Wales*, 222.

4. P. Morgan, "Keeping the Legends Alive," 19–41.

5. Tyler, "Occupational Mobility and Social Status," 2.

6. Berthoff, "Peasants and Artisans, Puritans and Republicans," 579.

7. E. Foner, *Free Soil, Free Labor, Free Men*, 11–13. See also Weber, *Protestant Ethic and the Spirit of Capitalism*.

8. E. Foner, *Free Soil, Free Labor, Free Men*, 17–20, 26. For an analysis of the extensive literature on "republicanism," see Rodgers, "Republicanism."

9. E. Foner, *Free Soil, Free Labor, Free Men*, 22–23, 32; Montgomery, *Beyond Equality*, 26–27.

10. E. Foner, *Free Soil, Free Labor, Free Men*, 33, 38–39; Cawelti, *Apostles of the Self-Made Man*, 125–64.

11. The literature on the modern industrial economy is very extensive. See, for example, these standards: Cochran and Miller, *Age of Enterprise*; Kirkland, *Industry Comes of Age*; Chandler, *Invisible Hand*; and Bensel, *Political Economy of American Industrialization*.

12. Gutman, *Work, Culture, and Society*, 50–51.

13. Quoted in *National Labor Tribune*, October 2, 1880.

14. Gwyther, "Sidelights on Religion and Politics in the Rhondda Valley," 30–43.

15. Evans, "Trusts and Trade Unions," 133–36 (quotations on 134–35). There are numerous examples of coal and iron workers who became ministers and articulated an ideology linking republicanism and evangelical religion in support of upward mobility as a reward for a virtuous life. See for example, *The Cambrian* 24 (April 1904): 177–79.

16. Gutman, *Work, Culture, and Society*, 51–52; *National Labor Tribune*, December 12, 1874 (quotation).

17. Gutman, *Work, Culture, and Society*, 221, 225, 233. (Gutman's essay is part of the larger work cited here.)

18. See, for example, Miller, *Men in Business*.

19. Ingham, *Iron Barons*, 14–16, 36–37.

20. Casson, *Romance of Steel*, 267.

21. Ingham, *Iron Barons*, 22.

22. Ingham, *Iron Barons*, 30, 32.

23. Gottlieb, "Immigration of British Coal Miners," 374–75; Harvey, *Best-Dressed Miners*, 85–86.

24. Knowles, *Calvinists Incorporated*.

25. R. Lewis, *Welsh Americans*.

26. Bodnar, "Socialization and Adaptation," 147–62.

27. Thomas, *Hanes Cymry America*, 22.

28. David Davies, "Pittsburgh, the Smoky City," *Western Mail* (Cardiff), December 6, 1898, 4. For a similar description see, "Away West!," *Cambrian Daily Leader*, July 29, 1913, 4.

29. Carter, "Industrial, Industrious, and Diverse."

30. Carter, "Industrial, Industrious, and Diverse," 308–9.

31. Carter, "Industrial, Industrious, and Diverse," 282–300. See also Knowles, *Calvinists Incorporated*; R. Lewis, *Welsh Americans*; Tyler, *Wales and the American Dream*; Van Vugt, *British Buckeyes*.

32. Carter, "Industrial, Industrious, and Diverse," 303–5. Population comparisons are for males ages sixteen and older, and Carter rounds off percentages to the nearest tenth.

33. Carter, "Industrial, Industrious, and Diverse," 291–300.

34. "A Welsh Pilgrim's View," *National Labor Tribune*, February 16, 1899, reprinted from the *Llanelly Mercury*, January 12, 1899.

35. Carter, "Industrial, Industrious, and Diverse," 311–14.

36. Carter, "Industrial, Industrious, and Diverse," 324–26.

37. "Joseph Corns," *The Cambrian*, 271–72.

38. "Thomas Rees Morgan, Sr.," *The Cambrian*, 290–91. See also Charles Wilkins, "Thomas Morgan, Ironmaster, United States," *Weekly Mail*, January 9, 1897, 9; and Heald, *Stark County Story*, 1:471–72.

39. "Thomas Rees Morgan, Sr.," *The Cambrian*, 290–91; Heald, *Stark County Story*, 1:472–73.

40. "Late T. R. Morgan," *The Cambrian*, 442–43.

41. "Thomas Rees Morgan, Sr.," *The Cambrian*, 291. The Welsh press eulogized Morgan when he died. See, for example, his obituary in the *Merthyr Times*, *Dowlais Times*, and *Aberdare Echo*, September 17, 1897, 7. The Rodman Library, Alliance, Ohio, has collected a large file of material on the Morgan family and Morgan Engineering. See Morgan Family, AF Biography, Rodman Public Library.

42. "Welsh of the Great West," *Western Mail*, December 6, 1898, 4. Davis had been acting editor of Cardiff's *Western Mail*, and he took a long sabbatical to tour America and file special reports to the *Western Mail*. Before leaving, he had agreed to resume his career as the editor of Swansea's *South Wales Daily Post*. Thanks to Bill Jones.

43. "Carnegie's Great Works," *Western Mail*, December 27, 1898, 4.

44. Carter, "Industrial, Industrious, and Diverse," 329–32.

45. R. Lewis, *Welsh Americans*, 44–50; Baines, *Migration in a Mature Economy*, 220–49; B. Thomas, *Migration and Economic Growth*, particularly chaps. 7 and 14; B. Thomas, "Wales and the Atlantic Economy."

46. Nash, *Conflict and Accommodation*, 109. See also US Congress, Senate, *Reports of the Immigration Commission* (1911), 8:83.

47. Carter, "Industrial, Industrious, and Diverse," 332–33.

48. Carter, "Industrial, Industrious, and Diverse," 334.

49. Carter, "Industrial, Industrious, and Diverse," 335–39.

50. David Davies, "Welsh of the Western World: Among the Ironworkers of Youngstown," *Western Mail*, November 22, 1898, 5.

51. "Tinplate Making in America," *South Wales Daily Post*, July 31, 1897, 3.

52. David Davies, "Homeward Bound," *Western Mail*, August 19, 1899, 6.

53. McKelvey, *Centennial History of Belmont County, Ohio*, 188, 191.

54. McKelvey, *Centennial History of Belmont County, Ohio*, 199–200.

55. Tyler, "Migrant Culture Maintenance," 71–72.

56. Tyler, "Migrant Culture Maintenance," 73.

57. Tyler, "Migrant Culture Maintenance," 84. Tyler's definition of "Welsh" includes only those having two parents born in Wales, because frequently the sons born to either Irish or English immigrants who had emigrated from Wales identified themselves as Irish or English.

58. Tyler, "Migrant Culture Maintenance," 85.

59. Tyler, "Migrant Culture Maintenance," 87–88.

60. Thomas, *Hanes Cymry America*, 116.

61. Tyler, "Occupational Mobility and Social Status," 10–11; Tyler, *Wales and the American Dream*, 71. In the latter source, Tyler examines the Welsh communities in Emporia, Kansas (farming/mercantile); Bevier, Missouri (coal mining); Sharon, Pennsylvania (steel, tinplate); and Poultney, Vermont (slate mining).

62. Tyler, "Occupational Mobility and Social Status," 10; Tyler, *Wales and the American Dream*, 79.

63. Tyler, "Occupational Mobility and Social Status," 17, 20; Tyler, *Wales and the American Dream*, 76, 80.

64. E. Summers, *Genealogical and Family History of Eastern Ohio*, 144.

65. Di Rocco, "In the Shadow of Steel," 133; Jobin, *Cleveland, Past and Present*, 324–26.

66. Ruminski, *Iron Valley*, 40–41, 52–53, 60; Di Rocco, "In the Shadow of Steel," 131; Blue et al., *Mahoning Memories*, 33–40; Sanderson, *20th Century History of Youngstown*, 247–48.

67. Froggett, "Mahoning Valley as an Iron Center: Originality in Practice Marked Steady Progress," 183 (quotation); Di Rocco, "In the Shadow of Steel," 131; *History of Trumbull and Mahoning Counties*, 2:92–98.

68. Sanderson, *20th Century History of Youngstown*, 248; Ruminski, *Iron Valley*, 53–55, 57.

69. Ruminski, *Iron Valley*, 57–58; Warren, *American Steel Industry*, 42, 56.

70. Ruminski, *Iron Valley*, 67–69; Di Rocco, "In the Shadow of Steel," 158–59; Brennan, *Bi-*

ographical Cyclopedia and Portrait Gallery, 398; Sanderson, *20th Century History of Youngstown*, 585, 607; J. Butler, *History of Youngstown and the Mahoning Valley*, 2:180–81; Hazen, *20th Century History of New Castle*, 69–70, 119–20.

71. Brennan, *Biographical Cyclopedia and Portrait Gallery*, 398 (quotations); Hazen, *20th Century History of New Castle*, 118, 120.

72. Ruminski, *Iron Valley*, 69–70; *Biographical History of Northeastern Ohio*, 601; White, *Twentieth-Century History of Mercer County*, 378; J. Butler, *History of Youngstown and Mahoning Valley*, 1:671, 2:180, 372; Di Rocco, "In the Shadow of Steel," 163; Froggett, "Mahoning Valley as an Iron Center [part 1]," 184.

73. Ruminski, *Iron Valley*, 122; Di Rocco, "In the Shadow of Steel," 163–64; Froggett, "Mahoning Valley as an Iron Center [part 2]," 225; Froggett, "Mahoning Valley as an Iron Center [part 1]," 184.

74. Ruminski, *Iron Valley*, 124; Thurston, *Pittsburgh and Allegheny in the Centennial Year*, 71.

75. Ruminski, *Iron Valley*, 125–26; Di Rocco, "In the Shadow of Steel," 165.

76. Ruminski, *Iron Valley*, 126; Temin, *Iron and Steel in Nineteenth Century America*, 97; Gordon, *American Iron*, 165–66.

77. Di Rocco, "In the Shadow of Steel," 166–67; Froggett, "Mahoning Valley as an Iron Center [part 2]," 227; J. Butler, *History of Youngstown and the Mahoning Valley*, 2:181; Ruminski, *Iron Valley*, 154; Sanderson, *20th Century History of Youngstown*, 608; Wilson, *Appletons' Cyclopedia of American Biography*, 7:36.

78. Ruminski, *Iron Valley*, 67.

79. Ruminski, *Iron Valley*, 129–30; J. Butler, "Early History of Iron and Steel Making in the Mahoning Valley," 426. For Cyfarthfa Iron Works, see C. Evans, *"Labyrinth of Flames."*

80. Ruminski, *Iron Valley*, 131–33; J. Butler, *History of Youngstown and Mahoning Valley*, 1:686; Jenkins, *History of Modern Wales*, 221; J. Butler, "Early History of Iron and Steel Making in the Mahoning Valley," 426.

81. Ruminski, *Iron Valley*, 134–35.

82. Thomas Family Genealogy, Niles Furnace-Niles Firebrick Company Papers, Archives of the Museum of Industry and Labor, Ohio Historical Society, Youngstown, Ohio.

83. J. Butler, *History of Youngstown and Mahoning Valley*, 3:805; Ruminski, *Iron Valley*, 165. See also Pallante, "To Work and Live."

84. J. Butler, *History of Youngstown and Mahoning Valley*, 3:806; Upton, *Twentieth-Century History of Trumbull County*, 2:31; "Thomas, William Aubrey," *Biographical Directory of the United States Congress*.

85. Biographies were drawn from E. Summers, *Genealogical and Family History of Eastern Ohio*; J. Butler, *History of Youngstown and Mahoning Valley*, vols. 2 and 3; and Upton, *Twentieth-Century History of Trumbull County*, vol. 2.

86. *Youngstown Vindicator*, undated clipping [1925], Ethnicity File, Mahoning Valley Historical Society. See also Pallante, "To Work and Live."

Epilogue

1. Murdoch, *British Emigration*, 111–12, 114–15; Baines, *Migration in a Mature Economy*, 128; Erickson, *Leaving England*, 104; Berthoff, *British Immigrants in Industrial America*, 82.

2. Murdoch, *British Emigration*, 122; Calavita, *U.S. Immigration Law*, 39–40; Berthoff, *British Immigrants in Industrial America*, 36.

3. Murdoch, *British Emigration*, 115, 122–23; Baines, *Migration in a Mature Economy*, 139–40; Ferguson, *Empire*, 284; Berthoff, *British Immigrants in Industrial America*, 209.

4. Murdoch, *British Emigration*, 116–17 (quotation on 116).

5. Glanmor Williams, *Religion, Language and Nationality in Wales*, 226; Berthoff, *British Immigrants in Industrial America*, 210.

6. Emrys Jones, "Some Aspects of Cultural Change," 36–40.

7. Emrys Jones, "Some Aspects of Cultural Change," 26–28.

8. Emrys Jones, "Some Aspects of Cultural Change," 31–34.

9. *Y Drych*, November 18, 1909, quoted in Emrys Jones, "Some Aspects of Cultural Change," 28.

10. W. D. Jones, "Welsh Language and Welsh Identity," 275.

11. Hazel Davies "Observations on Immigrants in America."

BIBLIOGRAPHY

Government Publications

United States

United States. *Statutes at Large.* 48th Cong. 2nd sess., 1885, vol. 23.

US Bureau of the Census. *Eleventh Census of the United States: 1890.* Vol. 2, *Population.* Washington, DC: Government Printing Office, 1891.

US Bureau of the Census. *Status of Population in the U.S. at the Tenth Census.* Washington, DC: Government Printing Office, 1883.

US Bureau of the Census. *Thirteenth Census of the United States, 1910.* Vol. 10, *Manufactures,* 1909, "Reports for Principal Industries," 205–61. Washington, DC: Government Printing Office, 1910.

US Bureau of the Census. *Twelfth Census of the United States: 1900.* Vol. 1, *Population,* part 1. Washington, DC: Government Printing Office, 1901.

US Bureau of the Census. *Twelfth Census of the United States: 1900.* Vol. 9, *Manufactures,* part 3. Arthur L. Lunt, "Canning and Preserving." Washington, DC: Government Printing Office, 1902.

US Bureau of the Census. *Twelfth Census of the United States: 1900.* Vol. 9, *Manufactures,* part 4. "Special Reports on Selected Industries," 3–95. Washington, DC: US Government Printing Office, 1901.

US Congress. House. Committee on the Investigation of the United States Steel Corporation. *Hearings.* 62nd Cong., 2nd sess., 1911–1912.

US Congress. House. Committee on the Judiciary. *Report 2447: Investigation of the Homestead Troubles.* 52nd Cong., 2nd sess., 1892–1893. Washington, DC: Government Printing Office, 1893.

US Congress. House. Committee on Ways and Means. *Revision of the Tariff: Hearings before the Committee.* Letter from A. B. Farquhar, March 21, 1890. 51st Cong., 1st sess., 1889–1890. Washington, 1890.

US Congress. House. Committee on Ways and Means. *Revision of the Tariff: Hearings before the Committee on Ways and Means, 1889–90.* 51st Cong., 1st sess., 1889–1890. Washington, 1890.

US Congress. House. Misc. Doc. No. 335, 52nd Cong., 1st sess., 1892.

US Congress. House. *Report of the Industrial Commission on the Relations and Conditions of Capital and Labor Employed in Manufactures and General Business.* Testimony of John Schaffer, September 23, 1899. House Doc. 495, 56th Cong., 2nd sess. Washington, 1901.

US Congress. House. *Tariff Hearings before the Committee on Ways and Means, 1896–1897.* Testimony of W. C. Cronemeyer, January 9, 1897. House Doc. 338, 54th Cong., 2nd sess. Washington, 1897.

US Congress. Senate. *Investigation of the Strike in the Steel Industries: Hearings before the Com-*

mittee on Education and Labor. 66th Cong., 1st sess., 1919. Washington, DC: Government Printing Office, 1919.

US Congress. Senate. *Report of the Committee of the Senate upon the Relations between Labor and Capital.* 4 vols. Washington, DC: Government Printing Office, 1885.

US Congress. Senate. *Report on the Conditions of Employment in the Iron and Steel Industry.* 62nd Cong., 1st sess., 1911. Washington, DC: Government Printing Office, 1913.

US Congress. Senate. *Reports of the Immigration Commission.* 61st Cong., 2nd sess. Multiple vols. Washington, DC: Government Printing Office, 1910, 1911.

US Congress. Senate. Speech of Senator Benjamin F. Shively (D-IN), June 1892. *Congressional Record*, 52nd Cong., 1st sess., 1891–1892, vol. 23.

US Department of Treasury. Special Report to the Secretary of the Treasury, by Ira Ayer, Special Agent, Treasury Department, relative to the Manufacture of Tin and Terne Plates in the United States during the quarter ending April 29, 1892, with comparative statements of production.

US Department of Treasury. Special Report to the Secretary of the Treasury, by Ira Ayer, Special Agent, Treasury Department, showing the Production of Tin and Terne Plates in the United States during the quarter ending June 30, 1894, with comparative statements of production.

Great Britain

Great Britain. Enumerators' Books, 1861 Census for England and Wales, Swansea Registration District, RG 9/4098 Enumeration Districts 1 and 6.

Great Britain. Enumerators' Books, 1891 Census for England and Wales, Swansea Registration District, RG 12/4473 E.E. 6 and E.D. 7.

Great Britain. House of Commons. Parliamentary Documents. *Report of the Chief Inspector of Factories and Workshops to Her Majesty's Principal Secretary of State for the Home Department for the Year Ending 31st October 1887.* N.p., 1888.

Great Britain. Parliamentary Documents. Home Office. *Report on the Conditions of Employment in the Manufacture of Tinplates with Special Reference to the Process of Tinning,* vol. 122, by Edgar L. Collis (H.M. Medical Inspector) and J. Hilditch (H.M. Inspector of Factories). Presented to both Houses of Parliament by order of His Majesty. London: His Majesty's Stationery Office, 1912.

Great Britain. Parliamentary Papers. *Report of the American Tin Plate Industry and the Welsh Tin Plate Export Trade to the United States,* 1897. Vol. 88 (C. 8278-25).

Great Britain. Parliamentary Papers. *Reports of the Commissioners of Inquiry into the State of Education in Wales,* 1847. Vol. 27, part 3.

Great Britain. Parliamentary Papers. *Report of the Foreign Commerce of the United States of America,* 1880. Vol. 72 (C. 2570).

Great Britain. Parliamentary Papers. *Report on the Effect of the McKinley Tariff on the Tin Plate Industry of the United States,* 1893. Vol. 91 (C. 6856–28).

Great Britain. Parliamentary Papers. *Reports of the Trade Union Commissioners,* 1867–1868. Vol. 39.

Pennsylvania

Commonwealth of Pennsylvania. Secretary of Internal Affairs. *Annual Report.* Part 3, *Industrial Statistics, 1895.* Vol. 23. Harrisburg, 1895.

Newspapers

United States

Amalgamated Journal (Pittsburgh)
Bulletin, The (Philadelphia)
Druid, The (Pittsburgh)
Homestead Times
Knoxville Daily Press and Herald
Knoxville Weekly Chronicle
National Labor Tribune (Pittsburgh)
New Castle News
Pittsburgh Chronicle-Telegraph
Pittsburgh Commercial Gazette
Pittsburgh Daily Gazette
Pittsburgh Daily Morning Post
Pittsburgh Dispatch
Pittsburgh Evening Telegraph
Pittsburgh Leader
Pittsburgh Morning Chronicle
Pittsburgh Morning Gazette
Pittsburgh Post
Pittsburgh Press
Pittsburgh Times
Scranton Republican
Wheeling Intelligencer
Wheeling Majority
Y Drych [The mirror] (Utica, NY)
Youngstown Telegram
Youngstown Vindicator

Wales

Aberdare Echo
Cambrian, The (Swansea)
Cardiff and Merthyr Guardian
Cardiff Times
Carmarthen Journal and South Wales Weekly Advertiser
Dowlais Times
Evening Express (Cardiff)
Herald of Wales and Monmouthshire Recorder (Swansea)
Industrial World (Swansea)
Llanelly Mercury and South Wales Advertiser
Llanelly Star
Merthyr Express
Merthyr Telegraph and General Advertiser for the Iron Districts of South Wales
Merthyr Times
South Wales Daily News (Swansea)

South Wales Daily Post (Swansea)
South Wales Echo (Cardiff)
Tarian y Gweithiur [The workman's shield] (Aberdare)
Weekly Mail (Cardiff)
Western Mail (Cardiff)

England

Times, The (London)

Primary and Secondary Sources

Adams, Sean Patrick. *Old Dominion Industrial Commonwealth: Coal, Politics, and Economy in Antebellum America*. Baltimore, MD: Johns Hopkins University Press, 2004.

Allen, Jay D. "The Mount Savage Iron Works, Mount Savage, Maryland: A Case Study in Pre-Civil War Industrial Development." MA thesis, University of Maryland, 1970.

American Iron and Steel Association. *Directory to the Iron and Steel Works in the United States.* Philadelphia, 1884.

American Iron and Steel Association. *Directory of Iron and Steel Works in the United States and Canada.* 12th ed. Philadelphia, 1894.

"American Tin Plate Industry." *American Artisan* 29 (May 25, 1895): 17–25.

"Another 'Nauseating' Writer from 'the Little Dependency of Wales'?" *NINNAU* 46 (September–October 2021): 17.

Armes, Ethel. *The Story of Coal and Iron in Alabama*. Birmingham, AL: Chamber of Commerce, 1910.

Ashton, Thomas Southcliffe. *Iron and Steel in the Industrial Revolution*. 1924. New York: August M. Kelley, 1968.

Baines, Dudley. *Emigration from Europe, 1815–1930*. 2nd ed. Cambridge: Cambridge University Press, 1995.

Baines, Dudley. *Migration in a Mature Economy: Emigration and Internal Migration in England and Wales, 1861–1900*. Cambridge: Cambridge University Press, 1985.

Bennett, John William. "Iron Workers in Woods Run and Johnstown: The Union Era, 1865–1895." PhD diss., University of Pittsburgh, 1977.

Bensel, Richard Franklin. *The Political Economy of American Industrialization, 1877–1900*. Cambridge: Cambridge University Press, 2000.

Berlin, Ira, and Herbert G. Gutman. "Natives and Immigrants, Free Men and Slaves: Urban Workingmen in the Antebellum American South." *American Historical Review* 88, no. 5 (1983): 1175–1200.

Berthoff, Rowland Tappan. *British Immigrants in Industrial America, 1790–1950*. Cambridge, MA: Harvard University Press, 1953.

Berthoff, Rowland Tappan. "Peasants and Artisans, Puritans and Republicans: Personal Liberty and Communal Equality in American History." *Journal of American History* 69 (December 1982): 579–98.

Berthoff, Rowland Tappan. "The Welsh." In *Harvard Encyclopedia of American Ethnic Groups*, edited by Stephan Thernstrom, 1011–17. Cambridge, MA: Harvard University Press, 1980.

Bezís-Selfa, John. *Forging America: Ironworkers, Adventurers, and the Industrious Revolution*. Ithaca, NY: Cornell University Press, 2004.

Bining, Arthur Cecil. *British Regulation of the Colonial Iron Industry.* Philadelphia: University of Pennsylvania Press, 1964.

Bining, Arthur Cecil. *Pennsylvania Iron Manufacture in the Eighteenth Century.* Harrisburg: Pennsylvania Historical Commission, 1938.

Bining, Arthur Cecil. "The Rise of Iron Manufacture in Western Pennsylvania." *Western Pennsylvania Historical Magazine* 16 (November 1933): 235–56.

Biographical History of Northeastern Ohio, Embracing the Counties of Ashtabula, Trumbull, and Mahoning. Chicago: Lewis Publishing Company, 1893.

Birch, Alan. *The Economic History of the British Iron and Steel Industry, 1784–1879.* London: Frank Cass, 1967. Reprint, New York: Augustus M. Kelley, 1968.

Bishop, James L. *History of American Manufactures from 1608 to 1860.* Philadelphia: Edward Young and Company, 1864.

Blewett, Mary H. *Constant Turmoil: The Politics of Industrial Life in Nineteenth-Century New England.* Amherst: University of Massachusetts Press, 2000.

Blewett, Mary H. "Deference and Defiance: Labor Politics and the Meanings of Masculinity in the Mid-Nineteenth-Century New England Textile Industry." *Gender and History* 5 (Autumn 1993): 398–415.

Blewett, Mary H. *Men, Women, and Work: Class, Gender, and Protest in the New England Shoe Industry, 1780–1910.* Urbana: University of Illinois Press, 1988.

Blue, Frederick J., et al. *Mahoning Memories: A History of Youngstown and Mahoning County.* Virginia Beach, VA: Donning, 1995.

Bodnar, John. "The Italians and Slavs of New Castle: Patterns in the New Immigration." *Western Pennsylvania Historical Magazine* 55 (July 1972): 269–78.

Bodnar, John. "Socialization and Adaptation: Immigrant Families in Scranton, 1880–1890." *Pennsylvania History* 43 (April 1976): 147–62.

Bodnar, John. *The Transplanted: A History of Immigrants in Urban America.* Bloomington: Indiana University Press, 1985.

Boston, Ray. *British Chartists in America, 1839–1900.* Manchester: Manchester University Press, 1871.

Boyle, James. *Minimum Wage and Syndicalism: An Independent Survey of the Two Latest Movements Affecting American Labor.* Cincinnati: Stewart and Kidd, 1913.

Brands, H. W. *American Colossus: The Triumph of Capitalism, 1865–1900.* New York: Doubleday, 2010.

Brennan, J. Fletcher, ed. *A Biographical Cyclopedia and Portrait Gallery of Distinguished Men with a Historical Sketch of the State of Ohio.* Cincinnati: John C. Yorkston and Company, 1879.

Bridge, James Howard. *The Inside History of the Carnegie Steel Company: The Romance of Millions.* New York: Aldine Book Company, 1903.

Brody, David. *In Labor's Cause: Main Themes on the History of the American Worker.* New York: Oxford University Press, 1993.

Brody, David. *Steelworkers in America: The Nonunion Era.* 1960. Urbana: University of Illinois Press, 1998.

Brown, Sharon A. *Cambria Iron Company: America's Industrial Heritage Project: Pennsylvania.* Washington, DC: US Department of Interior, National Park Service, 1989.

Bruce, Kathleen. *Virginia Iron Manufacture in the Slave Era.* 1930. New York: Augustus M. Kelly, 1968.

Bryce, James. *American Commonwealth*. 2 vols. New York: Macmillan, 1888.

Bukowczyk, John J. "*The Transplanted*: Immigrants and Ethnics." *Social Science History* 12 (Fall 1988): 233–41.

Burgoyne, Arthur G. *The Homestead Strike of 1892*. 1893. Pittsburgh: University of Pittsburgh Press, 1979.

Busch, Jane. "An Introduction to the Tin Can." *Historical Archaeology* 15, no. 1 (1981): 95–104.

Butler, Elizabeth Beardsley. *Women and the Trades, Pittsburgh, 1907–1908*. 1909. Pittsburgh: University of Pittsburgh Press, 1984.

Butler, Joseph G., Jr. "Early History of Iron and Steel Making in the Mahoning Valley." *Iron and Trade Review* 77 (August 20, 1925): 425–28.

Butler, Joseph G., Jr. *History of Youngstown and the Mahoning Valley*. 3 vols. Chicago: AHS, 1921.

Byington, Margaret F. *Homestead: The Households of a Mill Town*. New York: Russell Sage Foundation, 1910.

Cappon, Lester J. "History of the Southern Iron Industry to the Close of the Civil War." PhD diss., Harvard University, 1928. Microfilm ed. Alderson Library, University of Virginia.

"Captain William Richard Jones." *The Cambrian* 5 (September 1885): 264.

Carnegie, Andrew. *Autobiography of Andrew Carnegie*. Boston: Houghton Mifflin, 1920.

Carnegie, Andrew. *Triumphant Democracy, or Fifty Years' March of the Republic*. New York: Scribner, 1886.

Casson, Herbert. *The Romance of Steel: The Story of a Thousand Millionaires*. New York: A. S. Barnes, 1907.

Calavita, Kitty. *U.S. Immigration Law and the Control of Labour, 1820–1924*. London: Academic Press, 1984.

Carter, Matthew David. "Industrial, Industrious, and Diverse: Comparative Case Studies of the Welsh in Urban and Rural America during the Late Nineteenth Century." PhD diss., Cardiff University, 2011.

Cawelti, John G. *Apostles of the Self-Made Man: Changing Concepts of Success in America*. Chicago: University of Chicago Press, 1965.

Chandler, Alfred, Jr. "Anthracite Coal and the Beginnings of the Industrial Revolution in the United States." *Business History Review* 46 (Summer 1972): 141–81.

Chandler, Alfred, Jr. *The Invisible Hand: The Managerial Revolution in American Business*. Cambridge, MA: Harvard University Press, 1977.

Clapham, J. H. *An Economic History of Modern Britain*. Vol. 1, *The Early Railway Age, 1820–1850*. Cambridge: Cambridge University Press, 1926.

Clark, Joseph Harold. "History of the Knoxville Iron Company." MA thesis, University of Tennessee, 1949.

Clark, Victor S. *History of Manufactures in the United States, 1607–1860*. Vol. 1. 1929. New York: Peter Smith, 1949.

Clark, Victor S. *History of Manufactures in the United States, 1893–1928*. Vol. 3. New York: McGraw-Hill, 1929.

Cochran, Thomas C., and William Miller. *The Age of Enterprise: A Social History of Industrial America*. New York: Macmillan, 1961.

Conway, Alan. "Welsh Emigration to the United States." In *Dislocation and Emigration: The Social Background of American Immigration*, edited by Donald Fleming and Bernard Bailyn, 177–271. Cambridge, MA: Charles Warren Center for Studies in American History, Harvard University, 1974.

Conway, Alan, ed. *The Welsh in America: Letters from the Immigrants*. Minneapolis: University of Minnesota Press, 1961.

Conway, Alan. "Welshmen in the Union Armies." *Civil War History* 4 (June 1959): 143–74.

Council, R. Bruce, Nicholas Honerkamp, and M. Elizabeth Will. *Industry and Technology in Antebellum Alabama: The Archaeology of Bluff Furnace*. Knoxville: University of Tennessee Press, 1992.

Couvares, Francis G. *The Remaking of Pittsburgh: Class and Culture in an Industrializing City, 1877–1919*. Albany: State University of New York Press, 1984.

Cronemeyer, William C. "The Development of the Tin-Plate Industry: Memoirs of W. C. Cronemeyer [part 1]." *Western Pennsylvania Historical Magazine* 13 (January 1930): 23–54.

Cronemeyer, William C. "The Development of the Tin-Plate Industry: Memoirs of W. C. Cronemeyer [part 2]." *Western Pennsylvania Historical Magazine* 13 (April 1930): 123–35.

Cushing, Thomas. *History of Allegheny County, Pennsylvania*. Vol. 2. Chicago: A. Warren and Company, 1889.

Davies, Douglas James. *Mormon Spirituality: Latter Day Saints in Wales and Zion*. Nottingham: Nottingham University Press, 1987.

Davies, E. T. *Religion in the Industrial Revolution in South Wales*. Cardiff: University of Wales Press, 1965.

Davies, Hazel. "Observations on Immigrants in America." Presentation at the Conference of the North American Association for the Study of Welsh Culture and History, Rio Grande University, Ohio, 1998.

Davies, Huw. "The Hattie Williams Affair of 1895: Exposing the Family Roots and Uncovering More of the Hetty Ellen Evans (1864–1950) Story." *Llafur* 12, no. 3 (2018): 165–70.

Davies, John, Nigel Jenkins, Menna Baines, and Peredur I. Lynch, eds. *Welsh Academy Encyclopaedia of Wales*. Cardiff: University of Wales Press, 2008.

Davis, Evan E. *Industrial History, Oak Hill, Ohio*. 2nd ed. Portsmouth, OH: Compton Printing, 1980.

Davis, James J. *The Iron Puddler: My Life in the Rolling Mills*. Indianapolis: Bobbs-Merrill, 1922.

DeVault, Ileen A. "'Give the Boys a Trade': Gender and Job Choice in the 1890." In *Work Engendered: Toward a New History of American Labor*, edited by Ava Baron, 191–215. Ithaca, NY: Cornell University Press, 1991.

DeVault, Ileen A. *United Apart: Gender and the Rise of Craft Unionism*. Ithaca, NY: Cornell University Press, 2004.

Dew, Charles B. *Ironmaker to the Confederacy: Joseph R. Anderson and the Tredegar Iron Works*. New Haven, CT: Yale University Press, 1966.

Dieterich-Ward, Allen. *Beyond Rust: Metropolitan Pittsburgh and the Fate of Industrial America*. Philadelphia: University of Pennsylvania Press, 2016.

Dilts, James D. *The Great Road: The Building of the Baltimore and Ohio, the Nation's First Railroad, 1828–1853*. Stanford, CA: Stanford University Press, 1993.

Di Rocco, Samuel, II. "In the Shadow of Steel: Leetonia, Ohio, and Independent Iron Manufacturers in the Mahoning and Shenango Valleys, 1845–1920." PhD diss., University of Toledo, 2012.

Dodd, A. H. *Industrial Revolution in North Wales*. Cardiff: University of Wales Press, 1933.

Downs, Laura Lee. *Manufacturing Inequality: Gender Division in the French and British Metalworking Industries, 1914–1939*. Ithaca, NY: Cornell University Press, 1995.

Downs, Margaret Berry. "Industrial Structure and Pattern of the Wheeling District: Its Evolution and Development, 1840–1950." PhD diss., University of Maryland, 1956.

Dunbar, Donald E. *The Tin-Plate Industry: A Comparative Study of Its Growth in the United States and in Wales.* Boston: Houghton Mifflin, 1915.

Easterlin, Richard A. *Population, Labor Force, and Long Swings in Economic Growth: The American Experience.* Cambridge, MA: National Bureau of Economic Research, 1968.

Eavenson, Howard N. *The First Century and a Quarter of American Coal Industry.* Pittsburgh: privately printed, 1942.

Edwards, Robert. Interview by Keith Dix, October 10, 1974, Huntington, West Virginia. West Virginia and Regional History Center, Wise Library, West Virginia University, Morgantown.

Eggert, Gerald G. *Steelmasters and Labor Reform, 1886–1923.* Pittsburgh: University of Pittsburgh Press, 1981.

Elbaum, Bernard, and Frank Wilkinson. "Industrial Relations and Uneven Development: A Comparative Study of the American and British Steel Industries." *Cambridge Journal of Economics* 3 (September 1979): 275–303.

Elliott, Bruce S, David A. Gerber, and Suzanne M. Sinke, eds. *Letters across Borders: The Epistolary Practices of International Migrants.* New York: Palgrave Macmillan, 2006.

Erickson, Charlotte. *American Industry and the European Immigrant, 1860–1885.* Cambridge, MA: Harvard University Press, 1957.

Erickson, Charlotte. *Invisible Immigrants: The Adaptation of English and Scottish Immigrants in Nineteenth Century America.* Ithaca, NY: Cornell University Press, 1972.

Erickson, Charlotte. *Leaving England: Essays on British Emigration in the Nineteenth Century.* Ithaca, NY: Cornell University Press, 1994.

Ethnicity File, [1925]. Mahoning Valley Historical Society, Youngstown, Ohio.

Evans, Chris. *"The Labyrinth of Flames": Work and Social Conflict in Early Industrial Merthyr Tydfil.* Cardiff: University of Wales Press, 1993.

Evans, D. Gareth. *A History of Wales, 1815–1906.* Cardiff: University of Wales Press, 1989.

Evans, E. C. "Census Reports of the Welsh Population in the United States from 1850–1890." *The Cambrian* 13 (April 1893): 131–38.

Evans, E. Keri. *Cofiant Dr. Joseph Parry.* Llandybie, Carmarthenshire, Wales: Educational Publishing, 1921.

Evans, E. W. *Miners of South Wales.* 1961. Cardiff: University of Wales Press, 1989.

Evans, Henry Oliver. *Iron Pioneer: Henry W. Oliver, 1840–1901.* New York: E. P. Dutton, 1942.

Evans, Neil. "'As Rich as California': Opening and Closing the Frontier; Wales 1780–1870." In *The People of Wales*, edited by Gareth Elwyn Jones and Dai Smith, 111–44. Llandysul, Wales: Gomer Press, 1999.

Evans, Reverend William R. "Trusts and Trade Unions." *The Cambrian* 24 (April 1904): 133–36.

Faires, Nora. "Immigrants and Industry: Peopling the 'Iron City.'" In *City at the Point: Essays on the Social History of Pittsburgh*, edited by Samuel P. Hays, 3–33. Pittsburgh: University of Pittsburgh Press, 1989.

Ferguson, Niall. *Empire: How Britain Made the Modern World.* London: Penguin Group, 2004.

Firmstone, William. "Sketch of Early Anthracite Furnaces." *Transactions of the American Institute of Mining Engineers* 3 (October 1874): 152–56.

"The First Rolling of Iron Bars in America." *The Cambrian* 6 (November–December 1886): 328–29.

Fitch, John A. *The Steel Workers*. 1910. Pittsburgh: University of Pittsburgh Press, 1989.

Fleming, Donald, and Bernard Bailyn, eds. *Dislocation and Emigration: The Social Background of American Immigration*. Cambridge, MA: Charles Warren Center for Studies in American History, Harvard University, 1974.

Fleming, George Thornton. *The History of Pittsburgh and Environs*. Vol. 3. New York: American Historical Society, 1922.

Folsom, Burton W., Jr. *Urban Capitalists: Entrepreneurs and City Growth in Pennsylvania's Lackawanna and Lehigh Regions, 1800–1920*. Baltimore, MD: Johns Hopkins University Press, 1981.

Foner, Eric. *Free Soil, Free Labor, Free Men: The Ideology of the Republican Party before the Civil War*. New York: Oxford University Press, 1970.

Foner, Philip S. *History of the Labor Movement in the United States*. Vol. 3, *The Politics and Practices of the American Federation of Labor, 1900–1909*. New York: International Publishers, 1964.

Foner, Philip S. *History of the Labor Movement in the United States*. Vol. 4, *The Industrial Workers of the World, 1905–1917*. New York: International Publishers, 1965.

Fones-Wolf, Ken. *Glass Towns: Industry, Labor, and Political Economy in Appalachia, 1890–1930s*. Urbana: University of Illinois Press, 2007.

Fones-Wolf, Ken. "Transatlantic Craft Migrations and Transnational Spaces: Belgian Window Glass Workers in America, 1880–1920." *Labor History* 40 (August 2004): 299–321.

Forrester, Shannon. "The John E. Morris Story." *NINNAU* 45 (May–June 2020): 24–25.

Francis, Hywel, and Dai Smith. *The Fed: A History of the South Wales Miners*. Cardiff: University of Wales Press, 1998.

French, B. F. *History of the Rise and Progress of the Iron Trade of the United States from 1621 to 1857*. New York: Wiley and Halsted, 1858. Reprint, Clifton, NJ: Augustus M. Kelley 1973.

Fritz, John. *Autobiography of John Fritz*. New York: John Wiley, 1912.

Froggett, Joseph F. "The Mahoning Valley as an Iron Center: Originality in Practice Marked Steady Progress [part 1]." *Iron Trade Review* 44 (January 21, 1909): 181–85.

Froggett, Joseph F. "The Mahoning Valley as an Iron Center: Sheets and Tin Plate Supplant Iron Cut Nails [part 2]." *Iron Trade Review* 44 (January 28, 1909): 225–29.

Gabaccia, Donna R. *From the Other Side: Women, Gender, and Immigrant Life in the U.S., 1820–1990*. Bloomington: Indiana University Press, 1994.

Gabaccia, Donna R. "The Transplanted: Women and Family in Immigrant America." *Social Science History* 12 (Autumn 1988): 243–53.

Garis, Roy L. *Immigration Restriction: A Study of the Opposition to and Regulation of Immigration into the United States*. New York: Macmillan, 1927.

Gerber, David A. "Epistolary Ethics: Personal Correspondence and the Culture of Emigration in the Nineteenth Century." *Journal of American Ethnic History* 19 (Summer 2000): 3–23.

Gilmer, Harrison. "Birth of the American Crucible Steel Industry." *Western Pennsylvania Historical Magazine* 36 (March 1953): 17–36.

Goodspeed, Weston Arthur. *History of Tennessee, Knox County Edition*. Nashville: Goodspeed Publishing Company, 1887.

Gordon, Robert B. *American Iron, 1607–1900*. Baltimore, MD: Johns Hopkins University Press, 1996.

Gottlieb, Amy Zahl. "British Coal Miners: A Demographic Study of Braidwood and Streator, Illinois." *Journal of the Illinois State Historical Society* 72 (August 1979): 179–92.

Gottlieb, Amy Zahl. "Immigration of British Coal Miners in the Civil War Decade." *International Review of Social History* 23 (December 1978): 357–75.

Gottlieb, Peter. *Making Their Own Way: Southern Blacks' Migration to Pittsburgh, 1916–30.* Urbana: University of Illinois Press, 1987.

Greenwald, Maurine Weiner. Introduction to *Women and the Trades: Pittsburgh, 1907–1908*, edited by Elizabeth Beardsley Butler. 1909. Pittsburgh: University of Pittsburgh Press, 1984.

Greenwald, Maurine Weiner. "Women and Class in Pittsburgh, 1850–1920." In *City at the Point: Essays in the Social History of Pittsburgh*, edited by Samuel P. Hays, 33–67. Pittsburgh: University of Pittsburgh Press, 1989.

Griffiths, Ralph A. *Free and Public: Andrew Carnegie and the Libraries of Wales.* Cardiff: University of Wales Press, 2021.

Griffiths, Robert Huw. "The Welsh and the American Civil War." PhD diss., University of Wales, Cardiff, 2004.

Gruenwald, Kim M. *River of Enterprise: The Commercial Origins of Regional Identity in the Ohio Valley, 1790–1850.* Bloomington: Indiana University Press, 2002.

Guglielmo, Thomas A. *White on Arrival: Italians, Race, Color, and Power in Chicago, 1890–1945.* New York: Oxford University Press, 2003.

Gutman, Herbert G. *Work, Culture, and Society in Industrializing America: Essays in American Working-Class and Social History.* New York: Vintage Books, 1977.

Gwyther, Cyril E. "Sidelights on Religion and Politics in the Rhondda Valley, 1906–1926." *Llafur* 3 (Spring 1980): 30–43.

Hansen, Marcus Lee. *The Atlantic Migration, 1607–1860.* Cambridge, MA: Harvard University Press, 1940.

Harris, Frederick J. *Welshmen and the United States.* Pontypridd, Wales: Glamorgan County Times Offices, 1927.

Hartmann, Edward G. *Americans from Wales.* 1967. New York: Octagon, Books, 1983.

Harvey, Katherine A. *The Best-Dressed Miners: Life and Labor in the Maryland Coal Region, 1835–1910.* Ithaca, NY: Cornell University Press, 1969.

Harvey, Katherine A., ed. *The Lonaconing Journals: The Founding of a Coal and Iron Community, 1837–1840.* Philadelphia: American Philosophical Society, 1977.

Hays, Samuel P., ed. *City at the Point: Essays on the Social History of Pittsburgh.* Pittsburgh: University of Pittsburgh Press, 1989.

Hazen, Aaron L., ed. *20th Century History of New Castle and Lawrence County.* Chicago: Richmond-Arnold Publishing Company, 1908.

Heald, Edward Thornton. *The Stark County Story.* Vol. 1. Canton, OH: Stark County Historical Society, 1949.

Hendrick, Burton J. *The Life of Andrew Carnegie.* Garden City, NY: Doubleday, Doran, 1932.

Higham, John. "Current Trends in the Study of Ethnicity in the United States." *Journal of American Ethnic History* 2 (Fall 1982): 5–15.

History of Trumbull and Mahoning Counties: With Illustrations and Biographical Sketches. 2 vols. Cleveland: H. Z. Williams and Brother, 1882.

Hodges, A. H. *Flame in the Mountains: Williams Pantycelyn, Ann Griffiths and the Welsh Hymn.* Edited by E. Wyn James. Tal-y-bont, Wales: Y Lolfa, 2017.

Hoerder, Dirk. *Cultures in Contact: World Migrations in the Second Millennium.* Durham, NC: Duke University Press, 2002.

Hoerder, Dirk, ed. *"Struggle a Hard Battle": Essays on Working-Class Immigrants*. DeKalb: Northern Illinois University Press, 1986.

Hogan, William T. *Economic History of the Iron and Steel Industry in the United States*. 5 vols. Lexington, MA: Lexington Books, 1971.

Holmes, G. M. "The South Wales Coal Industry, 1850–1914." *Transactions of the Honourable Society of Cymmrodorion* (1976): 162–207.

Holt, James. "Trade Unionism in the British and U.S. Steel Industries, 1888–1912: A Comparative Approach." *Labor History* 18, no. 1 (1977): 5–35.

"Hon. David Richards." *The Cambrian* 26 (April 1906): 181–82.

Hughes, Glyn Tegai. *Williams Pantycelyn*. Cardiff: University of Wales Press, for the Welsh Arts Council, 1983.

"Humphreys, Miles S." Pennsylvania State Senate. https://www.legis.state.pa.us/cfdocs/legis/BiosHistory/MemBio.cfm?ID=4793&body=S.

Humphries, Jane. "'The Most Free from Objection': The Sexual Division of Labor and Women's Work in Nineteenth-Century England." *Journal of Economic History* 47 (December 1987): 929–49.

Humphries, Jane. "The Working-Class Family, Women's Liberation and Class Struggle: The Case of Nineteenth-Century British History." *Review of Radical Political Economics* 9 (Fall 1977): 25–42.

Humphries, John. *The Man from the Alamo: Why the Welsh Chartist Uprising of 1839 Ended in a Massacre*. Porth Glyndwr, Wales: Glyndwr Publishing, 2004.

Hunt, R. W. "A History of the Bessemer Manufacture in America." *Engineering* 22 (1876): 509, 532–33.

Hutchinson, Edward P. *Legislative History of American Immigration Policy, 1798–1965*. Philadelphia: University of Pennsylvania Press, 1981.

Hyde, Charles K. *Technological Change and the British Iron Industry, 1700–1870*. Princeton, NJ: Princeton University Press, 1977.

Ingham, John N. *The Iron Barons: A Social Analysis of an American Urban Elite, 1874–1965*. Westport, CT: Greenwood, 1978.

Ingham, John N. *Making Iron and Steel: Independent Mills in Pittsburgh, 1820–1920*. Columbus: Ohio State University Press, 1991.

Iriye, Akira. *Global and Transnational History: The Past, Present, and Future*. Basingstoke, UK: Palgrave Macmillan, 2013.

Irwin, Douglas A. *Against the Tide: An Intellectual History of Free Trade*. Princeton, NJ: Princeton University Press, 1996.

Irwin, Douglas A. "Did Late-Nineteenth-Century U.S. Tariffs Promote Infant Industries? Evidence from the Tinplate Industry." *Journal of Economic History* 60 (June 2000): 335–60.

Jarrett, John. AAISW President's Report. *Journal of the Proceedings of the Annual Convention of the Amalgamated Association of Iron, Steel, and Tin Workers* (held August 7–16, 1883, Philadelphia), 1105.

Jarrett, John. "The Story of the Iron Workers." In *The Labor Movement: The Problem of To-Day*, edited by George E. McNeill, 268–311. New York: M. W. Hazen, 1887.

Jarrett, John, and William Martin. Letter to the Iron and Steel Workers of England, Scotland and Wales. *Journal of the Proceedings of the Annual Convention of the Amalgamated Association of Iron, Steel, and Tin Workers* (held August 1–10, 1882, Chicago), 856.

Jenkins, Paul. *"Twenty by Fourteen": A History of the South Wales Tinplate Industry, 1700–1961.* Llandysul, Wales: Gomer Press, 1995.

Jenkins, Philip. *A History of Modern Wales, 1536–1990.* 1992. New York: Routledge, 2014.

Jobin, Maurice. *Cleveland, Past and Present: Its Representative Men, Comprising Biographical Sketches of Pioneer Settlers and Prominent Citizens with a History of the City.* Cleveland: Fairbanks, Benedict, and Co., 1869.

John, Arthur H. *Industrial Development of South Wales, 1750–1850: An Essay.* Cardiff: University of Wales Press, 1950.

Johnson, Keach. "The Genesis of the Baltimore Ironworks." *Journal of Southern History* 19 (May 1953): 157–79.

Johnston, W. Ross. "The Welsh Diaspora: Emigrating around the World in the Late Nineteenth Century." *Llafur* 6, no. 2 (1993): 50–74.

Jones, Aled. *Press, Politics and Society: A History of Journalism in Wales.* Cardiff: University of Wales Press, 1993.

Jones, Aled, and Bill Jones. *Welsh Reflections: "Y Drych" and America, 1851–2001.* Llandysul, Ceredigion, Wales: Gomer, 2001.

Jones, Aled, and Bill Jones. "*Y Drych* and American Welsh Identities." *North American Journal of Welsh Studies* 1 (Winter 2001): 42–58.

"Jones, Benjamin Franklin." *Dictionary of American Biography.* Vol. 10, 162–63. New York: Charles Scribner's Sons, 1933.

Jones, Bill [aka William D.]. "Banqueting at a Moveable Feast: Wales 1870–1914." In *The People of Wales*, edited by Gareth Elwyn Jones and Dai Smith, 145–78. Llandysul, Wales: Gomer Press, 1999.

Jones, Bill [aka William D.]. "Ethnic Journalism and the Reconstruction of Identity: The Welsh-Language Press in the USA in the Nineteenth and Early Twentieth Centuries." Paper presented at the Rush D. Holt Conference, April 2003, West Virginia University, Morgantown.

Jones, Bill [aka William D.]. "'Inspecting the Extraordinary Drain': Emigration and the Urban Experience in Merthyr Tydfil in the 1860s." *Urban History* 32 (May 2005): 100–113.

Jones, Bill [aka William D.]. "Raising the Wind: Emigrating from Wales to the USA in the Late Nineteenth and Early Twentieth Centuries." Annual Public Lecture 2003, Cardiff Centre for Welsh American Studies, Cardiff University, Wales.

Jones, Bill [aka William D.]. "'We Will Give You Wings to Fly': Emigration Societies in Merthyr Tydfil in 1868." *Merthyr Historian* 13 (2001): 27–45.

Jones, Bill [aka William D.]. "Writing Back: Welsh Emigrants and Their Correspondence in the Nineteenth Century." *North American Journal of Welsh Studies* 5 (Winter 2005): 23–46.

Jones, David. *Memorial Volume of the Welsh Congregationalists of Pennsylvania, U.S.A.* Utica, NY: Press of Utica Printing Company, 1934.

Jones, David J. *The Last Rising: The Newport Chartist Insurrection of 1839.* Cardiff: University of Wales Press, 1999.

Jones, Edgar R. *Toilers of the Hills.* Pontypool, Wales: Hughes & Son, 1959.

Jones, Emrys. "Some Aspects of Cultural Change in an American-Welsh Community." *Transactions of the Honourable Society of Cymmrodorion* (1952): 15–41.

Jones, J. H. *The Tinplate Industry with Special Reference to Its Relations with the Iron and Steel Industries.* London: P. S. King and Son, 1914.

Jones, Maldwyn A. "The Background to Emigration from Great Britain in the Nineteenth

Century." In *Dislocation and Emigration: The Social Background of American Immigration*, edited by Donald Fleming and Bernard Bailyn. Cambridge, MA: Charles Warren Center for Studies in American History, Harvard University, 1974.

Jones, Maldwyn A. "From the Old Country to the New: The Welsh in Nineteenth-Century America." *Flintshire Historical Society Publications* 27 (1975–1976): 85–100.

Jones, Samuel. *Pittsburgh in the Year 1826*. Pittsburgh: Johnston and Stockton, 1826.

Jones, Wendell M. "The Gymanfa Ganu." MA thesis, Ohio State University, 1946.

Jones, William D. [aka Bill]. "'Going into Print': Published Immigrant Letters, Webs of Personal *Relations*, and the Emergence of the Welsh Public Sphere." In *Letters across Borders: The Epistolary Practices of International Migrants*, edited by Bruce S. Elliott, David A. Gerber, and Suzanne M. Sinke, 175–99. New York: Palgrave Macmillan, 2006.

Jones, William D. [aka Bill]. "Wales in America: Scranton and the Welsh, 1860–1920." PhD diss., University of Wales, Cardiff, 1987.

Jones, William D. [aka Bill]. "The Welsh Language and Welsh Identity in a Pennsylvania Community." In *Language and Community in the Nineteenth Century*, edited by Geraint H. Jenkins. Cardiff: University of Wales Press, 1998.

Jones, William D. [aka Bill], and Ronald L. Lewis. "Gender and Transnationality among Welsh Tinplate Workers: The Hattie Williams Affair, 1895." *Labor History* 48 (May 2007): 175–94.

Jones, William Harvey. "Welsh Settlements in Ohio." *Ohio Archaeological and Historical Publications* 16 (April 1907): 198–203, 216–18.

Jordan, Ellen. "Exclusion of Women from Industry in Nineteenth-Century Britain." *Comparative Studies in Society and History* 32 (April 1989): 273–96.

Jordan, John W. *Genealogical and Personal History of Western Pennsylvania*. Vol. 2. New York: Lewis Historical Publishing, 1915. Google Online Library.

"Joseph Corns." *The Cambrian* 4 (October 1884): 271–72.

Kaltinick, Arnold. "Socialist Municipal Administration in Four American Cities (Milwaukee, Schenectady, New Castle, Pennsylvania, and Conneaut, Ohio), 1910–16." PhD diss., New York University, 1882.

Keeler, Vernon D. "An Economic History of the Jackson County Iron Industry." *Ohio Archaeological and Historical Quarterly* 42 (1933): 132–44.

Kenny, Kevin. "Diaspora and Comparison: The Global Irish as a Case Study." *Journal of American History* 90 (June 2003): 134–62.

Kessler-Harris, Alice. *Out to Work: A History of Wage-Earning Women in the United States*. New York: Oxford University Press, 1982.

Kirkland, Edward Chase. *Industry Comes of Age: Business, Labor, and Public Policy, 1860—1897*. New York: Holt, Rinehart and Winston, 1961.

Kitson, James. "The Iron and Steel Industries of America." *Contemporary Review* 59 (1891): 629.

Kleinberg, Susan J. "Technology and Women's Work: The Lives of Working-Class Women in Pittsburgh, 1870–1900." *Labor History* 17 (Winter 1976): 58–72.

Knowles, Anne Kelly. *Calvinists Incorporated: Welsh Immigrants on Ohio's Industrial Frontier*. Chicago: University of Chicago Press, 1997.

Knowles, Anne Kelly. "Labor, Race, and Technology in the Confederate Iron Industry." *Technology and Culture* 42 (January 2001): 1–26.

Knowles, Anne Kelly. *Mastering Iron: The Struggle to Modernize an American Industry, 1800–1868*. Chicago: University of Chicago Press, 2013.

Knox, Howard A. *Development of the American Tin Plate Industry*. Pittsburgh: Carnegie-Illinois Steel Corporation of the United States, [1965].

Kobus, Ken. *City of Steel: How Pittsburgh Became the World's Steelmaking Capital during the Carnegie Era*. Lanham, MD: Rowman & Littlefield, 2015.

Krass, Peter. *Carnegie*. New York: John Wiley & Sons, 2003.

Krause, Paul. *The Battle for Homestead, 1880–1892: Politics, Culture, Steel*. Pittsburgh: University of Pittsburgh Press, 1992.

Lamoreaux, Naomi R. *The Great Merger Movement in American Business, 1895–1904*. New York: Cambridge University Press, 1985.

"The Late Captain William R. Jones." *The Cambrian* 10 (April 1890): 98.

"The Late Capt. W. R. Jones: Biographical Sketch and Crown Memorial Poems." In *The Royal Blue Book*. Pittsburgh: International Eisteddfod Memorial Edition, 1913.

"The Late T. R. Morgan." *The Cambrian* 17 (October 1897): 442–43.

Lawyer, Charles E. "History of the Trade Unions: Tin Plate Workers." *American Federationist* 10 (September 1903): 841.

Levine, Susan. *Labor's True Woman: Carpet Weavers, Industrialization, and Labor Reform in the Gilded Age*. Philadelphia: Temple University Press, 1984.

Lewis, Jane, ed. *Labour and Love: Women's Experience of Home and Family, 1850–1940*. Oxford: Basil Blackwell, 1986.

Lewis, Ronald L. *Coal, Iron, and Slaves: Industrial Slavery in Maryland and Virginia, 1715–1865*. Westport, CT: Greenwood Press, 1979.

Lewis, Ronald L. *Welsh Americans: A History of Assimilation in the Coalfields*. Chapel Hill: University of North Carolina Press, 2008.

Lewis, W. David. "The Early History of the Lackawanna Iron and Coal Company: A Study in Technological Adaptation." *Pennsylvania Magazine of History and Biography* 96 (October 1972): 424–68.

Lewis, W. David. *Sloss Furnaces and the Rise of the Birmingham District: An Industrial Epic*. Tuscaloosa: University of Alabama Press, 1994.

Lillibridge, George Donald. *Beacon of Freedom: The Impact of American Democracy upon Great Britain, 1830–1970*. Philadelphia: University of Pennsylvania Press, 1955.

Linaberger, James. "The Rolling Mill Riots of 1850." *Western Pennsylvania Historical Magazine* 47 (January 1964): 1–18.

Livesay, Harold C. *Andrew Carnegie and the Rise of Big Business*. Boston: Little, Brown, 1975.

Long, Priscilla. *Where the Sun Never Shines: A History of America's Bloody Coal Industry*. New York: Paragon House, 1989.

Loveday, Amos J., Jr. *The Rise and Decline of the American Cut Nail Industry: A Study of the Interrelationships of Technology, Business Organization, and Management Techniques*. Westport, CT: Greenwood Press, 1983.

Lown, Judy. *Women and Industrialization: Gender at Work in Nineteenth-Century England*. Minneapolis: University of Minnesota Press, 1990.

Magda, Matthew S. *Monessen: Industrial Boomtown and Steel Community, 1898–1980*. Harrisburg: Pennsylvania Historical and Museum Commission, 1985.

Mapes, Lynn Gordon. "*Iron Age*: An Iron Manufacturer's Journal and the 'Labor Problem' in the Age of Enterprise." PhD diss., University of Rochester, 1973.

Martin, Louis C. "Causes and Consequences of the 1909–1910 Steel Strike in the Wheeling District." MA thesis, West Virginia University, 1999.

Martin, Louis C. "'So Nobly Struggling for Their Manhood': Masculinity and Violence among Steelworkers in the Wheeling District, 1880–1910." *Labor History* 60, no. 5 (2019): 429–43.

Martin, Louis C. "Tin Plate Towns, 1890–1910: Local Labor Movements and Workers' Responses to the Crisis in the Steelworkers' Union." *Pennsylvania History: A Journal of Mid-Atlantic Studies* 74 (Autumn 2007): 492–528.

May, Earl Chapin. *Principio to Wheeling, 1715–1945: A Pageant of Iron and Steel.* New York: Harper and Brothers, 1945.

May, Martha. "Bread before Roses: American Workingmen, Labor Unions, and the Family Wage." In *Women, Work, and Protest: A Century of U.S. Women's Labor History,* edited by Ruth Milkman, 1–21. Boston: Routledge and Kegan Paul, 1985.

McAdoo, William. "Immigration and the Tariff." *Forum* 11 (June 1891): 398–405.

McHugh, Jeanne. *Alexander Holley and the Makers of Steel.* Baltimore, MD: Johns Hopkins University Press, 1980.

McKelvey, A. T. *Centennial History of Belmont County, Ohio, and Representative Citizens.* Chicago: Biographical Publishing Company, 1903.

McKinley, William. *Speeches and Addresses of William McKinley from His Election to Congress to the Present Time.* New York: D. Appleton and Company, 1893.

Merry, Robert W. *President McKinley: Architect of the American Century.* New York: Simon and Schuster, 2017.

Milkman, Ruth. "Organizing the Sexual Division of Labor: Historical Perspectives on 'Women's Work' and the American Labor Movement." *Socialist Review* 49 (January–February 1980): 95–144.

Milkman, Ruth. *Women, Work and Protest: A Century of US Women's Labor History.* Boston: Routledge & Kegan Paul, 1985.

Miller, Kerby A. *Emigrants and Exiles: Ireland and the Irish Exodus to North America.* Oxford: Oxford University Press, 1885.

Miller, Kerby A., and Bruce D. Boling. "Golden Streets, Bitter Tears: The Irish Image of America during the Era of Mass Migration." *Journal of American Ethnic History* 10, no. 1–2 (1990–1991): 16–35.

Miller, William, ed. *Men in Business.* Rev. ed. New York: Harper & Row, 1962.

Minchinton, W. E. *The British Tinplate Industry: A History.* Oxford: Clarendon Press, 1957.

Minchinton, W. E. "The Diffusion of Tinplate Manufacture." *Economic History Review,* n.s., 9, no. 2 (1956): 349–58.

Misa, Thomas J. *A Nation of Steel: The Making of Modern America, 1865–1925.* Baltimore, MD: Johns Hopkins University Press, 1995.

Montgomery, David. *Beyond Equality: Labor and the Radical Republicans, 1862–1872.* 1967. Urbana: University of Illinois Press, 1981.

Morgan, Derec Llwyd. *The Great Awakening in Wales.* London: Epworth Press, 1988.

Morgan, H. Wayne. *William McKinley and His America.* Syracuse, NY: Syracuse University Press, 1963.

Morgan, Kenneth O. *Rebirth of a Nation: Wales, 1880–1980.* Oxford: Oxford University Press, 1981.

Morgan, Kenneth O. *Wales in British Politics, 1868–1922.* Cardiff: University of Wales Press, 1963.

Morgan, Owen. *A Souvenir of the Visit of the Iron and Steel Institutes of Great Britain and Germany to America.* Cardiff: Daniel Owen, 1890.

Morgan, Prys. "Keeping the Legends Alive." In *Wales the Imagined Nation: Essays in Cultural and National Identity,* edited by Tony Curtis, 19–41. Bridgend: Poetry Wales Press, 1986.

Morgan Family. AF Biography, Rodman Public Library, Alliance, Ohio.

Morris, John. "Coal and Steel." In *Wales through the Ages, from 1485 to the Beginning of the Twentieth Century*, edited by A. J. Roderick, 2:177–84. Llandybie, Wales: Christopher Davies Publishers, 1969.

Morris, J. H., and L. J. Williams. *South Wales Coal Industry, 1841–1875*. Cardiff: University of Wales Press, 1958.

Mosher, Anne Elaine. *Capital's Utopia: The Steel Industry's Search for Urban Order at Vandergrift, 1855–1916*. Baltimore, MD: Johns Hopkins University Press, 2004.

"Mr. John Jarrett, Pittsburgh, Pa." *The Cambrian* 9 (March 1889): 65–66.

Muller, Edward K. "Metropolis and Region: A Framework for Enquiry into Western Pennsylvania." In *City at the Point: Essays on the Social History of Pittsburgh*, edited by Samuel P. Hays. 181–211. Pittsburgh: University of Pittsburgh Press, 1989.

Murdoch, Alexander. *British Emigration, 1603–1914*. New York: Palgrave Macmillan, 2004.

Nasaw, David. *Andrew Carnegie*. New York: Penguin, 2006.

Nash, Michael. *Conflict and Accommodation: Coal Miners, Steel Workers, and Socialism, 1890–1920*. Westport, CT: Greenwood, 1982.

National Museum of Wales. Museum of Welsh Life, Cardiff. Sound Archive. Transcripts of interviews with Cecil Frederick Lewis (b. Morriston 1913), October 22, 1986, and Doris Rees (b. Morriston 1910), October 21, 1986.

O'Leary, Paul. *Immigration and Integration: The Irish in Wales, 1798–1922*. Cardiff: University of Wales Press, 2000.

O'Leary, Paul. "Power and Modernity: Transnational Wales, 1780–1939." *Llafur: Journal of Welsh People's History* 12, no. 4 (2019–2020): 33–55.

"Oliver, Henry William." *Dictionary of American Biography*. Vol. 14, 19–20. New York: Charles Scribner's Sons, 1934.

Owen-Jones, Sheila. "Women in the Tinplate Industry: Llanelly, 1930–1950." *Oral History Journal* 15 (Spring 1987): 42–49.

Palen, Marc-William. "Protection, Federation and Union: The Global Impact of the McKinley Tariff upon the British Empire, 1890–94." *Journal of Imperial and Commonwealth History* 38 (September 2010): 395–418.

Pallante, Martha I. "To Work and Live: Brickyard Laborers, Immigration, and Assimilation in an Ohio Town, 1890–1925." *Northeast Ohio Journal of History* 2 (Fall 2003): [1–11].

Parr, Joy. *Gender of Breadwinners: Women, Men, and Change in Two Industrial Towns, 1880–1950*. Toronto: University of Toronto Press, 1990.

Parr, Joy. "The Skilled Emigrant and Her Kin: Gender, Culture, and Labour Recruitment." *Canadian Historical Review* 68 (December 1987): 529–51.

Paskoff, Paul F., ed. *Iron and Steel in the Nineteenth Century*. New York: Bruccoli Clark Layman and Facts on File, 1989.

Perelman, Dale Richard. *Steel: The Story of Pittsburgh's Iron and Steel Industry, 1852–1902*. Charleston, SC: History Press, 2014.

Pietranton, Frank A. *History of Weirton and Holiday's Cove and Life of J. C. Williams*. Pittsburgh: Pittsburgh Printing Company, 1936.

"The Pittsburgh Eisteddfod." *The Cambrian* 8 (February 1888): 52–53.

Pollert, Anna. *Girls, Wives, Factory Lives*. London: Macmillan, 1981.

Porter, Glenn, and Harold Livesay. *Merchants and Manufacturers: Studies in the Changing Structure of Nineteenth-Century Marketing*. Baltimore, MD: Johns Hopkins University Press, 1971.

Proctor, R. G., comp. *Tariff Acts Passed by the Congress of the United States.* Washington, DC: Government Printing Office, 1898.

Pugh, Arthur. *Men of Steel, by One of Them: A Chronicle of Eighty-Eight Years of Trade Unionism in the British Iron and Steel Industry.* London: Iron and Steel Trades Confederation, 1951.

Pursell, Carroll W., Jr. "Tariff and Technology: The Foundation and Development of the American Tin-Plate Industry, 1872–1900." *Technology and Culture* 3 (Summer 1962): 267–84.

Pyle, D. S. *A Pioneer History of the Tin Plate Industry at New Castle, Pennsylvania.* 1936. Mimeographed pamphlet in New Castle Public Library.

Reitano, Joanne. *The Tariff Question in the Gilded Age: The Great Debate of 1888.* University Park: Pennsylvania State University Press, 1994.

Rhys, Dulais. *Joseph Parry: Bachgen bach o Ferthyr.* Cardiff: University of Wales Press, 1998.

Rhys, Dulais, ed. *The Little Hero: The Autobiography of Joseph Parry.* Aberystwyth, Wales: National Library of Wales, 2009.

Rhys, Dulais, and Frank Bott. *To Philadelphia and Back: The Life and Music of Joseph Parry.* Llanwrst, Wales: Gwasg Curreg Gwalch, 2010.

Richards, Bart. Interview by Joe Uehlein, February 21, 1974, Pittsburgh, Pennsylvania. Transcription in USA Archive and Oral History Collection, Pattee Library, Pennsylvania State University, State College.

Richards, Bart. *Lawrence County: A Compact History of Lawrence County, Pennsylvania.* New Castle, PA: New Castle Area School District, 1968.

Richards, Eric. *Britannia's Children: Emigration from England, Scotland, Wales and Ireland since 1600.* London: Hambledon and London, 2004.

Robbins, Michael W. *Maryland's Iron Industry during the Revolutionary War Era.* Annapolis: Maryland Bicentennial Commission, 1973.

Robbins, Michael Warren. "The Principio Company: Iron-Making in Colonial Maryland, 1720–1781." PhD diss., George Washington University, 1972.

Roberts, Gwyneth Tyson. *Language of the Blue Books: The Perfect Instrument of Empire.* Cardiff: University of Wales Press, 1998.

Robinson, Jesse S. *The Amalgamated Association of Iron, Steel, and Tin Workers.* Baltimore, MD: Johns Hopkins University Press, 1920.

Rodgers, Daniel T. "Republicanism: The Career of a Concept." *Journal of American History* 79 (June 1992): 11–38.

Rose, Sonya O. "Gender at Work: Sex, Class, and Industrial Capitalism." *History Workshop Journal* 27 (1986): 113–31.

Rule, William, George Mellen, and John Wooldridge, eds. *Standard History of Knoxville, Tennessee.* Chicago: Lewis Publishing Company, 1900. Reprint, Whitefish, MT: Kessinger Books, 2010.

Ruminski, Clayton J. *Iron Valley: The Transformation of the Iron Industry in Ohio's Mahoning Valley, 1802–1913.* Columbus: Ohio State University Press, 2017.

Rutherford, Roy. *Romancing in Tin Plate.* Warren, OH: Wean Engineering, 1951.

Sadie, Julie Anne, and Stanley Sadie. *Calling on the Composer.* New Haven, CT: Yale University Press, 2005.

Samuel, J. R. *A Short History of the Tin and Tinplate Trade.* Newport, Wales: Williams Press, 1924.

Samways, Norman L. "Welshman Installs First Revolutionary New Process in America Iron Puddling and Bar Rolling." *NINNAU* 41 (January–February 2016): 22.

Sanders, Vivienne. *Wales, the Welsh and the Making of America*. Cardiff: University of Wales Press, 2021.

Sanderson, Thomas W. *20th Century History of Youngstown and Mahoning County, Ohio*. Chicago: Biographical Publishing Company, 1907.

Santos, Michael. "Between Hegemony and Autonomy: The Skilled Iron Workers' Search for Identity, 1900–1930." *Labor History* 35 (Summer 1994): 399–423.

Schechter, Patricia. "Free and Slave Labor in the Old South: The Tredegar Ironworkers' Strike of 1847." *Labor History* 35 (Spring 1994): 165–86.

Schubert, H. R. *History of the British Iron and Steel Industry*. London: Routledge & Kegan Paul, 1957.

Scott, Henry Dickerson. *Iron and Steel in Wheeling*. Toledo, OH: Caslon, 1929.

Scrivenor, Harry. *History of the Iron Trade, from Earliest Records to the Present Period*. London: Longman, Brown, and Green, 1854.

Seccombe, Wally. "Patriarchy Stabilized: The Construction of the Male Breadwinner Wage Norm in Nineteenth-Century Britain." *Social History* 11 (January 1986): 53–76.

Shapiro, Karin. *A New South Rebellion: The Battle against Convict Labor in the Tennessee Coalfields, 1871–1896*. Chapel Hill: University of North Carolina Press, 1998.

Sheppard, Muriel Earley. *Cloud by Day: The Story of Coal and Coke and People*. 1947. Pittsburgh: University of Pittsburgh Press, 1991.

Shepperson, Wilbur S. *British Emigration to North America: Projects and Opinions in the Early Victorian Period*. Minneapolis: University of Minnesota Press, 1957.

Shepperson, Wilbur S. *Samuel Roberts: A Welsh Colonizer in Civil War Tennessee*. Knoxville: University of Tennessee Press, 1961.

Shergold, Peter R. *Working-Class Life: The "American Standard" in Comparative Perspective, 1899–1913*. Pittsburgh: University of Pittsburgh Press, 1982.

Skrabec, Quintin R., Jr. *William McKinley, Apostle of Protectionism*. New York: Algora, 2008.

Smith, Dai. *Wales: A Question for History*. Cardiff: Seren, 1999.

Smith, Dai. *Wales! Wales?* London: George Allen and Unwin, 1984.

Smith, Timothy L. "Religion and Ethnicity in America." *American Historical Review* 83 (December 1978): 1155–85.

Stapleton, Darwin. *The Transfer of Early Industrial Technology to America*. Philadelphia: American Philosophical Society, 1987.

Stephens, Thomas. *Madoc: An Essay on the Discovery of America by Madoc Ap Owen Gwynedd in the Twelfth Century*. London: Longmans, Green, 1893.

Sullivan, William A. *The Industrial Worker in Pennsylvania, 1800–1840*. Harrisburg: Pennsylvania Historical and Museum Commission, 1955.

Summers, Ewing. *Genealogical and Family History of Eastern Ohio*. Chicago: Lewis Publishing Company, 1903.

Summers, Mark Wahlgren. *Party Games: Getting, Keeping, and Using Power in Gilded Age Politics*. Chapel Hill: University of North Carolina Press, 2004.

Swank, James M. *History of the Manufacture of Iron in All Ages*. Philadelphia: American Iron and Steel Association, 1892.

Taussig, Frank W. "The Iron Industry in the United States [part 1]." *Quarterly Journal of Economics* 14 (February 1900): 143–70.

Taussig, Frank. W. *The Tariff History of the United States*. New York: G. P. Putnam's Sons, 1892. Reprint, New York: Augustus M. Kelley Publishers, 1967.

Temin, Peter. *Iron and Steel in Nineteenth-Century America*. Cambridge, MA: MIT Press, 1964.

Thomas, Brinley. "Growth of Industrial Towns." In *Wales through the Ages*, vol. 2, edited by A. J. Roderick, 185–92. Llandybie, Wales: Christopher Davies, 1971.

Thomas, Brinley. *The Industrial Revolution and the Atlantic Economy: Selected Essays*. London: Routledge, 1993.

Thomas, Brinley. *Migration and Economic Growth*. Cambridge: Cambridge University Press, 1954.

Thomas, Brinley. "The Migration of Labour into the Glamorgan Coalfield (1861–1911)." *Economica*, no. 30 (November 1930): 275–94.

Thomas, Brinley. "Wales and the Atlantic Economy." In *The Welsh Economy: Studies in Expansion*, edited by Brinley Thomas, 1–29. Cardiff: University of Wales Press, 1962.

Thomas, Brinley, ed. *The Welsh Economy: Studies in Expansion*. Cardiff: University of Wales Press, 1962.

Thomas, R. D. [Robert David]. *Hanes Cymry America: A History of the Welsh in America*. 1872. 2nd ed., translated by Martha A. Davies and Phillips G. Davies. Wymore, NE: Great Plains Welsh Heritage Project, 2008.

Thomas, Samuel. "Reminiscences of the Early Anthracite-Iron Industry." *Transactions of the American Institute of Mining Engineers* 29 (February–September 1899): 901–28.

"Thomas, William Aubrey." *Biographical Directory of the United States Congress*. Accessed August 9, 2022. https://bioguide.congress.gov/search/bio/T000186.

"Thomas C. Jenkins." *The Cambrian* 10 (June 1890): 163.

Thomas Family Genealogy. Niles Furnace-Niles Firebrick Company Papers. Archives of the Museum of Industry and Labor, Ohio Historical Society, Youngstown.

"Thomas Rees Morgan, Sr." *The Cambrian* 11 (October 1891): 290–91.

Thurston, George H. *Pittsburgh and Allegheny in the Centennial Year*. Pittsburgh: A. A. Anderson & Son, 1876.

"Tin Plates Abroad." *American Artisan* 29 (May 11, 1895): 24.

Toth, Anthony B. "The Syrian Community in New Castle and Its Unique Alawi Component, 1900–1940." *Western Pennsylvania Historical Magazine* 69 (July 1986): 221–39.

Tweedale, Geoffrey. *Sheffield Steel and America: A Century of Commercial and Technological Interdependence, 1830–1930*. Cambridge: Cambridge University Press, 1987.

Tyler, Robert Llewellyn. "Migrant Culture Maintenance: The Welsh Experience in Martins Ferry, Belmont County, Ohio, 1900–1940." *Ohio History* 125 (Spring 2018): 70–94.

Tyler, Robert Llewellyn. "Occupational Mobility and Social Status: The Welsh Experience in Sharon, Pennsylvania, 1880–1930." *Pennsylvania History: A Journal of Mid-Atlantic Studies* 83 (Winter 2016): 1–27.

Tyler, Robert Llewellyn. *Wales and the American Dream*. Newcastle upon Tyne, UK: Cambridge Scholars, 2015.

Upton, Harriet Taylor. *A Twentieth-Century History of Trumbull County, Ohio*. 2 vols. Chicago: Lewis Publishing Company, 1909.

Van Buskirk, William. "History of the Philanthropic Order of True Ivorites in Wales and in North America." *NINNAU* 45 (March–April 2020): 20.

Vance, James E., Jr. *The North American Railroad: Its Origin, Evolution, and Geography*. Baltimore, MD: Johns Hopkins University Press, 1995.

Van Tine, Warren. *Making of the Labor Bureaucrat: Union Leadership in the United States, 1870–1920*. Amherst: University of Massachusetts Press, 1973.

Van Vugt, William E. *Britain to America: Mid-Nineteenth-Century Immigrants to the United States.* Urbana: University of Illinois Press, 1999.

Van Vugt, William E. *British Buckeyes: The English, Scots, and Welsh in Ohio, 1700–1900.* Kent, OH: Kent State University Press, 2006.

Vecoli, Rudolph. "Contadini in Chicago: A Critique of *The Uprooted.*" *Journal of American History* 51 (December 1963): 404–17.

Wade, Richard C. *The Urban Frontier.* Chicago: University of Chicago Press, 1959.

Wall, Joseph Frazier. *Andrew Carnegie.* New York: Oxford University Press, 1970.

Wallace, Anthony F. *St. Clair: A Nineteenth-Century Coal Town's Experience with a Disaster-Prone Industry.* New York: Knopf, 1987.

Walters, R. H. *Economic and Business History of the South Wales Steam Coal Industry, 1840–1914.* New York: Arno Press, 1977.

Warren, Kenneth. *The American Steel Industry, 1850–1970.* Oxford: Clarendon Press, 1973.

Warren, Kenneth. *Big Steel: The First Century of the United States Steel Corporation.* Pittsburgh: University of Pittsburgh Press, 2001.

Watts, D. G. "Changes in Location of the South Wales Iron and Steel Industry, 1860–1930." *Geography* 53 (July 1968): 294–307.

Weber, Max. *The Protestant Ethic and the Spirit of Capitalism.* New York: Charles Scribner's Sons, 1958.

Wells, David A. *Recent Economic Changes and Their Effect on the Production and Distribution of Wealth and the Well-Being of Society.* 1889. New York: D. Appleton Company, 1896.

"Welsh Mills Idle." *American Artisan* 29 (May 18, 1895): 29.

Welsh Pioneers Society. Mahoning Historical Society, Youngstown, Ohio.

"Welsh Settlers a Boon to America." *The Cambrian* 11 (July 1890): 7.

White, John G. *Twentieth-Century History of Mercer County.* Chicago: Lewis Publishing Company, 1909.

Wilkins, Charles. *The History of the Iron, Steel, Tinplate, and Other Trades of Wales.* Merthyr Tydfil, Wales: Joseph Williams, Printer and Publisher, 1903.

Wilks, Ivor. *South Wales and the Rising of 1839.* Llandysul, Wales: Gomer Press, 1989.

Willard, Eugene B., ed. *A Standard History of the Hanging Rock Iron Region of Ohio.* 2 vols. Chicago: Lewis Publishing Company, 1916.

Williams, Daniel Jenkins. *One Hundred Years of Welsh Calvinistic Methodism in America.* Philadelphia: Westminster Press, 1937.

Williams, David. "John Evans' Strange Journey [part 1]." *American Historical Review* 54 (January 1949): 277–95.

Williams, David. "John Evans' Strange Journey [part 2]." *American Historical Review* 54 (April 1949): 508–29.

Williams, David. *John Frost: A Study in Chartism.* Cardiff: University of Wales Press, 1939.

Williams, David. *The Rebecca Riots.* 1955. Cardiff: University of Wales Press, 1986.

Williams, Glanmor. *Religion, Language and Nationality in Wales.* Cardiff: University of Wales Press, 1979.

Williams, Glyn. *Desert and the Dream.* Cardiff: University of Wales Press, 1962.

Williams, Glyn. *The Welsh in Patagonia: State and Ethnic Community.* Cardiff: University of Wales Press, 1991.

Williams, Gwyn A. "Emergence of a Working-Class Movement." In *Wales through the Ages*, edited by A. J. Roderick, 2:140–46. Llandybie, Wales: Christopher Davies, 1971.

Williams, Gwyn A. *The Merthyr Rising.* Cardiff: University of Wales Press, 1988.

Williams, Gwyn A. *The Search for Beulah Land.* New York: Holmes and Meier, 1980.

Williams, Gwyn A. *When Was Wales?* London: Penguin Books, 1985.

Williams, Peter. *David Thomas: Iron Man from Wales.* Trucksville, PA: National Welsh-American Foundation, 1995.

Williams, Stephen Riggs. *The Saga of Paddy's Run.* Privately printed, 1997.

Wilson, James Grant, ed. *Appletons' Cyclopedia of American Biography.* Supplementary vols. New York: D. Appleton and Company, 1901.

Wittke, Carl. *We Who Built America: The Saga of the Immigrant.* New York: Prentice-Hall, 1939.

Wright, Carroll D. "The Amalgamated Association of Iron and Steel Workers." *Quarterly Journal of Economics* 7 (July 1893): 400–32.

Wyman, Mark. *Round-Trip to America: The Immigrants Return to Europe, 1880–1930.* Ithaca, NY: Cornell University Press, 1993.

Yans-McLaughlin, Virginia, ed. *Immigration Reconsidered.* New York: Oxford University Press, 1990.

Yates, W. Ross. "Discovery of the Process for Making Anthracite Iron." *Pennsylvania Magazine of History and Biography* 98 (April 1974): 206–23.

Yearley, Clifton K. *Britons in American Labor: A History of the Influence of the United Kingdom Immigrants on American Labor, 1820–1914.* Baltimore, MD: Johns Hopkins Press, 1957.

Zieger, Robert H. "The Career of James J. Davis." *Pennsylvania Magazine of History and Biography* 48 (January 1974): 67–89.

INDEX